Policy and Program Planning for Older Adults

Elaine Theresa Jurkowski, MSW, PhD, is an associate professor and graduate program director at the School of Social Work, Southern Illinois University Carbondale (SIUC). Dr. Jurkowski also coordinates the Certificate in Gerontology through the College of Education and Human Services at SIUC. Dr. Jurkowski's professional background includes both social work (BSW, MSW) and public health (PhD). Her work in the policy arena began during her undergraduate degree program in social work and has continued throughout her career. Dr. Jurkowski has spent most of her career writing about access to care issues for older adults and people with disabilities. She has been effective in shaping policy and program efforts in several countries in addition to the United States, including Canada, India, and Niger, West Africa.

Policy and Program Planning for Older Adults

Realities and Visions

Elaine Theresa Jurkowski, MSW, PhD

SPRINGER PUBLISHING COMPANY
New York

Springer Publishing Company, LLC
11 West 42nd Street
New York, NY 10036
www.springerpub.com

Acquisitions Editor: Sheri W. Sussman
Production Editor: Carol Cain
Cover design: Joanne E. Honigman
Composition: Apex Publishing, LLC

10   11   12   /   5   4   3   2

Library of Congress Cataloging-in-Publication Data
Jurkowski, Elaine Theresa.
   Policy and program planning for older adults : realities and visions / Elaine
   Theresa Jurkowski.
     p. cm.
   Includes index.
   ISBN-13: 978-0826129444 (alk. paper)
   ISBN-10: 0-8261-2944-7 (alk. paper)
   1. Older people—Services for—United States.   2. Older people—Government
policy—United States.   3. Older people—Legal status, laws, etc.—United
States.   4. Population aging—United States.   I. Title.
   HV1461.J87   2008
   362.6—dc22   2007016188

Printed in the United States of America by Yurchak Printing, Inc.

To my parents
Lorraine and Eddie Jurkowski
whose vision for community-based policies and programs inspired this work

To my dear husband
Bill
whose unconditional support helped complete this work

Contents

PART I. UNDERSTANDING POLICY AND PROGRAM DEVELOPMENT

PART III. TOOLS FOR POLICY AND PROGRAM DEVELOPMENT

PART IV. PROGRAMS AND SERVICES: REALITIES AND VISIONS

List of Figures

List of Tables

Preface

Realities and Visions

Looking around oneself either at the grocery store, at a shopping mall, or in the workplace, a common thread may be seen—a graying population. The first of the baby boom cohort turned 60 in 2006, and by 2030, it is anticipated that 20% or more of the adult population in the United States will be 65 years of age or older. Consequently, social work, public health, human services, and allied health professionals will be at the forefront of service delivery and policy development. Thus, resources and tools to adequately prepare these individuals for the journey ahead, to meet this changing society, will be vital and critical.

In response to this need, this text, *Policy and Program Planning for Older Adults: Realities and Visions,* has been developed. This textbook offers some innovative features. Essentially, the book will take a public health/population health approach to the development of programs and services for older adults. The book attempts to build students' understanding of policy development through a critical analysis and review of policy frameworks, and the policy implementation process. Once the student understands how policies are formulated and implemented, a second innovation will include the development of skills to shape programs and the implementation of policies. Skills to shape policies and programs such as media advocacy, coalition building, and health promotion frameworks will also be addressed within the text. Last, community-based programs and services are addressed within the context of text. Existing policy texts neglect to triangulate skills, policies, and programs for the reader. Existing texts also neglect to blend a social welfare and public health approach into their conceptual designs.

Layout of this Book

This book has been developed with the notion that it will provide the reader with an overview of dimensions impacting policy development, apprise the reader of current mandated policies in the United States that will affect older adults, identify and present tools that are helpful in building both policy and programs for older adults, and showcase programs and services for older adults. Each chapter provides the reader with Web sites that can be used for additional reference information. Each chapter also presents some notion of the realities facing older adults within each topical area, and a summary chapter outlines both realities of today and visions for the future. It is the author's hope that this resource can be valuable for advocates working within the field of aging as they develop programs and policies for our next generation.

Part I of this book lays out a background as to the current and future demographic trends of older adults and makes the case for the reader that there are a variety of philosophical, political, economic, and social factors that affect public policy development. The chapters help the reader explore a range of perspectives that define, shape, and impact the development and implementation of public policy. This section is also intended to prepare the reader to be able to critically analyze public policies related to aging.

Chapter 1 provides a demographic profile of the aging population (60+ years) currently, and reviews how these demographics have changed from 1900 until the present time. Demographics are also reviewed from the perspectives of specific health outcomes, gender differences, ethnic composition, and rural/urban dimensions. The chapter concludes by looking at how these specific demographic changes will shape challenges for the future and gaps to be addressed through policy and program developments.

The second chapter takes the reader through a historical review of policy, economic, political, and social changes that have occurred both on the American and global fronts. It reviews such dimensions within 10-year increments, highlighting major innovations or developments from 1900 to 2005. The chapter concludes by challenging the reader to consider factors that have led to innovations in science and technology as opposed to aging-related policies and lays the groundwork to begin to explore philosophical paradigms that impact policy development.

Chapter 3 provides an overview of different philosophical paradigms that impact the development of policy proposals and eventually drafted or legislative bills. The chapter also explores various factors and policy frameworks that impact the implementation of aging policy. Philosophical paradigms include "blaming the victim," "elitism," "social welfare as a right," "econometric perspectives," "cause versus function," and "window of opportunity," to name a few. These philosophical frameworks help the reader understand the development of aging-related policies and programs, while the policy frameworks help the reader understand the implementation process related to aging policy. Implementation strategies will include frameworks such as "street-level bureaucrats," "incrementalism," "rationalism," and "window of opportunity." An important perspective of this chapter is that the reader is exposed to the view that a range of perspectives ranging from extreme liberal to conservative impact the development and implementation of public policy.

The fourth chapter of the book, and the last in Part I, lays out a variety of tools and government documents available and how these are used to provide evidence and rationale for public policy development and analysis. Sources include "Congressional Universe," "Thomas," Government Printing Office (GPO) documents, Government Accounting Office (GAO) documents, and various databases available through the national database sources. This chapter also makes the linkage between using data and evidence to support policy and program development decisions. Some exercises are provided at the conclusion of the chapter to help the reader understand and utilize these sources.

Part II of this text will provide an overview to major federal policies and programs that impact older adults and people with disabilities. Some historical developments leading up to the actual development and implementation of the policies are also examined. Policies include Social Security, Medicare, the Older Americans Act, the Americans with Disabilities Act, the Community Mental Health Centers Act, and Freedom Initiative.

Chapter 5 provides a backdrop to our current Social Security Program, provides an overview to some models for Social Security programs in Europe and Canada, and explores the genesis of the Social Security program in the United States. The contents of the original Social Security Act will be explored and compared to the current-day titles and programs mandated through the current Social Security Act. Chapter 6 reviews the history of Medicare and reviews some of the changes in Medicare legislation over time. It also provides an overview of the current services available through Medicare Parts A, B, C, and D.

The Older Americans Act has seen a growth of programs, legislative resources, and a series of amendments since its inception into law in 1965. This chapter reviews some of the history leading up to the signing, the original components of the act, amendments that have occurred over time, and, finally, the most recent amendments of 2006, which will serve as a guidepost until 2011.

Chapter 8 provides an overview to the Americans with Disabilities Act and examines how this landmark piece of legislation impacts the lives of older adults. Mobility impairments and other impairments associated with disability and chronic conditions have posed major barriers and challenges to people as they age and develop mobility or sensory limitations. Within the area of mobility and sensory deficits and challenges, older adults have greatly benefited from the work and accomplishment of the disability and independent living movements.

Chapter 9, the last in this part on legislative initiatives that impact older adults, reviews mental health legislation and its impacts for older adults living within the community. It also explores President Bush's Freedom Commission Initiative and explores how this legislation affects older adults' lives in the United States.

Part III provides some tools for the reader to use to be more adequately equipped to prepare program initiatives that flow from policy appropriations. The tools also are designed to prepare the practitioner or reader with some skills to more effectively advocate for policy change. This section helps bridge some of the skills and tools used both within the disciplines of social work and public health and begins to expand the boundaries of public policy development.

Chapter 10 addresses health behavior models and lays out the premise that understanding and programming with some concept of health behavior in mind will strengthen community-based programs and improve the return on investment in these programs. Health behavior models addressed within this chapter will include four specific models, including the "health belief model," "stages of change," and "theories of reasoned action." An overview of these models and their components will be presented and reviewed. These will then be examined relative to aging policies and the implementation of specific programs. The chapter concludes with making a case for the importance of using health behavior models in the development of aging programs and provides some "best practice" examples.

Chapter 11 provides an innovative tool for policy advocates, which is the use of media and advocacy strategies for change. This chapter provides an overview of the social marketing process and media/advocacy strategies inherent in the process of developing advocacy campaigns for creating public awareness. A variety of specific constituent groups are addressed, and media strategies are presented. Strategies include the use of preparing sound bites, developing fact sheets, letter writing campaigns, use of the Internet, infomercials, and "trinket techniques" (t-shirts, bumper stickers, visors, etc.).

The focus of tools presented in chapter 12 is on coalitions and coalition building. This chapter provides an overview of coalitions, and their development and use as a technique for policy development or program implementation.

Chapter 13 outlines and reviews tools used in the needs assessment process. This chapter outlines the use of needs assessment tools and how either one, or all five strategies discussed in this chapter are used in the development of community, agency, state, or national priorities. Strategies include community forums, social indicators, key stakeholders, service statistics, and surveys.

The third part of this text concludes with chapter 14, which attempts to pull together each of the chapters in this section on tools and make the linkage between the first three parts and the last part of this book. This chapter provides the reader with a short overview of how the tools presented are salient in the process of program development and sets the stage for the concluding part of this text.

This last part of the text outlines specific programmatic areas that flow from aging policies, and specific components that flow from federally mandated policies. Each chapter will be written with the same basic outline: an overview of the programs, specific features and strengths of the programs, gaps and areas for development, and challenges for the future. The tools and concepts presented earlier in this text will be integrated and woven throughout each of the chapters in Part IV.

Chapter 15 explores various models of community living and residential options for older adults. Traditional models of long-term care, home- and community-based, will be examined and innovative approaches presented, such as consumer-directed approaches. This chapter examines the current status of the long-term care system, seeks to provide different residential models of care for people as they require community-based settings or settings with supports, and addresses issues that will face the long-term and community-based care settings in the future.

Chapter 16 examines the mental health needs of older adults, addresses the programs and services available to meet this need, and addresses gaps such as counseling, peer support, and resources to meet the needs of dual diagnosis such as substance abuse and mental health. The prevalence of various mental health disorders is presented in this chapter, and the chapter concludes with an exploration of model programs around the United States to address the mental health needs of older adults.

Chapter 17 explores health care needs and services for older adults. This chapter will examine the traditional programs offered for preventative, acute, and chronic care within the Medicare program. Gaps such as oral health care, screening, and assessment will also be examined.

An issue that has been on the rise, that of grandparents raising grandchildren, is explored in Chapter 18. This chapter examines some of the legislation that affects grandparents raising grandchildren, such as child welfare components. It also addressees the unique dilemmas grandparents raising grandchildren face when straddling aging and child welfare policies. This chapter also provides an overview of the current status of grandparents raising grandchildren, as well as some background on the literature, and it provides an awareness of issues that grandparents face as primary caregivers. A literature review examines some of the current issues and services needed. Resources and services designed to meet the needs of grandparents raising grandchildren are discussed, and programmatic responses identified through the national resources. Lastly, some best practice interventions are outlined for review.

Elder abuse is addressed and gaps in services and public policy are presented in Chapter 19. The incidence and prevalence of elder abuse is probably largely underreported. While efforts are being made to understand the magnitude of the problem, limited resources hamper progress. The Older Americans Act has some resources in place to deal with the education of providers and screening/detection of individuals who have been at risk of abuse; however, Adult Protective Services plays a key role also in this intervention process. The role of one's cultural beliefs and help-seeking behavior also plays a significant role. Challenges in uncovering this silent epidemic face the health care provider, programs, and services.

Legal issues, including those related to power of attorney, enduring power of attorney, end-of-life care issues, are examined in Chapter 20. It also presents dilemmas in public policy development relative to how these are implemented. In addition, legal services provided to older adults as a result of the Older Americans Act are explored, and challenges within the realm of legal issues outlined.

The last chapter concludes by laying out realities, proposing visions for the future, and summarizing a top 10 list of challenges for the future, listed here.

1. Designing paradigms to meet the demographic and social needs of our graying population through evidence-based approaches.
2. Social Security—boom or bust?
3. Medicare: Will there be a pot at the end of the rainbow for preventative services?
4. Understanding health behavior and planning with this understanding in mind
5. Using the media, advocacy, and coalitions for social change
6. Home- and community-based care
7. Mental health programs, services, and issues
8. Health programs, services, and issues
9. Long-term care
10. Diversity and special populations

This text also offers various unique features, which include some of the following:

- The book is presented in four parts, addresses philosophical paradigms underlying policy making, addresses current policies impacting older adults, describes tools and strategies for policy making and program planning, and presents programs and services to address the needs of older adults.

- The book addresses some unique areas such as evidence-based policy development, the media, and coalition building.
- The book presents materials on the new Older Americans Act reauthorization.

In addition, this book addresses specific strategies and tools that can be useful in the development of renewed social policy for older adults or people with disabilities and equips the reader with tools and strategies to impact public health or health policies and programs. The reader is apprised of current legislative efforts that impact older adults in practice settings, or that impact program development. It also provides a conceptual or philosophical framework that guides the development of social policy. Tools, strategies, and resources that shape social policy efforts are also addressed, followed by programs and services currently in place. Since the text is sole authored, a linkage between chapters is possible, which lends itself to continuity throughout the text.

A graying society is a reality—thus we can be prepared to plan, or we can plan to fail. Planning promotes engagement, thus rendering a healthy community and a foundation for our generations to come.

Elaine Theresa Jurkowski
Carbondale, Illinois

Foreword

In the next 20 years the number of adults in the United States over the age of 65 is expected to double. This dramatic increase in the numbers of aging individuals has been referred to as "the demographic imperative." As a result of changes in medical care, health care policy, and technology, older adults are living longer than ever before, and their needs are changing. Today adults over the age of 65 represent 12.3% of the US population. By 2030 that percentage will increase to 20%, or 71.5 million people. The percentage of older minorities in the population will also increase from 16% in 2007 to 25% in 2030. By now it is recognized that this shift in the age of the United States population will seriously strain the medical, health care, and social services systems.

With the oldest members of the baby boom generation reaching the age of 65 in 4 years, the number of older adults in the U.S. population will present a profound challenge. The fields of medicine, social work, nursing, public health, gerontology, and others will have the opportunity to support older adults—those aging well and those who will need increased social services, medical, and long-term care—in order to help them maintain the highest level of quality of life.

Controversies are already emerging throughout our society about what the elderly should receive, what care and when, and who should pick up the bill and for how long. Aging-related issues are being debated in the halls of Congress, in the media, and in the privacy of our own homes. Whether we work with older adults or not, policy issues related to their needs are rampant and will have an intergenerational impact.

The emerging demographic, economic, and social realities have upset the foundation of existing paradigms regarding older adults. Can we afford to be our brother's keeper? Do older adults really need us like they did 50 years ago? And, considering the population explosion within this cohort, we are even asking how can older adults contribute to society?

Complicating the situation is that, unfortunately, we appear to be in an era of retraction rather than expansion of our safety net and, therefore, we may not meet this demographic imperative's demand. Given the perception of scarcity, even the 2005 White House Conference on Aging was focused on the importance of "individual responsibility" rather than "entitlements." The whole question of aged-based policy is controversial. Are people entitled to something simply because of their age? How do we translate policy into programs and vice versa to make sure we are attending to the diversity of not only the needs of older adults but also those who care for them?

Clearly, alternative strategies are needed to improve comprehensiveness and quality of care in view of the projected growth in the millions of Americans expected to have multiple chronic illnesses, the huge increase expected in the numbers of older adults as the baby boom generation ages, and the economic, demographic, political, and systemic pressures for services amidst greater challenges and declining resources.

My experience as a John Heinz Senate Fellow, when I took a sabbatical from my practitioner role to better understand and influence policy, was invaluable. Learning about policy development from the ground up gave me a better understanding of how to effectively address seemingly insurmountable issues by gathering evidence and forging coalitions. There is no question that government can move slowly at times; however, Senator Clinton and her staff taught me that the system can still serve its citizens' needs. I observed and believe that if people can frame their issues clearly and advocate for them before Congress, they can really make a difference by influencing the legislative agenda and future policy. Although some of the political and partisan truths that surface throughout the legislative process may be daunting, the ability to have a real effect on the course of the nation's older Americans is indeed possible. These effects may be incremental and slow in coming, but the immediacy and relevancy of the political and policy process is an awe-inspiring one.

We in the field of aging must involve ourselves in today's public debate and political struggles not only for the benefit of older adults but also for those who will be asked to support them. This book, *Policy and Program Planning for Older Adults: Realities and Visions,* provides us with a structured, comprehensive guide to policy development and planning that will be useful for the experienced practitioner and the neophyte as well. Dr. Elaine Jurkowski presents a realistic portrayal of policy and planning for aging issues. The hands-on case examples demystify the process, making the content accessible and comprehendible. The text is all encompassing and can be used in sections or as a whole. The challenges of an aging society can be met by engaging in Dr. Jurkowski's critical analysis and review of policy frameworks, the policy implementation process, and skill development to shape programs. This text will help us in the field and play a pivotal role in one of the greatest challenges of our times.

Robyn Golden, LCSW
Director of Older Adult Programs
Rush University Medical Center

Acknowledgements

A journey to complete a work such as this book, cannot be completed successfully without the guidance and help from many people. Firstly, I would like to acknowledge Sheri W. Sussman, Senior Editor at Springer Publishing for her vision and unwavering support through this process. Sheri, along with her assistant Alana Stein were wonderful resources to shape and redirect details to help bring some of my vision into reality.

This book also would not have been possible without the input from many of my students, especially students within the Certificate in Gerontology program and School of Social Work at Southern Illinois University Carbondale. Although many students have contributed insights and asked questions which have shaped the various chapters of this book, there are some students that should be acknowledged by name for their help with literature searches, media artifacts and technical details, such as Janelle Biver, April Green, Cherie Green, Ron Hillerman, Kimberly McCutcheon, Tsukasa Okino, Deenaz Patel and Theresa Walls. In addition, Imram Mohammed was helpful with the artwork, photos and computer technology issues, while Ms. Pat Martens was a lifesaver with her expertise in graphics and administrative details.

I would also like to acknowledge my colleagues who have been sources of input and offered valuable suggestions for the manuscript itself. Colleagues such as Charla Lautar, Sandra Beebe (Southern Illinois University Carbondale), Terry Koenig (The University of Kansas), Anissa Rogers (Portland State University) and Crystal Moore (Skidmoore College), Marla Berg-Weger (St. Louis University) were very helpful with insights from various aspects of the field. John Smith and Susan Patterson, (Egyptian Area Agency on Aging) and Bert Weber (Illinois Department on Aging) were very helpful with technical details related to the Older Americans Act. Robyn Golden, (Rush University Older Adult Program and the American Society on Aging) has been a source of enthusiasm and realism. In addition to these key individuals, I would like to acknowledge faculty from my doctoral program at the University of

Illinois Chicago, who enabled me to bring together my backgrounds in public health and social work, and synthesize these two professional arenas—Dr. Lou Rowitz and Dr. Regina Kulys.

Lastly, I would like to acknowledge my family for their patience, understanding, unconditional support, and never ending "cheerleading". Bill and Robert deserve special mention for the many nights they spent home alone while I tapped away on the computer keys!

Policy and Program Planning for Older Adults

PART I

Understanding Policy and Program Development

This part lays out a background as to the current and future demographic trends of older adults and makes the case for the reader that there are a variety of philosophical, political, economic, and social factors that affect public policy development. The chapters help the reader explore a range of perspectives that define, shape, and impact the development and implementation of public policy. This part is also intended to prepare the reader to be able to critically analyze public policies related to aging. It sets the stage for understanding the demographic, social, political, and philosophical perspectives to policy development. The policy overview journey sets out with a glimpse of factors that play a role in policy and program development.

CHAPTER 1

Background and Demographic Profile of Older Adults

PREPARING FOR THE "BOOM"

America is graying at a faster rate than ever before. In 2006, the first baby boomer turned 60 and became eligible for Older Americans Act Services. Baby boomers are a distinct group, with attitudes and values unlike the seniors who have preceded them. This group of aging individuals thrive on choice, seek out information, are consumer-oriented and demanding, and want their independence. Are we prepared to deal with the policy and program needs this group will present and need? Are we ready to address the gaps in services that this group will be demanding of us? How will social service and public health practitioners and policy makers be prepared for community and individual needs? What are the realities for current services, and what visions will be presented from baby boomers for new or revised services? What paradigms shape services that are currently in place, and how can we revise these services using tools for program planning and policy development?

Before we can address these issues, an exploration of the current demographic face in America is necessary. What does our landscape look like, and how do we anticipate that demographic changes will shape our social and community needs?

THE CHANGING DEMOGRAPHIC STRUCTURE AND AGING POPULATION

Life expectancy has dramatically increased over the past century. At the turn of the twentieth century (1900), life expectancy was 47 years of age (Pickett & Hanlon, 1995). In 1958 the life expectancy of adults increased to 68 years, and by 1991, the life expectancy was 76 years, while in 2003 life expectancy in the United States was 77.6 years of age (Centers for Disease Control and Prevention, 2005a). Hand in hand with these changes, there has been an increase in the number of elderly living within the United States over the past century. In 1900, 4% of the population was over 65 years of age, while it reached 12.7% by 1997 (nearly triple). The American Association of Retired Persons (AARP, 1998), based upon U.S. Census, estimates that by the year 2010, at least 28% of the population will be over 65 years of age. Table 1.1 illustrates these demographic changes over time.

Interestingly, approximately 1 out of about every 8 Americans falls into the older adult population. The number of older Americans has increased by nearly 11% since 1900 (compared to a 9% increase in the under-65 population) (USDHHS AoA, 2006). As the clock ticks away, every 8 seconds a baby boomer turns 60 (U.S. Census Bureau, 2006). Figure 1.1 provides an overview of this demographic shift.

The older population is expected to double over the next 30 years. The 85 and older group is expected to grow faster than any other group (Federal Interagecy Forum on Aging-Related Statistics, 2006). In the last U.S. census, there were an estimated 66,000 centenarians; by 2050 there are expected to be 834,000. See Figure 1.2. Thus, our population profile appears to be growing older and grayer.

TABLE 1.1 Demographic Changes of an Aging Population in the United States Over Time

Year	Percentage of the population 65 years of age or older.
1900	4.0
1920	4.6
1940	6.8
1980	11.3
1990	12.4
2000	12.0
2005	12.3

Source: U.S. Bureau of the Census, 1900, 1920, 1940, 1980, 1990, 2000, 2005 (assorted years).

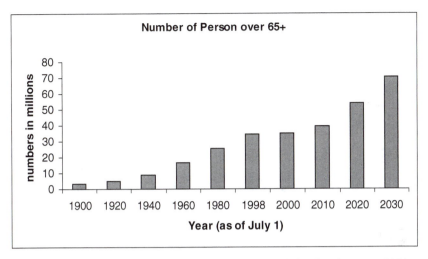

FIGURE 1.1   Population projections of older adults for the year 2030.
Source: Administration on Aging, 2000.

CHANGES IN OUR POPULATION PROFILE

It has been estimated that the fastest growing group of older adults is the 85-year and older group. It is estimated by the U.S. Census Bureau that approximately 19 million people will be 85 or older in the United States by 2050 (see Figure 1.3).

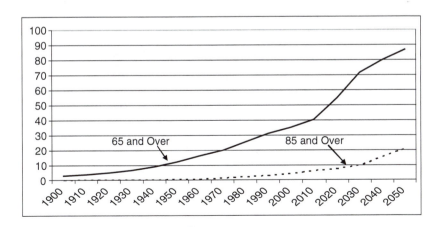

FIGURE 1.2   Population breakdown by age group.
Note: Data for 2010–2050 are projections of the population.
Data refers to resident populations and noninstitutionalized individuals.
Source: U.S. Census Bureau, Decennial Census and Projections.

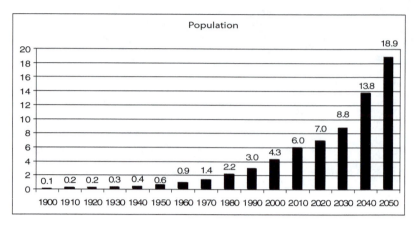

FIGURE 1.3   Population estimates.
Note: Data for 2010–2050 are projections of the population.
Data refer to resident populations and noninstitutionalized individuals.
Source: U.S. Census Bureau, Decennial Census and Projections.

During the twentieth century in the United States there was a significant gender shift among the aging (65+ years). In 1900, The U.S. Bureau
of the Census reported that there were 108.5 men for every 100 women.
In 1950, this ratio declined slightly; however there were still more men per
100 women (102.3 men per 100 women). In 1960, there were equal numbers of women per men (100 men per 100 women). By 1980, there were
only 69.7 men per 100 women, and by 1990 the ratio had dropped to
64.1 men per 100 women, as shown in Table 1.2. By 2005, this ratio has
increased to 74.5 men per every 100 women at 65 years of age or older.

TABLE 1.2   Changes in Population Profile: Males and Females

Year	Number of males per 100 females
1870	111.4
1900	108.5
1950	102.3
1960	100
1980	69.7
1990	64.1
2000	63.3

Source: U.S. Bureau of the Census, 1870, 1900, 1950, 1960, 1980, 1990, 2000 (assorted years).

These dramatic shifts in numbers, especially over the past 40 years, will leave more women living alone and widowed, while men will be more likely to remain married or attended by women. Other implications of this will include the need to target income support mechanisms and social support programs for widowed and single women. This will have multiple effects on policies related to supplementary security income (SSI), Disability Insurance (DI), and Medicare, especially funding. Statistically, more men are married who are older adults (77%), when compared to women (43%), and more women are widowed (45%) as compared to men (14%). Only 4% of men and women are found to be single (never married) and 8% of both groups are separated or divorced (U.S. Bureau of the Census, 2005). Figure 1.4 provides an illustration of these statistics.

Living Arrangements *Less likely to have a spouse + kids to provide caregivers*

As to marital status, it is no surprise that men were more likely to live with spouses (72.4%) as compared to women (41.6%), while more women tended to live alone or with nonrelatives (41.6%) as compared with their male counterparts (21.5%). Women were also more likely to live with other relatives (16.8%) as compared to men (6.1%). Figure 1.5 provides an illustration of these data (USDHHS AoA, 2003).

A number of interesting trends have occurred between 1970 and 2004 among both men and women with regard to living alone. The number of men living alone has steadily increased among men aged 65 to 74

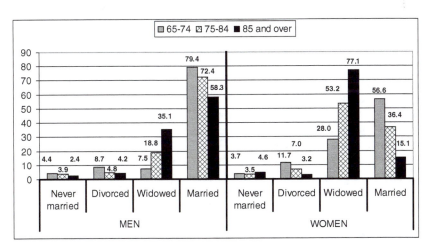

FIGURE 1.4   Marital status of people 65+ years.
Source: United States Census Bureau (2006).

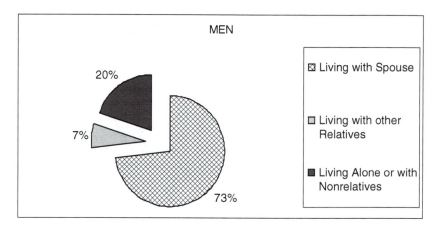

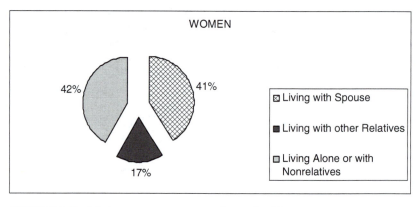

FIGURE 1.5   Living arrangements of people 65+ years.
Source: Administration on Aging, 2001.

years of age (11.3% in 1970 to 15.5% in 2004). Men living alone in the 75 and over age category have also steadily risen from 19.1% in 1970 to 23.1% in 2004. Women between the ages of 65 and 74 have slightly dropped in number in terms of women living alone (31.7% in 1970 versus 29.4% in 2004). The age group that has had the most drastic rise in people living alone is the 75 years of age and over category (37% in 1970 as compared with 49.9% in 2004) (USDHHS AoA, 2003). Figure 1.6 provides an overview of these data.

Education Level

Today older adults are increasingly more educated than the previous generation. In 1965 only 23.5% of adults 65 years of age and older had

FIGURE 1.6   Percentage of people living alone by age, sex.
Note: Data refer to the civilian, noninstitutionalized population.
Source: U.S. Current Population Survey, Annual Social and Economic Supplement.

completed high school degrees as compared to 48.2% in 1985 and 73.1% in 2004 (USDHHS, AoA, 2006). Similarly, there has been an increasing trend to attend college and complete a bachelor's degree. In 1965, only 5% of older adults 65 years of age and older had completed a bachelor's degree, as compared to 9.4% in 1985 and 18.7% in 2004. Figure 1.7 provides an illustration of these data.

Despite improvements in the overall education level of older adults over the past few decades, disparities still exist across ethnic groups. In 2004, non-Hispanic whites were the most educated when compared to African Americans, Blacks, Asians, and Hispanics. Whites aged 65 years and older were more likely than any other group to complete high school (73.1%) and a bachelor's degree (18.7%), as compared to Blacks (52.5% completing high school and 10.7% completing a bachelor's degree) or Hispanics (37.6% completing high school and 8.3 percent completing a bachelor's degree). These variations in education level pose implications for the development of innovative resources, teaching tools, and training initiatives that may need to be tailored for the various educational levels. Figure 1.8 provides an overview of this data.

Economic Well-Being

Over the past several years there has been much debate about privatizing the Social Security program. Although there may be a portion of the population within a high income bracket category that could afford to invest money for their future (15% of people over the age of 65 years

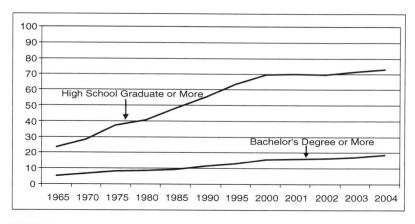

FIGURE 1.7   Education attainment of people 65+.
Notes: Data are based upon the Census Bureau question: "What is your highest grade or degree completed?"
Data refer to noninstitutionalized civilians, 65 years of age or older.
Source: U.S. Census Bureau, Current Population Survey, Annual Social and Economic Supplement.

have incomes of $75,000 or more), the majority of families with the head of the household over 65 years of age (53%) are families living below $35,000 per year (see Figure 1.9). When one further explores this issue and examines the distribution of income among people 65 years of age and older, it is found that 87% of this group are receiving less than $35,000 per year (see Figure 1.10). These limited funds make survival difficult within one's retirement years, without some financing alternatives such as "reverse mortgages" and other creative financing options.

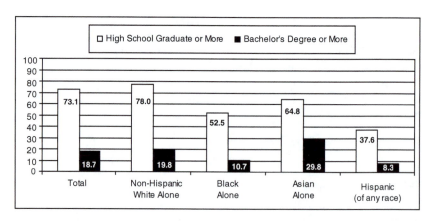

FIGURE 1.8   Education by race and Hispanic origin.

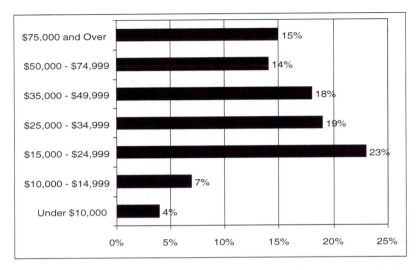

FIGURE 1.9   Economics: Percentage distribution by income with the head of the household 65+.

Source: Administration on Aging, 2004.

When considering sources of income for people 65 years of age and over, it appears that there is a trend towards reliance upon Social Security income, more so in 2004 (39%) as compared to 1962 (31% support). Pensions were also increasingly important (20% of income in 2004) as compared to 1962 (9% pension income). Asset income in 2004

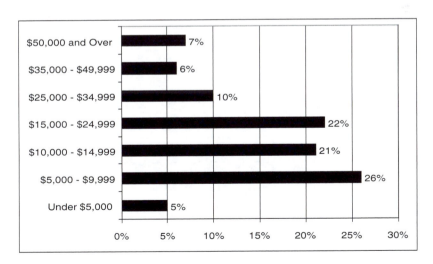

FIGURE 1.10   Percentage distribution by income 65+.

Source: Administration on Aging, 2004.

accounted for 13% of total income as compared to 16% of total income in 1962. Table 1.3 provides an overview of these data.

Despite these concerns about income, older adults 65 years of age and over are not actually the most prevalent group living in poverty over time. When compared to individuals younger than 18 years of age, or people 18 to 64, more of the youngest age group were noted to be in poverty (17.8%) when compared to other age groups. Among individuals over the age of 65, the oldest group of people were the most likely to be living in poverty. People 85 years of age and older were noted to have 12.6% of their cohort living in poverty, as compared to 9.8% for all individuals 65 years of age and older. Figure 1.11 shows these data.

agri → urban

Changes in Rural Population

Although there has been a well-documented shift from agrarian/rural-based population to urban settings, the proportion of people living in rural settings (<9,999 people) has remained relatively stable over the past 30 years. At the turn of the twentieth century, 39.8% of the population lived in rural settings. This percentage increased steadily until 1950, when nearly three-fourths of all Americans lived in rural settings (71.2%). Between 1950 and 1960, nearly 50% of people living in rural

TABLE 1.3   Sources of Income for Adults 65+ Years of Age (represented by percent values)

Source	1962	1976	1980	1990	1998	2000	2004
Social Security	31	39	39	36	38	38	39
Asset income	16	18	22	24	20	18	13
Pensions	9	16	16	18	19	18	13
Earnings	28	23	19	18	21	23	26
Other	16	4	4	4	2	3	2
Total	100	100	100	100	100	100	100

Notes: Income is aggregated by source for selected years, 1962–2004, represented as percentages. The definition of "other" includes, but is not limited to, public assistance, unemployment compensation, worker's compensation, alimony, child support, and personal contributions.
Data refers to noninstituionalized populations.
Sources: Social Security Administration, 1963 Survey of the Aged, 1968 Survey of Demographic and Economic Characteristics of the Aged; U.S. Census Bureau, Current Population Survey, Annual Social and Economic Supplement, 1976–2002.

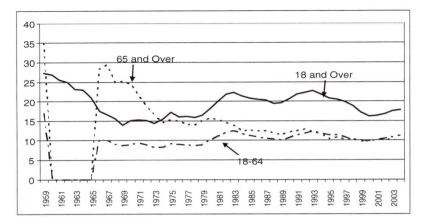

FIGURE 1.11   Percentage living in poverty—a comparison across the life span.

Source: U.S. Census Bureau, Current Population Survey, Annual Social and Economic Supplement, 1960–2005.

settings migrated to urban settings, dropping from 71.2% to 37.5%. The percentages have remained relatively stable over the last 40 years with slight decreases in rural populations from year to year.

The rural demographic portrait becomes more descriptive, particularly with regards to the proportion of people living in rural areas who are 65 years of age and over and who live in very small rural communities (<2,500 people). Table 1.4 outlines this demographic shift.

TABLE 1.4   Shift in Percentage of People Living in Rural Settings

Year	Percentage of the population living in rural settings
1900	59.8
1950	71.2
1960	37.5
1970	33.5
1980	32.7
1990	30.8
2000	24.6
2005	n/a

Source: U.S. Bureau of the Census, 1900, 1950, 1960, 1970, 1980, 1990, 2000, 2005 (assorted years).

This demographic picture is further compounded by those who were foreign-born and are living in rural areas, as shown in Table 1.5. These are foreign-born people who immigrated to the United States and are living in Frontier Rural Communities (referred to areas of <2,500 people) or who live in rural communities (2,500–9,999). While there has been a decrease (over 50%) of foreign-born people living in rural areas (59.8% in areas of <2,500 people; 14.3% in areas of 2,500–9,999 in 1900 versus 24.8% Frontier Rural in 1990 and 6.0% in rural communities with a population of 2,500–9,999, respectively), there have been more women than men 65 years of age and older and more foreign-born people residing in smaller rural centers.

The number of foreign-born people residing in small rural areas or Frontier Communities (<2,500) who are over 65 years of age raises some serious concerns about the need for services, which may need to be culturally sensitive and culturally diverse. These services may also need to address such issues as cultural expectations around help-seeking behaviors, the role of religion and mortality, the aging process, loss of independence, and expectations around social supports. Language barriers may also play a role in the delivery of services and access to services within rural communities. (See Table 1.5.)

Trends in Morbidity and Mortality

Over the last century there have been dramatic changes in the facts of morbidity for older adults. This is due to technological advances, changes

TABLE 1.5   Percentage of People Foreign Born

Year	<2,5000	2,500–9,999	%65+	Males	Females	Rate: Males/Females
1900	59.8	14.3	9.2	8.8	9.7	108.5
1910	53.7	24.3	8.9	8.1	9.9	105.3
1920	48.6	25.4	9.7	9.0	10.5	104.7
1930	43.8	26.6	12.0	11.6	12.5	107.7
1950	43.5	27.7	26.3	26.2	26.5	100
1960	30.1	7.4	32.6	33.4	31.9	100
1970	26.5	7.0	32.0	31.5	32.3	82.4
1980	26.3	6.4	21.2	18.6	23.4	69.7
1990	24.8	6.0	13.6	10.9	16.3	64.1
2000	22.4	5.7	10.7	4.2	6.5	65.6

Sources: Gibson & Lennon (1999) and United States Census Bureau (2005).

in quality of life and living conditions, and advances in medicine. In 1900, the leading cause of death for people 40 years of age and older was tuberculosis, while for women it was childbirth (Picket & Hanlon, 1995). According to the National Health Interview Survey (CDC NHIS, 1997) the leading cause of morbidity in 1994 for people 65 years of age and over was arthritis (50 per 100). Hypertension was the second leading cause of morbidity (36 per 100) followed by heart disease (32 per 100). The changes in morbidity leads to a need for renewed public health, health promotion, and health education strategies. New approaches will be necessary to accommodate these health promotion efforts, which have recently been identified within the Older Americans Act amendments of 2006. (See Table 1.6 and Figure 1.12.)

Recently there has been a change in perceptions about health among older adults. In 1995, 20.3% of the population 65 and older rated their health as fair to poor, as compared to 9.4% for the general population. However, there was a difference between general perceived health status of African Americans, 43% of whom reported their health as fair to poor. This compares to only 28% of Caucasians who reported their health as fair to poor (CDC NHIS, 1995). This suggests that there is a growing percentage of the population over the age of 65 who perceive themselves to be in poor health and an increase in disparity among people of color (CDC, 2005b). These data serve to illustrate the importance of interventions to target diverse groups. The differences in perceived health status will also have an impact on health promotion programs to target older adults and reach minority groups in meaningful ways. (See Figure 1.13.)

One's perceived health status is also compounded by difficulties reported with carrying out activities of daily living (ADLs) by people 65 and over. Respondents in the National Health Interview Survey (1995) who identified themselves as being over 65 years old and were living independently within their community reported difficulties with carrying out both activities of daily living and instrumental activities of daily

TABLE 1.6 Rates of Morbidity

Type of illness	Rate per 100 in the population
Arthritis	50 per 100
Hypertension	36 per 100
Heart disease	32 per 100
Hearing	29 per 100
Cataracts	17 per 100
Orthopedic impairments	15 per 100

Source: National Health Interview Survey, 1997.

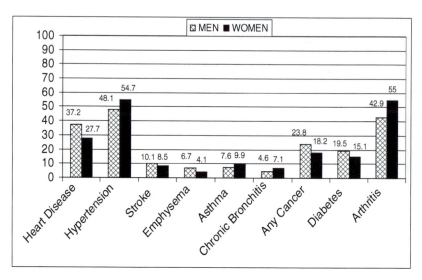

FIGURE 1.12 Health status related to chronic conditions of older adults.

Notes: Data are based upon the question "Have you EVER been told by a doctor or other health professional that you have some form of arthritis, rheumatoid arthritis, gout, lupus or fibromyalgia?"

Data refers to civilian, noninstitutionalized population.

Source: Centers for Disease Control and Prevention, National Center for Health Statistics, National Health Interview Survey.

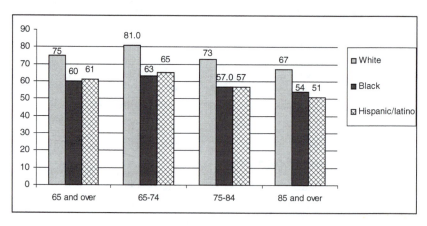

FIGURE 1.13 Perceived health status—comparing for ethnic diversity.

Notes: Respondents reported that they were in good to excellent health. Target population was noninstitutionalized civilian adults, 2002–2003.

Data is averaged.

Source: National Health Interview Survey, National Center for Health Statistics, Centers for Disease Control and Prevention.

16

living (IADLs). Activities of daily living, characterized as bathing, dressing, feeding, mobility, toileting, and transferring were reported as problematic for 14% of the noninstitutionalized population who were over 65 years of age.

In addition, 6.5% of the population reported having difficulty with IADLs. These activities included meal preparation, shopping, managing money, taking medication, doing housework, and using the telephone. These difficulties will translate into needs for services to allow people to remain in their homes and communities. Increasingly, there will be people living in communities who will require assistance with basic ADLs and services to promote functional status and healthy living. Given that current health policies only support services that are "medically necessary," a challenge for health educators and health promotion experts will be the development of health policy provisions to include health education and health promotion programs.

CHANGES WITHIN THE SOCIAL, POLITICAL, AND CULTURAL EXPECTATIONS OF COMMUNITIES

Up to this point, this chapter has highlighted some of the current health programs and policies in place and changes in demographic trends for older adults living within American society. In addition, there have been substantial changes within the social, political, and cultural expectations of communities over the past century that will pose challenges for policies and programs serving older adults.

Socially, health care has been impacted by numerous changes in gender roles and expectations over the last century (Kinsella & Gist, 1998). Women have become and continue to be active members of the community and maintain a high degree of civic engagement long into retirement. They have also retired after having had careers (GAO, 1997). Women have also begun to outnumber males, as they grow older. Along with this demographic shift, there are growing numbers of women who are independent of their husbands or in same sex/gender relationships. These social changes have generated new social policy needs for women (GAO, 1998).

As noted, there has been an increased mobility to urban centers from rural communities and a shift from agrarian to industrial communities. Despite this, many of the older foreign-born population and minorities have remained in rural communities, especially those with more severe functional impairments and disabilities. Coupled with smaller and more mobile families, this will lead to the need for alternative care models for people in rural areas as they grow older, and for service paradigms that will address the unique needs of rural communities.

Emerging service models that include community care and assisted living care models will serve as alternatives to traditional care of elders (Kovner & Jonas, 1999; Kronenfeld, 2000). Many of the traditional cultural expectations for families have eroded away as a result of cross-cultural or interracial marriages, smaller families, and more mobile family units. These changes to the social structure of families are resulting in changes and the need for differences in service composition for the older adult.

The shift from family to community support systems is another social change that will impact health care services (Atchley, 2000). Support provided by extended families and large families caring for the elderly has evolved into greater reliance on informal systems including the faith community, and formal systems such as local community-based service and philanthropic organizations. This leads to implications for the delivery of social programs through faith-based initiatives associated with local religious communities. Funding appropriations for such programming will need to be supported through some mechanism, either private donations or through some legislative mandate (Kaiser Commission on Medicaid and the Uninsured, 2001).

In summary, demographic changes; educational levels; income levels; and shifts in social, cultural, and service expectations of communities will contribute to changes in social services, programs, and policy initiatives as we move into the twenty-first century. These will pose challenges to the aging arena and to aging policies and programs.

CHALLENGES FOR AGING POLICIES AND PROGRAMS

Several issues emerge as realities within the context of policy development and program planning for older adults, as we have seen in this chapter. These include: changes in living arrangements, education levels, economic well-being, rural population settings, trends in morbidity and mortality, and changes within the social, political, and cultural expectations of communities. These changes lead to challenges to the current realities of our aging policies and service delivery network. Communities and service providers will also be challenged to prepare for the upcoming onslaught of baby boomers, who will challenge paradigms, and will be consumer-driven. The realities of our system will require professionals working within the field of aging to challenge the current contexts, take a hard look at what exists in reality, and develop strategies to envision an innovative set of interventions, services, and policy/legislative initiatives(Binstock, 1998, Derthick, 1979, Hiller

& Barrow, 1999). Such an approach will demand a new skill set that may be foreign to the current workforce. Such skills will include an in-depth understanding of what factors and contexts impact legislative initiatives, paradigms that affect the development of legislation, and data that may influence or contribute to policy development. Tools such as coalition building, media advocacy, and theoretical perspectives on health behavior are also going to be critical in this endeavor. Finally, building an awareness of what programs and services currently exist will also be a part of this process. Hence, this lays the groundwork for the remainder of this text, which is broken out into four distinct parts, and designed to address each of the skill areas required to enable reflective practitioners to build on their skills and be effective program and policy advocates in the aging arena.

REALITIES AND VISIONS

In summary, health policies related to aging in the United States have focused on in-kind medical services, supportive state and local services, and antipoverty benefits. Despite the availability of programs and services resulting from health policies, many programs are focused upon "medically necessary" services and lack a health promotion or health education focus (Torres-Gil, 1998; Torres-Gil & Villa, 2000). A challenge for health professionals working with the elderly will be to lobby for social policies that will offer health education and health promotion options to maintain a healthy elderly population. The benefits of such advocacy efforts will include the development of a more active and healthy elderly population leading to cost containment and the preservation of current benefits and programs available to the elderly living in the United States.

REFERENCES

American Association of Retired Persons (AARP). (1998). *Global aging report: Aging everywhere*. Washington, DC: Author.

Atchley, R. (2000). *The social forces of aging: An introduction to social gerontology*. CA: Wadsworth Publishing.

Binstock, R. H. (1998). Health care policies and older Americans. In J. S. Steckenrider and T. M. Parrott (eds.), *New directions in old-age policies* (pp. 13–35). Albany, NY: State University of New York.

Centers for Disease Control and Prevention, National Center for Health Statistics. (2007). *Summary health statistics for the U.S. population, the National Health Interview Survey, 2007*. Hyattsville, MD: U.S. Department of Health and Human Services.

Centers for Disease Control and Prevention, National Center for Health Statistics. (2005a). *Life expectancy hits record high.* Retrieved April 29, 2007, from http://www.cdc. gov/nchs/pressroom/05facts/lifeexpectancy.htm

Centers for Disease Control and Prevention, National Center for Health Statistics (2005b). *Summary health statistics for the U.S. population, the National Health Interview Survey, 2005.* Hyattsville, MD: U.S. Department of Health and Human Services.

Derthick, M. (1979). *Policy making for Social Security.* Washington, DC: The Brookings Institute.

Federal Interagency Forum on Aging-Related Statistics. (2006) *Older Americans update 2006: Key indicators of well-being. Federal Interagency Forum on Aging-Related Statistics,* Washington, DC: U.S. Government Printing Office.

GAO. (1997). *Social Security reform: Implications for women's retirement income.* Report to the ranking minority member, Subcommittee on Social Security, Committee on Ways and Means, House of Representatives. Washington, DC: U.S. Government Printing Office.

GAO. (1998). *Social Security reform: Raising retirement age improves program solvency but may cause hardship for some.* Testimony: Statement by D. Bovbjerg, Associate Director, Income Security Issues, Health Education and Human Services Division. Washington DC: U.S. Government Printing Office.

Gibson, C. J. & Lennon, E. (1999). *Historical census statistics on the foreign-born population of the United States: 1850–1990.* Population Division Working Paper. No. 29. Washington, DC: U.S. Bureau of the Census.

Hiller, S., & Barrow, G. (1999). *Aging, the individual and society.* CA: Wadsworth Publishing.

Kaiser Commission on Medicaid and the Uninsured. (2001). In P. R. Lee & C. L. Estes (Eds.), *The nation's health* (pp. 403–407). Boston: Jones and Bartlett Publishers.

Kinsella, K., & Gist, Y. (1998). Gender and aging. *International Brief, 98(2).*

Kovner, A., & Jonas, S. (1999). *Health care delivery in the United States.* New York: Springer Publishing Company.

Kronenfeld, J. J. (2000). Social policy and health care. Social policy and the elderly. In J. Midgley, M. B. Tracy, & M. Livermore (Eds.), *The handbook of social policy* (pp. 222–236). Thousand Oaks, CA: Sage Publications.

Pickett, G., & Hanlon, J. (1995) *Public health administration and practice.* St. Louis, MO: Times Mirror Publishing.

Torres-Gil, F. M. (1998). Policy, politics, aging: Crossroads in the 1990s. In J. S. Steckenrider & T. M. Parrott (Eds.), *New directions in old-age policies* (pp. 75–87). Albany, NY: State University of New York.

Torres-Gil, F. M., & Villa, V. (2000). Social policy and the elderly. In J. Midgley, M. B. Tracy, & M. Livermore (Eds.), *The handbook of social policy* (pp. 209–220). Thousand Oaks, CA: Sage Publications.

United States Census Bureau. (2005). *Census 2000 special tabuiations (STP-159)* Washington, DC: Author.

United States Census Bureau. (2006). *current population survey, annual social and economic supplement,* 1960–2005. Retrieved June 15, 2007, from http://www.census.gov/cps

United States Department of Health and Human Services. (1999). *Health, United States, 1999 with Health and Aging Chartbook.* MD: U.S. Department of Health and Human Services.

United States Department of Health and Human Services, Administration on Aging (USDHHS AoA). (2003). *A statistical profile of older Americans aged 65+.* Washington, DC: Administration on Aging.

United States Department of Health and Human Services, Administration on Aging (USDHHS AoA). (2005). *Older population by age: 1900–2050.* Retrieved April 29, 2007, from http://www.aoa.gov/prof/Statistics/online_stat_data/AgePop2050.asp

U.S. Department of Health and Human Services, Administration on Aging (USDHHS AoA). (2006). *A statistical profile of older Americans aged 65+.* Washington, DC: Administration on Aging.

CHAPTER 2

Social, Political, Economic, and Demographic Factors and Historical Landmarks Impacting Aging Policy

AN OVERVIEW OF THE ROLE HISTORICAL LANDMARKS PLAY IN SHAPING SOCIAL TRENDS AND PUBLIC POLICIES

Landmarks serve as essential tools to help us recall specific historical events in time and mark specific historical junctures. Historical landmarks are also integral in the development of social trends and social policies. As landmark events have occurred throughout history, we witness the evolution of new trends and the development of specific social mores, values, and institutions. Along with these specific institutions we also witness the development of new trends in social welfare, technology, science, and social life. Historical landmarks, such as the development of the "talking pictures" in Hollywood, enabled women to expand their roles beyond the wife and mother. World War II, an event that saw the exodus of the male workforce to fight for freedom, opened up opportunities for women to enter and engage in the workforce. The upshot of this historical landmark also saw the making of social welfare policy designed to help women maintain their role within their homes if they chose to do so, such as through the Aid to Families with Dependent Children

(AFDC) legislation. Historical landmarks, science, and technology have played significant roles in the evolution of social policies; however, aging policy may not have made as many strides as other areas throughout history. This next segment explores the relationship between historical landmarks and aging policy and presents both developments within science, technology, and historical landmarks (Glennon, 1995), and compares some of these historical landmarks to those of labor, gender, and racial/ethnic developments (Day, 2006) over the same course of time.

THE RELATIONSHIP BETWEEN HISTORICAL LANDMARKS AND AGING POLICY

Social policy can be dramatically influenced by trends in social issues, the political climate, and labor/economic perspectives during a given time frame. All three factors play a role in the social fabric of one's culture or the prevailing culture in communities (Compton, 1980). It is interesting to examine the development of aging policy, vis-à-vis other economic, social, and cultural trends that took place over the course of time. We begin to see the initial steps that make up some of our current aging policies evolve in the United States in 1920 with the passing and enactment of the Civil Service Retirement Act. Prior to 1920, although other countries worldwide had begun to make strides towards evolving some legislation for social security and a mandatory retirement age, we did not actually see any such legislation until at least a decade later in the United States. Commencing with the 1920s, we began to see the development of legislation for retirement benefits; however, aging policy does not mirror other policy development initiatives or social developments that took place during the past century.

TRENDS IN POLICY, SOCIAL, AND POLITICAL INFLUENCES AND LANDMARKS

The Roaring 20s: 1920–1929

Aging Policy Landmarks

The pioneer efforts to develop a retirement system for government employees emerged with the passing of the *Civil Service Retirement Act*, which was enacted in 1920 and included members of the U.S. Congress, and uniformed and civil servants. While we see just the emergence of a society to care for the aged, which seems like a bare essential, we see burgeoning developments elsewhere within American society. This same time period was characterized with major developments within the fields of technology and science.

Industry/Technology and Social Landmarks

During the 1920s, widespread availability of petroleum and electricity occurred, along with the advent of many new products such as refrigerators, vacuum cleaners, wristwatches, foam rubber, disposable tissues, and frozen foods. During this era, Charles Lindbergh made his historic transatlantic flight, which was a first step towards revolutionizing travel. This first solo flight for Lindbergh was also unique in that it did not have a fleet of support resources to travel as "ground" support beneath him. Technology had also advanced the movie industry, and the first feature-length "talking picture" was released—*The Jazz Singer* starring Al Jolson. Women viewed this era also as a time of social experimentation and enjoyed dances like the Charleston. Their sexual freedom may have been encouraged by the popularity of Freud. Despite this, women realized that securing the right to vote (1920) did not improve their economic position nor did this lead to any improvements in social policies to advance women.

Labor

The labor movement was trying to organize; however, unionists efforts were resisted through the "trickle down" economic policy. In 1926, the United States Senate passed a law to allow unions to organize. Jane Addams, the "mother of social work," and Elizabeth Gurley Flynn, among others, became founding members of the American Civil Liberties Union (ACLU) in 1920.

Racial/Ethnic

Legislation on other fronts included the Immigration Act (1921), which attempted to levy controls on the diverse nature of society, and attempted to "maintain the racial preponderance of the basic strain of people." Racial/ethnic groups like blacks, Hispanics, Native Americans, and Asian Americans were systematically discriminated against by legislative efforts. Quotas were set for immigration based upon one's national origin, and the Immigration Act set quotas to restrict people of African descent (1924).

Poverty

In terms of poverty, a perception existed that all would share in prosperity as the economic climate improved; however, with the stock market crash in 1929, this illusion was shattered. The New York Stock Market crash of 1929 led to what was known as the Great Depression.

The Dirty 30s: 1930–1939

Aging Policy Landmarks

The "dirty thirties," or the time span characterized by the Great Depression, saw the development of hallmark legislation impacting older adults in the United States, that is, the Social Security Act of 1935. This piece of legislation was passed and signed into legislation by President Franklin D. Roosevelt to ensure that protection into old age was a right for older workers in America, and to establish social insurance programs. Some of the titles also signed as components of the Social Security Act established provisions for the Old Age Insurance (OAI) programs, Workers' compensation programs, and unemployment compensation. In addition, the Social Security Act provided for public health programs such as maternal and child health services, vocational rehabilitation programs, and public health clinics. Public assistance programs such as Aid to the Blind (AB) and Aid to Dependent Children (ADC) were also components of the Social Security Act.

In addition, the Railroad Retirement Act signed into legislation in 1937 was enacted to ensure that pensions or annuities were available for retired railroad employees and their spouses. President Roosevelt, who had been instrumental in signing the Social Security Act into legislation, was reelected in 1936 as president of the United States.

Provision for widows and children through Survivor's Insurance (OASI) was added in 1939, thus providing some financial pension for those left behind once a retired worker was deceased. On face value, this amendment could have been perceived to have been costly by the House and Senate when moving through the legislative process. However, OASI was presented as an insurance program based on the myth that benefits would be based upon some actuarial contribution. Although the formulary presents itself as being progressive, women are not necessarily the benefactors, and those who were the most poor were least likely to benefit from this provision.

Industry/Technology and Social Landmarks

The Indian Reorganization Act (1934) was passed, which was responsible for partially repealing the Dawes Act and restored tribal rights. Native Americans began to acknowledge their roots and restore their birthrights to their tribal organizations. The act put a halt to the allotment of tribal lands to white people and also put an end to the assimilation of cultures between Native Americans and the white dominant culture. It also enabled Native Americans to develop their own constitution for tribal councils and develop tribal business councils.

While the United States was working towards devising opportunities to improve the lives of older adults, events were brewing on the international scene that led to the decline of economic growth. Hitler assumed leadership in Germany in 1933, which resulted in the onset of World War II (1939). The resulting war effort saw an end to the economic slowdown and depression of the decade; however, it laid the groundwork for a number of changes politically and economically, as countries developed new political alliances throughout the world to combat Hitler and restore the world to some peaceful order.

Labor

During the 1930s, labor unions were legalized and empowered using the 1928 *National Labor Relations Act* or the *Wagner Act*. In addition, this decade began to see a coalition emerge between unions and the Democratic party. Unions gained momentum and force during this decade.

Racial/Ethnic/Gender

The Social Security Act actively excluded blacks and some other minority groups from coverage. In addition, women for the most part were also excluded from Social Security, except as widows.

The Tuskegee study on syphilis recruited African Americans and then left them untreated. African American veterans were recruited unknowingly from their health care providers to examine the course of syphilis. Rather than receiving treatment, these recruits were told that they had a "bad blood" disease and were simply given a placebo.

President Roosevelt appointed a "Black Cabinet" including Mary McLeod Bethune, A. Phillip Randolph, and Robert Weaver. In turn, Bethune also appointed the National Council of Black Women.

Poverty

Despite the passage of the Social Security Act, a number of social factors still played a role in who was included and excluded. African Americans and other minority groups were excluded from coverage when the act was first drafted. Women for the most part were also excluded, except for widows, and even at that, some widows were excluded. During this time frame poverty was rampant, and Roosevelt's New Deal programs were thought to be temporary, including the Federal Emergency Relief Act (FERA), the National Industrial Recovery Act (NIRA), the Public Works Administration (PWA), and the Civil Works Administration (CWA).

The War-Torn 40s: 1940–1949

Aging Policy Landmarks

During the 1940s we see the first visage of a state agency on aging. The state of Connecticut was the first to establish a state-based agency on aging and titled the agency the State Commission on the Care and Treatment of Chronically Ill, Aged and Infirm.

Industry/Technology and Social Landmarks

On the international scene after World War II ended, the United Nations was established in 1945 in response to the universal feeling that there should be some mediating body in place to assure that the world would not face another world war. The United Nations split Palestine into two nations in 1947, resulting in Israel and Palestine. Other significant events on the international front included India's independence from Britain, through the influence of Mohandas Gandhi. Gandhi's leadership called attention worldwide to the notion of nonviolent negotiation strategies.

Labor/Racial

There were a number of advances politically, but this did not mean necessarily that these advances were felt by minority groups or oppressed populations. Labor unions consolidated their power both economically and politically, which resulted in post–World War II compromises that led to an increase in both prices and wages. Discrimination was rampant toward blacks and women. Despite the active roles these two groups played during the World War II, returning African American soldiers were discriminated against, even though President Truman ordered that the army desegregate in 1948. There was a rise in activity of civil rights groups, and African Americans began to migrate north.

Gender

Although women entered the workforce in large numbers during World War II, they were driven out afterward, and women were encouraged to enjoy their time at home. Thus, the "Cleaver" phenomena began to emerge during this decade, which encouraged women to be the "head of their home" as domestic engineers and homemakers. This resulted in the growing market targeting women as consumers. The decade drew to a close with the baby boom.

The Golden Ages: 1950–1959

Aging Policy Landmarks

During this decade, developments within the aging arena began to emerge. This decade witnessed the first National Conference on Aging held in Washington, D.C., sponsored by the Federal Security Agency. In 1956, a special staff on aging was assigned to coordinate responsibilities for the field of aging within the office of the Secretary of the Department of Health, Employment, and Welfare. In 1958 Representative John E. Fogarty introduced a bill in Congress calling for a White House Conference on Aging. This was to be the first White House Conference held. In 1959, the Housing Act was passed, which authorized a direct loan program, making nonprofit rental projects available for the elderly at low interest rates. In addition, the U.S. Senate Special Committee on Aging was created.

Some amendments to the Social Security Act were also passed during this decade. In 1950 incapacitated fathers were included as recipients of aid through the Aid to Families with Dependent Children (AFDC) program. In 1956, people with mental illness were classified as disabled for the purpose of receiving disability support and Old Age Security and Disability (OASDI) through the Old Age Security Insurance program (OASI).

Industry/Technology and Social Landmarks

As a society socially there were a number of advances. Although abroad the Korean War began (1950), people began to move out into the suburbs and began to be served by the development of shopping malls. As people left their agricultural homesteads, movement towards urban centers forced housing expansions outside of the centers of cities and people began to need nearby suburban shopping centers.

The Geneva Accord split Vietnam into two parts, one communist and one noncommunist. This split eventually brought the United States military into the Vietnam war.

The development of psychotropic medications provided new help to people with mental illness. This development led to the vision and goal that people with severe persistent mental illnesses could live outside institutions and become a part of the community.

Most homes were furnished with televisions during this decade, which revolutionized the entertainment patterns for families. Other lifestyle changes included the appearance of sugar-free soft drinks (1952), the debut of *MAD* magazine (1952), and the debut of the Barbie doll (1959).

Racial/Ethnic/Gender

The rise of civil rights activism became pivotal during this decade with the first groundbreaking case challenging the notion of segregation. Brown versus Topeka Board of Education, a case that ordered the desegregation of the public school system (1954) led the way for groundbreaking desegregation movements within local communities through the school system. This was further augmented by Rosa Parks, a fatigued office worker from the NAACP who refused to move from the front of a bus one evening in 1955 in Montgomery, Alabama, to the segregated back section of the bus. This shocking event led to challenging the practice of segregation.

The Age of Technology Explosion: 1960–1969

Aging Policy Landmarks

The Social Security Program went through a number of changes during this decade. In 1960, Social Security amendments made a number of changes in the law, including: (a) eliminating age 50 as a minimum age to qualify for disability benefits, and (b) liberalizing the retirement test and requirement for fully insured status.

In addition, on July 14, 1965, the Medicare health insurance program for the elderly was legislated, along with Medicaid (a health insurance program for the poor). The Older Americans Act was passed and signed into law by President Johnson in 1965.

In 1961, the First White House Conference on Aging took place, under the Kennedy administration. Following this White House Conference, in 1962, more than 160 bills were introduced in Congress that related to the aged and aging. Of these, eight were enacted.

The passage of the Older Americans Act also led to a number of amendments during this decade. For example, in 1967, amendments to the Older Americans Act extended its provisions for 2 years and directed the Administration on Aging to undertake a study of personnel needs in the aging field. Another change took place in 1969 when amendments to the Older Americans Act extended its provisions for 3 years and authorized the use of Title III funds to support area-wide model projects. Another advance within the civil rights arena, was related to age, and the Age Discrimination Act of 1967 was passed and signed into law by President Johnson.

The Administration on Aging was placed in a newly created department of Social and Rehabilitative Services. The face of human services changed dramatically when John F. Kennedy was elected as president of the United States (1960). This introduction of social democracy led to the appointment of two president's commissions—the President's Commission on Mental Health and the President's Commission on Mental Retardation. Unfortunately, some of Kennedy's vision may not have been fully materialized due to his assassination in 1963. Despite the loss of Kennedy, many of the recommendations were carried out by the Johnson Administration.

Industrial/Technological and Social Landmarks

Additional landmarks included the Cuban missile crisis (1962) and the U.S. entry as advisors to the Vietnam War (1963). Racial parity was on its way with the enactment and passage of the Civil Rights Act (1964), a result of the rise in the civil rights movement. In 1963, the Community Mental Health Act was passed. This and the Great Society legislation changed social work and the face of human services.

Several landmark civil rights efforts occurred during this decade. Martin Luther King Jr.'s "I Have a Dream" speech symbolized the movement for civil rights and paved the way for laws and cultural norms accepting people regardless of race, color, or creed. Regardless of gains within the aging arena, several events occurred that led to an impact on social development. Martin Luther King was assassinated in Memphis, Tennessee, during one of his rallies in 1968.

Technology and science passed a new frontier as United States astronauts from the Apollo XI mission landed on the moon on July 21, 1969.

On the political front, farm workers began to organize, and gender also began to be an issue in legislation. In an effort to embarrass the supporters of civil rights legislation, opponents included gender in the legislation. Although the power of this was not immediately recognized, it later became the basis of several lawsuits. The "pill" and sexual revolution were also in full swing.

Poverty

The war on poverty was declared in 1964. Within one year, 1,000 community action centers opened. These community action centers became the training grounds for many community organizers who became active in many of the movements that followed.

The Decade of Presidential Resignation: 1970–1979

Aging Policy Landmarks

The 1970s marks a decade of development within the aging arena. The second White House Conference on Aging convened in Washington, DC. Some of the major resolutions during this decade included:

The Supplemental Security Income (SSI) program was created in 1972 and was implemented to provide economic supplements to low-income individuals in their old age and to care for widows or children of the deceased. SSI benefits were available to beneficiaries if money had been paid into the system for the requisite number of quarters.

In 1973, The Older American Comprehensive Service Amendments established area agencies on aging, and amendments authorized model projects for senior centers.

The Domestic Volunteer Service Act provided for foster grandparent programs. This is the first acknowledgment of grandparents' role.

The Comprehensive Employment and Training Act (CETA) provided job training for those facing barriers to employment, including older workers. CETA became an employment agency for temporary public service jobs, thus creating a labor opportunity for talented older workers.

The Age Discrimination Act of 1975 was passed and signed into law by President Nixon. Some of the hallmarks of this legislation included penalties to employers who discriminate against older workers on the basis of their age.

Industry/Technology and Social Landmarks

During this era, John Lennon was murdered, which led to an end to the rock revival and era. Along with this end to the rock revival, a change of tide associated with recreational drugs also was seen.

The rise of technology led to innovations and changes in communication through computers. Industry was also brought into the computer era, which began to systematize administrative and data management procedures.

In 1973, *Roe vs. Wade* was part of the growth of the women's movement. Poverty was addressed through the food stamp program, which nationalized and established national eligibility standards nationwide.

The poor also saw an end to their "voice" through President Nixon's dissolution of the ability for legal aid recipients to file class action lawsuits against governmental agencies.

The Era of Economic Entrenchment: 1980–1989

Aging Policy Landmarks

During the 1980s the aging arena once again saw a number of new developments. Commencing in 1981, amendments to the Older Americans Act extended the program for 3 years, through September 30, 1984. In 1984, additional amendments to the Older Americans Act clarified the roles of state and area agencies on aging in coordinating community-based services and in maintaining accountability for the funding of national priority services (legal, access, and in-home services). In 1985 *A Compendium of Papers Honoring the Twentieth Anniversary of the Older Americans Act* was compiled by the U.S. House of Representatives Select Committee on Aging. In 1987, amendments to the Older Americans Act authorized new initiatives on mental health, elder abuse, home health care for the frail elderly, and outreach to eligible SSI recipients.

Industry/Technology and Social Landmarks

On the international scene, Reagan and Gorbachev signed the historic INF arms treaty (1987). This arms treaty led to alliances between the two superpowers of the world—the United States and Russia.

In 1988, the Free Trade Agreement (FTA) between the United States and Canada began, which opened up trade and commerce between the two North American countries. The FTA was later expanded to include Mexico through the North America Free Trade Agreement (NAFTA).

Racial/Ethnic/Gender

From a racial/ethnic perspective, there was increased recognition for affirmative action and hiring quotas. This led also to the increased presence of women in the labor market and nontraditional sector. Sandra Day O'Conner is a good example of women in nontraditional roles, as she was appointed the first woman Supreme Court Judge (1982).

Poverty

Despite these advances, we see an increased rate of poverty, particularly among people with disabilities and people with severe persistent mental illness. Some may argue that the decreased support to social programs through "Reagonomics" impacted poverty, since spending for social services was reduced by 50% or more; however, massive cuts to federal and social programs began following the passage of the Gramm-Rudman-Hollings Act (GRH) in 1986. Protected programs, which received only moderate or modified cuts in fiscal spending, included OASDI, AFDC, Child Nutrition, Food Stamps, Medicaid, SSI, Veterans' Compensation and Veterans' Pensions, and Medicare and Social Services block grants, to name a few. Unprotected programs included Headstart programs, programs and services for the elderly and disabled, and rural development programs, to name a few. Unfortunately, GRH failed miserably at the reduction of spending, since it did not address some of the tax policies, which led to deficits in spending.

The Era of Globalization: 1990–1999

Aging Policy Landmarks

In 1992 amendments to the Older Americans Act included the addition of Title VII, the Vulnerable Elders Rights Protection Title, and funded efforts to increase education on how healthy lifestyles reduce the risk of chronic health problems in later life. These are major advances to the Older Americans Act and lay the groundwork to showcase the importance of prevention programs for maintaining one's health.

The Balanced Budget Act of 1997 impacts older adults, through the enrollment of eligible Medicaid retirees, into managed care entities. This act enabled individual states to force Medicaid recipients to enroll in managed care organizations (MCOs) or primary care case managers (PCCMs).

Industry/Technology and Social Landmarks

On the international front, Iraq invaded Kuwait (1990). Operation Desert Storm also prevailed (1991) following the development of "Operation Desert Shield" (1990), and the world also saw the collapse of the Soviet Union (1990). Undoubtedly, the collapse of the Soviet Union moved Russia from being considered one of the world's superpowers to a struggling economic capitalistic nation. This also led the way for other communist European nations to become capitalist. The Berlin wall came down in 1990, forging Germany into one nation.

The Americans with Disabilities Act was signed into law in 1990 by President George H. W. Bush, and through its five titles, paved the road for inclusion of older adults into community life. Although intended for people with disabilities, people who are nondisabled older adults were also benefactors of this legislative effort.

Changes in technology made worldwide communications more efficient through the Internet and the World-Wide Web. Search engines such
as "Google" and "Yahoo" expanded the use of the home computer into
the virtual gateway of information. Libraries also benefited remarkably
through the use of technology for database management.

In Michigan, under the leadership of Dr. Jack Kevorkian, the notion
of assisted suicide was challenged. Dr. Kevorkian, although eventually
arrested, disbarred from practicing medicine, and imprisoned, prescribed
medication to chronically ill patients interested in assisted suicide as an
option to care. Although illegal in the United States, and in most states,
the state of Oregon used the Kevorkian paradigm to develop state legislation in support of physician-assisted suicide as an option for patients
with chronic health conditions.

Labor Front

The North American Free Trade Agreement (NAFTA) was approved by
Congress (1993), which led to changes in the labor market pool within
the U.S., and realizes shifts in jobs and industries to Mexico. While NAFTA
was used to stimulate business across North American countries, business
was stimulated in the United States through Empowerment/Enterprise
zones during the Clinton administration (1993).

Racial/Ethnic/Gender

The United States also witnessed a growing ethnic diversity and women
challenged the "glass ceiling." Carol Moseley-Braun succeeded with this
challenge as the first African American woman to be elected to the United
States Senate.

During this decade, the United States Supreme Court also ruled that
the use of race as a factor when creating congressional districts was un-
constitutional. This landmark decision was made in *Bush v. Vera* and
Shaw v. Hunt.

Poverty

Welfare reform and changes in AFDC impacted people in poverty. New
legislation known as Temporary Aid to Needy Families (TANF) led to a
ceiling in the number of years one could collect funds (5 years). TANF,
spearheaded by the then Secretary of Health and Human Services Tommy
Thompson, was modeled after Thompson's Wisconsin welfare initiative,
which had been successfully implemented while he was governor.

The Dawning of a New Century: 2000–2007

Aging Policy Landmarks

A number of advances within the aging policy arena have already occurred during the twenty-first century. In 2000, Social Security earnings tests were eliminated for full retirement age. In 2003, the Medicare Part D prescription drug benefit was passed, which opened up options for people seeking financial assistance for pharmaceutical medications.

The fifth White House Conference on Aging took place in 2005, in Washington, DC. This conference was, according to many professionals within the field, mired in politics and devoid of meaningful constituent input. Fifty priorities were developed as a result of the conference, and these priorities helped shape the 2006 amendments to the Older Americans Act.

These amendments laid the groundwork for some significant changes in community services, which can address prevention services as well as services for existing conditions. The concept of Centers for Prevention to address mental health and health care are welcome additions to the act. Dealing with self-neglect is also introduced in the Older Americans Act.

Industry/Technology and Social Landmarks

A number of events have taken place in the twenty-first century, including terrorist attack, the toppling of dictatorships (for example, Saddam Hussein), and natural disasters (for example, Hurricane Katrina).

On September 11, 2001, the United States witnessed a number of terrorist attacks on American soil. These began with two planes crashing into the Twin Towers of the World Trade Center in New York City and were followed by one crashing into the Pentagon in Washington, DC. A fourth plane was forced into a field in Pennsylvania, which was perhaps intended to crash into the Capitol building in Washington, DC. These attacks spurred President George W. Bush's "War on Terror."

In 2002, the world witnessed the toppling of a major dictatorship, that of Saddam Hussein in Iraq. The United States sought to topple this dictatorship as one of its strategies to address the war on terror. At the time of the writing of this chapter (2006), the presence of United States military forces still exists within Iraq, as an attempt to bring about a democracy within the country.

In the spring of 2005, the world bid farewell to Pope John Paul II, who passed away in Rome. The pontiff was known for his vision to bring about world peace, and he impacted religious leadership well beyond the Roman Catholic faith, to include Christians, Muslims, Jews, Buddhists, and other world religions.

TABLE 2.1 Historical Landmarks, Social and Political Trends, and Their Relationship With Aging Policy

Decade	Policy landmarks in the aging arena	Social landmarks	Political influences and landmarks
1920–29	1920—The Civil Service Retirement Act: provides a retirement system for many government employees. Includes members of the U.S. Congress, uniformed and civil servants.	Widespread availability of petroleum and electricity. The advent of new products: refrigerators, vacuum cleaners, wristwatches, foam rubber, disposable tissues, frozen foods. 1920 League of Nations begins. 1927—Charles Lindbergh makes his first transatlantic flight. 1927—The first sound movie, *The Jazz Singer*, is released. Dancing of the "Charleston." This is an era of social experimentation. The Scopes trial is in 1925. Prohibition is enacted in 1919. In 1924, the Immigration Act seeks to control immigration, to maintain the "racial preponderance of the basic strain of our people." 1929—The Great Stock Market crash.	*Labor*: Labor is trying to organize but meets with major resistance. In 1926 Senate passes law to allow unions to organize. It is an era of trickle down economics and company unions. *Racial/ethnic*: Blacks, Hispanics, Native Americans and Asian Americans are systematically discriminated against, often by laws. Quotas are set based on national origin. Immigration Act sets immigration quotas to restrict people of African descent. *Gender*: Women are realizing that getting the vote does not improve their economic position nor lead to improved social policies. There is a new sexual freedom, characterized by the flappers and encouraged by the popularity of Freud. *Poverty*: It is assumed that all will share in prosperity as the economy grows, with this era.

(continued)

TABLE 2.1 Historical Landmarks, Social and Political Trends, and Their Relationship With Aging Policy (continued)

Decade	Policy landmarks in the aging arena	Social landmarks	Political influences and landmarks
1930–39	1935—The Social Security Act is passed and signed into law by President Roosevelt "to provide protection as a matter of right for the American workers." 1937—The Railroad Retirement Act is enacted to provide annuities (pensions) for retired railroad employees and spouses. 1939—Social Security Administration adds survivor's insurance.	Hitler assumes leadership (1933) in Germany. Roosevelt is elected President of the United States (1936). Indian Reorganization Act passes (1934). World War II (1939–45) begins.	*Labor:* Unions are legalized and empowered through the 1938 National Labor Relations Act (Wagner Act). A coalition between unions and the Democratic party emerges. New York Association of Social Workers organizes social workers into unions. *Racial/ethnic:* The Social Security Act actively excludes Blacks and some other minority groups from coverage. The syphilis study recruits African Americans, then leaves them untreated. Mary McLeod Bethune founds the National Council of Negro Women. Roosevelt appoints "Black cabinet" including Bethune, A. Phillip Randolph Randolph, and Robert Weaver. *Gender:* For the most part women are excluded from Social Security, except as widows. *Poverty:* Poverty is rampant. The New Deal programs are assumed to be temporary, until the economy rights itself. Roosevelt (1933) drafts "grand design" to include: Federal Emergency Relief Act (FERA) National Industrial Recovery Act (NIRA)

	Aging	World Events	Social/Economic Context
1940–49	1945—State of Connecticut is the first to establish a state agency on aging through its designation of a State Commission on the Care and Treatment of Chronically Ill, Aged and Infirm.	Japan attacks Pearl Harbor (1941). Soviet victory at Stalingrad (1943). United Nations is established (1945). UN splits Palestine into two nations (1947), Palestine and Israel. India gains independence from Britain through the efforts of Ghandi (1947).	Public Works Administration (PWA) Civil Works Administration (CWA). Under Harry Hopkins, Francis Perkins appointed the Secretary of Labor. *Labor:* Unions consolidate their power both economically and politically. The post–World War II compromise allows wages and prices to grow. *Racial/ethnic:* Returning Black soldiers are again discriminated against. President Truman orders the Army desegregated in 1948. There is growing dissatisfaction, and civil rights groups are beginning to become active. Blacks migrate north. *Gender:* Women enter the workforce in large numbers during the war, but are driven out after the war. The June Cleaver phenomenon begins to develop. Marketers begin targeting women as consumers. The Baby Boom begins. *Poverty* is ignored. Social work is in the Freudian stage.
1950–59	1950—First National Conference on Aging in DC, sponsored by Federal Security Agency. 1956—A special staff on aging is assigned coordinative responsibilities for aging.	Korean War begins (1950). People move from farms into suburbs. Development of psychotropic medications unleashes potential for people with mental illness. *Brown vs. Board of Education*	*Labor:* Unions consolidate their power both economically and politically. The post–World War II compromise allows wages and prices to grow. Truman seizes the steel mill industry to avert a strike (1952). AFL-CIO Merger creates an organized super-power (1955)

(continued)

TABLE 2.1 Historical Landmarks, Social and Political Trends, and Their Relationship With Aging Policy (continued)

Decade	Policy landmarks in the aging arena	Social landmarks	Political influences and landmarks
1950–59 (*Cont.*)	within the Office of the Secretary of Department of Health, Employment and Welfare. 1958—Representative John E. Fogarty introduces bill in Congress calling for a White House Conference on Aging. 1959—The Housing Act is enacted, authorizing a direct loan program of nonprofit rental projects for the elderly at low interest rates. Also the U.S. Senate Special Committee on Aging is created.	(1954) Rosa Parks refuses to move from the front of a bus to the segregated section (1955) Most homes are furnished with televisions. The Baby Boom. The birth of rock and roll (Elvis Presley, Jerry Lee Lewis, etc.). The Geneva Accord splits Vietnam into two parts, one Communist, one noncommunist. *MAD Magazine* appears at newsstands (1952). Sugar free soft drinks appear (1952). Puerto Rico becomes an independent commonwealth of the United States (1952). Polio vaccine becomes widely available (1955). Barbie doll debuts (1959).	*Racial/ethnic:* Blacks migrate north. "Family of Man" exhibition displayed by curator Edward Streichen at the Metropolitan Museum of Art (1955). Jim Crow laws are struck down (1954). *Gender:* Women enter the workforce in large numbers during the war, but are driven out after the war. The Clever phenomenon begins to develop. Marketers begin targeting women as consumers. The Baby Boom begins. Ann Launders (1955) revolutionizes women's expectations. *Poverty:* The AFDC population increased dramatically along with the *baby boom.* Accessibility to public assistance did not encourage productivity or employability, and over the decade public aid expenditures rose from $2.30 to $3.30 million.
1960–69	1960—Social Security amendments made a number of changes in the law, including: (a) eliminating age 50 as a minimum to qualify for disability benefits and (b) liberalizing the retirement test and requirement for fully insured status.	John F. Kennedy elected as President of the United States (1960). Kennedy assassinated in 1963 United States enters as advisors to the Vietnam War (1963). Cuban missile crisis (1962). Civil Rights Act passes (1964).	*Labor:* Farm workers begin to organize. *Racial/ethnic:* The civil rights movement catches the popular eye. Several civil rights acts are passed. *Gender:* In an effort to embarrass the supporters of civil rights legislation, opponents included gender in the acts. Although the power of this was not immediately

1961—First White House Conference on Aging.

1962—More than 160 bills introduced in Congress related to the aged and aging; eight are enacted.

1965—Medicare health insurance program for the elderly is legislated. Also the Older Americans Act is passed and signed into law by President Johnson on July 14.

1967—Amendments to the Older Americans Act extend its provisions for 2 years and directed the Administration on Aging to undertake a study of personnel needs in the aging field.

Age Discrimination Act of 1967 is passed and signed into law by President Johnson.

The Administration on Aging is placed in a newly created Social and

Martin Luther King Jr.'s "I Have a Dream" speech.

U.S. astronauts land on the moon (1969).

Haight-Ashbury sit in takes place in San Francisco with the hope of social change.

recognized, it later becomes the basis of several lawsuits. The birth control pill and sexual revolution are in full swing.

Poverty: The war on poverty is declared in 1964. In a year, 1,000 community action centers are opened. They are training grounds for many community organizers who are active in many of the movements that follow.

In 1963, the Community Mental Health Act is passed. This and the Great Society legislation change social work.

(continued)

TABLE 2.1 Historical Landmarks, Social and Political Trends, and Their Relationship With Aging Policy (continued)

Decade	Policy landmarks in the aging arena	Social landmarks	Political influences and landmarks
1960–69 (Cont.)	Rehabilitative Service Agency (SRS) within the Department. 1969—Amendments to the Older Americans Act extend its provisions for 3 years and authorize the use of Title III funds to support area-wide model projects.		
1970–79	1971—Second White House Conference on Aging convened in Washington, DC. 1972—Supplemental Security Income (SSI) programs created 1973—The Older American Comprehensive Service Amendments established areas agencies on aging, and amendments authorized model projects for senior centers. The Domestic Volunteer Service Act provided for Foster Grandparent programs.	Martin Luther King is assassinated. Nixon reduces troops to Vietnam, which leads to an end of the Vietnam war (1972). The rise of technology improves the age of mechanization through computers. President Reagan's fiscal policies (Reaganomics) affect nations worldwide.	*Labor:* 1970—OSHA passed. *Racial/ethnic:* A time of consolidating gains. *Gender:* 1973—*Roe vs. Wade.* Women's movement grows. *Poverty:* Food stamp program is nationalized and national eligibility standards are established. Nixon takes away the ability of Legal Aid to file class action suits against government agencies.

| 1980–89 | The Comprehensive Employment and Training Act (CETA) provided job training for those facing barriers to employment commonly experienced by older workers. Age Discrimination Act of 1975 was passed and signed into law by President Nixon. 1981—Amendments to the Older American Act extended the program for 3 years, through September 30, 1984. 1984—Amendments to the Older Americans Act clarified the roles of state and area agencies on aging in coordinating community-based services and in maintaining accountability for the funding of national priority services (legal, access and in-home services). 1985—*A Compendium of Papers Honoring the Twentieth Anniversary of the Older Americans Act* is compiled | Reagan and Gorbachev sign historic arms treaty (1987). John Lennon is murdered, an end to an era of rock revival (1980). | *Labor:* 1980—OSHA amendments. *Racial/ethnic:* Increased recognition for affirmative action and hiring quotas. *Gender:* Women increase presence in the labor market and nontraditional sector. *Poverty:* Increased poverty particularly among people with disabilities and people with severe persistent mental illness. Decreased support to social programs through the impact of "Reagonomics" on poverty—impacts those with fewest resources and creates a narrowing of the middle-class income. |

(continued)

TABLE 2.1 Historical Landmarks, Social and Political Trends, and Their Relationship With Aging Policy (continued)

Decade	Policy landmarks in the aging arena	Social landmarks	Political influences and landmarks
1980–89 (*Cont.*)	by the U.S. House of Representatives Select Committee on Aging. 1987—Amendments to the Older Americans Act authorized new initiatives on mental health, elder abuse, home health care for the frail elderly, and outreach to eligible SSI recipients.		
1990–99	1992—Amendments to the Older Americans Act include the addition of Title VII, the Vulnerable Elders Rights Protection Title, and fund efforts to increase education on how healthy lifestyles reduce the risk of chronic health problems in later life. 1995—The fourth White House Conference on Aging convenes in Washington, DC. 1997—The Older Americans Act is up for re-authorization.	Iraq invades Kuwait (1990). The Americans with Disabilities Act is signed (1990). Nelson Mandela is released from prison in South Africa (1990). The Clean Air Act is passed (1990). Desert Storm (1991). Collapse of the Soviet Union (1991). Changes in technology make world wide communications more efficient. Assisted suicide movement begins under the leadership of Dr. Jack Kevorkian in MI.	*Labor:* North American Free Trade Agreement (NAFTA) is approved by Congress (1993), leads to changes in the labor market pool within the United States, and sees shifts in jobs and industries to Mexico. *Racial/ethnic:* Growing ethnic diversity changes the face of America (23.9% white). *Gender:* Women challenge the "glass ceiling." *Poverty:* Welfare reform and changes in Aid to Families and Dependent Children (AFDC) impact people in poverty. Stewart B. McKinney Assistance Act for the Homeless reauthorized. TANF replaces AFDC and subsumes other assistance programs (1996).

| 2000–2006 | 2000—Social Security earnings test eliminated for full retirement age.
2003—Medicare Part D Prescription drug benefit passed. | 2001—Terrorist attack at the Twin Towers, New York, Pentagon, Washington, DC.
2002—Overthrow of Saddam Hussein in Iraq.
2004—Death of Ronald Reagan.
2005—Hurricane Katrina.
2005—Death of Pope John Paul II.
2005— Same sex marriage passed as a constitutional right in Canada, several states in the United States follow suite.
2006—Execution of Saddam Hussein.
2007—Massacre of 39 victims (students and faculty) on Virginia Technology University campus. | *Labor:*
Racial/ethnic:
Gender: Same sex marriage is legalized in Canada and several U.S. states. |

Hurricane Katrina, in 2005, stormed through New Orleans and other parts of Louisiana, Mississippi, and the Gulf areas in the United States leaving many people homeless, particularly the marginalized and poor. This devastating natural disaster led to the displacement of many people.

In 2007, the most devastating massacre in the history of postsecondary institutions took place in Virginia. Over 35 victims (students and faculty) were shot by a troubled student one warm day on a college campus, just weeks before the end of the spring semester.

Racial/Ethnic/Gender

A major issue was same-sex marriages. Canada legalized same sex marriages, with at least five states in the United States, by 2006. This will continue to lead to major challenges to the paradigm of the family, and the contract of marriage.

SUMMARY

A number of changes have occurred within the field of aging over the last century. These changes, however, do not come close to the changes we have witnessed within the social, technological, and political arenas in the United States or worldwide. This relative dearth in changes can also be attributed to the fact that economic climate plays a tremendous role in social programs. Philosophical perspectives also play a major role in the development of our social fabric. The next chapter will lay out a range of philosophical paradigms that may play a part in the development of social programs. See Table 2.1.

REFERENCES

Compton, B. R. (1980). *Introduction to social welfare and social work: Structure, function, and process*. Homewood, IL: The Dorsey Press.

Day, P. J. (2006). *A new history of social welfare*. Boston: Allyn & Bacon.

Glennon, L. (1995). *Our times: The illustrated history of the 20th century*. Atlanta: Turner Publishing.

CHAPTER 3

Philosophical Paradigms and Policy Frameworks

Public policy is a fabric woven from threads of numerous sources and through various influences. In the first two chapters we have seen that aging policy is shaped by a variety of demographic, social, and economic factors. However, these factors are not the only influences that play a role in the development of public policy or aging policies. While these factors have some influence in the development of public policy, philosophical paradigms influence the actual development of policy and play a strong implicit role in how public policy is actually drafted. So, how exactly do these philosophical paradigms and theoretical frameworks play a role in the development of aging policy?

INTRODUCTION TO PHILOSOPHICAL PARADIGMS AND THE RELATIONSHIP TO AGING POLICY AND POLICY ANALYSIS

A number of benefits exist to having a working knowledge of the social welfare and policy arena, including how to analyze public policy. All too often, policy decisions have been made on the basis of economic and political considerations, while the experiences of those who are directly affected, such as the constituents, have been given little attention. Human service specialists are often called upon to provide insight into programs and policies, and within this context often have a vision for what they would like to see implemented in terms of policy or programs. However, the reality is that there is often a mismatch between what planners and public health/human service professionals have in mind for aging policy and what is either signed into legislation or becomes a program/service. This is often the result of competing philosophical paradigms or the implementation process. An explanation of these issues as a part of the policy analysis process helps facilitate an understanding of these competing philosophical paradigms.

WHAT IS POLICY ANALYSIS?

Policy analysis can be explained as an investigation and inquiry into the causes and consequences of public policies. Public policy is the general term for decisions, laws, and regulations put forth by governing bodies. Information gained through the analysis of public policies can be used to develop policy alternatives for the future, to assess existing or previous policies, or to explain public problems and social phenomena (Dobelstein, 1996). Within this framework of policy analysis, various philosophical paradigms play a role in the development of healthy public policy, and various implementation strategies play a role in the process of moving policy from a legislative effort to programs and services. In the next sections these factors, such as philosophical paradigms and implementation strategies, will be explored, within the context of policy development and implementation.

PHILOSOPHICAL PARADIGMS

Public policy is never shaped in a vacuum, and it is strongly influenced by a variety of philosophical perspectives, which may run the range from very conservative to very liberal. These perspectives are essential to understanding the prevailing views that influence or shape the current social policy that we have in place. Understanding these various views can help build strategies to promote new perspectives, directions, or amendments to current and existing policy/legislation. In this chapter a variety of philosophical paradigms is presented.

Individual values and ideology greatly influence the content and structure of public policy, although theories explain how social problems receive recognition and then become the objects of the policy debate. One's individual values color how public policy can be developed, and how public policy may either be introduced as a bill, or eventually be signed into legislation. In fact, a close examination of public hearings and personal testimonies and legislative proceedings can reveal some very significant value-laden perspectives. These values can be categorized into paradigms, which can help serve as a framework to understand social policy, or the values that underpin social policy. Although no one paradigm stands clearly as the best explanation of why and how certain public policies came to be, paradigms do help to provide a framework for the analysis of the current welfare system and aging system. Some specific paradigms include blaming the victim, elitism, social welfare as a right, econometric perspectives, cause versus function and the window of opportunity. An exploration of each of these paradigms will help shape our understanding of how public policy can be developed.

Cycle of victimization

Blaming the Victim

The philosophical paradigm of blaming the victim embraces the notion that individuals are at fault for their shortcomings or their status in society, rather than considering the systemic or universal issues (Ryan, 1976). This concept helps explain inequity in our society, by suggesting that there are individuals who are inherently in a cycle of poverty, culturally deprived, or career criminals due to their choice, rather than because of an inherent problem in society, or with the social care system. Ryan characterizes these cycles of victimization due to three dimensions: (1) perceived differences versus similarities; (2) individual behaviors versus collective action; and (3) internal factors versus external forces. The exclusion of specific groups of people from legislative efforts incorporates this blaming the victim perspective. For example, people with addictions and substance abuse histories are excluded from policies like the Americans with Disabilities Act. This also explains why self-neglect has only recently been added to the Older Americans Act. Both of these social issues are perceived to be attributed to behaviors that are not similar to the majority of older adults and people with disabilities. Secondly they are as a result of individual behaviors, and lastly due to individual weaknesses. Hence, legislative efforts for programs and services do not address the needs of these specific groups of people, since these individuals are perceived to be responsible for their own problematic behaviors and thus responsible for their own solutions, rather than requiring solutions as a result of collective efforts or broad social and public response. Unfortunately, historically speaking, many legislative efforts have not been as comprehensive as possible due to this paradigm of blaming the victim.

This concept can be further articulated if we examine a basic premise in American culture—the belief that all older Americans have access to adequate food, clothing, and shelter. For the most part, we would assume that this is true, and the majority of our educated program planners and policy makers would subscribe to this perspective. Hence, if an older adult is at risk of being homeless due to an inappropriate pension, we often perceive this as an individual difference, and a problem for the individual, not the collective; thus we blame the victim.

Elitism

In the paradigm of elitism, policy development is in the hands of a few stakeholders. This group of stakeholders tends to dictate the rules and influence public policy largely in response to their own values and preferences (Bruggerman, 1997, Domhoff, 1956, 1974, Dye, 1975). Individuals with financial resources tend to play a critical role in the policy making arena, due to their wealth, than those who do not have access to such resources (Galbraith, 1973). Corporate giants or their executive have been thought to utilize government as a resource in efforts to influence public policy in their favor (Wright-Mills, 1956).

John Kenneth Galbraith argues that the "public bureaucracy . . . can be effectively and durably influenced by another organization. And between public and private organizations there can be a deeply symbiotic relationship"(Galbraith, 1973, p. 46). Hence, the elite have access to opportunities that other groups may not be privy to, which enhance their ability to influence public policy. To illustrate: "the president of General Motors, has a prescriptive right, on visiting Washington, to see the president of the United States. The president of General Electric has a right to see the secretary of defense" (Galbraith, 1973, p. 46). This illustrates how corporate elites use their opportunities to shape the legislative fabric of our state through their values (Galbraith, 1973).

Additionally, many of these same individuals may have been appointed to high-level policy-making positions within government. Since many may have a track record of running effective corporations, they are often appointed to run massive federal bureaucracies. Through these positions, they can often wield tremendous influence on public policy by imposing their own policy and value preferences within the federal agencies they direct.

"The power," argues Galbraith, of this elite system "rests on its access to belief." What is good for the specific elite group in question is believed to be good for the general public. People in "elite power" believe that a model of public policy making is best because "the masses are largely passive, apathetic, and ill-informed." Public policy results in "not reflecting the demands of the people in so much as it does the interests and values of the elites" (Dye, 1975, p. 25).

Social Welfare As a Right

The paradigm of social welfare as a right dates back to the Elizabethan Poor Laws of 1654, in which the deserving poor were perceived to have a

COST + Economic always consider

right to services and support. Under this philosophical paradigm, a group in society is perceived to have a right to services—people such as widows, and people with congenital disabilities. It is seen that these individuals are widowed or disabled, not through their doing, but through some negative or adverse event. The original Aid to Families and Dependent Children (AFDC) program, a title which was a component of the Social Security Act, was drafted to care for mothers who had been widowed, or affected by the loss of their husbands through honorable service. This program was intended as a right for women and children whose spouses were assuming responsibility for their country. As civil rights expanded in the United States for people who were minorities, and particularly African Americans, the inclusion of minority groups into Social Security was seen as a right, rather than a privilege.

Econometric Perspectives

Within an econometric paradigm, costs and the economic impact are always considered, when developing programs and drafting policy. The Government Accounting Office is mandated to conduct evaluations on policy initiatives, with cost in mind. Unfortunately, the costs of programs and of implementation are often a major deterrent to building incremental changes to current public policy. Support for public policy is weighed through the lens of costs to society, and a quantitative view of how many people will benefit from such investment (Kemp & Denton, 2003). An example to illustrate how the econometric paradigm plays a role in the development of public policy can be seen with some of the amendments to the retirement ages that must be attained for the receipt of Social Security benefits.

Cause Versus Function

Through the cause versus function paradigm, policy and programs are drafted in an attempt to placate the cause, rather than have any utilitarian value or functional value or impact (Karger & Stoesz, 1990; Piven & Cloward, 1979; Wilensky & Lebeaux, 1965). Hence, with this approach, the very purpose of the drafted policy or legislation is to create the impression to the general public that some effort has been taken to care for a specific social problem or issue. However, in reality, the program or legislative effort really plays a limited role or function for the individual or group. An example of this paradigm at play was seen after Hurricane Katrina in Louisiana, in 2005. As a result of the Homeland Security Act, all skilled nursing care and nursing home facilities were to have an emergency response evacuation plan, in the event of a community-wide emergency. The "cause" was to be responsive in time of public emergency; however, in reality, these plans failed because of other systemic features within the larger community. Hence, the actual function of these plans was ineffectual, but as a result of the legislative efforts, the impression was that an emergency response plan was in effect.

In summary, various paradigms are at play when legislation is drafted or programs/services developed. Insight into these various philosophical perspectives can help enable the public policy advocate to become better prepared with responses or rebuttals to support their own perspective, and to help equip them with responses to assure that some of the gaps within legislation or programs are addressed. In the next segment of this chapter, specific policy implementation strategies are addressed.

IMPLEMENTATION STRATEGIES

Social policy is developed and implemented within the context of both philosophical paradigms and specific implementation strategies. These implementation strategies help one to understand why specific policies and programs are implemented versus others, and once understood; enable the reader to develop strategies to use to more effectively recognize the implementation of public policy. Values and ideology greatly influence the content and structure of public policy, although theories explain how social problems receive recognition and then become the objects of the policy debate. Although no one theory stands clearly as the best explanation of why and how certain public policies came to be, theories do help to provide a framework for the analysis of the current welfare system and aging system. Implementation strategies include window of opportunity, implementation, incrementalism, rationalism and street-level bureaucrats.

Window of Opportunity

The timing of a public decision has been characterized by Kingdon (1984) as the opening of a policy window of opportunity, and an essential consideration in the implementation of public policy. Three elements need to be present for the success of the window of opportunity, which include (1) a compelling public problem, (2) a solution, and (3) broad political support for the solution. When these three elements come together, there is a strong likelihood that public policy will be developed. The events of the 1930s demonstrate the three streams coming together to develop the Social Security Act. Timing was right, depression brought about economic hardship, and a solution had been debated by political leaders and advocates for years. The Homeland Security Act is another example of the window of opportunity implementation theory. At the time of its passing, the social problem was impending attacks from terrorist sources, the solution was controls imposed through the Homeland Security Act, and since this was a compelling social issue, broad bipartisan political support ensued.

Implementation

It is no surprise that what develops as a policy and what actually gets implemented as a program or service will often differ. This reality is often considered the implementation theory of policy development. Pressman and Wildavsky (1979) suggest that the implementation of public policy is an evolutionary process, and the actual legislated policy changes when it is implemented. Although policy makers develop policy, the initial perception of what had been written in the legislation, or even what had been initially envisioned is seldom what is implemented. Unfortunately, this may be accounted for by the reality that those who devise the policy are not the same people who are responsible for actually putting the ideas into practice. This leaves room for interpretation and values, especially for social welfare programs. What might make sense politically, when passed in the legislature, may make no sense once this same policy is implemented at a local level or in rural communities, for example. An example to illustrate this theory is the implementation of Medicare Part D. While seniors are required to apply on a computer, using a URL and through a specific Medicare Part D web site, a vast number of older adults, particularly those living in rural communities, are in serious need of technology support in order to apply for Medicare Part D. Ironically, Barbara Bush, George W. Bush's mother, also cited problems with attempting to apply.

Incrementalism

Charles Lindblom (1959), in "The Science of Muddling Through," articulates that public policy is developed through small changes to existing policies. In the implementation process, Lindblom suggests that there is never enough time to consider all information, that information on all possible choices is not possible, that choices are not readily available, and that it is easier to make small changes to existing policies than to create something entirely new. The Social Security Act and The Older Americans Act are good examples of how policy development occurred through incrementalism, since amendments over time have shaped both pieces of legislation to include important updates that enable the policies to address programs and services needed by the general population.

Rationalism

Rational policy making requires knowledge of the values of all segments of society, all possible policy alternatives, the consequences of those alternatives, and the costs and benefits. This knowledge is often hard to come by because it is not necessarily realistic, but rather, the ideal. Numerous factors affect this rational process, such as values, attitudes, interest groups with varying resources, lack of time to weigh all possibilities, and lack of adequate information. Unfortunately, within the policy-making process, there is often not the time or the resources to really examine all possible alternatives, such as short-term and long-term implications, costs, and benefits to a particular proposal. Although a number of interest groups may present themselves to the legislature, it may not be possible to hear from all groups that may be affected by a specific legislative effort, due to time and resources. Consequently, interest groups that have the resources and person power to be heard are often those whose perspectives are considered, rather than the perspectives of all who will be affected, and the end result is that a rational policy-making approach is not carried out.

Street-Level Bureaucrats

The implementation theory known as street-level bureaucrats is best characterized by Lipsky (1980), who suggests that the implementation process should focus on what happens after policy is implemented. He calls the power to shape social policy exercised by public services workers the power of street-level bureaucrats, since the administrative and human service workforce play a tremendous role in the actual implementation of the intended public policy. Street-level bureaucrats have significant power and control over people's lives, making decisions that affect who gets what, how quickly, and under what circumstances (Moore, 1987, 1990). Actions affecting policy can be as simple as how quickly applications are processed or whether phone calls are returned. These resources and their implementation are further controlled by administrative structures that may include severe person shortages, thus leading to additional constraints upon a public care system (Jewell & Glasser, 2006; Smith, Novak & Frank, 2001; Vinzant & Crothers, 1996).

An understanding of specific implementation strategies is an initial step to the development of effective public policies. Developing an awareness of specific strategies such as rationalism, implementation, incrementalism, window of opportunity, and street-level bureaucrats can help the policy advocate better understand the system and why specific policies may be limited in their impact, or why specific policies do not meet the intended goals. The next step in this process is to conceptualize a model for social welfare policy analysis.

A MODEL FOR SOCIAL WELFARE POLICY ANALYSIS

Within the context of philosophical paradigms and implementation strategies, one must consider how to pull these together to best understand the implementation of social welfare policy analysis. Although public policies such as aging policy are developed for a purpose (that is, to meet a specific community need) within this purpose, one can examine what values or philosophical paradigms were at play in the development and intention of the policy, and second, what specific strategies are or can be used to help address the intended and actual impact. Hence, within this framework, one must consider several key concepts that will help build a model for social welfare policy analysis. These concepts include the social problem/social issue, the goal, the affected population, the intended impact, and the actual impact. Let us review each of these to help build an understanding of how these develop an overall framework or model for policy analysis.

Social Problem/Social Issue

The first step in this process is to understand what is the social problem or social issue. How is this social issue shaped by demographic, social, technological, or economic factors? How prevalent is it within the community of concern? Is this a universal issue, or is it localized within a specific region? What data is available to support that this is indeed an issue of concern? Within this phase, a community needs assessment can be very useful in articulating the incidence and prevalence of a specific social issue.

Goal

The second step in this process is to articulate a goal. This goal can be developed to meet the need or social problem. The goal may thus help identify the purpose of the specific legislation—what is the intended purpose and how this will be designed to meet the social problem or need. An important question to consider is how does this help us address the issue of the social problem. What values and philosophical paradigms underlie this goal? How are these values used to meet the goal or address the social problem?

Policy or Legislation

In this step within the framework of public policy analysis, one must consider the actual policy or piece of legislation. What is it? What does it attempt to do in terms of meeting the social needs or social problem? What are the specific features of the legislation? What programs or services does the legislation mandate?

IMPLEMENTATION OF POLICY OR LEGISLATION

What are the actual features of the policy or legislation? How has the implementation process altered the original intention of the policy or legislation? Who are the affected populations? What was the intended impact of the policy or legislation? What is the actual impact? How does this impact mirror or come close to meeting the original goal and addressing the social problem that was initially cited?

Affected Population

In this stage of the policy analysis, consider who is the affected population. What role do they play and who in fact are impacted by the legislative efforts described? It is important to note that many times the affected population may not necessarily be the same population as those intended to be addressed, especially if a policy or legislation is developed to meet the needs of a specific group. For example, the Social Security Act was intended to provide a safety net for people in their retirement. Since African Americans were originally excluded from this legislation, the affected population in the original legislation became White civil servants. Thus the affected population may not have necessarily been those identified within the original social problem or issue.

Intended Impact

An important step within the analysis framework is to ask what was the intended impact of the legislation? How was it developed to meet the needs of the social problem identified initially? What goals did the policy or legislation have in mind?

Actual Impact

Finally, within this framework, it is essential to identify what is the actual impact. Who was affected and to what degree? What role did the policy play and to what extent was the social issue/social problem addressed?

Figure 3.1 provides an overview of this policy analysis framework. Using this framework and the questions addressed within this text helps one to more effectively analyze what was a social problem or issue, and how this has been addressed within the context of social policy/legislation. Lastly, it enables one to examine how both philosophical paradigms and implementation strategies play a role in meeting the intended goal and addressing a gap in social policy or legislation and how these address a specific social issue or problem.

THE USE OF NEEDS ASSESSMENTS FOR POLICY DEVELOPMENT AND COMMUNITY PLANNING

Community-based needs assessments can be very useful in the process of identifying specific community needs and specific issues or problems to be addressed. In fact, community needs assessments can be vital tools in the process of policy development and community planning, and are addressed in Part III of this text, as a specific tool in the process of policy development. What is important, however, at this juncture is to understand how these needs assessments fit with the overall model for policy analysis. It is also important to keep in mind that within the policy development process, needs assessments can be objective and provide some measure of evidence to support an objective view of a problem. Philosophical paradigms, however, will color this process, as well as the implementation strategies, hence it is important to consider how paradigms impact the social issue at hand. Needs assessments help one to be able to use specific objective evidence to better address how paradigms and the implementation process then play a critical role in this process. The following chapter will address the use of evidence in policy development and will revisit the concept of using evidence as part of a needs assessment.

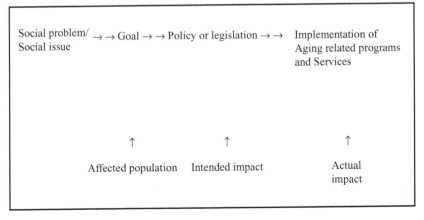

FIGURE 3.1   A framework for public policy analysis.

SUMMARY

Public policy, especially aging policy, is not created in a vacuum, nor is it value free. Values and philosophies guide the development of specific philosophical paradigms and shape how aging policy is developed and implemented. This chapter has attempted to explore how these realities play a role in the development and implementation of public policy and aging policy. Although advocates for aging policy may have a vision for policies and programs that address issues in a more utopian manner, this chapter showcases some of the realities of why this vision may nor always be possible As a safeguard against a subjectively devised policy and program base, objective evidence and empirically driven initiatives can be developed by aging policy advocates. The next chapter facilitates these skills within the policy development process.

REFERENCES

Bruggerman, W. G. (1997). *The practice of macro social work.* Chicago: Nelson Hall Publishers.

Dobelstein, A. W. (1996). *Social welfare policy and analysis* (2nd ed.) Chicago: Nelson-Hall.

Domhoff, G. W. (1956). *Who rules America?* Englewood Cliffs, NJ: Prentice-Hall.

Domhoff, G. W. (1974). *The powers that be.* New York: Random House.

Dye, T. (1975). *Understanding public policy.* Englewood Cliffs, NJ: Prentice-Hall.

Galbraith, J. K. (1973). *Economics and the public purpose.* Boston, MA: Houghton-Mufflin.

Kemp, C. L., & Denton, M. (2003). The allocation of responsibility for later life: Canadian reflections on the roles of individuals, government, employers and families. *Aging and Society, 23*(6), 737–760.

Jewell, C. J., & Glasser, B. E. (2006). Toward a general analytic framework. Organizational settings, policy goals, and street-level behavior. *Administration & Society, 38*(3), 335–364.

Karger, H. J., & Stoesz, D. (1990). *American social welfare policy: A structural approach.* New York: Longman.

Kingdon, J. W. (1984). *Agendas, alternatives and public policies.* Boston: Little, Brown.

Lindblom, C. E. (1959). The science of muddling through. *Public Administration Review, 19,* 79–88.

Lipsky, M. (1980). *Street level bureaucrats.* Thousand Oaks, CA: Sage Publications.

Moore, S. T. (1987). The theory of street-level bureaucracy. A positive critique. *Administration & Society, 19*(1), 74–94.

Moore, S. T. (1990). Street-level policymaking: Characteristics of decision and policy in public welfare. *The American Review of Public Administration, 20*(3), 191–209.

Piven, F. F., & Cloward, R. A. (1979). *Poor people's movements: How they succeed and how they fail.* New York: Random House.

Pressman, J. L., & Wildovsky, A. (1979). *Implementation.* Los Angeles: University of California Press.

Ryan, W. (1976). *Blaming the victim.* New York: Random House Books.

Smith, B. W., Novak, K. J., & Frank, J. (2001). Community policing and the work routines of street-level officers. *Criminal Justice Review, 26*(1), 17–37.

Vinzant, J., & Crothers, L. (1996). Street-level leadership: Rethinking the role of public servants in contemporary governance. *The American Review of Public Administration*, 26(4), 457–476.

Wilensky, H. L., & Lebeaux, C. N. (1965). *Industrial society & social welfare*. New York: The Free Press.

Wright-Mills, C. (1956). *The power elite*. New York, NY: Oxford University Press.

CHAPTER 4

Evidence-Based Policy Development: Tools for Public Policy Development and Analysis

WHAT IS AN EVIDENCE BASE?

Evidence seems to be the buzz word that is used repeatedly; however, what does it really imply and how can it be used in the process of program planning and policy development? Witkin and Harrison (2001) define evidence based as using the "best available" evidence, or empirically based/research-driven "knowledge" about specific issues or concerns. Evidence is defined as "something that tends to prove ground or a belief"(Webster, 2001). In the previous chapter, the case was made that philosophical paradigms play a major role in the development of public policy, and within the context of many philosophical paradigms, a rational, data-driven evidence base is often negated. Hence, an evidence base provides some research-based theory and/or empirically driven background/rationale to support the need for specific directions for policy development or program planning. Historically, we have been acclimated to the idea of needs assessment and have been familiarized with this concept in order to identify issues that require redress, and in essence, the process of a needs assessment provides an evidence base for decision making and planning efforts.

WHAT IS EVIDENCE-BASED PROGRAM AND POLICY DEVELOPMENT?

Evidence-based needs assessment and program development is the use of data and benchmarks to inform one's decision making and the development of resource allocation.

Professional judgments and policy development should be guided by two principles:

- Policy should be grounded upon prior findings, likely to produce predictable and effective results.
- Client systems over time should be evaluated to determine the efficacy of the intervention (i.e., policy decision)(Howard, McMillen, & Pollio, 2003).

Thus, at the core of policy development and program-planning initiatives should be the best evidence, which would include integrating knowledge that one gleans from practice, clinical trials, and practice experience (Institute of Medicine, 2003; Johnson & Austin, 2006; Proctor, 2003, Rosen, 2003). An evidence base to policy development envisions a scientifically based approach that uses the best available evidence to guide policy and practice decisions. It also strives to move beyond one's cultural perspective for decision making and bridges the cultural perspective about what power relations tell us is real (Witkin & Harrison, 2001), and what data showcases as real (Jurkowski, 2005) when developing policy or building programs for older adults.

WHY AN EVIDENCE BASE?

An evidence base provides several advantages. First, it strives towards policy development from a rational philosophical paradigm perspective. An evidence base also minimizes values that may be political as opposed to objective reasons for policy development. In addition it provides a measure of accountability and solicits data for the basis of policy and program-related decisions (McNeill, 2006). The field of public health is steeped in epidemiologic data, much of which is used for decision making, program planning, and policy development. Other allied health professions, like social work, have been lagging in their use of epidemiologic data and available data sources to assist in building a case for program planning and policy development (Morago, 2006, Plath, 2006). In fact, some professions, like social work, have been considered "authority based" and have relied upon this authority basis for the development of programs, policies, and services. The heart of this authority may be the need to identify what constitutes an evidence base, and how empirical knowledge and evidence are really defined (Gibbs & Gambrill, 2002; Rubin & Parrish, 2007).

SOCIAL WORK AND PROGRAM PLANNING FOR OLDER ADULTS: AN AUTHORITY-BASED OR EVIDENCE-BASED PROFESSION?

Traditionally our profession has been seen as "authority based practice (ABP)" (Gambrill, 1999), which means we utilized our expertise to make the best possible clinical judgments, as opposed to driving our decisions. Although a move has been popularized to address the dearth of evidence, through the integration of practice wisdom and evidence-based approaches, this next section will address some of the dilemmas of an authority-based approach and the need for an evidence-based approach (Gambrill, 2001). Based upon this notion, several dilemmas of the authority-based profession exist. These include:

- Clients may not be adequately informed of the range of options available to them.
- Social workers may lack adequate information and evidence to support programs or policies that have been developed to guide practice.
- Decisions may not be informed by empirical or realistic outcomes and findings.

While social work is being critiqued here for not being an authority-based profession, other allied health professions may also follow with some of the same limitations when evidence supporting the authority is concerned. Thus, the debate around what is evidence-based practice, and how does this play into program planning and policy development also emerges. What strategies can be used to create an evidence-based approach to program planning and policy development for older adults? Do clinical trials alone provide adequate evidence to develop an implementation framework for policy development, or do we need to consider alternative sources of evidence to support program and policy decisions, while waiting for our clinical trials to gestate data? Such alternative approaches will provide for substance, while assuring that some of the objections to evidence-based practice are negated, such as value-driven approaches to discipline specific practice (Gibbs & Gambrill, 2002). The profession of social work has struggled with the concept of evidence-based approaches to practice (EBP), since the concept of an evidence base is dependent upon clinical trials in the broadest sense of the definition of EBP. In addition, the profession, and documentation of outcome measures, is still in its childhood; thus some alternative ways to consider sources of evidence at this time, while building policy and program initiatives within the aging arena, will be necessary.

APPROACHES TO EVIDENCE-BASED POLICY DEVELOPMENT

A number of approaches guide the process to assure an evidence-based policy development approach. These approaches include efficiency, effectiveness, cost, cost-benefit studies, and cost-effectiveness. In terms of efficiency, one must consider the question: does the policy/intervention work? In terms of effectiveness: does the policy meet the stated objectives under normal conditions? In addition, do the service outcomes associated with a policy differ across consumer subpopulations? In terms of cost, how much does it cost to deliver an intervention per unit of service? And finally, one must consider the cost-benefit of the process or policy in question. From this perspective, do the dollar benefits exceed the dollar costs of the policy/programs? If in fact policies lead to programs that are cost-effective, how do these policies compare with regard to the resources required to implement them? Thus, each of these questions leads to a different approach that can be used in the process of gathering evidence to build an evidence base for policy development.

The National Association of Social Workers (NASW) Code of Ethics challenges social workers to develop policies and programs that draw from practice-related research. Through this challenge, one makes use of data, evaluation, and outcomes measures to evaluate practice (and policy) decisions. This process enables one to monitor progress and trends over time and can also be translated into impact assessment.

Public health, on the other hand, can be considered an empirically based profession, which utilizes a variety of tools that incorporate the use of counts, incidence, and prevalence. These epidemiologic sources of data are useful for building a case to showcase the impact of specific public policy or the need for revision of social policy.

SOURCES OF EVIDENCE

A number of sources that can be used to provide evidence and support policy directions or programmatic choices are available to practitioners and advocates within the health and human service arenas. Some of these include Congressional Universe, Congressional Record, *Thomas*, Government Printing Office, Government Accountability Office, and databases from secondary data sources. This section provides an overview of these evidence-based sources that can be used.

Congressional Universe

A comprehensive online resource known as "Congressional Universe" enables the researcher/policy advocate to search for Congressional hearings, public issues, legislation, history, and legal research. This tool also provides the ability to research using an in-depth approach to access the full text of congressional information, dating back for at least 200 years. This resource provides detailed information about Congress, including member biographies, committee assignments, voting records, financial data, and the full text of key regulatory and statutory resources. Specifically Congressional Universe can enable some of the following:

- Pinpoint expert testimony on the leading issues of the day.
- Tap authoritative sources of statistics, projections, and analyses.
- Discover a law's intent by tracing its legislative history.
- Gauge Congressional attitudes toward current topics.
- Find out how members of Congress voted on legislation.
- Investigate the finances of members of Congress.
- Monitor legislation and public policy on almost any topic.
- Review the federal regulations that implement legislation.
- Learn the makeup and mission of Congressional committees.
- Access "hot bills" and topics of Congress.

This tool can provide the background necessary to enable a policy advocate to identify the philosophical paradigms behind either a proposed bill or current legislative efforts. Congressional Universe provides an up-to-date holding of federal United States Congressional Record.

Thomas Search Database

The *Thomas* search database is a publicly funded resource that makes United States federal policy-related materials available to the general public through a variety of links to current federal legislative information. This resource was first launched in January of 1995, at the inception of the 104th Congress, and it resulted from leadership in this Congress directing the Library of Congress to assure that federal information was easily available to the general public. Since 1995, *Thomas* has been expanded to include a range of resources of interest to the policy advocate. These include bills and resolutions, activity in Congress, Congressional Record, schedules and calendars, committee information (House and Senate), presidential nominations, treaties, government resources, and a segment for teachers.

Bill resolutions can be found through *Thomas's* home page, which provides the text of legislation for the current Congress. In addition, one can search a bill summary and the status of a particular bill. The summary and status information includes: sponsor(s); cosponsor(s); official, short, and popular titles; floor/executive actions; detailed legislative history; Congressional Record page references; bill summary; committees of referral; reporting and origin; subcommittees of referral; links to other committee information provided by the House of Representatives; amendment descriptions (and text, when available); subjects (indexing terms assigned to each bill); a link to the full text versions; and if the bill has been enacted into law, a link to the full text of the law on the Government Printing Office Web site.

Bill summary and status information is searchable by word/phrase, subject (index) term, bill/amendment number, stage in the legislative process, dates of introduction, sponsor/cosponsor, and committee. Lists of all legislation, public laws, private laws, vetoed bills, and bills/amendments sponsored/cosponsored by each member during each Congress are also available.

Search Bill Text or Bill Summary and Status for Previous Congresses

The Bill Text and Bill Summary and Status features both contain the ability to search previous Congresses. Users can select a Congress from the menu on the search pages.

Public Laws by Law Number

This feature contains Bill Summary and Status records for each bill that became public law. Laws are listed both by law number order and in bill number sequence (House Joint Resolutions, House Bills, Senate Joint Resolutions, and Senate Bills).

House and Senate Roll Call Votes

Roll call votes are recorded votes, from the House of Representatives and the Senate. Votes are listed in reverse chronological order by roll call vote number. The vote summary page lists roll call vote number, vote date, the issue (bill/amendment number being voted on, quorum call or Journal approval), the question (description of the vote), the result (passed, failed, or agreed to) and the title/description of the legislation. Detailed vote pages show individual member votes and vote totals by party.

Legislation by Sponsor

Legislation can be browsed by sponsor (senator or representative) for the current Congress. Legislation sponsored by a particular member or members can also be found for previous Congresses.

Search Committee Reports

Committee Reports include the full text of House and Senate committee reports (including conference reports and joint committee reports) printed by the Government Printing Office (GPO). Most committee reports are printed by the GPO. Reports can be searched by word/phrase, report number, bill number and committee. Searches can be limited by type of report (House, Senate, Conference, Joint). Reports can be browsed sequentially by House/Senate committee report number, conference report, and joint committee report.

Treaties

Information provided about treaties includes treaty number, the date the treaty was transmitted, short title, formal title, treaty type, legislative actions, and index terms. New information is added throughout the day by the executive clerk of the Senate. It becomes available early the next morning. This feature does not contain the actual text of the treaty itself. The full text of treaties can be searched at GPO Access.

Government Resources

Thomas contains a list of legislative and other government resources. *Thomas* also provides resources for learning about the legislative process and resources for legislative researchers. *Thomas* also provides resources for teachers, including classroom activities, lesson plans, guides to congressional information, and more.

Government Printing Office (GPO)

The Government Printing Office (GPO) is the federal government's primary centralized resource for gathering, cataloging, producing, providing, authenticating, and preserving published information in all its forms. GPO is responsible for the production and distribution of information products and services for all three branches of the federal government. GPO's main mission is to ensure the American public has access to government information.

The U.S. Government Printing Office's core mission, which is stated as "Keeping America Informed," dates to 1813 when Congress determined the need to make information regarding the work of the three branches of government available to all Americans. This is the inherent function of government, which GPO carries out for federal agencies on behalf of the public.

Many of the United States's most important information products, such as the Congressional Record and Federal Register, are produced at the GPO's main plant in Washington, DC, a 1.5 million square-foot complex that is the largest information processing, printing, and distribution facility in the world, located just five blocks from the Capitol. In addition to the agency's production facilities, GPO procures between 600 and 1,000 print-related projects a day through private sector vendors across the country. The majority of the government's printing needs are met through a long-standing partnership with America's printing industry. GPO competitively buys products and services from thousands of private sector companies in all 50 States. It is one of the government's most successful procurement programs, assuring the most cost-effective use of the taxpayers' printing dollars. The GPO also publishes reports drafted through GAO and makes these available to the general public and Federal Book Depositories. Thus the materials are easily available to the general public, public health and human services policy advocates, and lobbyists interested in building evidence-based cases for aging-related causes.

Government Accountability Office (Formerly Government Accounting Office, GAO)

The Government Accountability Office (GAO) is an agency that works for Congress and the American people. Congress asks GAO to study the programs and expenditures of the federal government. GAO, commonly called the investigative arm of Congress or the congressional watchdog, is independent and nonpartisan. In the recent past, the GAO was known as the Government Accounting Office. This GAO entity studies the impact of how the federal government spends taxpayer dollars. GAO advises Congress and the heads of executive agencies (such as Environmental Protection Agency, EPA, Department of Defense, DOD, and Health and Human Services, HHS) about ways to make government more effective and responsive to current social, economic, and political issues. GAO evaluates federal programs, audits federal expenditures, and issues legal opinions. When GAO reports its findings to Congress, it recommends actions. GAO's work leads to laws and acts that improve government operations, and hopefully will save dollars for the public purse strings. An example of how the GAO interfaces with policy developments in the aging arena can be found with evaluation reports, which advise legislative amendments to the Older Americans Act or Social Security amendments.

The Government Accountability Office (GAO) is not subject to the Freedom of Information Act (FOIA) (5 USC 552). However, GAO's disclosure policy follows the spirit of the act consistent with GAO's duties and functions as an agency with primary responsibility to the Congress.

Secondary Data Sources Useful in an Evidence-Based Approach

A number of data sources are also available from state-based and federal agency sources, which can also be used to advise policy and program developments in the aging arena. Although a comprehensive listing from a recent publication entitled *Data Sources on Older Americans 2006*, compiled by the Federal Interagency Forum on Aging Related Statistics (2006), this segment will provide a short overview of some of the existing data sources available from publicly available data sources. Table 4.1 also provides an overview of data sources that can provide empirical data.

TABLE 4.1   Secondary Data Sources That Can Provide Empirical Data

Source	Web site
Census bureau	www.census.gov
Centers for Disease Control and Prevention	www.cdc.gov/brfss
Behavioral Risk Factor Surveillance System	www.cdc.gov/brfss/pubs/index.htm
Longitudinal Studies on Aging	www.cdc.gov/nchs/lsoa.htm
Trends in Health and Aging Warehouse	www.cdc.gov/nchs/agingact.htm
National Ambulatory Medical Care Survey	www.cdc.gov/nchs/namcs.htm
National Death Index	www.cdc.gov/nchs/ncndi.htm

(continued)

TABLE 4.1   Secondary Data Sources That Can Provide Empirical Data (continued)

Source	Web site
National Health and Nutrition Examination Survey	www.cdc.gov/nchs/nhanes.htm
National Health Interview Survey	ww.cdc.gov/nchs/nhis.htm
National Home and Hospice Care Survey	www.cdc.gov/nchs/nhhcs.htm
National Hospital Ambulatory Medical Care Survey	www.cdc.gov/nchs/nhamcs.htm
National Hospital Discharge Survey	www.cdc.gov/nchs/nhds.htm
National Mortality Follow-Back Survey	www.cdc.gov/nchs/nmfs.htm
National Nursing Home Survey	www.cdc.gov/nchs/nnhs.htm
National Nursing Home Survey Follow-Up	www.cdc.gov/nchs/nnhsf.htm
National Vital Statistics System (Vital Statistics)	www.cdc.gov/nchs/nvss.htm
Centers for Medicare and Medicaid Services	www.cms.hhs.gov/medicaid
Health and Retirement Study	http://hrsonline.isr.umich.edu
National Long Term Care Survey	http://nltcs.cds.duke/edu/
New Immigrant Survey	http://nis.princeton.edu
Panel Study on Income Dynamics	http://psonline.isr.umich.edu
Drug Abuse Warning Network	http://dawninfo.samhsa.gov/default.asp
National Survey on Drug Use and Health	http://aas.samhsa.gov/nsduh.htm
The Survey of Mental Health Organizations	wwwdasis.samhsa.gov/webt/NewMapv1.htm
American Time Use Survey	www.bls.gov/tus/
The Consumer Expenditure Survey	www.bls.gov/cex/
Current Population Survey	www.census.gov/cps
National Longitudinal Surveys	www.bls.gov/nls/home.htm
National Survey of Veterans	www.va.gov/vetdata
FEDSTATS	www.fedstats.gov
New Beneficiary Data System	www.ssa.gov/policy/docs/microdata/nbds/

State Departments of Public Health (Data for Community Assessment)

Every state-based health department currently has a data system available that provides a composite picture of the health of communities. Although the actual variables within each data set may differ from state to state based upon health priorities, essentially all states collect data on acute and chronic conditions across the life span; thus policy and program advocates can secure data related to health conditions of older adults. These data have been collected in a standardized manner based upon the APEX-PH model for public health practice and are readily available to constituents through the state-based departments of public health. Many state-based departments of public health also have these data available through state-based Web sites. State-based data are also compared to the benchmarks identified in the *Healthy People 2010's Health Objectives for the Nation.*

U.S. Bureau of the Census

The U.S. Bureau of the Census collects data on its residents on a decennial basis for two specific purposes. The first is to apportion the 435 seats in the U.S. House of Representatives among the 50 states. According to the U.S. Constitution (Article 1, Section 2), apportionment of representatives among the states must take place every 10 years (decennially). The second reason to carry out the census is to enumerate the resident population. The census can provide data on sex, race, Hispanic origin, and age for 100% of the enumerated population, and data on income, education, housing, occupation, and industry from a representative sample. Data are enumerated from a short form with seven basic questions, and a long form, which includes the same seven questions and an additional set of questions. Although all residences are enumerated, only one in every six households receives the long form. Data are available from the census through the census bureau at http://www.census.gov.

Department of Health and Human Services

The Department of Health and Human Services provides resources to fund a variety of products that provide data related to older adults, and conditions of aging and across the life span. These resources are available through the Centers for Disease Control and Prevention, the National Center for Chronic Disease Prevention and Health Promotion, the National Center for Health Statistics, and the Centers for Medicare and Medicaid Services. This section will describe each of the secondary data sets available through these entities, which can be useful in the process of building a vision for developing an evidence base for program planning or policy development.

Centers for Disease Control and Prevention (CDC)

Within the Centers for Disease Control and Prevention (CDC), the National Center for Chronic Disease Prevention and Health Promotion is responsible for the Behavioral Risk Factor Surveillance System (BRFSS). The BRFSS is designed to collect state-specific data on behaviors that can relate to leading causes of morbidity and mortality. Since comparable methods are used from year to year, states can compare risk factors and the prevalence of specific behaviors across states and over time. Thus, it becomes possible to track the impact of health interventions over time as well. The questionnaire used within the BRFSS has four components: a fixed core, a rotating core of questions, standardized optional modules, and some specific state-devised questions. State and local health departments take advantage of the data provided from the BRFSS to:

- identify priority health needs and populations most at risk for illness and disability
- develop strategic plans and target prevention programs and activities
- examine trends in behaviors over time and monitor the effectiveness of interventions vis-à-vis Healthy People 2010 objectives
- support community policies and programs that promote health and prevent disease

The data from the BRFSS can be exceedingly helpful for program planners interested in examining the impact of specific programs and policies that will impact older adults within state-based initiatives. The data is available from the BRFSS Web site at http://www.cdc.gov/brfss/technical_infodata/index.htm. Surveillance summaries and reports relevant to the BRFSS are also available through the Web site.

National Center for Health Statistics

The National Center for Health Statistics in collaboration with the National Institute on Aging sponsors a data site with a Longitudinal Study on Aging (LSOA), and the Supplement on Aging (SOA). These surveys provide data to measure changes in health, health-related behaviors, health care, and causes/consequences of such changes across two cohorts of elderly Americans. Variables covered within the questionnaires include housing characteristics, family structure and living arrangements, relationships and social contacts, use of community services, occupation and retirement (income sources), health conditions and impairments, functional status and assistance with basic activities, utilization of health services and nursing home stays, and health opinions. The sample includes adults 55 years of age or older. Table 4.1 provides the Web site to find this data.

Trends in Health and Aging

Trends in Health and Aging is a database available to provide up-to-date information on trends in health behaviors, health status, health costs, and utilization, along with other specific health-related topics on the older population in the United States. The data are organized within eight general topic areas to include demography, vital statistics, health status and well-being, functional status and disability, risk factors and health behavior, health care utilization, health care expenditures, and insurance and injuries. All data is drawn from National Center for Health Statistics surveys and other data systems, and data are organized in a user-friendly format through Beyond 20/20 dissemination tools. The trends warehouse of data can be found through accessing http://www.cdc.gov/nchs/agingact.htm.

National Center for Health Statistics

Other secondary database products available through the National Center for Health Statistics include some of the following databases:

- National Ambulatory Medical Care Survey (NAMCS)
- National Death Index (NDI)
- National Health and Nutrition Examination Survey (NHANES)
- National Health Interview Survey (NHIS)
- National Home and Hospice Care Survey (NHHCS)
- National Hospital Ambulatory Medical Care Survey (NHAMCS)
- National Hospital Discharge Survey (NHDS)
- National Mortality Followback Survey (NMFS)
- National Nursing Home Survey (NNHS)
- National Nursing Home Survey Follow-Up (NNHSF)
- National Vital Statistics System (Vital Statistics)

All of these surveys can be accessed through the Centers for Disease Control and Prevention (CDC) and National Health Statistics (NHS) Web site links.

Centers for Medicare and Medicaid Services

Data sources collected through the Centers for Medicare and Medicaid Services are collected for the purpose of assessing the Medicare and Medicaid programs. These secondary data sets include the following:

- Consumer Assessment of Health Care Providers and Systems (CAHPS)
- Medicaid (Claims and Enrollment) data
- Medicare (Claims and Enrollment) data
- Medicare Current Beneficiary Survey (MCBS)
- Medicare Health Outcomes Survey (HOS)
- Minimum Data Set (MDS)
- Outcome and Assessment Information Set (OASIS)
- Section 723 Chronically Ill Medicare Beneficiary Research and Data Initiative (Section 723)

National Institutes of Health

The National Institutes of Health include two institutes that house data relevant to aging. These include the National Cancer Institute (NCI) and the National Institute on Aging (NIA). NIA provides a database on surveillance epidemiology and end results (SEER), while NIA supports four specific data sets of interest to aging policy advocates. These four data sets include the Health and Retirement study (HRS), the National Long Term Care Survey (NLTCS), the New Immigrant Survey (NIS), and the Panel Study on Income Dynamics (PSID).

Office of the Assistant Secretary for Planning and Evaluation

The office of the Assistant Secretary for Planning and Evaluation hosts two national studies. The first is the National Survey of Residential Care Facilities, and the second is the National Study of Assisted Living for the Frail Elderly, 2000.

Substance Abuse and Mental Health Services Administration (SAMHSA)

The SAMHSA program provides oversight to mental health and substance abuse programs nationwide in the United States. In efforts to develop programs and services that are meaningful to the aging population, several databases are available that provide data on the usage and attitudes of older adults and substance use or mental health service provision. These include the following:

- Client/Patient Sample Survey (CPSS)
- Drug Abuse Warning Network (DAWN)
- National Survey on Drug Use and Health (NSDUH)
- National Survey of Substance Abuse Treatment Services (N-SSATS)
- The Survey of Mental Health Organizations (SMHO)
- Treatment Episode Data Set (TEDS)

The Drug Abuse Warning Network (DAWN) was developed as an ongoing, national public health surveillance system that collects data related to adverse health consequences resulting from drug misuse and abuse. Data are collected from hospital emergency room visits drawn from a national probability sample of hospitals. DAWN provides data to showcase emerging drug-related trends and provides this data to communities, member facilities, local public health authorities, federal agencies and policy makers.

The National Survey of Substance Abuse Treatment Services (N-SSATS) collects information from all facilities in the United States, both public and private, that provide substance abuse treatment. Some of the objectives of collecting this information include: to assist SAMHSA and state/local governments to assess the nature and extent of services provided in state-supported and other treatment facilities; to analyze treatment service trends and provide a comparative analysis for the nation, regions, and states; and to provide a national directory of drug abuse treatment facilities.

The Survey of Mental Health Organizations (SMHO) provides a biannual review of organizations that provide mental health services in efforts to gain timely data on the availability and use of mental health services. These reviews are exceedingly helpful to provide insight into mental health services, and areas for development and areas of service utilization, as the policy development process unfolds. The sample includes 4,500 mental health organizations nationwide.

The Treatment Episode Data Set (TEDS) is compiled annually and provides demographic data on the characteristics and substance abuse problems of people admitted for substance abuse treatment. The records are not compiled per individual, but rather per admission, and agencies included within this data set are receiving funds for alcohol or drug services along or Federal Block Grant money. The TEDS system includes both an Admissions Data Set and a Discharge Data Set.

Department of Housing and Urban Development

The Department of Housing and Urban Development, through the Office of Policy Development and Research, disseminates the American Housing

Survey (AHS). This survey addresses the nation's housing situation. The AHS provides data on the characteristics, conditions, financing, and costs of housing nationally, and in selected metropolitan areas, on neighborhood conditions and amenities and on households. Specifically, the AHS conducts a national survey every 2 years, and a metropolitan areas survey once every 6 years. Public use data files are available through http://www.huduser.org/datasets/ahs.html.

Department of Labor

The Department of Labor, through the Bureau of Labor Statistics, provides for four specific surveys with relevance to aging adults. These include the American Time Use Survey (ATUS), The Consumer Expenditure Survey (CEX), Current Population Survey (CPS) and the National Longitudinal Surveys (NLS).

Department of Veterans Affairs

The Department of Veterans Affairs collects data on their veterans through the National Survey of Veterans (NSV). The intent of this survey is to describe characteristics of the veteran population and of users and nonusers of Department of Veterans Affairs (VA) benefit programs. The survey topics include sociodemographic and economic characteristics, military background, health status measures, and VA and non-VA benefits usage. The sample is based upon a population of veterans 65 years of age and older.

Office of Management and Budget

The Office of Management and Budget produces a product entitled FEDSTATS, which is an interagency effort that provides access to a full range of official statistical information available to the public through the federal government. Users can access official statistics, which are collected and published by more than 100 federal agencies.

Social Security Administration

Social Security Administration compiles a system of data on their new beneficiaries known as the New Beneficiary Data System (NBDS). The NBDS provides important data on the changing circumstances of aged and disabled beneficiaries. The data system includes two studies, the New Beneficiary Survey (NBS) and the New Beneficiary Follow-Up (NBF). A wide range of topics are covered, including demographic characteristics, marital and childbearing history, employment history, current income and assets, and health status. Some data are also gathered from spouses and added to the administrative records. Data are available from http://www.ssa.gov/policy/docs/microdata/nbds.

BENCHMARKS USED IN THE HEALTH CARE ARENA FOR PROGRAM PLANNING AND POLICY DEVELOPMENT

A blueprint for the health of the United States has been developed through the use of a document entitled *Healthy People 2010: Health Objectives for the Nation*. The Department of Health and Human Services has undertaken this initiative that provides benchmarks for the progress of the health of Americans for the next 10 years, with supporting objectives in disease prevention and health promotion. The two main goals of the health objectives are (1) to increase quality and years of health life and (2) to eliminate health disparities. The Future of Public Health (Institute of Medicine, 1988) called for a national system of benchmarks to articulate the health objectives of the nation, and these have been revised for 1990, 2000, and 2010. Benchmarks currently have been established in order to identify where health goals for the nation and individual states should be, and the program is evaluated routinely by local and state health departments. Healthy People 2010 also is used to gauge the impact of health policy. Within the objectives, benchmarks are listed for a variety of health issues that impact older adults, including mental health, access to care, physical activity, oral health care, and disability. The data sources cited within this chapter are used in the process of identifying how closely benchmarks have been met.

EVIDENCE AND ITS ROLE IN POLICY DEVELOPMENT AND COMMUNITY PLANNING

Thus far this chapter has focused on sources of evidence for evidence-based policy development. Now we need to ask the question: "What role does evidence play in the development of policy and community resources for aging services?" How can this information be put to use in the development of revised policies to benefit older adults and programs or services to improve the health and well-being of older adults? The first step in this process is to use the information through needs assessments.

What Is a Needs Assessment?

Needs assessments take on a variety of different meanings and definitions; however, Witkin & Altschuld (1995) sum this up in their definition, which suggests that needs assessments are "a systematic set of procedures undertaken for the purpose of setting priorities and making decisions about program or organizational improvement and allocation of resources. These priorities are based upon identified needs"(p. 4).

Several strategies can be used in the process of developing this inventory of community resources and gaps in the resources. Kirst-Ashman and Hall (2002) identifies five specific strategies that can be used. These include social indicators, key informants, community forums, surveys, and agency-related data. Each is important and can make a significant contribution in part or in combination with other methods in order to create a composite sketch of a community's needs. Although presented cursively here, these approaches will be revisited as a tool for policy and program development in a later section of this text (chapter 13) and will be elaborated upon. These needs are based upon evidence or data, much of which can also be obtained from the sources cited earlier in this chapter.

SUMMARY

The struggle to reach a vision of rational policy development based upon evidence is paramount at this juncture in our journey to build aging policies and services. This chapter has explored some of the dilemmas with developing an evidence base and provided a range of empirical sources within the aging arena that can be used in building an evidence-based approach to policy development. The journey, however, will not be without struggle—since philosophical paradigms, and social and economic factors will interface and play a role in the development of evidence-based policy. Policy advocates, however can help with this cause through the use of data-driven and evidence-based approaches to building public policy and program planning for older adults.

USEFUL WEB SITES

Centers for Disease Control and Prevention: http://www.cdc.gov
    The official site for the Centers for Disease Control and Prevention, which provides links to the host of national data sets, collected through the National Center for Health Statistics.

Congressional Record: http://www.gpoaccess.gov/crecord/index.html

Government Accountability Office (GAO): http://www.gao.gov/

Government Printing Office (GPO): http://www.gpoaccess.gov
There are approximately a quarter of a million titles available to the public via the Internet on the GPO Access Web site at http://www.gpoaccess.gov. Through GPO's partner Web sites, an additional half a million titles are accessible to the public. Printed copies of more than 5,500 of those documents ranging from Supreme Court opinions to reports from the Bureau of Labor Statistics may also be purchased from the GPO Sales Program in person, online, via phone, fax, e-mail, or postal mail.

Healthy People 2010: http://www.healthypeople.gov/
The official Web site for Healthy People 2010 containing the health objectives for the year 2010, as well as midcourse progress reports.

Thomas: http://thomas.loc.gov/home/abt_thom.html

World Health Organization: http://www.who.org
This site provides links to the World Health Organization. Data collected for countries worldwide in the areas of health and social indicators are available.

REFERENCES

Federal Interagency Forum on Aging Related Statistics. (2006). *Data sources on older Americans, 2006.* Washington, DC: Government Printing Office.

Gambrill, E. (1999). Evidence-based practice: An alternative to authority-based practice. *Families in Society, 80*(4), 341–350.

Gambrill, E. (2001). Social work: An authority-based profession. *Research on Social Work Practice, 11,* 166–175.

Gibbs, L., & Gambrill, E. (2002). Evidence-based practice: Counterarguments to objections. *Research on Social Work Practice, 12*(3), 452–476.

Howard, M., McMillen, C., & Pollio, D. (2003). Teaching evidence-based practice: Toward a new paradigm for social work education. *Research on Social Work Practice, 13*(2), 234–259.

Institute of Medicine. (1988). *The future of public health.* Washington, DC: National Academies Press.

Institute of Medicine. (2003). *The future of the public's health in the 21st century.* Washington DC: National Academies Press.

Johnson, M., & Austin, M. J. (2006). Evidence-based practice in the social services: Implications for organizational change. *Administration in Social Work, 30*(3), 75–104.

Jurkowski, E. (2005, Dec. 14). *Evidence based policy development.* A paper presented to the American Public Health Association, Philadelphia, PA.

Kirst-Ashman, K., & Hall, G. H. (2002). *Understanding generalist practice.* Belmont, CA: Brooks Cole Publishing.

McNeill, T. (2006). Evidence-based practice in an age of relativism: Toward a model for practice. *Social Work, 51*(2), 147–156.

Morago, P. (2006). Evidence-based practice: From medicine to social work. *European Journal of Social Work, 9*(4), 461–477.

Plath, D. (2006). Evidence-based practice: Current issues and future directions. *Australian Social Work, 59*(1), 56–72.

Proctor, E. K. (2003). Evidence for practice: Challenges, opportunities, and access. *Social Work Research, 27*(4), 195–196.

Rosen, A. (2003). Evidence-based social work practice: Challenges and promise. *Social Work Research, 27*(4), 197–208.

United States Department of Health and Human Services (USDHHS). (1999). *Healthy People 2010: Health Objectives for the nation.* Washington, DC: Government Printing Office.

Webster's new world college dictionary, 4th ed. (2001). Foster City, CA: IDG Books Worldwide.

Witkin, R. W., & Altschuld, J. W. (1995). *Planning and conducting needs assessments: A practical guide.* Thousand Oaks, CA: Sage Publications.

Witkin, S., & Harrison, D. (2001). Whose evidence and for what purpose? *Social Work, 46*(4), 293–296.

PART II

The Legislative Basis for Programs and Services Affecting Older Adults and/ or People With Disabilities

Part II of this text will provide an overview to major federal policies and programs that impact older adults and people with disabilities. Some historical developments leading up to the actual development and implementation of the policy are also examined. Policies include Social Security, Medicare, the Older Americans Act, the Americans with Disabilities Act, the Community Mental Health Centers Act, and the President's Freedom Commission Initiative.

CHAPTER 5

The Social Security Act

OVERVIEW

Can you imagine a system where there is no safety net for one's economic and medical resources upon retirement or disability within our current industrialized and technological society? In agrarian societies, people bore many children as insurance for themselves when they were into their old age—thus, they would have person power to provide for them in their golden years. In today's society, with families opting to have one or two children, it hardly seems realistic that one would rely upon their children to care for them in their old age. In fact, these were some of the dilemmas that Franklin D. Roosevelt faced when he considered the passage of the Social Security Act.

This chapter will provide a backdrop to our current Social Security Program, provide an overview to some models for Social Security programs in Europe and Canada, and explore the genesis of the Social Security program in the United States. The contents of the original Social Security Act will be explored and compared to the titles and programs mandated through the current Social Security Act. The chapter will also provide some guidelines for the current administration of the program, examine the debate around current proposals for revision, and review why these proposals are current issues for consideration. The chapter will conclude with an overview of useful Web sites that can provide current and up-to-date information.

BACKDROP TO OUR CURRENT SOCIAL SECURITY PROGRAM

Social Security in the United States is a program that by worldwide standards was a relative latecomer to this country. Although the original Social Security program was signed into legislation by President Franklin

81

D. Roosevelt in 1935 to provide for the welfare and financial security of older Americans, programs from other corners of the world may have been more comprehensive in nature than what we began with in the United States. The early social insurance schemes were designed in Western Europe to address three fears of industrial workers:

- poverty in old age
- illness
- unemployment

The German Chancellor Otto Von Bismarck established and designed Europe's first social insurance program in 1880; however, the program was not officially adopted until 1889, thus leading the campaign for an old-age social security program. The idea was first put forward, at Bismarck's behest, in 1881 by Germany's emperor, William I, in a groundbreaking letter to the German Parliament. William wrote: "... those who are disabled from work by age and invalidity have a well-grounded claim to care from the state" (Mann, 1970, p. 269).

Two specific motivations can be credited for Bismarck's introduction of a social security program in Germany. The first was to encourage the health and well-being of workers as an effort to promote and maximize the efficiency of the German economy, while the second was to thwart any more radical "socialist alternatives." Despite Bismark's right-wing perspective and commitment to commerce and trade, Bismarck would be coined a socialist for introducing these programs, similar to President Roosevelt 70 years later.

The German system provided contributory retirement benefits and disability benefits as well. Participation was mandatory and contributions were taken from the employee, the employer, and the government. Coupled with the workers' compensation program established in 1884 and the "sickness" insurance enacted the year before, this gave the Germans a comprehensive system of income security based on social insurance principles.

An interesting myth has prevailed throughout history, to suggest that Bismarck chose an arbitrary retirement age of 65, since he himself has been told in legend to have been 65 years of age at the time. In reality, however, Germany initially set their retirement age at 70 years of age, while Bismarck himself was 74 at the time. The retirement age was lowered to 65 in 1916, although Bismarck had been deceased since 1898. The myth is significant, however, because the United States examined the German model and utilized its features as a blueprint, when designing its own Social Security program, including a retirement age of 65.

Social Security in Europe

In England, the first vestiges of a social security act were seen in the early 1900s through England's Pension Act of 1908. France was a latecomer to the development of a Social Security System and did not evolve their program until 1930.

European models for a social security system were based upon investment schemes as opposed to a "pay as you go" system. Essentially, this meant that systems invested the taxation revenues and used the proceeds to finance a social security or disbursement plan. In contrast the "pay as you go" approach has revenue coming into a system, and paid out at the same time, with no, or limited investment of the resources.

Social security programs enhanced workers' loyalty to the state by giving laborers a stake in the government, especially if they were not landowners. In some cases labor unions revolted.

The Genesis of Social Security in the United States

In the United States, the Great Depression served as a major economic upheaval. Hence, reform proposals suggested taking taxes to fund guaranteed incomes in old age. The 1932 presidential election brought Roosevelt (FDR) into office with a clear mandate to "do something." Roosevelt established a cabinet-level Committee on Economic Security (CES). The mandate of CES was to draft a proposal for a New Deal program in collaboration with Francis Perkins (a trained social worker with a master's degree in social work) appointed to serve as the Secretary of Labor. In 1935 the Social Security Act was passed into legislation, which provided programs to address the unemployed, women, children, and the elderly within one single piece of legislation.

Initially, Social Security paid benefits in the form of a single, lump-sum payment (1937–1940). These one-time payments were designed to give some payback to those people who contributed to the program but wouldn't participate long enough to be vested for monthly benefits. Under the 1935 law, monthly benefits were to begin in 1942; however, the time span between 1937 and 1942 was designed to be a period of time to build up the Trust Funds and to provide a minimum period for participation in order to qualify for monthly benefits.

The original Social Security legislation provided only retirement benefits, and only to the worker. In 1939 amendments made a fundamental change in the Social Security program. The amendments added two new categories of benefits: payments to the spouse and minor children of a retired worker (so-called dependents benefits) and survivors benefits paid to the family in the event of the premature death of a covered worker. This change transformed Social Security from a retirement program for workers into a *family-based* economic security program.

Amendments made to the Social Security program in 1954 initiated a disability insurance program that lent support to the public with additional coverage against economic insecurity. Although the disability program did not offer any cash benefits, it did prevent disability from reducing or wiping out one's retirement and survivor benefits. In 1956, once again the Social Security Act was amended to provide benefits to disabled workers, 50 to 64 years of age, and disabled adult children of recipients. Additional amendments to the Social Security program were made by President Eisenhower in September 1960, which amended the disability rules to permit payment of benefits to disabled workers regardless of their age and to their dependents.

In 1961 (June 30), President John Kennedy signed additional Social Security amendments that permitted workers to elect a reduced retirement age and would enable people to retire at 62 years of age. The decade of the 1960s brought major changes to the Social Security program. Under the Amendments of 1961, the age at which men are first eligible for old-age insurance was lowered to 62, with benefits actuarially reduced (women previously were given this option in 1956).

Medicare

The Medicare bill was signed on July 30, 1965, by President Lyndon Johnson. This bill provided health coverage to all Americans who were 65 years of age and older.

Contents of The Original Social Security Act (SSA)

The original Social Security Act of 1935 was comprised of 11 titles, including the following arenas:

- Grants to states for OAA
- Federal old age benefits
- Grants to states for unemployment compensation administration
- Aid to dependent children
- Maternal and child welfare
- Public health work
- Social Security Board
- Taxes with respect to employment
- Tax on employers of eight or more

- Grants to states for aid to the blind
- General provisions

These are summarized in Table 5.1.

THE CURRENT SOCIAL SECURITY ACT

Over time the original 11 titles of the Social Security Act have expanded to now cover 21 titles; however, two have been repealed (Barusch, 2002). Within these titles, there is now a provision that includes special benefits for certain World War II veterans. SSA also includes block grants for social services and the state children's health insurance program. Health insurance for the aged and disabled are also included through the Medicare program (which was enacted in 1965). The following chapter of this textbook will elaborate on the Medicare program. The titles of the current program are summarized in Table 5.2.

TABLE 5.1   Contents of the Social Security Act of 1935

Preamble: An act to provide for the general welfare by establishing a system of Federal old-age benefits, and by enabling the several States to make more adequate provision for aged persons, blind persons, dependent and crippled children, maternal and child welfare, public health and the administration of their unemployment compensation laws; to establish a Social Security Board, to raise revenue; and for other purposes.

Title I: Grants to States for Old Age Assistance

Title II: Federal Old-Age Benefits

Title III: Grants to States for Unemployment Compensation Administration

Title IV: Grants to States for Aid to Dependent Children

Title V: Grants to States for Maternal and Child Welfare

Title VI: Public Health Work

Title VII: Social Security Board

Title VIII: Taxes with respect to Employment

Title IX: Tax on Employers of Eight or More

Title X: Grants to States for Aid to the Blind

Title XI: General Provisions

Source: Social Security Act of 1935 [H.R. 7260].

TABLE 5.2   Titles of the Social Security Act (2000)

Title I: Grants to states for Old-Age Assistance (Supplemental Security Income)

Title II: Old Age, Survivors, and Disability Insurance Benefits

Title III: Grants to States for unemployment compensation

Title IV: Grants to States for Aid and Services to Needy Families with Children and for Child Welfare Services

Title V: Maternal and Child Health Services Block Grant

Title VII: Administration

Title VIII: Special benefits for certain WWII Veterans

Title IX: Miscellaneous Provisions Relating to Employment Security

Title X: Grants to States for Aid to the Blind—Supplemental Security Income

Title XI: General Provisions

Title XII: Advances to State Unemployment Funds

Title XIII: Special benefits for Certain World War II Veterans

Title XIV: Supplemental Security Income (Grants to States for Aid to the Permanently and Totally Disabled)

Title XVI: Supplemental Security Income for the Aged, Blind and Disabled

Title XVII: Grants for Planning Comprehensive Action to Combat Mental Retardation

Title XVIII: Health Insurance for the Aged and Disabled

Title XIX: Grants to States for Medical Assistance Programs

Title XX: Block Grants to States for Social Services

Title XXI: State Children's Insurance Program

Note: Titles VI and XV have been repealed.
Source: Social Security Act, 2000.

Some Guidelines for Social Security Programs

The Social Security Act and related laws establish a number of programs that have the following basic purposes:

A.   to provide for the material needs of individuals and families
B.   to protect aged and disabled persons against the expenses of illnesses that may otherwise use up their savings
C.   to keep families together
D.   to give children the chance to grow up healthy and secure

Although we tend to think that Social Security is specifically retirement benefits, at the current time, a number of social welfare programs designed for families, women and children are also a part of this initiative.

The following programs are included within the Social Security program:

A. retirement insurance
B. survivors insurance
C. disability insurance
D. hospital and medical insurance for the aged, the disabled, and those with end-stage renal disease
E. prescription drug benefit
F. extra help with Medicare prescription drug costs
G. supplemental security income
H. special veterans benefits
I. unemployment insurance
J. public assistance and welfare services, including:
    1. temporary assistance for needy families
    2. medical assistance
    3. maternal and child health services
    4. child support enforcement
    5. family and child welfare services
    6. food stamps
    7. energy assistance

Individuals are eligible for Social Security Benefits if they fall into the following categories:

A. a disabled insured worker who has not reached full retirement age
B. a retired insured worker age 62 or over
C. the spouse of a retired or disabled worker entitled to benefits who:
    1. is age 62 or over
    2. has in care a child who is either under age 16, or over age 16 and disabled, who is entitled to benefits on the worker's Social Security record
D. the divorced spouse of a retired or disabled worker entitled to benefits if at least 62 and married to the worker for at least 10 years
E. the divorced spouse of a fully insured worker who:
    1. has not yet filed a claim for benefits if both they and their ex-spouse are at least 62
    2. was married for at least 10 years
    3. has been finally divorced for at least 2 years in a row
F. the dependent, who is an unmarried child of a wage earner who is retired, disabled, or a deceased insured worker is entitled to benefits if he or she is:
    1. under age 18

2. under age 19 and a full-time elementary or secondary school student
3. age 18 or older but under a disability which began before age 22
G. the surviving spouse (including a surviving divorced spouse) of a deceased insured worker age 60 or older
H. the disabled surviving spouse (including a surviving divorced spouse in some cases) of a deceased insured worker if they are age 50 to 59 and become disabled within the period specified
I. the surviving spouse (including a surviving divorced spouse) of a deceased insured worker, regardless of age, if caring for an entitled child of the deceased who is either under age 16 or was disabled before age 22
J. the dependent parents of a deceased insured worker age 62 or over

Note: In addition to monthly survivors benefits, a lump-sum death payment is payable upon the death of an insured worker.

Supplemental Security Income (SSI) is a federal program administered by SSA.

The SSI program was established to provide cash assistance to individuals who:

A. have limited income and resources
B. are age 65 or older
C. are blind
D. are disabled

Disabled and blind children are also included in the SSI program.

SOME REFORMS WORTH NOTING

The notion of revising or reforming the Social Security system is definitely not a new concern or issue and has been a subject of concern and discussion in previous administrations, prior to George W. Bush. In 1981 President Reagan appointed the National Commission on Social Security Reform, headed by Alan Greenspan. The four areas of recommendations included:

1. revisions in the cost of living adjustment
2. taxation of benefits
3. increased retirement ages
4. work incentives

The end result has included revisions particularly in increased retirement ages. Although many of the recommendations that Greenspan identified did not take place during the Reagan administration, some of these revisions did come to pass, and particularly full retirement ages have increased and continue to increase to age 67, based upon one's year of birth (Ball, 1996). One may begin to collect retirement benefits at age 62; however, there will be a reduction in benefits, depending upon one's year of birth. Table 5.3 provides a listing of one's year of birth and retirement year (USDHHS, 2007). See Table 5.3.

PROPOSALS FOR REVISION AND WHY

During President Clinton's administration, an effort was made to privatize Old Age Survivors and Disability Insurance (OASDI). At this point in time, President Clinton had appointed Jose Obera (the former labor minister of Chile, 1979) to head up this task force through the Social Security Advisory Council. President Clinton's Social Security Advisory Council

TABLE 5.3 Retirement Ages at Which One Can Collect Social Security Benefits

Year of Birth	Full retirement age	Number of months of reduction
1937 or earlier	65	36
1938	65 years and 2 months	38
1939	65 years and 4 months	40
1940	65 years and 6 months	42
1941	65 years and 8 months	44
1942	65 years and 10 months	46
1943–1954	66 years	48
1955	66 and 2 months	50
1956	66 years and 4 months	52
1957	66 years and 6 months	54
1958	66 years and 8 months	56
1959	66 years and 10 months	58
1960 and later	67 years of age	60

developed three proposals, based upon a successful model used in Chile to privatize social security benefits. The three proposals included:

1. Maintenance of Benefits Plan
2. Individual Accounts
3. Personal Savings Accounts

These three proposals, although different, all had similarities, and most importantly, they were all in support of maintaining a mandatory, universal, public social insurance program, and within this program retirement, survivor, and disability benefits were paramount (Quinn & Mitchell, 1996). None of the proposals called for a revision of the Social Security system into a welfare-oriented system that would be means tested.

The Maintenance of Benefits Plan proposed to raise the revenues to restore the system's solvency. A proportion of this increase could be accomplished through an investment of up to 40% of the trust fund reserves within private capital markets. This plan would also result in a two-point increase in payroll taxes, which would begin in 2050.

The Individual Accounts proposal would end up reducing benefits, and increasing benefits through the establishment of individual contribution accounts that would be ultimately funded through increasing payroll taxes. Individual participants would have some discretion (not completely) in how their accounts are invested.

The Personal Savings Accounts (PSA's) would completely replace the Social Security System, into a two-tier system. This is the most radical of all the proposals. The first tier would provide a low flat rate of benefits for people with at least 10 years of contributed benefits, regardless of their earning history. Those individuals with 35 years of contributions would have their benefits pro-rated. At a maximum, this approach could provide benefits to about two-thirds of the poverty levels for older adults. The second tier would provide for a mandatory personal savings account (PSA), which would be directed and held by the individual. After the age of 62, these accounts could be withdrawn as lump sum payments.

One must also consider why these proposals came to the forefront and what hidden agendas were at play in this process as a 16-member bipartisan Commission on Social Security was appointed in 2001. Their task was to modernize and restore financial soundness to Social Security. The end result of this commission has been a task force report offering three possible scenarios that are fairly similar, for how the long range financing for Social Security should be addressed.

Implications of a Privatized System

There are several implications that accompany a privatized social security system and leave this proposal in great debate. One of these implications includes the loss of bond treasury. Funds are used to invest in the bond treasury, and thus are paid out in benefits. As a result of the inability for many working-class people to save and/or invest for their older age, we can predict that there will be an upsurge of the elderly poor (2/3 of our older adult population), which is dramatic, especially in a country that is known to be one of the most affluent countries in the world.

A second implication of a privatized system would be an increase in stock market investments. While this could prove to be an advantage and lucrative, it may only benefit about 10% of the population. Hence, the remaining 90% of the population may be left to struggle to their own devices. Another consideration is that while investments may benefit a narrow segment of the population, one cannot guarantee how long this benefit may last. There could be disaster if there were a crash in the stock market such as occurred in 1929. It is also interesting to note in testimony presented by Alan Greenspan, the former chair of the Federal Reserve Board in 1999. In his testimony, he argued that it would be impossible to keep politics out of the stock market if major public funds were invested there by the Social Security system.

The most important implication of major revisions to the program would be the loss of a safety net program that benefits millions of older adults within the United States. The outcome and implication of this initiative could potentially leave huge pockets of people who will be poverty stricken. This may also have some serious impacts for a nation that has people growing older and living longer.

DILEMMAS FOR THE FUTURE

A number of issues discussed within this chapter also lead to dilemmas for the future. Specifically, poverty and the threat of a dismantled Social Security system are two major factors that will lead to some profound impacts in a safety net system that was originally envisioned for older adults. A central question to examine includes how these specific issues lead to specific concerns for our current Social Security system.

A Culture of Impoverished Older Adults

The dilemma of a potential culture that will emerge with impoverished older adults can be a reality, if corporate pension plans continue to erode.

This so-called erosion could potentially place more pressure on the current Social Security system and lead to more older adults with fewer resources and thus a specific subculture of poverty. These factors, coupled with smaller families and more fragmented families and social networks, could potentially lead to more people who, in their old age, become impoverished. The Government Accountability Office has studied this issue, with projections for 2030 and 2050, only to raise alarming concerns about a growing culture of poverty.

Older Women and Poverty

Women who survive to age 65 can plan to outlive men of the same age by at least 7 years. They face far more challenges today, and will continue to face challenges into the future. One of the most important of these challenges is that of poverty. A significant proportion of women who reach retirement age today may not have worked at their capacity during their lifetime and may not have accumulated a comfortable pension, which can result in women living at or far beneath the poverty level. Two additional factors that lead to older women living in poverty will include the reality that women will live longer than their male counterparts and the changing family structure. Far more frequently within the last two decades women have lost secure marriages due to divorce or death and have become victim to a limited safety net. Pension splitting, as a result of divorce, often does not provide ample funds for a divorced spouse to live comfortably, or even to live far above the poverty level. Thus, a dilemma for the future will be the significant increase of women living in poverty.

An Empty Pot at the End of the Rainbow

Last, a dilemma for the future is the reality that the "pot," or resources available to retirees through the Social Security Fund, may not exist. Thus, the "pot" that people looked towards as income to support in retirement may no longer exist or may be either depleted and empty or close to empty by the time an individual reaches his or her retirement or the end of their rainbow.

SUMMARY

This chapter has presented the current Social Security system, which provides for older adults, but has also grown to cover women and children. The historical background behind the program and its evolution have also been discussed. Although many people have argued for their vision to privatize the system, the reality is that there is much more political support to maintain the program as a safety net program rather than a means-tested program, and hopefully this universal retirement program will be maintained.

USEFUL WEB SITES

The official Web site of Social Security: http://www.ssa.gov
This Web site provides a comprehensive array of materials to address every possible question regarding Social Security and Disability benefits. This official governmental Web site provides the reader with background information on the Social Security and Disability programs, as well as current publications.

The Social Security Network: A Century Foundation Project: http://www.socsec.org/
This Web site provides some essays that review some of the current issues that the Social Security program faces at the current time. Debates about privatization of the Social Security program are also discussed.

National Committee to Preserve Social Security Movement: http://www.ncpssm.org/
This Web site provides the reader with the opportunity to participate as a consumer in the preservation of the Social Security movement. It serves as a portal to a number of essays that address strategies to preserve the Social Security program and Social Security Trust funds.

The Urban Institute Tool Kit on Social Security: http://www.urban.org/toolkit/issues/socialsecurity.cfm
This Web site provides a wide array of materials that address issues for and against the Social Security program. A variety of educational materials are also available.

REFERENCES

Ball, R. M. (1996). Medicare's roots: What Medicare's architects had in mind. *Generations,* *20*(2), 13–18.

Barusch, A. S. (2002). *Foundations of social policy: Social justice, public programs, and the social work profession.* Itasca, IL: Peacock Publishers.

Mann, G. (1970). *The history of Germany since 1789.* New York: Praeger Publications.

Quinn, J. F., & Mitchell, O. S. (1996). Social Security on the table. *American Prospect, 26,* 6–81.

Social Security Act of 1935 [H.R. 7260] Retrieved June 14, 2007 from http:///www.ssa.
    gov/history/35actionx.html
United States Department of Health and Human Services. (2007). *Retirement planner:
    Social Security online.* Retrieved May 20, 2007, from http://www.ssa.gov/retire
    chartred.htm

CHAPTER 6

Medicare

[handwritten notes:]
medicare beneficia
half income below 22000 per year
usdo have 3+ chronic conditions
2/3 do have cognitive impairment
2/3 poor health
¼ live in nursing one

In a country as prosperous as the United States, one would expect all people to be healthy and prosperous. The inception of Medicare in 1965 gave many people the illusion that there would be a "pot" at the end of the rainbow to take care of their health care concerns, once they reached the magic, tender age of 64, and were ready to move into their retirement. Despite this illusion, at the turn of the century Medicare only covered 13.4% of those insured in the United States. While the Medicare/managed care programs have expanded the health care market, there are still many people without health care insurance who are struggling for coverage.

Despite these limitations, Medicare serves as a guaranteed source of insurance coverage, hence contributing to billable services in situations where research and development with older adults or people with disabilities will take place (Ball, 1996). The Centers for Medicare and Medicaid Services (CMS) administer Medicare, the nation's largest health insurance program, which covers nearly 40 million Americans. Medicare is a health insurance program for people 65 years of age and older, some disabled people under 65 years of age, and people with end-stage renal disease (permanent kidney failure treated with dialysis or a transplant).

HISTORICAL PERSPECTIVE

Congress enacted Medicare and Medicaid in 1965 as Titles XVIII and XIX of the Social Security Act. Medicare is a social insurance program available to all citizens of the United States if they have worked and contributed into the program. While this is not a means-tested program, and all who have contributed can benefit, an additional benefit is available known as Medicaid, which is a means-tested public assistance program.

Robert Ball, the architect for the program, argued that Medicare was the first step towards a universal health care coverage program (Ball, 1996). Ball, who had served as commissioner of Social Security under Presidents Kennedy, Johnson, and Nixon, also suggested that when the initial thoughts of a universal health care program came into play in 1916, the American Medical Association was in support of the plan. In actual fact, a prior version of the Medicare program had been developed in the 1930s, along with the Social Security Act, with the intention of serving as universal health care coverage. This began with a Committee on Economic Security created by President Roosevelt (June, 1934), which subsequently filed a report regarding the feasibility of a Social Security and health insurance program. This Report of the Committee on Economic Security was sent to Congress (January, 1935) without any health insurance recommendations, but spelling out principles and promising further efforts to evolve a plan.

The first government health insurance bill introduced in Congress, the "Epstein bill" (S. 3253) sponsored by Senator Capper, occurred in July, 1935. Although struck down, President Franklin D. Roosevelt continued his campaign to develop a health care coverage plan, appointed a National Health Survey to be conducted, and in 1938, a Report of the Technical Committee on Medical Care, A National Health Program, was published. As a direct result of this survey, in 1939 Senator Robert F. Wagner introduced a "National Health Bill" (S. 1620) incorporating recommendations of the National Health Conference. This was struck down and died in committee. However, after several attempts to introduce versions of a universal health coverage plan for older adults and the poor by Presidents Truman, Eisenhower, and Kennedy, a version of a health care coverage program known as Medicare was developed, debated, and eventually signed into legislation, by President Johnson in 1965.

Unfortunately, business groups, especially those associated with the insurance industry, were in opposition to a universal health care program; thus Medicare was a compromise with bipartisan support. Leaders of the labor movement sought to develop Medicare coverage as early as 1957; however, this legislation was not successfully passed until Johnson's expansion of the Great Society programs, in the mid 1960s. Thus the labor movement used a window of opportunity to see these programs come to passage.

Medicare, in 1965, initially did not include coverage for people with disabilities. This target group was given coverage for Medicare as a result of the 1972 Social Security amendments, which added coverage for the disabled and people with end-stage renal disease. The amendments also included a venue for quality control through the Professional Standards Review Organizations (PSRO). This oversight, however, was replaced with Peer Review Organizations (PRO) through the 1982 Social Security amendments. These amendments also included benefit expansion which added coverage for hospice care to Medicare enrollees.

The freedom of choice waivers and home- and community-based care waivers were established for Medicaid through 1981 legislative amendments. In 1987, the Omnibus Budget Reconciliation Act (OBRA) strengthened the protection for residents of nursing homes.

In 2003, the Medicare Prescription Drug Improvement and Modernization Act (MMA) probably impacted the Medicare program the most since its inception in 1965. MMA created a drug prescription card, valid until 2006, which then rolled over into a new voluntary program known as Medicare Part D. This outpatient prescription drug program makes prescription drugs available to beneficiaries from private drug plans, as well as Medicare Advantage plans (Centers for Medicaid & Medicare, n.d.).

HOW DOES MEDICARE WORK?

Currently there are four components of Medicare insurance available—specifically Part A, Part B, Part C, and Part D. Each of these specific programs will be outlined more concisely.

Hospital Insurance (Part A)

Medicare Part A is a hospital insurance, which is funded through mandatory contributions through employment and payroll taxes (1.45% each or 2.9% if self-employed). These funds are held in the Hospital Insurance Trust Fund. Some of the specific services and provisions that are covered through Medicare Part A include care in hospitals as an inpatient, critical access hospitals (small facilities that give limited outpatient and inpatient services to people in rural areas), skilled nursing facilities, hospice care, and some home health care. Services covered under Medicare Part A are those considered "medically necessary."

More specifically, some of the medically necessary services fall under the categories of blood, home health services, hospice care, hospital stays, and skilled nursing facility care. Blood that one receives through a hospital or skilled nursing facility during a covered stay, although perceived as a minute detail, is one item covered under Medicare Part A. Enrollees pay all costs for the first three pints of blood received as an inpatient, then 20% of the Medicare-approved amount for the additional pints of blood.

A second area of services covered under medically necessary services includes home health services. These services must be ordered by one's physician and be provided for by a Medicare-certified home health agency. Home health services are limited to intermittent skilled nursing care and home health aide services, physical therapy, occupational therapy, and speech-language pathology. Medically necessary services also include medical social services, other services, durable medical equipment such as wheelchairs, hospital beds, oxygen, walkers, and medical supplies that can be used in one's home. Under Medicare coverage, individuals pay nothing for home health care services and 20% of the Medicare-approved amount for durable medical equipment.

A third area of services under Medicare Part A includes hospital stays. Medicare enrollees are eligible for semi-private rooms, meals, general nursing care, and other hospital services and supplies. Inpatient care that one receives through critical access hospitals and mental health care are also covered. Private rooms are not considered an eligible hospital stay unless such a stay is considered medically necessary. Other areas within this category of hospital stays that are not included as Medicare benefits are private-duty nursing services and a television or telephone in one's room. Inpatient mental health care within psychiatric hospitals is limited to 190 days within one's lifetime. As of 2007, one pays $952 for the first 60 days of each benefit period. Following this first six-day period, individuals are levied at least $238 per day for days 61 to 90 of the benefit period (note: $238.00 is a 2007 rate). From days 91 to 150, individuals will pay $476 per day for care. Individuals also may take advantage of "lifetime reserve days" or 60 extra days of coverage that can be used during their lifetime. As of 2006, one pays $476 per day during the 60 days of coverage. Beyond these lifetime reserve days, all costs for each day of care beyond the 150 days are the responsibility of the individual.

A fourth area of services covered under Medicare Part A is skilled nursing facility care. Although Medicare does not cover long-term care, one can take advantage of 100 days in a benefit period of skilled nursing facility care (SNFC). SNFC includes a semi-private room, meals, skilled nursing and rehabilitative services, and other services and supplies. This period of 100 days per benefit period kicks in after a 3-day inpatient hospital stay for a related illness or injury. The costs of SNFC care as of 2006 is nothing for the first 20 days of each benefit period, then $119 per day for days 21 to 100 of each benefit period, and then 100% for each day after day 100 in the benefit period.

One additional area covered within Medicare Part A is hospice care. Hospice care is available to individuals receiving Medicare, if in fact they are deemed to have only 6 months or less to live. Services one can utilize include drugs for symptom control and pain relief, medical and support services from a Medicare-approved hospice, and other services not otherwise covered by Medicare, such as grief counseling. Hospice care is generally provided within one's home, or in a nursing facility if that is considered one's home. Hospice also covers short-term hospital and inpatient respite care, which generally takes the form of care that is given to a hospice patient so that the usual caregiver can rest. Under hospice care benefits, an individual pays a copayment of up to $5.00 for outpatient prescription drugs and 5% of the Medicare-approved amounts for inpatient respite care (short-term care given by another caregiver so that the usual caregiver can rest).

Medical Insurance (Part B)

Medicare Part B is an optional voluntary supplemental insurance that subscribers may opt into for coverage. This component of Medicare insurance can help pay for medical services such as physicians' services, outpatient care, and additional medical services that are not covered under Part A. Part B can be helpful in paying for items considered medically necessary, but not covered under part A, and it also covers preventative services. "Medically necessary" has been defined for the purposes of Medicare as "an item or service that is needed for the diagnosis or treatment of one's medical condition." It should be noted, however, that not all preventative services are covered under Medicare Part B. Services that are available and covered under Medicare Part B include the following:

Ambulance services
Ambulatory surgery centers
Blood administered through blood transfusion
Bone mass measurement
Cardiovascular screenings
Chiropractic services (limited)
Clinical laboratory services
Clinical trials
Colorectal cancer screenings
Diabetes screenings
Diabetic self-management training
Diabetic supplies
Durable medical equipment
Emergency room services
Eyeglasses (limited)
Flu shots
Foot exams and treatment
Glaucoma tests
Hearing and balance exams

Home health services
Kidney dialysis services and supplies
Mammograms (screening)
Medical nutrition therapy services
Mental health care (outpatient)
Occupational therapy
Outpatient hospital services
Outpatient medical and surgical services and supplies
Pap test and pelvic exams (including clinical breast exams)
Physical exams
Physical therapy
Pneumococcal shots
Practitioner services
Prescription drugs
Prostate cancer screening
Prosthetic/orthotic items
Second surgical opinions
Smoking cessation
Speech-language pathology services
Surgical dressings
Telemedicine
Transplant services
Travel services (health care required when traveling outside the
    United States in Canada); and
Urgently needed care.

Table 6.1 provides an overview of the services and a thumbnail sketch of what they entail.

Despite coverage that appears to identify a wide range of items, there still remain a number of services that are considered preventative in nature that are not covered in Medicare Part A and B. Some of these services include acupuncture, cosmetic surgery, dental care and dentures, hearing tests not ordered by a physician, eye care, custodial care, and long-term care. A more detailed list of services not covered is available in Table 6.2.

Medicare insurance (part B) is based upon voluntary contributions and is financed through general revenues. One voluntarily enrolls in the program. In 2006 subscribers paid for a Medicare Part B premium $88.50 per month; however, there have been changes to this amount effective January 1, 2007, and the premium amounts are based on income. If an individual did not choose part Medicare Part B when eligible at age 65, the cost of Part B may go up 10% for each 12-month period that one could have had Part B but did not sign up for it, except in special cases.

TABLE 6.1   Services Covered Under Medicare Part B

Service	Overview of what is covered
Ambulance services	Transportation to a hospital or skilled nursing facility, when transportation by any other means would be considered a danger to one's health.
Ambulatory surgery	Facility fees covered for approved services.
Blood	Pints of blood received during outpatient services for Part B-covered services.
Bone mass measurement	Covered once every 24 months for patients at risk for bone fractures. Certain medical conditions may qualify for assessments more frequently than once every 24 months.
Cardiovascular screenings	Cholesterol, lipid, and triglyceride levels tested once every 5 years for prevention of stroke or heart attack.
Chiropractic services	Limited services for manipulation of the spine to correct for subluxation (one or more of the bones out of position within the spine).
Clinical laboratory services	Blood tests, urinalysis, and some screening tests.
Clinical trials	Routine costs associated with qualifying clinical trials to test new regimens of medical care. Costs for the drugs or devices being tested within the clinical trial may not be covered.
Colorectal cancer screenings	1. Fecal Occult Blood Tests: once every 12 months if 50 years of age or older. Although one does not pay for the test, a fee for the doctor's visit may be levied.
	2. Flexible Sigmoidoscopy: Once every 48 months if 50 years of age or older, or once every 120 months when used instead of a colonoscopy for those not at high risk.
	3. Screening Colonoscopy: Once every 120 months (high risk every 24 months). No minimum age.
	4. Barium enema: Once every 48 months if age 50 or older (high risk every 24 months) when used instead of a sigmoidoscopy or colonoscopy.

(continued)

TABLE 6.1   Services Covered Under Medicare Part B (continued)

Service	Overview of what is covered
Diabetes screenings	Screenings up to two times per year based upon specific eligibility criteria including hypertension, dyslipidemia (history of abnormal cholesterol and triglyceride levels), obesity, or a history of high blood sugar.
Diabetic self-management training	Provided for people with diabetes with a written physician order.
Diabetic supplies	Supplies to include glucose testing monitors, blood glucose test strips, lancet devices and lancets, glucose control solutions, and in some cases, therapeutic shoes. Syringes and insulin are covered if used with an insulin pump or if one has Medicare prescription drug coverage.
Durable medical equipment	Oxygen, wheelchairs, walkers, and hospital beds needed for use in one's home.
Emergency room services	Coverage for visits when one's health is in serious danger, following a bad injury, sudden illness, or an illness that quickly causes physical deterioration.
Eyeglasses	Limited coverage for eyeglasses is available for one pair of eyeglasses with standard frames following cataract surgery that implants an intraocular lens.
Flu shots	Once per flu season.
Foot exams and treatment	For individuals with diabetes-related nerve damage.
Glaucoma tests	Tests to detect eye disease glaucoma, once per 12-month period for people with high risk for glaucoma (i.e., with a pre-existing condition of diabetes or family history of glaucoma, or specific risk factors).
Hearing and balance exams	Coverage is based upon physicians' requests to determine if medical treatment is required for condition. Exams for the purpose of fitting hearing aids are not covered.
Home health services	Limited to reasonable and necessary services to include part-time or intermittent skilled nursing care, home health aid services, physical therapy, occupational therapy, and speech-language pathology ordered by a physician.

TABLE 6.1 (continued)

Service	Overview of what is covered
	These services must also be provided for through a Medicare-certified home health agency. Medical supplies for use within the home are also covered and include medical social services and durable medical equipment to include wheelchairs, hospital beds, oxygen, and walkers.
Kidney dialysis services	Covered within a facility setting or at home.
Kidney dialysis supplies	Covered within a facility setting or at home.
Mammograms (screening)	For women 40 years of age or older, preventative (screening) mammograms are covered once every 12 months.
Medical nutrition therapy	Individuals with diabetes or renal disease (prior to dialysis services or transplant), or for people up to 3 years post-kidney transplant with a doctor's order. Mental health care (outpatient). Some limits and conditions will apply.
Occupational therapy (OT)	OT services to facilitate one's ability to resume activities of daily living following an illness episode.
Outpatient hospital services	Services provided as an outpatient, as part of a doctor's care.
Outpatient medical and surgical services and supplies	Based upon approved procedures.
Pap test and pelvic exams	Women considered low risk are covered once every 24 months, while women considered high risk for cervical and vaginal cancer, and those past childbearing age who have had an exam that indicated cancer or other abnormalities in the past 3 years are covered once every 12 months.
Physical exams	A one-time physical exam within the first 6 months of enrollment in Medicare Part B.
Physical therapy	Treatment for injuries and disease through heat, light, exercise, and massage.
Pneumococcal shots	To aid in the prevention of pneumococcal infection. Currently shots last one's lifetime.
Practitioner services	Services provided for by clinical social workers, physician assistants, and nurse practitioners.

(continued)

TABLE 6.1 Services Covered Under Medicare Part B (continued)

Service	Overview of what is covered
Prescription drugs	Limited at the current time to drug coverage through Medicare Part D.
Prostate cancer screening	Once every 12 months for all men over 50 years of age. Exam includes preventative digital rectal exam and prostate specific antigen (PSA) test.
Prosthetic/orthotic items	Arm, leg, and neck braces; artificial eyes; artificial limbs and replacement parts; breast prostheses (following mastectomy); prosthetic devices needed to replace an internal body part or function (including ostomy supplies and parenteral and enteral nutrition therapy).
Second surgical opinions	If surgery is not an emergency, subscribers may seek second and third opinions for potential surgical options.
Smoking cessation	Up to eight face-to-face visits during a 12-month period, if ordered by a physician, provided that one is diagnosed with a smoking-related illness or is using medications that may be affected by tobacco use.
Speech-language pathology services	Treatment to regain or strengthen speech skills.
Surgical dressings	Treatment of surgical or surgically treated wound.
Telemedicine	Services within some rural communities, provided within a practitioner's office, a hospital, or federally qualified health center.
Transplant services	Within a Medicare-certified facility, services for heart, lung, kidney, intestine, and liver, bone marrow, and some cornea transplants. If transplant was paid for by Medicare Part A or an employer/union group, and one is entitled to Medicare Part B, immunosuppressive drugs can be covered.
Travel services	Medical services provided for in Canada when one travels the most direct route to Canada between Alaska and another state.
Urgently needed care	Treatment for a sudden illness or injury not identified as a medical emergency.

TABLE 6.2   Services Not Covered by Medicare Parts A and B

Acupuncture

Chiropractic services (except those listed in Table 6.1)

Cosmetic surgery

Custodial care (help with activities of daily living—bathing, dressing, toileting or eating) either at home or within a nursing home setting

Dental care, oral health screenings, and dentures

Eye care (routine eye exams), eye refractions, and most eyeglasses

Foot care such as cutting corns or calluses

Hearing aids and hearing exams related to fitting a hearing aid

Hearing tests outside of physician's orders

Laboratory tests for screening purposes outside those listed in Table 6.1

Long-term care and custodial care in a nursing home

Orthopedic shoes (with the exception of people who are diabetics, and under certain conditions)

Physical exams (routine or annual)

Preventative vaccinations (outside of those listed in Table 6.1)

Screening tests (outside of those listed in Table 6.1)

Travel (health care received outside of the United States, except Canada, under certain conditions

This penalty of an additional 10% is a premium that follows an individual requiring payment for the rest of one's life. Enrolling in Part B is an individual choice, and one is eligible to sign up for Part B anytime during a 7-month period that begins 3 months prior to one's 65th birthday.

Although subscribers may opt into Medicare Part B and receive the services that are not considered medically necessary in Part A, some co-payments or costs are still assigned to particular services and items. For example, in the case of blood received as an outpatient, subscribers will pay for all costs of the first three pints and then 20% of the Medicare-approved amount for additional pints of blood. No additional fees are levied for clinical laboratory services utilized under Medicare Part B if the services are deemed medically necessary. Under home health services, one pays nothing for Medicare-approved services, and 20% of the Medicare-approved amount for durable medical equipment. While medical and other services will require one to pay 20% of the Medicare-approved amount for most doctor services, outpatient therapy (note that in 2007 some limits to physical therapy, occupational therapy, and speech language pathology services may exist), most preventative services, and durable medical equipment. Mental health services require subscribers to pay for 50% of the outpatient mental health care. Other services require the subscriber to pay for the copayment and coinsurance amounts, while outpatient hospital services require that the subscriber pay a coinsurance or copayment amount that varies by service. The subscriber initially pays the first $124 yearly for Part B-covered services or items.

Medicare Part C

Medicare Part C is a program that combines one's hospital coverage (Part A) and medical coverage (Part B) through a health maintenance organization (HMO) or preferred provider organization (PPO). This plan is designed to enable private insurance companies approved by Medicare to provide coverage to subscribers at a cost that may be lower than the original Medicare plan, with some additional benefits. The down side of this plan is that individuals must see physicians within the group assigned to provide coverage. Such a scheme works well for individuals who may be stationary, and remain within their home-based community; however, for people who travel frequently, or spend a portion of their time at a second residence, this plan may not offer the flexibility necessary.

Three specific options are available within the Part C Medicare Advantage Plans, each of which operates slightly differently. For the most part, providers are paid per enrollee, regardless of whether services are used or not. Within each of the three plans (PPO, HMO, or private fee for service plan [PFFS]), there are also some slight variations, and one should consider their needs and what plans would work best. In most cases prescription drugs are covered in all three of the schemes (PPO, HMO, and PFFS). In the HMO scheme one must see a primary care physician in order to receive a referral elsewhere. Under the PPO and PFFS schemes, personal autonomy is limited in choosing a primary care physician.

Effective in 2007, Medicare Medical Savings Account Plans (MSAs) will be offered. These plans are similar to the Health Savings Account plans available outside of Medicare, and have two distinct parts. The first part, known as the Medicare Advantage Health Plan, does not begin to pay covered costs until a subscriber has met their annual deductible (which varies by plan). The second part is a Medical Savings Account into which Medicare deposits money that a subscriber can use to pay health care costs (Centers for Medicare and Medicaid Services, 2006).

How is Medicare Managed Care Different From
Other Managed Care Plans?

Medicare Part C, known as Medicare+ Choice, was the result of the Balanced Budget Act in 1997. In this component of the plan recipients enroll in an HMO plan; however, many plans have been found to discriminate against older adults (Etheredge, 1999, RPRI, 1999a). The act expanded prevention services and created incentives for managed care plans to enter underserved rural areas, which has been a real asset to improving access to care within rural and underserved areas.

Medicare Part D

Medicare Part D offers prescription drug coverage for everyone eligible to enroll and utilize Medicare. This coverage was intended to help lower prescription drug costs and help protect against higher costs in the future. It can give enrollees greater access to drugs that can be used to prevent medical complications of diseases and to promote health and wellness. These plans are run by insurance companies and other private companies approved by Medicare. While Part D is optional, one may face a penalty if enrolling at a later date than the initial enrollment period in 2005/06. Individuals with limited income and resources can qualify for extra help paying Part D costs. If one's income is below $14,700 (or $19,800 if married and living with a spouse) they may qualify for extra help. One's total assets generally must be limited to $11,500 (or $23,000 if married and living with a spouse).

HOW DOES MEDICARE AFFECT ACCESS TO HEALTH CARE, COST CONTAINMENT, AND QUALITY?

Medicare costs have been rising steadily, which has been a concern to governmental authorities. According to Brown, Clement, Hill, Retchin, and Bergeron (1993), costs savings accrued through reduced utilization of health care services do not balance the high overhead rates charged by HMOs, resulting in no net savings to the Medicare program. Quality is also inconsistent across providers. Finally, fraud has risen steadily over the past decade.

WHAT IS MEDICAID AND HOW DOES IT DIFFER FROM MEDICARE?

A program designed to enable individuals who are below the poverty line to pay for health care was designed by and is delivered through the program instrument known as Medicaid. This provision is actually a title under the Social Security Act (Title XIX). Medicaid was designed to provide insurance for older adults, people with disabilities, dependent children, and mothers. States participate in the Medicaid program on a voluntary basis, although all states participate. In order for a state to receive federal funding, states must provide a range of prescribed services. However, each state identifies eligibility criteria, remuneration schedules, and poverty guidelines. Although individual states may establish their own eligibility criteria, note that reimbursement from the federal government will not occur for services provided beyond the currently established guidelines (GAO, 1998, Rosenbach & Lamphere, 1999).

Eligibility

The Medicaid program has some mandatory and optional eligibility criteria. The mandatory criteria target five specific categories of poor or low income people:

- Pregnant women
- Children
- Older adult Medicare recipients
- Adults under 65 with dependent children
- Children and adults with disabilities

Although Medicaid is a federally mandated program, each state identifies and develops its own eligibility criteria. The Social Security Act authorizes multiple waiver and demonstration authorities to allow individual states flexibility in operating Medicaid programs. Each authority has a distinct purpose, and distinct requirements. Within the legislation, some specific sections provide for waivers to enable some flexibility to individual states to develop their own demonstration projects or carve out specific Medicaid opportunities that can meet specific community needs. These specific components of the act include Sections 1115, which addresses research and demonstration projects, and Section 1915, which addresses managed care waivers or home- and community-based services waivers.

Medicaid Waiver Opportunities

Section 1115: Research and Demonstration Projects

This section gives the Secretary of Health and Human Services broad authority to approve projects that test policy innovations likely to further the objectives of the Medicaid program. These may include innovative primary care health and preventative health care delivery options to meet the needs of the elderly who have been subject to low income.

Section 1915(b) Managed Care/Freedom of Choice Waivers:

This section provides the secretary authority to grant waivers that allow states to implement managed care delivery systems, or otherwise limit individuals' choice of provider under Medicaid. Under this option, older adults may be guaranteed some providers if living below the poverty level, and these providers may care for the health care needs of the elderly, especially in medically designated shortage areas.

Section 1915(c) Home- and Community-Based Services Waivers

This section provides the secretary authority to waive Medicaid provisions in order to allow long-term care services to be delivered in community settings. This program is the Medicaid alternative to providing comprehensive long-term services in institutional settings. This waiver program expands the opportunities for community living and assisted living opportunities for older adults that live in the community, who may otherwise be limited in their housing options or options for community-based care and assistance.

In summary these options within the Medicaid legislation provide for the opportunities to carve out and develop innovations within the health care service delivery networks for older adults who are low income. It also enables individual states to develop model programs that address the cultural and economic contexts of their population base.

WHAT ARE THE EFFECTS OF REIMBURSEMENT ON HEALTH CARE QUALITY, ACCESS, AND COSTS?

Despite the fact that services are available to meet the medical needs of older adults and the elderly poor, Medicaid and CHIP (State Children's Health Insurance Programs) reimbursement rates are not always consistent with the cost of delivering services. Hence, providers are often dubious about providing services to older adults on Medicaid. Certain neighborhoods in urban areas and certain rural communities may not have access to providers who will accept Medicaid. Prolonged periods of time to wait for reimbursements lead to disinterest in serving as a provider.

DILEMMAS FOR THE FUTURE

Although comprehensive in nature, Medicare faces a number of dilemmas when we look toward the future. Health care expenses appear to be most costly during one's last year of life, thus pouring a financial burden onto the current Medicare system. Dilemmas for the future include the burden of costs of financing a comprehensive health care system, the rationing of health care services, and accessibility of health care services to older adults living in medically designated shortage areas (GAO, 1998; RPRI, 1999b) .

An Empty Pot at the End of the Rainbow?

Medicare has been perceived by many to be the "pot of gold" at the end of the rainbow, or a benefit to be treasured in retirement. It was intended to provide medical coverage to older adults, upon retirement age and beyond; however, with the costs of health care exploding over the past decade, will this pot be empty in years to come, or will it be limited? Health care economists predict that the costs of care will far exceed the monies available for reimbursement to physicians and for hospital inpatient treatment. In addition, a number of services are currently not covered (see Table 6.2), which are not necessarily elective services, but necessary and required. Prevention and screening services are not covered, nor is there any vision that these services will be covered in the near future. In addition, Medicare only covered about 20% of all health care expenses (a more detailed discussion of health care expenses can be found in chapter 17). Thus, these issues leave one to wonder if the pot will continue to "evaporate" over the years to come, and if it will be empty in years to come? Unfortunately experts (Derickson, 2005; Barush, 2002) who have critiqued the system argue that this pot may be close to empty, if not empty, in years to come.

Rationing of Health Care Services—To Be or Not to Be?

A second dilemma for the future is the rationing of health care services. At the current time, rationing does not occur in most states, although it has been argued that Oregon's protocol for health care delivery prioritizes care and procedures based upon life-tables, and in effect, care is rationed as one moves across the life span. This approach is also apparent in some countries that provide socialized medicine, such as Britain. As the cost of health care continues to increase, and as our cohort of older adults (people 65+ years of age) continues to grow, will the rationing of health care services come to be? Since the philosophical paradigm underlying

Medicare at the time of its inception was that "health care was a right," will this concept of rationing come to pass, or will another philosophical paradigm prevail, which can lead to a rationing of health care for older adults through the Medicare program?

SUMMARY

Medicare, a health care program perceived to be a universal program rather than based upon a needs test, currently provides health care to people who reach the age of 64. Comprised of four parts, it can provide hospital care, general health care, hospice care, home health care, and prescription drug coverage. This chapter provided an overview of the Medicare program, its various components, and aspects of health care that are covered through its component parts. Although at the current time there are no needs tests or limitations as to who qualifies for services, the chapter concluded with presenting some dilemmas for the future relative to health care coverage, including "an empty pot at the end of the rainbow" and rationing of health care services and procedures.

USEFUL WEB SITES

Medicare: http://www.hcfa.gov/Medicare
This governmental Web site is orchestrated through the health care financing administration and provides an overview of Medicare and its programs, and a user's guide is available.

Medicaid: http://www.cms.hhs.gov
This governmental Web site is orchestrated through the health care financing administration and provides an overview of the Medicaid program, guidelines for use, and issues for debate. An overview of the Medicaid programs is provided, and a user's guide is available.

Kaiser Family Foundation: http://www.kff.org
This site for the Kaiser Family Foundation provides a background of current studies and up-to-date information on both the Medicaid and Medicare programs.

Strengthening Medicare: http://www.whitehouse.gov/infocus/medicare/
This Whitehouse site provides an overview of initiatives, speeches, and key summaries of roundtable discussions related to Medicare and Medicare modernization.

Medicare Publications Search: http://www.medicare.gov/Publications/ Search

This site provides a range of up-to-date publications and fact sheets that help simplify the process of understanding Medicare and its component parts.

REFERENCES

Ball, R. M. (1996). Medicare's roots: What Medicare's architects had in mind. *Generations, 20* (2), 13–18.

Barusch, A. (2002). *Foundations of social policy: Social justice, public programs, and the social work profession.* Itasca, IL: Peacock Publishers.

Brown, R. S., Clement, D. G., Hill, J. W., Retchin, S. M., & Bergeron, J. W. (1993). Do health maintenance organizations work for Medicare? *Health Care Financing Review, 15*(1), 7–23.

Centers for Medicare & Medicaid Services. (2006). *Medicare and you, 2007: Official government handbook.* Baltimore, MD: Government Printing Office.

Centers for Medicare and Medicaid Services. (n.d.). *Key milestones in CMS programs.* Retrieved May 16, 2007, from http://www.cms.hhs.gov/History/Downloads/CMS Program KeyMilestones.pdf

Derickson, A. (2005). *Health security for all: Dreams of universal health care in America.* Baltimore, MD. Johns Hopkins Press.

Etheredge, L. (1999). Medicare's governance and structure: A proposal: One expert's prescription for fixing what ails the management of Medicare and other federal health programs. *Health Affairs, 19*(5), 60–71.

GAO. (1998). *Medicaid: Early implication of welfare reform for beneficiaries and states.* Washington, D.C.: US Government Printing Office.

Rosenbach, M. L., & Lamphere, J. (1999). *Public policy institute: Bridging the gaps between Medicare and Medicaid: The case of QMBs and SLMBs.* Washington, DC: AARP.

Rural Policy Research Institute (RRPI). (1999a). *A rural perspective on Medicare policy: An initial assessment of the premium support approach.* Columbia, MO: RUPRI Office.

Rural Policy Research Institute (RRPI). (1999b). *Taking Medicare into the 21st century: Realities of a post BBA world and implications for rural health care.* Columbia, MO: RUPRI Office.

CHAPTER 7

The Older Americans Act

BACKGROUND AND OVERVIEW

Prior to the 1920s, limited attention was placed upon aging services or older adults' needs and concerns. The passage of the Civil Service Retirement Act provided for a retirement system for a number of government employees and served as a pioneer effort to consider social welfare needs for aging adults. However, this did not provide for any programs or services to meet the needs of older adults living in the community. Ironically, no development was apparent in this area until 1950, when President Truman initiated the first National Conference on Aging, sponsored by the Federal Security Agency. This resulted in the first federal funds being appropriated for social service programs for older people (1952); however, these funds were appropriated under the Social Security Act. In 1956, a special staff on aging was established and housed within the Office of the Secretary of Health, Education, and Welfare, with its main function to coordinate responsibilities for the aging. In addition, a Federal Council on Aging was created by President Eisenhower. Legislation introduced in Congress in 1958 called for a White House Conference on Aging, which was held in 1961. This led to legislation introduced in Congress, to establish an independent and permanent Commission on Aging. A direct result of this commission was the development of the Older Americans Act of 1965, which was first signed into law on July 14.

THE OLDER AMERICANS ACT OF 1965

The Older Americans Act (PL-89–73) signed into legislation on July 14, 1965, has been the cornerstone of community services for older adults in the United States. It is based upon 10 objectives that identify how older adults should be valued and treated, including conditions for an adequate income in concert with a standard of living in the United States; the most up-to-date physical and mental health care guided by scientific findings; affordable and suitable housing; complete rehabilitative or restorative services for people in institutional care; opportunities for nondiscriminatory employment, regardless of age; a retirement that offers dignity and honor in return for one's contribution to the nation's economy; the freedom for autonomy and independence and sufficient and effective community care services that promote independence. In the original act, these principles are defined in six specific Titles.

Title I: Definitions

In the original Older Americans Act (OAA) legislation, Title I outlined the objectives and defined the administrative oversight for the OAA. In addition to laying the groundwork to assure that the programs and services preserve the dignity and worth of the individual, Title I lays out definitions for the administrative structure to carry out the OAA. This includes the Secretary, Commissioner, and the role that individual states will take on in the administration of the act.

Title II: Administration on Aging (AoA)

Title II establishes the infrastructure for the administration of aging services and outlines the main activities of this administrative structure. The Administration on Aging is housed within the Department of Health, Education, and Welfare (as of 2007 this is known as the Department of Health and Human Services) and is headed by a commissioner, appointed by the president. The functions of the Administration on Aging include:

a. to provide a clearinghouse of information related to aging
b. to assist the secretary on all matters that pertain to aging and aging issues
c. to administer grants provided by the OAA
d. to develop, plan, execute, and disseminate research and demonstration programs within the field of aging
e. to provide consultation and technical assistance to individual states on issues related to aging
f. to prepare, publish, and disseminate information that relates to older adults
g. to collect data on issues pertinent to aging, which was not currently collected by other federal authorities
h. to encourage the use of services to promote healthy aging

Title III: Grants for Community Planning, Services, and Training

Title III outlines the authorization process of appropriations for the purpose of community planning, services, and training. Outlined within this title are allotments, reallotments, and monies available for grants, time limitations for grants, and an outline of how state plans filter into the grants process. This title also outlines how state agencies can administer a plan, the development of programs and activities, personnel, and how to prioritize projects and maintain records. An appeals process for state-based entities is also outlined.

Title IV: Research and Development Projects

Under section 401 of the original OAA, the secretary can authorize grants for the purpose of conducting research and development projects in up to four specific areas. These include: (a) to study patterns and living conditions of older adults to assure and maximize their well-being; (b) to develop new approaches, techniques and models of service delivery that will promote the well-being and maximize the potential for healthy lifestyles for older adults; (c) to evaluate approaches to promote and maximize service delivery models for community-based services; and (d) to promote best practice methods in social welfare.

Title V: Training Projects

Under Section 502 of the original OAA, title V outlines the provision of funds for training projects to benefit individual states, which are identified within the specific state's plan of priorities. Funds, although appropriated from the Secretary of the AoA, sanction must also be provided for by the individual state to receive funds.

Title VI: General

Title VI outlines the advisory committees that govern the administration of the OAA. Membership on the advisory committee is also outlined, the terms of office, compensation and travel expenses, and guidelines for the publication of informational materials.

Although the Older Americans Act is still in operation and serves as the mandate to guide service delivery for community-dwelling older adults, a number of legislative amendments have been enacted over the past 40 years. The next section will provide a thumbnail sketch of some of these amendments, including the most recent amendments of 2006 to the Older Americans Act.

AMENDMENTS TO THE OLDER AMERICANS ACT:
1967–2000

Since the inception of the Older Americans Act a number of amendments have been passed, which have both extended the initial appropriations and expanded the amounts budgeted for the act. However, with many of the amendments, the act has been expanded to address new issues, or additional concerns for older adults living within communities. In 1967, for example, with the first set of amendments, the Older Americans Act was extended for 2 years, with an expansion of the original act to study the personnel needs within the aging field. Two years later, in 1969, amendments to the act included the provision of funds for foster grandparent and retired senior volunteer programs, and model demonstration projects. The development of nutrition programs resulted following the amendments of 1972, when Title VII was created to authorize funds for such programs for the elderly. The establishment of area agencies on aging was the result of the 1973 Comprehensive Services Amendments. Title V authorized grants to community agencies for multipurpose senior centers, and created community service employment grants for people 55 years of age and older and considered in a low income bracket.

Title III of the Older Americans Act was expanded in 1974 to include transportation, and in 1975 grants were authorized for Indian tribal organizations. In addition, priority services were defined in the areas of transportation, home care, legal services, and home renovation/repair.

Changes to Title VII were made in 1977 that focused on nutrition programs. These changes led to nutrition sites, making use of surplus commodities through the Department of Agriculture. Further changes were seen in 1978, when Older Americans Act Amendments consolidated the Title III Area Agency on Aging administration and social services, the Title VII nutrition services, and the Title V multi-purpose senior centers into a new Title III and added a new Title VI for grants to Indian tribal organizations. The former Title V became the Community Service Employment grant program for low-income persons, age 55 and older (created under the 1978 amendments as Title IX). In addition, in 1978, amendments mandated each state to develop a long-term care ombudsman program to address issues of concern from residents and their families in nursing homes.

Amendments that took place in the 1980s to the OAA emphasized the support for community-based care and the principle of maintaining independence within the community. In 1981, the ombudsman program was expanded to provide coverage to board and care homes through OAA amendments. The subsequent reauthorizations that took place in 1984 reaffirmed the roles of the state and the local area agencies on aging to coordinate community-based services, and to assure funding to enable state and local entities to maintain accountability and funding of nationally prioritized services such as legal, in-home care, and accessibility. The reauthorization of the Older Americans Act added six additional distinct appropriations for services: in-home services for the frail elderly; long-term care ombudsman; assistance for special needs; health education and promotion; prevention of elder abuse, neglect, and exploitation; and outreach activities for persons who may be eligible for benefits under supplemental security income (SSI), Medicaid, and food stamps. Additional emphasis was given to serving those in the greatest economic and social need, including low-income minorities. In addition, the OAA reauthorization charged states to guarantee ombudsman access to facilities and patient records, provided important legal protections, authorized state ombudsmen to designate local ombudsman programs, and required that ombudsman programs have adequate legal counsel. See Figure 7.1.

Older Americans Act Amendments of 2000 (P.L. 106–501), which reauthorized the OAA for 5 years, was signed into law on November 13,

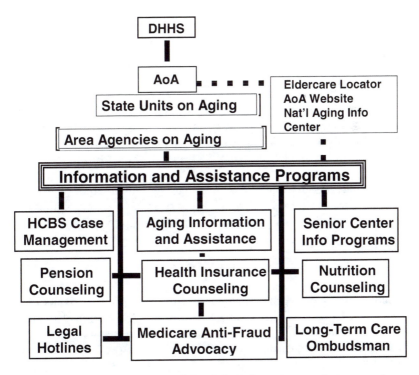

FIGURE 7.1   An overview of the Administration on Aging services.

2000. It included the establishment of the National Family Caregiver Support Program. (Lexis-Nexis Congressional Universe, 2000).

The National Family Caregiver Support Program

Caregivers provide a tremendous service to individuals requiring support, and they are often not regarded as an integral component of a service delivery system when examining care strategies. The National Family Caregiver Support Program acknowledges this vital role and provides assistance to family caregivers. Within the National Family Caregiver Support Act, a family caregiver is defined as an adult family member, or other individual, who is an informal provider of in-home and community care to an older individual. This definition provides some scope and flexibility in order to meet the needs of those responsible for caring for their loved ones. It also acknowledges the fact that other relatives, friends, neighbors, and domestic partners will also share the responsibility of caring for loved ones.

The National Family Caregiver Support Program provides services within five areas of support service, including: (1) information about services available; (2) assistance in gaining access to these services; (3) counseling, organization of support groups, and caregiver training; (4) respite care; and (5) supplemental services on a limited basis to augment the care provided by caregivers. The act also places a high priority for services to (1) older caregivers who demonstrate the greatest social and economic needs (with attention being paid to low-income individuals), and (2) older caregivers of persons with mental retardation and related developmental disabilities. The act also allows each state to use no more than 10% of their total funds to provide support services to eligible caregivers raising their grandchildren (under the age of 18 years). It should be noted that an eligible grandparent caregiver would be defined as someone who is at least 60 years of age or older; is a grandparent, step-grandparent, or relative by blood or marriage of the child; is the primary caregiver of the child; and lives with the child regardless of the legal relationship to the child.

LEGISLATIVE AMENDMENTS OF 2006

On Sept 29, 2006, legislative amendments to the Older Americans Act expanded the existing act and moved towards assuring that older Americans could maintain their dignity and independence, while segments of the act sought to put prevention efforts into place for services (N4A, 2006). Amendments known as Public Law 109-365 bring some specific new areas for consideration to include:

- Enhanced coordination of long-term care services to be developed in home- and community-based settings;
- Support for community planning efforts at the state level in order to begin to address some of the long-term care needs that the baby boom generation will face;
- An increased focus on prevention and treatment of psychiatric disorders;
- An expansion of the category of caregivers served under the National Family Caregiver Support Program;
- An increased focus on civic engagement and volunteerism;
- An expansion of programs designed to address elder abuse, neglect, and exploitation.

The amendments of 2006 expanded on the president's New Freedom Commission Initiative and affirmed the commitment to some specific values. These values included health promotion and disease prevention, independence, empowerment, and community-based care.

The Older Americans Act Amendments of 2006 (PL 109-365) are the primary source for the delivery of social and nutrition services for older individuals. First enacted in 1965, the act's programs include supportive services, congregate and home-delivered nutrition services, community service employment, the long-term care ombudsman program, and services to prevent the abuse, neglect, and exploitation of older individuals. The act also provides grants to Native Americans and research, training, and demonstration activities.

Title I of the Older Americans Act sets broad social policy objectives to improve the lives of all older Americans. Although the definitions have been updated in order to be consistent with other statutes and proposals, the objectives have been retained, and remain unchanged, from previous legislation. It recognizes the need for an adequate income in retirement, and the importance of physical and mental health, employment in community services for older individuals, and long-term care services. Definitions related to assistive technology have been made consistent with the Assistive Technology Act of 1998. The definitions for elder abuse, neglect and exploitation have also been made consistent with the definitions used by the Justice Coalition in the Elder Justice Act. See Figure 7.2.

Title II establishes the Administration on Aging (AoA), within the Department of Health and Human Services, to be the primary federal advocate for older individuals and to administer the provision of the Older Americans Act. It also establishes the National Eldercare Locator Service to provide nationwide information with regard to resources for older individuals; the National Long-Term Care Ombudsman Resource Center; the National Center on Elder Abuse; the National Aging Information Center;

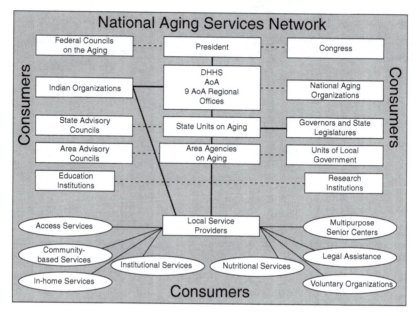

FIGURE 7.2   The Aging Services Network.
Source: Administration on Aging, 2006

and the Pension Counseling and Information Program. The 2006 amendments authorize the designation of a person to have responsibility for elder abuse prevention to develop a long-term plan and national response to elder abuse prevention, detection, treatment, and intervention. It also authorizes the assistant secretary to designate an individual to be responsible for administration of mental health services and authorizes aging and disability resource centers. Further, the 2006 amendments strengthen the leadership of the Department of Health and Human Services through an interagency coordinating committee to guide policy and program development across the federal government with respect to aging and demographic changes.

Within Title II, definitions for numerous key issues impacting older adults have been expanded within the new legislative amendments. These include exploitation, self-neglect, and at risk for institutional placement, (which were not included in the past. The definition of disease prevention and health promotion was changed to include an evidence-based approach, includes examples of chronic disease, and adds to the examples of health promotion activities: "falls prevention, physical activity and improved nutrition." Aging and Disability Resource Centers (ADRC—see Chapter 8 for a more comprehensive description) have also been added to the list of definitions. The functions of AoA are also expanded to include elder abuse prevention, benefits enrollment, choices for independence, federal partnerships, mental health, civic engagement, evidence-based nutrition services, and private pay options. Healthy lifestyles are also promoted through the use of evidence-based disease prevention interventions.

Title III authorizes grants to fund 655 area agencies on aging and more than 29,000 service providers nationwide. Title III services are targeted to those with the greatest economic and social need, particularly low-income minority persons and older individuals residing in rural communities. The 2006 amendments will authorize organizations with experience in providing volunteer opportunities for older individuals to be eligible to enter cooperative arrangements; require state agencies to promote the development and implementation of state systems that enable older individuals to receive long-term care and community-based settings in accordance with needs and preferences; encourage both states and area agencies on aging to plan for population changes; improve access to supportive services that help foster independence; require nutrition projects to prepare meals that comply with the most recent dietary guidelines; and reauthorize the National Family Caregiver Support Program.

The reauthorization of the National Family Caregiver Support Program broadens the population to be served, and will now include caregivers of individuals with Alzheimer's disease, grandparents or older relation caregivers who are 55 years of age or older (it was formerly 60 years of age) caring for a child related by blood, marriage, or adoption and also considers individuals responsible for an adult child with a disability.

Title IV supports a wide range of ongoing research and demonstration activities that will enhance innovation, identify best practices, and provide technical assistance for older individuals. The 2006 amendments will permit competitive grants for planning activities that will benefit the aging population, and assessment of technology-based models to aid in remote health monitoring systems, communication devices, and assistive technologies. These activities include naturally occurring retirement communities (NORCs), innovations to improve transportation, mental health services, and screening, and civic engagement. Further, it includes Hispanic-serving institutions among those eligible to compete for grants to provide education and training in the field of aging; reauthorizes grants to improve transportation services for older individuals; ensures increased awareness of mental health disorders among older individuals; and authorizes development of innovative models of service delivery to ensure older individuals may age in place, as they are able, and as they choose.

Title V authorizes the community service employment program for older Americans—known as the Senior Community Service Employment Program, or SCSEP—to promote part-time opportunities in community service for unemployed, low-income persons who are 55 years or older and who have poor employment prospects. It is administered by the Department of Labor. This program represents approximately one-quarter of Older Americans Act funds—$432 million out of $1.78 billion in fiscal year 2006. This program is operated by states, and national grantees were awarded competitive grants, supporting 61,050 jobs and serving approximately 91,500 individuals in fiscal year 2005. The 2006 amendments establish 4-year grant cycles for the competitive program and prohibit poor-performing grantees from competing during the next grant cycle. It expands participation for eligible individuals who are underemployed and establishes a 48-month time limit for participation in the program, with a waiver for particularly hard-to-serve individuals. It establishes an overall grantee average participation cap of up to 27 months and authorizes a waiver of up to 36 months.

Title VI provides funds for supportive and nutrition services for older Native Americans. The 2006 amendments will increase the Native American caregiver support program through 2011. Also, Title VII authorizes programs for the long-term care ombudsman; elder abuse, neglect, and exploitation prevention; legal service developers; and vulnerable Native American elder rights. The 2006 amendments will enhance the elder abuse prevention activities by awarding grants to States and Indian tribes to enable them to strengthen long-term care and provide assistance for elder justice and elder abuse prevention programs. It will create grants for prevention, detection, assessment, treatment of, intervention in, investigation of, and response to elder abuse; safe havens demonstrations for older individuals; volunteer programs; multidisciplinary activities; elder fatality and serious injury review teams; programs for underserved populations; incentives for long-term care facilities to train and retain employees; and other collaborative and innovative approaches.

Finally, the National Resource Center for Women and Retirement is a highly successful program run by the Women's Institute for a Secure Retirement—WISER—a nonprofit organization dedicated to ensuring the security of women's retirement income through outreach, partnerships, and policy development. We know that many older Americans lack financial knowledge, and that financial education is needed. This program provides a helpful service and should continue to be funded so as to expand its various programs for older Americans, including financial literacy.

PHILOSOPHICAL PARADIGMS IMPACTING LEGISLATIVE AMENDMENTS

In view of these legislative amendments to the Older Americans Act (OAA), one can ponder on the philosophical paradigms that have been influential in these amendments. The OAA changed slowly and incrementally over the past 40 years, thus one can suggest that the philosophical paradigm known as *incrementalism* is at play. In addition, one may argue that street-level bureaucrats may have an influence on how the act is administered, since area and state plans have a tremendous influence in how services are prioritized and delivered from state to state and region to region.

SUMMARY

In summary, the Older Americans Act has been a significant piece of legislation, which has impacted the face of services for older adults and enabled older adults at risk of institutionalization to remain within their homes and communities. Over the past 40 years the range of services has grown and its reach has extended to a number of services within the community and noninstitutionalized environments.

USEFUL WEB SITES

The Administration on Aging's official Web site: http://www.aoa.gov
This is the official Administration on Aging Web site and provides an overview of specific links related to the administration of the Older Americans Act.

Family Caregiver Alliance, National Center for Caregiving: http://www.caregiver.org/caregiver/jsp/home.jsp
This Web site provides an overview of the National Caregiver Support Program and materials and resources associated with this program. The program is one supported through amendments to the Older Americans Act.

National Caregiver Support Clearinghouse: http://www.aoa.gov/prof/aoaprog/caregiver/overview/overview_caregiver.asp
This Web site provides caregiver support information through the Administration on Aging.

National Association of Area Agencies on Aging: http://www.n4a.org/
This is the official Web site of the national body organizing individual area agencies on aging. The organization attempts to provide some unity to local entities and helps bring policy to practice and from a national to local level.

REFERENCES

Code of Federal Regulations. (n.d.). *Older Amercians Act: Title III Regulations* Title 45, 4, 45CFR1321, Washington, DC: Government Printing Office.

Egyptian Area Agency on Aging. (2001). *Area plan summary for FY 2002–2004.* Carterville, IL: Author.

Enzi, M. (2006). Testimony to the Senate, September 29, 2006.

LEXIS-NEXIS Congressional Universe. (2000). *Older Americans Act.* Retrieved October, 6, 2001, from http://web.lexis-nexis.com/congcomp/document

National Association of Area Agencies on Aging (N4a). (2006, October 7). *Side by side comparison of House and Senate Older Americans Act reauthorization bills.*

Public Law 89-73. 90th Congress, H.R. 3708, July 14, 1965.

The National Family Caregiver Support Program. (2006). Retrieved January 16, 2007, from http://www.aoa.gov

Older Americans Act of 2006, Public Law No. 109-365, Congressional Record, Vol. 152, USC 3001, 2006.

Walker, E., Burns, F., & Wren, J. (2006). Amendments to the Older Americans Act, PL 109-365. A presentation to the United States Administration on Aging.

CHAPTER 8

The Americans With Disabilities Act

THE INTERSECTION BETWEEN
DISABILITY AND AGING

Increasingly, people with activity limitations (one or more limitations to their activities of daily living), or limitations to mobility due to chronic disabilities, will opt to remain in the community. Consequently, community-based options have been influenced by the philosophical paradigms driving the independent living movements over the past half-century. Increasingly, Centers for Independent Living are also providing resources to adults over the age of 60 for the sole purpose of making their lives more comfortable within a community-based setting.

HISTORY OF THE DISABILITY MOVEMENT

Prior to World War II, people with disabilities or chronic health care needs were dehumanized and often left to the care of the Poor House or Settlement Movement, despite the prevailing notion that these individuals should be cared for by the state, an idea resulting from the Elizabethan Poor Laws. Despite these acts of charity, returning soldiers from World War I were not content with the status quo arrangement to be admitted and remain in a nursing home. Hence in the late 1940s activists began to argue for training the veteran to be a productive citizen and to be a part of their entire community (Jurkowski, 1987). Despite the provisions of the Rehabilitation Act of 1978, some people were not able to return to productive work: thus they returned to a nursing care facility. Lex Frieden, a paraplegic himself, questioned the validity of this approach and made the argument that every person deserved the right to remain in the community with community-based supports (Jurkowski, 1987). This then led to the development of the Independent Living Movement, which gained momentum and popularity following the civil rights legislation in the 1960s (Albrecht, 1992; Essex-Sorlie, 1994), and a prelude to the Americans with Disabilities Act (ADA).

THE JOURNEY TOWARDS THE AMERICANS WITH DISABILITIES ACT

In the later 1980s, prior to the signing of the ADA, more than 43 million Americans had one or more physical disabilities and it was anticipated that as people age, this number would only increase. Coupled with this staggering number was the reality that historically, society has had a tendency to isolate and/or segregate people with disabilities. Regardless of movements such as the Independent Living movement (DeJong, 1979) discrimination and segregation towards people with disabilities continued to be a pervasive social issue. In addition, discrimination against people with disabilities had a pervasive impact financially both in terms of dependency and under-productivity for people with disabilities. These issues grew as people with disabilities were considered across the life span, and people who were older adults and those with a disability were more likely to be discriminated against.

THE AMERICANS WITH DISABILITIES ACT OF 1990 (ADA)

The Americans with Disabilities Act of 1990 was established to fulfill a fourfold purpose:

1) To provide a clear and comprehensive national mandate for the elimination of discrimination against individuals with disabilities;
2) to provide clear, strong, consistent enforceable standards addressing discrimination against individuals with disabilities;
3) to ensure that the Federal Government plays a central role in enforcing the standards established in this Act on behalf of individuals with disabilities; and
4) to invoke the sweep of congressional authority, including the power to enforce the fourteenth amendment and to regulate commerce, in order to address the major areas of discrimination faced day-to-day by people with disabilities. (U.S. Department of Justice, 1999).

Disability, within ADA, refers to a person with a physical or mental impairment that substantially limits one or more major life activities for a person. The ADA excludes people with substance use or chronic drug histories from being addressed or covered within this act (U.S. Department of Labor, 2007).

The Americans with Disabilities Act of 1990 (Public Law 101-336), signed into legislation by George H. W. Bush, consists of five specific titles. Title I lays out provisions within the area of employment. Title II relates to public services; Title III focuses upon public accommodations and services operated by private entities; Title IV relates to accommodations; and Title V relates to miscellaneous provisions. This segment will lay out some of the provisions within each of the titles.

Title I: Employment

This title attempts to assure that individuals are not discriminated against within the employment sector as a result of their disability. Reasonable accommodations must be made for individuals with a disability who are qualified to perform the essential functions of a specific job. Reasonable accommodations are also specified within Title 1, which includes making existing job resources accessible to the individual and job restructuring so as to accommodate the handicapping condition for the individual. This also includes acquiring or modifying equipment or devices, adjusting training materials to provide for the person with a disability, or providing qualified readers and interpreters when necessary. Employers can be exempt, however, if they can prove undue hardship financially on their business if accommodations are pursued.

An employer is required to make an accommodation to the known disability of a qualified applicant or employee if it would not impose an "undue hardship" on the operation of the employer's business. Undue hardship is defined as an action requiring significant difficulty or expense when considered in light of factors such as an employer's size, financial resources, and the nature and structure of its operation. An employer is not required to lower quality or production standards to make an accommodation, nor is an employer obligated to provide personal use items such as glasses or hearing aids.

Title II: Public Services

This title of ADA provides for accommodations within the transportation arena. According to Title II of ADA, all new public transit buses and rail cars ordered after Aug. 26, 1990, must be accessible to individuals with disabilities. In addition, local transportation authorities must provide comparable paratransit or other special transportation services to individuals with disabilities who cannot use fixed route bus services, unless they can prove that an undue burden would result from providing these services. According to the ADA, the existing rail transportation systems were required to have at least one accessible car per train by July 26, 1995. While there is not much that can be expected of existing train and bus stations, new bus and train stations must be accessible. Within this segment of Title II, key stations in rapid, light, and commuter rail systems must be made accessible by July 26, 1993, with extensions up to 20 years for commuter rail (30 years for rapid and light rail). All existing Amtrak stations must be accessible by July 26, 2010. State and local governments may not discriminate against qualified individuals with disabilities. All government facilities, services, and communications must be accessible consistent with the requirements of section 504 of the Rehabilitation Act of 1973.

Title III: Public Accommodations and Services Offered Through Private Entities

Within Title III of the ADA, private entities such as restaurants, hotels, and retail stores may not discriminate against individuals with disabilities; this has been in effect since January 26, 1992. Reasonable modifications must be made to policies, practices, or procedures to avoid discriminating unless a fundamental alteration to the nature of the goods or services would result. In addition, auxiliary aids and services must be provided to ensure effective communication with individuals with disabilities that substantially limit the ability to communicate, such as vision, hearing or speech impairments, unless an undue burden or a fundamental alteration would result. Physical barriers in existing facilities must be removed, if removal is readily achievable. If not, alternative methods of providing the services must be offered, if they are readily achievable. All new construction and alterations of facilities must be accessible as of 1998.

Title IV: Telecommunications

Companies offering telephone service to the general public must offer telephone relay services to allow communications access for people with speech and hearing impairments who cannot use telephones. Closed captioning is also required by "any television public service announcement that is produced or funded in whole or in part by any agency or instrumentality of Federal Government" for public service announcements.

Title V: Miscellaneous Provisions

Title V of the ADA covers items such as building construction, prohibition against retaliation and coercion, federal wilderness areas, transvestites, the illegal use of drugs, amendments to the Rehabilitation Act of 1973, coverage of Congress and the agencies of the legislative branch, and alternative means of dispute resolution and severability.

IMPLICATIONS OF THE ADA ON THE AGING AND OLDER ADULT POPULATIONS

The Americans with Disabilities Act, although originally intended for a community-based population of individuals with disabilities, also has numerous implications for older adults who acquire mobility and sensory disabilities. A number of implications can be identified within each of the titles. In the next segment of this chapter we will review implications of the ADA for an older adult population.

Title I: Employment

Individuals qualify for services under the Older Adults Act when they reach 60 years of age. Ironically, the same definition of older adult is not followed in the administration of retirement benefits from Social Security, whose effective date is becoming later and will eventually be at least 67 years of age. It is possible that one may develop some mobility or sensory problems during the course of this lapse in time, in which case job modifications will be required. Older adults may also develop chronic health issues that would require employers to provide job modifications in order to accommodate them, such as stroke or sensory impairment. Under Title I, individuals with some physical and sensory impairments could not be discriminated against when seeking employment on the basis of some condition that may be detected during a company physical. This can also be an advantage for older adults, since many health conditions begin to emerge in one's 40s 50s, and 60s. Hence, the ADA and its provisions under Title I can be a real asset to protect older workers.

Title II: Public Services

The implications of Title II for older adults will have the most impact in the area of transportation and preserving one's dignity and autonomy. Lack of ability to travel in one's own vehicle, or the loss of one's driver's license can be a tremendous blow to one's autonomy and impact one's ability to travel independently through their community. Transportation systems within both urban and rural communities that can accommodate people with disabilities can be a tremendous asset to maintaining one in their home and within their community. In addition, transportation systems such as rail and air can assure that older adults continue to travel and maintain recreational outlets previously enjoyed by people in their younger years. With the increase in family mobility these days, more and more older adults travel and want to remain active with their loved ones. Accommodations to public transportation services make this possible and increase the likelihood that people with some mobility impairments are able to travel freely using rail or public transportation systems.

Title III: Public Accommodations and Services Offered Through Private Entities

Title III also promotes the inclusion of older adults into community-based activities. Public accommodations such as parking spaces, curb cuts, and longer period of time to travel across streets with traffic lights, although simple changes, make it possible for older adults to continue to participate within the community. Accommodations available to older adults to assist with some "instrumental activities of daily living" (Katz, 1983) can include assistance within stores when shopping, banking, doing laundry at public facilities, or traveling to churches or local recreational events. Architectural barriers are also minimized as a result of Title III and can have a profound effect on one's ability to navigate a community.

Title IV: Telecommunications

Title IV enables older adults the opportunity to enjoy major communication with a wealth of resources, which may not necessarily be possible without this piece of legislation. Aging individuals with sensory impairments will be able to enjoy television as a result of the closed caption subtitles. People who have hearing deficits will be able to carry on conversations with loved ones or conduct business transactions as a result of TTY relay equipment.

In the decades to come, the ADA will become much more significant within the lives of people who are aging with a disability. As more people who are aging and who have disabilities remain living in the community, we see an increase in the number of people who will utilize services from the disability resource community. One specific provision for access has occurred through the Aging and Disability Resource Centers (ADRC) legislated by Congress in 2002.

AGING AND DISABILITY RESOURCE CENTERS

In response to the growing numbers of older adults with disabilities found in communities, the Centers for Medicaid and Medicare, in conjunction with the Administration on Aging, have developed a cooperative grant program to support and assist states in efforts to create a single coordinated system of care and long-term support. This system provides funding for Aging and Disability Resource Centers (ADRC). The goal of these centers is to provide a single, coordinated system of information and access for people seeking long-term support. This approach will reduce the confusion, and maximize opportunities for older adults and their families to make informed choices. As of fall 2006, 43 states have received ADRC initiative grants. Planning grants were awarded in 2003, 2004, and 2005, with another round to be awarded in 2006.

Some of the activities undertaken through grantee states include information, referral, and educational services. Some of the anticipated outcomes of these projects include the following:

- Maximize the abilities of older people, persons with physical disabilities, and persons with developmental disabilities to make informed choices and to meet their long-term care needs.
- Provide direct assistance to family caregivers in planning for the future needs of family members who have physical disabilities and/or developmental disabilities.
- Enable consumers the ability to choose services tailored to their needs through tools connecting them to streamlined assessment.
- Enable consumers to experience less confusion and enhance their choices since they will receive information in a more timely way.
- Enable the long-term care system of services to be managed through a single, coordinated method of intake, assessment, and eligibility with quality monitoring through centralized data collection and evaluation.
- Develop databases that will enable professionals to have access to a single, coordinated system of intake, assessment, and eligibility.
- Improve capacity for state and local governments to connect consumers to needed services and supports from publicly and privately funded services.
- Increase the number of physicians and other professionals who refer their patients and clients to the resource centers.
- Develop non-stigmatizing public places of service that can be used to promote independence and accessibility by a range of diverse people.
- Promote the accessibility of information and assistance by both public- and private-pay individuals.

- Develop a sustainable single coordinated system of information and access for all persons seeking long-term support.
- Increase the numbers of elderly/disabled individual living in their own homes in their own communities.
- Increase early planning for long-term care.
- Increase referrals of persons over 60 to community mental health centers (CMHC).
- Streamline access to long-term support services.
- Improve outreach to underserved populations.
- Empower individuals in need, or planning for long-term supports, to make informed choices.
- Reduce and potentially eliminate barriers to community living and support consumer-driven home- and community-based service options.
- Develop technology system, forms, software, and other necessary tools to provide streamlined access to all long-term care services.
- Increase collaboration among providers of services to the aging and people with disabilities.
- Improve marketing and public awareness campaigns related to aging and disability.
- Increase requests for information, referral to services, and enrollments in home- and community-based service.
- Improve knowledge for health and long-term support professionals and others providing services to the elderly and people with disabilities.
- Maximize consumer choice and provide services in a consumer-friendly manner, respecting and ensuring dignity of all served.
- Create a more balanced system of long-term care to include more home- and community-based services.

Key stakeholder groups involved within the aging and disability networks include:

- Representatives of aging and disability advocacy groups;
- Departments on Aging;
- Departments of Human Services;
- Departments of Public Aid;
- Departments of Public Health;
- Departments of Rehabilitation Services;
- Area Agencies on Aging;
- Benefit-planning assistance outreach programs;

- State health assistance programs;
- Employment centers, Alzheimer's associations;
- Community service providers;
- Long-term care ombudsmen;
- Developmental disabilities councils;
- Independent living centers;
- State assistance technology projects;
- Housing development authorities;
- AARP; and
- Local university and community college programs.

States receiving ADRC grants in 2003 included Louisiana, Maine, Maryland, Massachusetts, Minnesota, Montana, New Hampshire, New Jersey, Pennsylvania, Rhode Island, South Carolina, and West Virginia.

In 2004 a handful of other states received ADRC grants: Alaska, Arkansas, California, Florida, Georgia, Illinois, Indiana, Iowa, New Mexico, North Carolina, Northern Marina Islands, and Wisconsin.

As of 2006, 43 states of been awarded funds to develop Aging and Disability Technical Resource Centers (ADRC). Awardees include Alabama, Arizona, Colorado, District of Columbia, Guam, Hawaii, Idaho, Kansas, Kentucky, Michigan, Mississippi, Nevada, Ohio, Tennessee, Texas, Vermont, Virginia, Washington, and West Virginia. See Table 8.1.

The ADRC Technical Assistance Exchange (TAE) supports Aging and Disability Resource Center program grantees. Some of the resources that the TAE will provide for the ADRC include technical assistance for one-on-one support, weekly newsletters, semi-annual ADRC national meetings, and monthly Webcasts.

SUMMARY

The Americans with Disabilities Act, while groundbreaking, was not initially intended for older adults, but rather people with disabilities. As time progressed, however, the benefits of the ADA were much more far-reaching than originally intended, especially for aging adults with disabilities. The individual titles of the ADA have had some dramatically positive and specific impact for older adults wishing to remain in their homes, or in their communities as long as possible. Although the ADA is still in its adolescence, it is expected that the benefit of the ADA can only grow as new and further linkages, such as the Aging and Disability Resource Centers, are further developed around each state.

TABLE 8.1   States That Have Received ADRC Grants Over the Past 3 Years

State	Year Grant Received
Louisiana	2003
Maine	2003
Maryland	2003
Massachusetts	2003
Minnesota	2003
Montana	2003
New Hampshire	2003
New Jersey	2003
Pennsylvania	2003
Rhode Island	2003
South Carolina	2003
West Virginia	2003
Alaska	2004
Arkansas	2004
California	2004
Florida	2004
Georgia	2004
Illinois	2004
Indiana	2004
Iowa	2004
New Mexico	2004
North Carolina	2004
Northern Marina Islands	2004
Wisconsin	2004
Alabama	2005
Arizona	2005
Colorado	2005
District of Columbia	2005
Guam	2005
Hawaii	2005
Idaho	2005
Kansas	2005
Kentucky	2005
Michigan	2005
Mississippi	2005
Nevada	2005
Ohio	2005
Tennessee	2005
Texas	2005
Vermont	2005
Virginia	2005
Washington	2005
West Virginia	2005

USEFUL WEB SITES

Disability Information and Resource Center: http://www/disabilityinfo.gov

This online connection provides a link to the U.S. government's disability-related information and resources. It serves as a one-stop Web site for information to a range of groups including people with disabilities, their families, employers, service providers, and others. This site was developed following President George W. Bush's New Freedom Initiative, in an effort to support its goals.

Americans with Disabilities Act Guidelines: http://www/access-board.gov

This Web site provides a comprehensive listing of accessibility guidelines as defined in the Americans with Disabilities Act accessibility standards.

ADA Technical Assistance Program: http://www.dbtac.vcu.edu

This Web site provides a comprehensive resource for information on the Americans with Disabilities Act and information about accessible technology. The site enables one to use a drop-down menu to find a specific state, and secure information specific to one's state.

U.S. Department of Justice, Americans with Disabilities Act Home Page: http://www.usdoj.gov

This Web site, a federal resource, provides a comprehensive guide to standards, regulations, and status in the implementation of the Americans with Disabilities Act. It includes information on ADA design standards, ADA information line, technical assistance programs, enforcement of the ADA, ADA business connection, new and proposed regulations, ADA mediation programs, and links to other federal agencies with ADA responsibilities, including the EEOC, Department of Transportation (DOT), telephone relay service (FCC), education, health care, and labor.

Aging and Disability Resource Center (ADRC): http://www.adrc-tae.org

This provides a link to the Aging and Disability Resource Center and its Technical Assistance Exchange. It provides contact information for consumers, information about the ADRC grant program, a link to the Technical Assistance Exchange program, and links to helpful background information that supports the ADRC.

REFERENCES

Albrecht, G. L. (1992). *The disability business: Rehabilitation in America.* Thousand Oaks, CA: Sage Publications.

DeJong, G. (1979). Independent living: From social movement to analytic paradigm. *Archives of Physical Medicine and Rehabilitation, 60,* 435–446.

Essex-Sorlie, D. (1994). The Americans with Disabilities Act: History, summary, and key components. *Academic Medicine, 68*(7), 519–524.

Jurkowski, E. T. (1987). *Leadership and community participation for people with and without disabilities.* Ann Arbor, MI: Dissertation Abstracts International.

Katz, S. (1983). Assessing self-maintenance: Activities of daily living, mobility, and instrumental activities of daily living. *Journal of American Geriatric Sociology, 31,* 721–727.

United States Department of Justice. (1999). *ADA regulations and technical assistance.* Retrieved September 28, 1999, from http://www.usdoj.gov/crt/ada/publicat.html

United States Department of Labor. (2007). *The Americans with Disabilities Act of 1990.* Retrieved April 27, 2007, from http://www.dol.gov/esa/regs/statutes/ofccp/ada.htm

Mental Health: The Community Mental Health Act and the President's Freedom Commission Initiative

WHAT IS MENTAL HEALTH?

The concept of mental health, especially mental health for older adults, has evolved over time. The same holds true of legislation to play a role in the preservation of mental health conditions for older adults. This chapter will explore some of the changes in legislation over time and explores some of the currently mandated/legislated programs available for older adults in the United States.

Mental health can be defined as the successful performance of mental function, resulting in productive activities, fulfilling relationships with other people, and the ability to adapt to change and to cope with adversity, from early childhood to late life (USDHHS, 1999). The Surgeon General's Report on Mental Health was a seminal report released in 1999, which provided a blueprint for the development of services, research, and policy in the mental health arena, including older adults. There are four overarching themes in the report:

1. A public health perspective;
2. The realization that mental disorders are disabling;
3. The realization that mental health and illness are on a continuum; and
4. The realization that the mind and body are inseparable.

Although the concepts of utilizing a public health perspective, considering mental disorders as potentially chronic, and moving from a labeling perspective to a continuum of care seem obvious and practical, these are actually new concepts and paradigms, which have not been historically valued, nor represented in legislative efforts.

As we move through history, various paradigms have affected legislative efforts within the mental health legislative arena (Geller, 2000). Institutionalization was once the preferred mode of intervention, and thus legislative efforts focused upon institutional care rather than community care. There were probably elements of this paradigm that affected the development of institutions that housed people with mental illness and older adults with chronic depression or mental illness.

The medical model prevails within most of the legislative efforts, since disease-specific diagnostic categories generally serve as eligibility criteria. In the medical model, disease or illness is treated medically and is not reversible. In many of the early legislative efforts for mental health initiatives, the concept of disease prevailed and played a critical role in the eligibility for disability benefits through Social Security Insurance (SSI).

The advent of psychotropic medications led to the de-institutionalization movement and paradigm. In this paradigm, hospital care is limited, and the notion of having people move back into their home environments is the key. The advent of psychotropic medications unleashed the potential for chronically mentally ill to participate in the community. An example of where this paradigm plays a role is with Medicare options for mental health care. Within Medicare Part A, in-patient day treatment is limited, with partial hospitalization being the preferred mode of care and treatment. Many of the community day hospital programs and community mental health programs administered through the Community Mental Health Act are based upon the de-institutionalization paradigm, since the goal is to treat people outside the institution and within community settings.

The rehabilitation paradigm makes the argument that people have the potential to be capable of returning to meaningful activities outside of a treatment setting, and within the community, given the appropriate therapeutic options. This concept places value and dignity upon the individual and their unique value to their community and social support network.

The civil rights movement paradigm sets the tone for treatment options to be a right, not a privilege for individuals. This paradigms flows directly from the civil rights movement, whereby individuals regardless of color, ability, or gender should be granted the same rights and privileges as people considered in the dominant majority of the population. This movement, which piggy-backed onto the Vietnam War protests, used the "window of opportunity" to push forward issues for people representing diverse groups.

The self-help and peer support paradigm relies upon peer helpers and supports to move through or assist in the rehabilitation process, rather than relying solely upon professional intervention. Some state-based programs that operate with gero-psychiatry also operate peer support groups either modeled after the Alcoholic Anonymous concept or the GROW group concept.

Demedicalization is a paradigm that attempts to move issues outside of the medical arena and examine the person in the environment, pointing to environmental causes for specific issues of concern.

Consumerism is a paradigm that suggests the consumer is a key player and/or partner in the rehabilitation or intervention process. Consumers are at the forefront of the planning and evaluation process within service development and delivery. President Bush's Freedom Commission Initiative is based upon the paradigm of consumerism.

The independent living paradigm makes the argument that all people, regardless of their functioning level, have the ability to participate in the community with the right community-based supports (DeJong, 1979). Assertive community treatment programs work with this paradigm in mind.

HISTORY OF LEGISLATIVE EFFORTS AFFECTING PEOPLE WITH MENTAL DISORDERS AND OLDER ADULTS

The earliest indications of legislative efforts within a progressive venue for people with mental health issues and older adults suffering from mental illness can be seen with the initial federal legislation that provided land grants for mental institutions initially on the east coast, and eventually across the nation in the United States. This initiative was spearheaded by a social change reformer—Dorothea Dix. Dix lobbied for the appropriation of land grants from the federal government to state governments in order to provide for land that could be used to build state-based institutions. In 1840 there were only eight asylums for the insane in the United States. Dorothea Dix's crusading led to establishment or enlargement of 32 mental hospitals, and transfer of the mentally ill from poorhouses and jails. These institutions would thus serve to protect people with mental health issues and provide them a place to convalesce. The paradigms of institutionalization and medical model can be seen as prevalent themes within the context of care here; however, at the point in history when these programs were developed, it seemed reasonable to develop structural opportunities within which people could be somewhat protected from the stigma that prevailed in communities (Gollaher, 1995).

In 1962, President John Kennedy appointed a group of experts and community representatives to spearhead the President's Commission on

Mental Illness. This 19-member task force set forth to examine the face of services for people afflicted with mental illness, and to make recommendations for legislation, service delivery, and intervention efforts. One outgrowth of the President's Commission on Mental Illness report was a recommendation for community-based treatment and outpatient centers, currently known as community mental health centers (Boroug, Ozarin & Sharfstein, 1978).

Kennedy expressed great optimism in his special message to Congress on February 5, 1963, in which he proposed a national mental health program to inaugurate "a wholly new emphasis and approach to care for the mentally ill." The Mental Retardation Facilities and Community Mental Health Centers Construction Act of 1963 (Public Law 88–164) was signed just a few weeks before President Kennedy's assassination. This legislation led the legislative mandate for community mental health treatment centers and led to the construction of community mental health centers. These centers were intended for the priority target group of people who had been deinstitutionalized and moved from institutional care to community-based care. Funding from the federal government to state-based governments came in the form of Medicaid funds, to support efforts related to treatment for people with severe, persistent mental illness. The context for the Community Mental Health Centers Act is important to consider, as it has played a role for the past 40 years. For example, this piece of legislation was originally intended to address the needs of individuals who were institutionalized and chronically mentally ill and served as a strategy to provide humane community-based treatment for this target group. In addition, it was perceived that the cost of community-based care was a fraction of institutional care.

A closer analysis of the legislation reveals that no mention or appropriation is given to individuals who were aging. In fact, since mental illness is not a normal part of the aging process, chronic care for people suffering from mental illness or some mental health condition, and who are older adults, is not a component of the Community Mental Health Centers Construction Act. Thus, this imposes some interesting dilemmas with respect to service delivery for older adults with mental health issues (Ray & Finley, 1994). Currently, there is a limited legislative mandate to address these issues. However, the Older Americans Act Amendments of 2006 will provide a legislative mandate to provide screening and detection services for mental health issues among older adults.

The 1973 National Rehabilitation Act (HR 8070) provides for funds to support programs and services to assist people with disabilities to return to the community and promotes maximum independence. The issue at hand, however, is that this legislation is framed to consider individuals whose goal is to become self-sufficient economically, through paid work. Since the goal for many people who are in their golden years is retirement, rather than full employment, many individuals who are older adults are excluded from services and provisions allotted through the 1973 National Rehabilitation Act.

President Reagan signed the Omnibus Budget Reconciliation Act (OBRA) of 1981. This act repealed the Mental Health Systems Act and consolidated devolved funding for treatment and rehabilitation service programs into a single block grant that enabled each state to administer its allocated funds. With the repeal of the community mental health legislation and the establishment of block grants the federal role in services to the mentally ill became one of providing technical assistance to increase the capacity of state and local providers of mental health services. The target group most impacted as a result of OBRA, relative to mental health services, was older adults. Service delivery was retrenched and cut back to assure that the initial priority and target group (people at risk of institutionalization and/or chronically mentally ill) were served first and foremost. This further eroded away aspirations for a system of care that would be responsive to people with some mental health conditions, especially acute conditions, and who are older adults.

The 2000 National Family Caregivers' Support Act

The National Family Caregivers' Support Act, passed by Congress in November 2000, gives federal grants to states to provide information and referral, training, counseling, respite care, and other supportive services to (1) people caring at home for chronically ill, frail, elderly relatives or relatives with mental retardation or other developmental disabilities and (2) grandparents and other relatives caring for children at home. The states must provide the services through their existing Area Agencies on Aging (AAA), established by the federal Older Americans Act of 1965. Local AAAs or their contractors will provide the services, which include caregiver counseling and some respite services, as well as information and referral services. Specifically, the AAAs must provide:

1. Information about available services;
2. Help in accessing the services;
3. Training, counseling, and support groups to help caregivers make decisions and solve problems concerning their caregiving roles;
4. Temporary relief from caregiver responsibilities through respite care; and
5. Limited supplemental services not available through other programs (to be defined by each state).

Under the program, states must give priority to services for older people with the greatest social and economic need (with particular attention to low-income older people) and to older people who are taking care of relatives with mental retardation or other related developmental disabilities.

The New Freedom Commission on Mental Health

The New Freedom Commission on Mental Health was established by President George W. Bush in April 2002 to examine in a comprehensive manner the status of the U.S. mental health service delivery system and to develop a series of recommendations based on the commission's findings. The president directed the commission to identify policies that could be implemented by federal, state, and local governments to maximize the utility of existing resources, improve coordination of treatments and services, and promote successful community integration for adults with serious mental illness and children with a serious emotional disturbances.

Perhaps one of the more significant pieces of legislation has been the Ronald Reagan Alzheimer's Breakthrough Act of 2004 (S2533, HR 4595). Clearly this piece of legislation took advantage of the window of opportunity in its passage. Some of the features of this piece of legislation to benefit older adults include the doubling of funding for National Institute of Health (NIH) Alzheimer's research by increasing authorization levels to $1.4 billion beginning in 2005. In addition, funding to assure that there is a hosted national summit, and the codification of three existing Alzheimer's research programs into law are all features of this legislation.

INFLUENCES TO CONSIDER IN THE DEVELOPMENT OF MENTAL HEALTH LEGISLATION

A number of influences in the treatment process are significant in the development of legislation that affects older adults. Some of these influences impacting treatment include patterns of service utilization, who uses services and where these services thus are located, health beliefs, the role of culture, family influences, the role of location (rural versus urban) and family/consumer movements.

Patterns of Service Utilization

Although the legislative base may suggest that services be provided regardless of location and socioeconomic environment, the reality is that patterns of service utilization may differ, based upon the availability of trained mental health professionals. Rural communities are more likely to face this scenario, since a lack of trained professionals exists to begin with, and the census count often does not make it attractive to build a practice for specialty psychiatrists within rural communities.

Health Beliefs and the Role of Culture

Furthermore, service delivery within rural communities may also be affected by the reality that older adults associate the receipt of mental health care with institutional care and feel somewhat concerned that their health beliefs will guide their need for more severe intervention than may actually be required.

The role of culture and mental health services plays a role in both the development of legislation and programs/services. Increasingly, the health disparities gap is widening due to cross-cultural issues and differences in health status. Mental health legislation needs to consider cultural differences. Health beliefs, perceptions of services and outcomes, and perceived seriousness of potential mental illness and its conditions all require consideration as legislation is drafted, in efforts to assure that the role of culture is considered in the intervention process.

FUTURE ISSUES

There are a number of issues for consideration when looking towards the need for resources and policy development to promote the mental health of older adults. One of the first and significantly important is the need to continue to build an evidence base and best practice interventions, through legislated initiatives. The issue of stigma still surfaces and prevents individuals and/or their aging loved ones from seeking mental health treatment. Hence, the need for legislation and funding to support and improve public awareness of effective treatment interventions is also paramount.

In an effort to ensure the supply of mental health services and providers, legislative initiatives that examine workforce issues will be a necessary future consideration. This will include support and benefits to medically designated shortage areas to help build both the professional workforce and also a workforce that is aware and trained in the delivery of state-of-the-art treatments.

Finally, legislative efforts within the mental health arena should assure that we tailor treatments to age, race, gender, and culture. Financial resources that can support clinical trials when developing norms for interventions specific to older adults and their caregivers should also be considered.

SUMMARY

Despite attempts to develop legislation to meet the needs of people with mental illness, throughout history, these legislative efforts have had limited benefit to older adults, unless the person has been afflicted with a long-standing chronic mental illness. This chapter has presented a brief overview of some legislative efforts within the mental health arena and examined their limitations and application with respect to older adults.

USEFUL WEB SITES

John F. Kennedy Special Message to the Nation on Mental Illness and Mental Retardation: http://www.presidency.ucsb.edu/ws/index. php?pid = 9546

This Web site provides an interesting background and the presidential speech from John F. Kennedy, and his vision for the legislative efforts impacting mental illness and mental retardation.

REFERENCES

Boroug, M., Ozarin, L. D., & Sharfstein, S. S. (1978). The aftermaths of deinstitutionaliza-tion: problems and solutions. *Psychiatric Quarterly, 50,* 128–132.

DeJong, G. (1979). Independent living: From social movement to analytic paradigm. *Archives of Physical Medicine and Rehabilitation, 60,* 435–446.

Geller, J. L. (2000). The last half-century of psychiatric services as reflected in Psychiatric Services. *Psychiatric Services, 51,* 41–67.

Gollaher, D. (1995). *Voice for the mad: The life of Dorothea Dix.* New York: Free Press.

Ray, C. G, & Finley, J. K. (1994). Did CMHCs fail or succeed? Analysis of the expectations and outcomes of the community mental health movement. *Administration and Policy in Mental Health, 21,* 283–293.

PART III

Tools for Policy and Program Development

Part III of this text provides some tools for the reader to use to be more adequately equipped to prepare program initiatives that flow from policy appropriations. The tools also are designed to prepare the practitioner or reader with some skills to more effectively advocate for policy change. This section helps bridge some of the skills and tools used both within the disciplines of social work and public health and begins to expand the boundaries of public policy development.

CHAPTER 10

Health Behavior Models and Health Promotion Frameworks

WHAT ARE HEALTH PROMOTION FRAMEWORKS?

A vital tool in the development and design of programs and services for older adults should include health promotion frameworks or at least some features of these behavioral intervention models. The focus in this chapter will be to explore health promotion frameworks, to showcase their role vis-à-vis health policy and programs, and to discuss three specific frameworks. Health promotion frameworks are theoretical conceptions of how health behavior can be addressed. These frameworks are developed for the purpose of program and policy development. The health promotion frameworks to be discussed will include the Health Belief Model, the Theory of Reasoned Action, the Trans-theoretical Model of Stages of Change.

HEALTH PROMOTION FRAMEWORKS AND HEALTH POLICY

The use of health promotions frameworks leads to three specific questions that play a role in the development of health policy: (1) what role do health promotion frameworks play in the development of health policy? (2) how are health promotion frameworks utilized in the health policy arena? and (3) what role does health promotion play with public policy and program development? This chapter will attempt to address these three questions; however, prior to discussing these questions

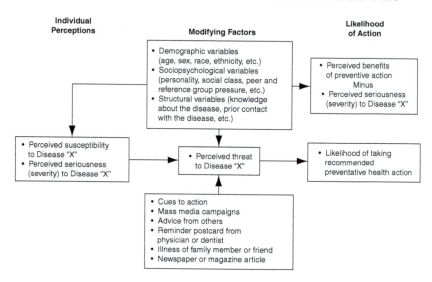

FIGURE 10.1   The Health Belief Model.

From: Rosenstock, strecher & Becker. (1988).

and answers, it is essential to first understand some well-known health promotion frameworks. Although a number of health promotion frameworks exist in the literature (Glanz, Lewis, & Rimer, 1997), this chapter will focus on three that can be specifically applied to older adults.

The Health Belief Model

The Health Belief Model (HBM) was originally conceptualized in the 1950s by social psychologists in an effort to understand why people did not use services for preventative or detection purposes. Although public health efforts in the 1950s evolved to provide for immunizations at no or little cost to the consumer, few people made use of these services. Thus, the question became apparent that there must be some reason why services were not being utilized, and understanding people's perception of their susceptibility to infectious diseases might be a key to improve utilization (Rosenstock, 1966). As the model evolved, it was used to help understand people's responses to symptoms (Kirscht, 1974) and compliance with medical regimens (Becker, 1974). See Figure 10.1.

The Health Belief Model (HBM) was originally developed to provide a systematic approach or method to understand and predict one's behavior relative to preventative strategies. The initial model focused upon the relationships between health behaviors, health practices, and the use of health care services. As time progressed, the HBM was updated to include health motivation, which led to an understanding of the distinction between illness and sick-role behavior from health behavior. This theory has also been labeled as the genesis of systematic, theory-based research in health behavior. The HBM tries to predict health-related behavior through an understanding of specific "beliefs" one holds. The model is used in explaining and predicting preventive health behavior, as well as outlining responses to sick-role and illness behavior. A person's motivation to act in specific ways when it comes to their health behavior can be categorized into three main arenas: individual perceptions, modifying behaviors, and likelihood of action. Individual perceptions are factors that affect the perception of illness or disease; they deal with the importance of health to the individual, perceived susceptibility, and perceived severity. Modifying factors include demographic variables, perceived threat, and cues to action. The likelihood of action discusses factors in probability of appropriate health behavior; it is the likelihood of taking the recommended preventive health action. The HBM also suggests that the perception of one's personal health behavior and threats to one's behaviors is influenced by at least three specific factors: (1) one's general health values, which include one's interests and concern about their own health; (2) specific health beliefs about vulnerability to a particular health threat; and (3) one's beliefs about the consequences of the a specific health issue or diagnosis. Once an individual perceives a threat to his or her health and is simultaneously cued to action, and that person's perceived benefits outweigh his or her perceived benefits, then that individual is most likely to undertake the recommended preventive health action. There may be some variables (demographic, sociopsychological, and structural) that can influence an individual's decision.

The components of the HBM include components identified by the authors as "perceived susceptibility," "perceived severity," "perceived benefits," "perceived barriers," "cues to action," and "self-efficacy." Understanding what these components mean, and how they interface with each other to explain one's behavior towards their own health, can help program planners and practitioners better plan and utilize health care resources.

Perceived Susceptibility

The authors of the health belief model and its reiterations (Rosenstock, 1966; Rosenstock & Kirscht, 1984) define perceived susceptibility as *one's perception of the likelihood that they will receive the disease or the condition.* In the application of this concept, it is important to consider the target population, define the population, and examine their at-risk levels. In addition, one may identify risk based upon the person's characteristics or behaviors. Each person has their own perception of the likelihood of experiencing a condition that would adversely affect their health and well-being. People's reaction to their perception of susceptibility to a disease or condition varies considerably. At one extreme are people who deny the possibility of contracting an adverse condition, while on the other end are people who are very obsessed with the possibility that they can be adversely affected by a given disease. People who are moderately susceptible seem to think that there is some chance of being affected by a specific disease or condition.

Perceived Severity

One's perceived severity refers to one's understanding of what the potential effects a given disease or condition would have on one's lifestyle and the consequences of this. These effects can be considered from the point of view of the difficulties that a disease would create. Examples are pain and discomfort, loss of work time, financial burdens, difficulties with family, relationships, and susceptibility to future conditions. It is important to include these emotional and financial burdens when considering the seriousness of a disease or condition.

Perceived Benefits

Taking action toward the prevention of disease or toward dealing with an illness is the next step to expect after an individual has accepted the susceptibility of a disease and recognized it is serious. One's perception of the impact (or efficacy) that an advised action will have in an effort to reduce the risks or seriousness of the impact will dramatically affect one's perceived benefits. In an effort to identify perceived benefits, one should define the actions to be taken, how should they be taken, when should they be taken, and what positive effects can be expected.

Perceived Barriers

Action may not take place, even though an individual may believe that the benefits to taking action are effective. This may be due to barriers. Barriers relate to the idea that a treatment or preventive measure may be inconvenient, expensive, unpleasant, painful, or upsetting. These ideas may lead a person away from taking the desired action. Perceived barriers can also include one's opinion of the tangible and psychological costs associated with the actions or treatments advised. These barriers can be reduced

TABLE 10.1   Components of the Health Belief Model

Component	Definition
Perceived susceptibility	One's perception of how likely they are to contract a disease or condition
Perceived severity	The seriousness of a disease or event/condition to oneself
Perceived benefits	The benefits one sees in pursuing a specific intervention
Perceived barriers	Blocks that impede involvement for older adults; transportation or lack of insurance coverage could be perceived barriers
Cues to action	Reminders that influence one's ability to comply
Self-efficacy	One's confidence in their ability to follow through

through reassurance, correcting misconceptions or misinformation, developing incentives to action, and providing assistance to assure actions.

Cues to Action

Cues to action related to an individual's perception of the levels of susceptibility and seriousness provide the force to act. Benefits (minus barriers) provide the path of action. However, a cue to action may be required for the desired behavior to occur. These cues may be internal or external. These cues are strategies used to activate one's readiness. Cues can include providing information on how-to, creating awareness, and using reminder systems. Some common examples may be refrigerator magnets with reminders to go and get a flu shot.

Self-Efficacy

Self-efficacy relates to confidence in one's ability to take action. In the self-efficacy phase, one accepts training and guidance in performing actions that lead to personal empowerment and control. In this stage, progressive goal setting is used. Coaching (verbal reinforcements), role modeling (demonstrating desired behaviors), and reducing anxiety are all components of this phase. This phase of the HBM was an addition, modeled from the work of Bandura, based on social learning theory (Bandura, 1977, 1982). A summary overview of these components is available in Table 10.1.

How Does This Model Apply to Health Policy, Program Planning, and Older Adults?

Essentially, the development of programs and resources, keeping in mind the mind-set of the specific target group of older adults you would like to reach, can only enhance the benefit of any programs developed for older adults. A clear understanding of older adults' perceived benefits and barriers to action can make a striking difference in their compliance with specific regimes. For example, if an older adult perceives that they are susceptible to catching the flu, they may be more likely to pursue seeking a vaccination against influenza. However, in other areas of health behavior, which may be more taboo, for example sexual behaviors—an older adult may be less likely to feel that they are susceptible or may have a wider range of barriers. HIV/AIDS awareness and protection may be an illustrative example here. An older adult, recently widowed, new to the dating scene, may not perceive themselves to be at risk for sexually transmitted diseases (STDs) or consider protective measures against STDs because they may not perceive themselves to be of reproductive age. Consequently, these factors may play a role in one's overall willingness to exercise caution or take action against STDs.

Investing in Meaningful Health Interventions

Interventions are often embarked upon with great vigor, and often little foresight or planning from a theoretical perspective. Unfortunately, this leads to a diluted and limited impact when programs or interventions are developed. The HBM can be used as a guide to identify perspectives from consumers, and enable the development of programs/resources to best utilize the resources invested in a program or intervention. A clear understanding, for example, of the specific benefits and barriers older adults may have to seeking help or engaging in a specific program can be very useful and helpful in the planning of the program and marketing of the program or intervention. Focus group approaches or community needs assessments can be very helpful in this process of identifying specific barriers and benefits.

The Theory of Reasoned Action

The Theory of Reasoned Action (TRA) and its companion Theory of Planned Behavior (TPB) (Fishbein & Ajzen, 1975) have both come from studying human behavior and attempting to develop meaningful interventions to address such behaviors. The goal behind this theory is threefold: (1) to predict and understand motivational influences on behavior that is not under the individual's control; (2) to identify how and where to target strategies for changing behavior; and (3) to explain human behavior. This theory also assumes that human beings are rational and make systematic use of information given to them and that people consider the implications of their decisions and actions before they decide to engage or not engage in certain activity.

The TRA framework is concerned with a person's motivation as a determinant of the likelihood for performing a specific behavior. The most important determinants of behaviors are behavioral intentions. Attitudes are determined by an individual's perception about outcomes of one's actions as a result of one's evaluation of this outcome or attribute. One's evaluation of the outcome or impact of taking action can seriously have some bearing on one's intentions toward taking some action. These intentions are also evaluated based upon the norms of one's culture and peer group and these two entities' influence on the person.

The components of TRA include behavioral beliefs, an evaluation of behavioral outcomes, attitude towards behavior, normative beliefs, subjective norms, the motivation to comply, behavioral intentions, and behavior. Behavioral intention refers to the perceived likelihood of performing the behavior.

One's attitude is influenced by both behavioral belief and one's subjective evaluation. The behavioral belief refers to the belief that one's actions or behaviors are associated with certain attributes or outcomes. One's subjective evaluation relates to the values one attaches to a behavioral outcome or attribute.

Subjective normative beliefs refers to the belief about whether there is approval or disapproval (acceptance level) for specific behaviors. The motivation to comply is the belief that one is motivated to do what a referent thinks.

Perceived behavioral control refers to the belief about one's sense of control that relates to the likelihood of the condition happening and its associated condition. If one does not perceive that they will be impacted by a situation or condition, they may not pursue any action. Perceived power relates to how much power an individual has insofar as they can impact change or undergo behavior to pursue a specific action or task. Hence, the question one must consider is going to be "what is the effect of each condition in making behavioral performance difficult or easy?"

The application of this Theory of Reasoned Action to health and help-seeking with older adults can be illustrated through two examples: mammography screening and Latino elders seeking mental health care (Godin & Kok, 1996). Although both sets of procedures may be necessary, they may not necessarily be used by older adults if the social support network does not perceive these as of value, does not see the benefits, and does not feel that they can control the outcomes or results once results are presented.

Limitations to this model are several. This model does not take into consideration factors such as personality or basic demographic variables (Ajzen, 1998). Perceived behavioral control is also a variable that is difficult to measure and thus is difficult to ascertain or get a handle on. The theory is also based upon an assumption that human beings are rational, and they make systematic decisions based upon available information (Ajzen, 1980). Unconscious motives are not considered, and issues that may mitigate rational behavior for older adults (such as dementia or early onset of Alzheimer's disease) may influence one's rational behavior.

Transtheoretical Model and Stages of Change Theory

This theory integrates stages of change into the processes and principles of change. It integrates the components from theories of psychotherapy and behavior changes. This model helps assess the readiness of individuals to follow through with interventions, which becomes critical when assessing where to invest health resources in order to maximize the impact of the investment. The stages of change actually run along a continuum from precontemplation to termination follow-up, as illustrated in Figure 10.2. These steps include:

- Precontemplation;
- Contemplation;
- Preparation planning;
- Action;
- Maintenance; and
- Termination follow-up.

Processes of Change

Each stage of change within this model provides for different stages, along a continuum towards success and institutionalization of new behaviors. The process of change may focus on one or several components of a model, and each stage will be utilized to facilitate change (Prochaska & Velicer, 1997). The individual stages are often components of health education or health interventions, shaped by specific health policies (Prochaska & DiClemente, 1983). This section will provide an overview of the stage and the specific behavioral components and changes that can be expected at the respective stages. See Table 10.2.

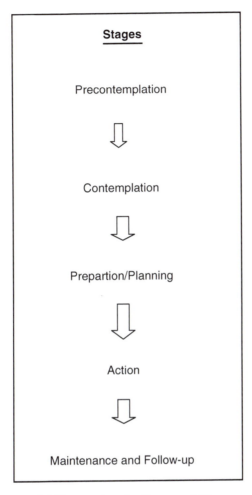

FIGURE 10.2   A model illustrating the Stages of Change continuum.

Precontemplation/Contemplation Stage

This stage can be characterized as a consciousness-raising stage. At this stage, although an individual may have a specific problem or issue, whether they recognize or acknowledge it or not, they literally have no intention of changing their behavior. The intervention strategies used during this stage will focus on consciousness raising, dramatic relief, self-evaluation and self- reevaluation, and environmental reevaluation. In the process of consciousness raising, information is provided and the goal is

TABLE 10.2   Components of the Stages of Change Model

Concept	Definition	Application
Precontemplation	Unaware of the problem. Has not thought about change.	Increase awareness. Identify need for change, tailor info to address risks and benefits.
Contemplation	Thinking about change.	Encourage specific plans.
Planning	Develop a plan for change. Set gradual goals.	Assist in the development of concrete action or plan for change.
Action	Implementation of specific action plans.	Provide feedback. Help with social support, reinforcement, and problem-solving skills.
Maintenance	Continue desired actions. Repeat periodic recommended steps.	Help with coping, give reminders, find alternatives, avoid relapses.

to target one's knowledge base. Advertisements and billboard campaigns often address this step. In the process of dramatic relief, role playing is often used as an intervention strategy, with the goal of creating awareness and insight into the problem. The process of environmental reevaluation examines how a problem affects one's physical environment. In the case of older adults, a falls prevention program may target not only creating an awareness for an older adults, but the fact that one's frailty and need for additional support may be taxing on furniture in the absence of grab bars or aids for walking (cane or walker).

During the contemplation stage, an individual may recognize the problem and may actually be seriously thinking about changing their behavior. This stage is marked by an individual's self-evaluation, and reflection. During this phase, some serious thought goes into thinking about changes that can be made, and there is recognition of a problem.

Preparation Stage

During the preparation stage, an individual recognizes the problem and has an intention to change their behavior within the next moth. Behavioral changes may occur but may not be consistent. This stage is also marked with some specific attempts to plan activities to put one's affairs in order, in order to pursue a change effort plan consistently. An older adult may be contemplating attending a meal support program or nutrition site. Part of the planning process may include transportation or some assurance that handicapped accessible parking is available.

Action/Maintenance Stage

In the action and maintenance stages, an individual has demonstrated a consistent behavior change; however, the length of time for which this behavior change has been consistent will determine which stage the individual is actually engaged in. If the behavior change is consistent for 6 months or less, then the individual is considered to be in the action phase, as compared to the maintenance phase, in which one's behavior can be consistent for 6 months or more. Within this phase, an individual or group engages in specific action plans. The role of a program or facilitator during this phase is to assist with feedback, problem solving, social support, and reinforcement. During the maintenance phase of the plan, one may see assistance with coping strategies, reinforcements for prolonged behavior, seeking out alternatives, and strategies to avoid relapses. Helping relationships at this phase are focused on contingencies and rewards, as well as stimulus and controls. Reminder messages or cues to action can be built into this phase, to help promote changes. Some examples may include reminder notices for check-ups or check lists, which summarize several of the healthy behaviors originally undertaken.

Termination Stage

During the termination stage, social liberation is achieved, and the individual moves from an approach where they were on the recipient end for services to becoming more of a peer helper, and interested in sharing some of their own successes with others. In this stage, one can characterize an increase in social opportunities or alternatives, especially for those who are relatively deprived or oppressed. Empowerment approaches, policy development, and advocacy efforts can improve and increase opportunities for health promotion efforts for minority elders, and those traditionally impoverished or ignored. Some of the same strategies can be implemented to help all people with change efforts, such as smoke-free zones, and healthy food choices.

The transtheoretical model offers promise for the development and implementation of specific interventions, particularly within the area of recruitment of subjects, retention of subjects, progress of individuals, the process of developing interventions, and outcomes.

Recruitment of a population using this model can yield high rates of participation. Since the model is structured so that people move through a process, based upon their readiness to change, the model can target participants at a range of stages, rather than simply those most prepared or ready for a commitment to action. Since this model makes no assumptions about people's readiness for change, and assumes people will be at different levels, this model will engage many more individuals with differing levels of participation.

Retention rates are another major positive consideration that can be seen when using this model. Traditional programs quickly realize a mismatch between the program delivery or polices undergirding programs. If a program does not meet an individual's needs, or they are not ready to pursue change, they may quickly tire and drop out. In contrast, this model is designed to meet specific stages of change and needs of individuals; thus people are less likely to drop out, and more likely to remain within a specific stage until they are ready to move forward.

Another advantage of building programs or services around this framework is the notion of progress, which can be recognized much more readily and easily among individuals through the process of breaking down intervention strategies using the transtheoretical approach to program development (Prochaska, 1994). Unfortunately, most action-oriented programs identify a single outcome or set of outcomes that define success. If one fails to meet these criteria, they also fail to meet success. Conversely, when people, especially older adults, are grappling with the notion of making change, they may not easily or readily see success, when it is defined as an outcome, maintained for 6 months or more. The transtheoretical model offers the opportunity for measures to be collected, keeping in mind a full range of cognitive, emotional, and behavioral steps, which may take place through incremental stages, and much more slowly (Prochaska, Velicer, DiClemente, & Fava, 1988). Addiction or smoking-cessation programs have effectively integrated this model to help target where individuals or group interventions should begin (DiClemente, 1981, 1986; DiClemente, Prochaska, et al., 1991).

Programs or interventions using these stages can be effective, especially if they take into consideration specific stages, and develop materials or interventions accordingly (Prochaska, DiClemente, Velicer, Ginpil & Norcross, 1985). For example, educational materials and psycho-educational programs can best be developed to target the various stages from precontemplation to action using this model. Incorporating this approach also reframes the notion of success: that is, rather than recognizing success based on the successful completion of new skills or mastering one's goals, one may recognize success if there has been movement from one stage to another, such as precontemplation to action (Prochaska & Velicer, 1997).

IMPLICATIONS OF THE HEALTH PROMOTION MODELS AND PROGRAM DEVELOPMENT FOR AGING-RELATED PROGRAMS AND SERVICES

The use of health promotion frameworks in the program planning process for older adults can have a number of positive outcomes, some of which have already been showcased in this chapter. Capturing health beliefs can enable program planners to tailor interventions and programs to meet the needs of different education levels, or groups with ethnic variation. Another strength of using the models, especially a model such as Prochaska and DiClemente's (1983) Stages of Change model, can relate to resources. If a program has a fixed amount of funding or resources, breaking down the stage and strategy to meet the needs of a specific change in your target group can have strong implications for success of a program and maximizing the use of one's resources. Finally, in a climate with finite and limited resources, these models can be helpful in the process of defining and targeting effective strategies for service intervention and program delivery.

SUMMARY

The Health Belief Model, Theory of Reasoned Action, and Stages of Change are only three health promotion models used to help shape and understand health behavior. The models are vital to the development of aging policy and aging programs/services and interventions because they help practitioners stage interventions based upon the specific needs of a community or target group. They will become increasingly important and of value as we implement the legislative amendments to the Older Americans Act of 2006, which calls for health promotion and screening efforts within public health and mental health arenas.

USEFUL WEB SITES

The National Commission for Health Education Credentialing: http://www.nchec.org

This is the official Web site for the National Commission for Health Education Credentialing and provides background to the reader on the responsibilities and competencies required of health educators. The competencies include assessing the individual and community needs for health education; planning effective health education programs; implementing health education programs; evaluating the effectiveness of health education programs; coordinating the provision of health education services;

and acting as a resource person for health education and communicating health and health education needs, concerns, and resources. This site also provides information on how to become a certified health education specialist (CHES).

The American Journal of Health Behavior: http://www.ajhb.org

This site provides direct access to the *American Journal of Health Behavior*, which serves as the office publication of the American Academy of Health Behavior. The journal strives to improve the approach of health education, health promotion, and other multidisciplinary efforts through improving our understanding of systems approaches to health behaviors.

The Communication Initiative: www.comminit.com

This Web site provides a host of information that can assist the novice or inexperienced health educator to understand both health education and health education change strategies. The Web site also has links to various organizations worldwide that support health and education efforts both nationally and internationally. The Web site also deals with various change theories.

The American Public Health Association (APHA)/Health Education Special Interest Group: www.apha.org

This site provides access to APHA's special interest group, which addresses health education and health promotion concerns.

REFERENCES

Ajzen, I. (1980). *Understanding the attitudes and predicting social behavior.* Englewood Cliffs, NJ: Prentice-Hall Inc.

Ajzen, I. (1998). *Attitudes, personality and behavior.* Chicago: The Dorsey Press.

Bandura, A. (1977). Self-efficacy: Toward a unifying theory of behavior change. *Psychological Review, 84,* 191–215.

Bandura, A. (1982). Self-efficacy mechanism in human agency. *American Psychologist, 37,* 122–147.

Becker, M. H. (1974). The Health Belief Model and personal health behavior. *Health Education Monographs, 2,* 324–473.

DiClemente, C. C. (1981). Self-efficacy and smoking cessation maintenance: A preliminary report. *Cognitive Therapy and Research, 5,* 175–187.

DiClemente, C. C. (1986). Self-efficacy and the addictive behaviors. *Journal of Social and Clinical Psychology, 4,* 302–315.

DiClemente, C. C., Prochaska, J. O., Fairhurst, S., Velicer, W. F., Rossi, J. S., & Velasquez, M. (1991). The process of smoking cessation: An analysis of precontemplation, contemplation and contemplation/action. *Journal of Consulting and Clinical Psychology, 59,* 295–304.

Fishbein, M., & Ajzen, I. (1975). *Beliefs, attitudes, intention and behavior: An introduction to theory and research.* Reading, MA: Addison-Wesley.

Glanz, K., Lewis, F. M., & Rimer, B. K. (Eds.) (1997). *Health behavior and health education: Theory, research and practice.* San Francisco, CA: Jossey-Bass.

Godin, G., & Kok, G. (1996). The theory of planned behavior: A review of its applications to health-related behaviors. *American Journal of Health Promotion, 11*(2), 87–98.

Kirscht, J. P. (1974). The Health Belief Model and illness behavior. *Health Education Monographs, 2,* 387–408.

Prochaska, J. O. (1994). Strong and weak principles for progressing from precontemplation to action on the basis of twelve problem behaviors. *Health Psychology, 13,* 47–51.

Prochaska, J. O., & DiClemente, C. C. (1983). Stages and processes of self-change of smoking: Toward an integrative model of change. *Journal of Consulting and Clinical Psychology, 51,* 390–395.

Prochaska, J. O., DiClemente, C. C., Velicer, W. F., Ginpil, S., & Norcross, J. C. (1985). Predicting change in status for self-changers. *Addictive Behaviors, 10,* 395–406.

Prochaska, J. O., & Velicer, W. F. (1997). The Transtheoretical Model of health behavior change. *American Journal of Health Promotion, 12,* 38–48.

Prochaska, J. O., Velicer, W. F., DiClemente, C. C., & Fava, J. L. (1988). Measuring the processes of change: Applications to the cessation of smoking. *Journal of Consulting and Clinical Psychology, 56,* 520–528.

Rosenstock, I. M. (1966). Why people use health services. *Milbank Memorial Fund Quarterly, 44,* 94–124.

Rosenstock, I. M., & Kirscht, J. P. (1984). The Health Belief model and personal health behavior. *Health Education Monographs, 2,* 470–473.

United States Department of Health and Human Services. (1999). Mental health and older adults. Chapter five appearing in report of the surgeon general on mental health needs. Bethesda, MD: U.S. Government Printing Office.

CHAPTER 11

Media and Advocacy Strategies for Change

ADVOCACY AND ITS ROLE IN PROGRAM AND POLICY DEVELOPMENT

Public advocacy has been at the heart and soul of policy development in aging services (Hudson, 2004). This advocacy effort has targeted social development and social change, in efforts to develop and broaden the face of social policy over the past several decades. Initially, when policy development strategies were in the process of enactment, the advocacy forces driving policy development were elite groups working within governmental systems (i.e., policy advisors drafting the Social Security Act of 1935). Over time, an "interest group" era arose within the aging arena, and in the 1960s a proliferation of aging-oriented interest groups arose. These advocates were effective in shepherding legislation such as Medicare (1965) and the Older American Act (1965). Groups such as the National Council of Senior Citizens, the National Association of Social Workers, and the National Association of Retired Federal Employees were all instrumental in developing policy and legislative changes. Further evolution of the policy advocacy arena included older adults and consumers themselves in this process. As advocacy organizations evolved, it also seemed to be prudent to include older adults as a component of the advocacy equation. Older adults, or consumers themselves, add credence to the importance of legislative efforts and the reasons for the development of new or revised policies or programs.

Within the efforts of advocacy for program and policy development, a number of initiatives are used to facilitate the advocacy process. Within this entire section of this text (Part III) tools for advocacy development are discussed; however, this chapter will deal with one subset of these strategies, notably using media as a part of this advocacy process.

Advocacy efforts count, and who better to consider developing and voicing these efforts than individuals who have expertise in the field of aging, and have professional credentials (Coalition of National Health Education Organization Partners, n.d.). Advocacy efforts do not have to be time-intensive, for 1 minute can lead to a message to a legislator, 5 minutes can lead to photocopying and sharing an article with a colleague or legislator, and 10 minutes can generate enough time to send an e-mail, fax, or letter to a legislator. This being said, it may be helpful to gain some skills in being savvy to use media strategies to develop advocacy efforts.

A number of successful efforts to improve health status or change health policy have been targeted using media advocacy strategies. Media advocacy and communications strategies have been effective in reducing health disparities through health communications or changing public perception on key health policy issues (Dorfman, 2005; Friemuth & Quinn, 2004). Effective media campaigns and the use of visual tools such as photography have been the key to success in public education and action on major issues such as the anthrax scare in 2001 or HIV/AIDS awareness (Bernhardt, 2004; Moore, 2004). Mueller, Page and Kuerbis (2004) have analyzed how communication through media sources has influenced U.S. Congressional hearings and have concluded that communication of information strategies and media advocacy has been the single most influential force in the development of policy for social movement issues.

Although health education campaigns have been found to be successful in the development of health policy or program development, researchers have also found that mass media campaigns have also influenced the changing of health behaviors (Cavill & Bauman, 2004; Randolph & Viswanth, 2004). Integrating a theoretical background into the development of health promotion messages, and targeting the messages to a specific stage of behavioral change or mastery, increases the chances of health promotion and media advocacy campaign efforts being effective. Changes in knowledge and attitudes have been possible in behavioral change campaigns through the use of advocacy efforts.

One can draw from the field of health education, where health educators have developed a number of competencies revolving around the use of advocacy to advance health and health education efforts. Within their credentialing body, the National Commission for Health Education Credentialing, a framework for competencies have been developed. This "Competency-Based Framework for Graduate Level Health Educators," developed in 1999, lays out a number of competencies required for advocacy to advance the profession, and several can be borrowed by the aging profession. These include the use of a variety of methods and techniques for providing information through the use of oral and written presentations and culturally sensitive methods and techniques, and exercise of organizational leadership through strategies to influence public policy. It is within this framework that we develop the use of media advocacy to educate on a specific topic of interest and attempt to advance policy and program development initiatives.

THE USE OF MEDIA ADVOCACY

What Is Media Advocacy?

Media advocacy is the strategic use of any form of media to help advance an organization's objectives or goals. In this context, media is a tool—not an end in itself, but a means to an end. Most health and human service professionals including social work and public health have not taken advantage of using media strategies for public education. Conversely, journalism and media specialists have not taken social welfare and health concerns under their wing for the promotion of health-related issues (APHA, n.d.). Through media advocacy, one can frame issues and showcase their importance for the community.

Media advocacy explores a number of key issues and serves to present strategies that can be helpful in the development of innovative human service opportunities and educate the general public. Media advocacy can change both public perception and perception of key stakeholders, elite power or key individuals within communities that impact policy or program-related issues for community development or community-based problems.

Media advocacy can be used to create a reliable, consistent stream of publicity or media focus for one's agency's issues and activities. It takes a focused approach to explain very specifically how targeted social problems or issues could and should be solved. Consequently, such a targeted approach will motivate community members and policy makers to step up to the plate and help with community change or endorse change efforts.

The Administration on Aging (2006), in their media advocacy kit, suggest that one can use the media to inform, recast, encourage, and promote. More specifically, media efforts can be used to inform the general public about specific causes or influences that impact older adults. Such problems or issues can be recast or reframed so that they affect all people, and not just a distant group of individuals. Once problems are reframed, media strategies can be used to encourage community members, voluntary organizations, community leaders, and the faith-based community to find out more about problems or issues for older adults and establish some engagement from these stakeholders to get involved. Finally, media advocacy can be used to promote services within the community that address and meet the needs of a wide array or people including older adults.

When Using Media for Advocacy

Developing a media-based approach does not simply imply developing flyers or newspaper articles, but rather it attempts to develop a concerted approach to developing strategies for social change. These strategies include the message, the messengers, and devising strategies to meet the target audience.

The message should be carefully crafted to include a specific message one wants to convey, as well as the messengers or vehicles to convey the message. In Chapter 10, health behavior models and various stages of the models were discussed. The stages of change model would require different sound bites or messages, depending upon the stage that the information is targeted to address. Sound bites are also crucial in the process as well because they help frame what one hears, and how one is called to action. Overburdening one with steps or activities may do more harm than good.

A second important step when considering using media for advocacy is to pick the right messengers. Questions to consider in this process would be "Do they have name recognition in the community?" or "Do they represent the class of individuals who are targeted?" and "Are they considered credible sources of information?" Examples of good messengers include elected officials, respected aging officials, and well-known volunteer advocates.

FORMS OF MEDIA ADVOCACY

Media strategies come in a variety of forms, including newspaper articles, letters to the editor, articles, advertisements, radio spots, news conferences, and media artifacts. While these are effective strategies, they are only a fraction of strategies or approaches available. A number of creative approaches can also be used with media artifacts such as bumper stickers, refrigerator magnets, baseball caps, door knockers, t-shirts, posters, billboard advertisements, newsletters, postcards, and flyers.

Newspaper Articles

Newspaper articles can be used to effectively target people who are literate and subscribe to a local paper. Articles are generally written at a fifth-grade reading ability and can be effectively persuasive and educational on specific issues. Developing a strong relationship with a newspaper columnist can help enhance one's ability to advocate on specific issues, and this individual can also be used to provide background on specific community-based issues.

News Releases

News releases are mechanisms to provide the "W-5's" of a story, meaning the who, what, when, where and why of an upcoming news story. Usually this "W-5" approach provides a news reporter with the background to be able to decide if an article will be newsworthy or not. According to the Media Advocacy manual from the American Public Health Association, the standard format for a news release is as follows:

- Organization's name: Although the name of the organization should be across the top of the release, using letterhead will also help with the legitimacy of the release.
- Contact information: This information should follow the organization's name. Ideally one would want to put the contact name and telephone number/fax number/e-mail address for one who can speak on behalf of the organization, such as a staff person, who is knowledgeable and easy to contact. This information is usually presented on the top right-hand corner of the page.
- Release date: The release date alerts the reporter when a press release item should be either published or broadcast. If it is available for immediate release, then it should be labeled as "For Immediate Release," and this can appear on the left-hand corner of your page, immediately following the title. If it is preferable that the news release be held until a particular date, the release date should read "Embargoed until (release date/time)."
- Headline: This component of your news release is probably the most important and will be what sparks attention. It generally is a short phrase or "sound bite" that will summarize the point of your news release. It is generally found under the contact information, and before the body of the release.
- Body: This is the portion of your document where the story is told. It contains the "who, where, what ,when, and why" of the

story. Generally speaking, one can see the news release framed as what is known as the inverted pyramid style of disclosure. In such a format, the conclusion, or most important of the details, is found initially, followed by supporting information. This inverted pyramid style is attractive because readers are often overwhelmed with information and news release items, hence they find the most important information summarized in the headline and initial paragraphs.

A few additional pointers that may be helpful to the writer when preparing a news release item can include:

- The first paragraph, which becomes the lead, should be the most powerful paragraph. It should captivate the interest of the reader.
- Sentences and paragraphs should be kept short and in layperson's language. Jargon and slang should be avoided. Ideally, your final product should be one or two pages, single spaced.
- Conclude the release with a "tag": This "tag usually consists of one paragraph and provides a background on the organization, its goals, and so forth. Generally it is prewritten and consists of what is known as a "boiler plate," outlining the background, goals, and mission of the not-for profit organization sponsoring the news release.
- End your release. In the news industry, news releases usually include some symbols to denote that the news release has been concluded. This can be symbolized in one of three ways, at the end of the release, such : —30—, END, or ####, and can be found centered on the end of the page. If a news release has two pages, always end the first page with: —more— to suggest that there is a second page.

Letters to the Editor

Letters to the editor are often considered simple ways to communicate one's opinion to the general public. One can increase their chances of having a letter published if they target smaller newspapers or magazines. A general rule of thumb is that shorter pieces are better and have more likelihood of getting printed. In addition to checking for how letters to the editor appear in specific magazines, some rules to follow include the following:

- Be brief: Try to focus your perspective to include only one idea or concept. Limit yourself to no more than 300 words.
- Refer to previous stories: Refer to stories that have been recently published in the news.
- Include contact information: Not only would one want to include their daytime contact information (name, telephone, e-mail addresses), but also their organizational affiliation and any degrees attained or titles that are relevant. The use of titles will help legitimize one's expertise.

Radio Spots or Television Interviews

Interviews with the media can be an effective way to share a message. Radio stations often have talk shows, which are interested in newsworthy information that can educate the public. Talk show hosts also often look for guests, so these can also be effective ways to promote one's message.

One must exercise care to ensure that they do not share too much information and overwhelm the readers or listeners. We generally refer to the technique of using "sound bites" of information. Some additional tips to help prepare for the interview include:

- Arrange an appearance: The first step is to communicate with the talk show host or the producer. Writing or calling directly is acceptable. In your introduction explain why people would be interested in the material you have to share about aging programs or policy issues. If the information can be tied to a local event, it also adds to the appeal for the producer.
- Do your homework prior to the program: One cannot stress enough the importance of getting to know both the host and their program. It is also a good idea to be pragmatic and find out about the interview—that is, will it be live or taped, how long is the interview, and will there be call-in questions. It might also be helpful to listen to at least a couple of broadcasts beforehand in order to get an idea of what to expect from the program.
- Plan ahead for the interview: Preparing ahead of the interview can ensure that the most important points one wants to make are covered. Prepare in written format, ahead of time, the most important points to be made, and include anecdotes or personal stories that will put a human touch to the face of the interview. Consider questions that you can anticipate and arguments and counterarguments that may come your way during the interview

so that you can prepare ahead for them. Since the media likes to give air time to opposing points of view and both sides of a story, it is prudent to prepare for these. Role-playing ahead of time with a colleague can also be very helpful in the preparation process.

Once the planning for the interview has been established, a few tips to keep in mind during the actual interview process can help assure success. These include:

- Speak naturally and enunciate so you can be heard clearly: Maintaining a calm and poised self are key to a successful interview situation. Avoid being defensive or showing any signs of anger, especially if challenged during the interview. Exercise caution not to say anything that you would prefer not seen on a tabloid or on the evening news.
- Avoid initials, trade language or jargon, and acronyms: Since advocacy using the media may involve reaching an audience who is not familiar with aging issues or trade terms like AAA's for Area Agencies on Aging, use language that will be easily understood by other people.
- Use the opportunity to share your message first: Use an interview situation as an opportunity to bring out a clear and consistent message repeatedly. Clarify and restate your message at every opportunity, then utilize the interview time to make points that will support your message. Prepare one main message that you want to see spoken, repeatedly, over and over in an effort to assure that it is heard.
- Be concise: Prepare "sound bites" or short statements ahead of time that can be used in the interview process. These will aid in keeping messages short and concise. It has been estimated that sound bites usually last 8 seconds; hence, it is important that these are quick and easily roll off one's tongue. A media trick has been reported to be dead space between questions. Generally people who are not prepared for this dead space jump in and say something that could be regretted later on, which can be picked up on by a reporter. Having prepared sound bites ahead of time enables one to avoid this pitfall.

Some people have been known to bring tape recorders in order to tape themselves during the interview. In this manner, they have the opportunity to see if they have made any errors or omissions that they would like to have corrected prior to airing their interviews.

A few additional pointers of being interviewed for television of public viewing:

- Attire: Clothing creates images whether on or off the camera screen. On camera, however, does pose some challenges that one must be prepared for. Jewelry, if loud and flashy, can create a reflection off TV camera lights. Clothing colors that seem to work best on television are solid designs in gray, blue, and brown. Solid black or white on camera creates too much of a contrast with the lights and can sometimes blend in with the background scenery.
- Focus on the host and not the camera: Make a point of focusing on the host, interviewer, or commentator. Maintaining eye contact with this individual, along with a comfortable style and smile, will go a long way.
- "Smile, you're on candid camera": Above all else, keep in mind that you are always on stage. With this knowledge, be guarded with your actions and comments. It is when one least expects it that their candid comments are caught.

At the conclusion, remember that this may be only the beginning of a long-standing working relationship with the reporter, so consider sending a personal thank-you note to the reporter. Generally speaking, they will also provide a tape of the interview, which can be used as a learning tool to evaluate your performance and things to consider for the next interview opportunity.

Media Events or Press Briefings

Media events or press briefings are the two most comment venues used for disseminating information about programs, policies, services, or issues. The difference between the two strategies is that a press briefing is held to provide journalists with information or background on a particular topic as well as new developments or key findings and updates. These events can be informal, and also be used as a venue to develop a relationship with the media. A news conference, on the other hand, usually is an opportunity to announce a major story such as a new initiative, research development, policy change, or program initiative.

Both media events and press briefings can actually be time-intensive, so they may not always be the best way to share information with a mass of people, if resources are slim. This being said, if one chooses to move into the realm of media events or press briefings, it is usually preferable to host these in a large group setting. Several points should be kept in mind when planning media events:

- *Consider the location:* Choosing a location that is easily accessible and well known assures that it is convenient for journalists to find and attend. When considering a location, keep in mind that journalists may need to bring their equipment; hence, it will be important to assure that there is adequate space at the back of a room, and plenty of electrical outlets. Popular sites to consider are usually hotels or press clubs, but a local aging or public health service provider, a local area agency on aging, or a public health department can all be adequate choices for a location.

- *Consider the time:* Timing of events is important to assure journalists will show up. Experts suggest that midweek events (Tuesdays, Wednesdays or Thursdays) are best, and events scheduled in the morning (10:00 or 11:00) meet the needs of journalists who are on the run.

- *Follow up prior to the event:* Prior to the event, forward an advisory to remind journalists of the event. This may be faxed or e-mailed to remind journalists of the event. Once initiated, follow-up with a telephone call can always be helpful since newsrooms are swamped with requests. This trail of contacts also helps to build rapport with the media.

- *Develop a press kit:* A press kit is generally a way of providing educational materials on a given topic that can be distributed the day of a media event. It can contain news releases, fact sheets, biographies of speakers or key individuals, case studies related to your event, and general information about an aging agency or services. The materials should provide a backdrop on issues for those receiving the information and can provide some background information for the journalists, which can be drawn from when producing some articles or other related materials.

- *Prepare an agenda beforehand:* Since it is important to assure that an event is well orchestrated, select a moderator for the event ahead of time, as well as an agenda and speakers, and determine who will make introductions, prepare remarks, and so on.

- *Presentations:* Formal statements should be prepared to be as brief as possible not to exceed 15 to 20 minutes. Experts suggest that a general rule to consider is to limit presentations to five speakers during a press conference, and limit speakers' time availability to 5 minutes. The setting for a media conference is not to provide dissertations to the audience, but to educate and provide plenty of opportunities for the media to ask questions.

- *Helping hands:* Press conferences can be time-sensitive; thus, having as many individuals as possible available who can help orchestrate an event and make it appear to move smoothly is helpful. Pairs of hands can assist with passing out press kits, attending to sign-in sheets, directing journalists to telephones or key presenters, or being available to manage any last-minute details or crises.
- *Interviews and photo opportunities:* Ensure some time at the end of the event for both interviews and photo opportunities.
- *Initiate some follow-up once the event is over:* Minding one's manners such as following up with personal thank-you notes can go a long way toward building relationships with reporters. Forwarding a press kit to journalists who were unable to attend also fosters relationships. Finally, if your press conference reaps any news stories, respond to these in writing and provide some commentary that can be woven by journalists into future stories. Each attempt to communicate with a journalist provides the opportunity to build a relationship.

Fact Sheets

Fact sheets are resources that can be very helpful to educate on a topic quickly and provide a summary of important points. Fact sheets generally identify the main message, and provide some empirical data (statistics, graphs etc.), as well as some anecdotal stories to put a human touch on the materials. Fact sheets are excellent resources to use when educating local legislators about a problem or issue that requires being addressed, and they are commonly used by local advocates. A key to keep in mind when developing fact sheets is to be brief, and keep them to one page.

Media Artifacts

In addition, there are also a variety of other methods and techniques that utilize media artifacts and present a message. The key to using media artifacts is to find something that can be useful and valued to your target population, and use either the distributor, a printer, or one's own ability to use the computer and office supplies to develop sound-bite messages. Many people are familiar with the use of artifacts by marketing companies to develop items that can be used to promote goods or services. In this vein, the ideas are similar; however, this slogan may include a sound-bite that will help convey a message regarding a particular service or issue.

The author's bias is that these media artifacts can be very useful to convey a message that reaches the majority of people through some creative mechanism. These artifacts are also a creative way to encourage students to transform policy or program development term papers into mechanisms that can impact older adults and their caregivers.

The following list provides a range of artifacts that can be used to develop these materials:

- Web sites;
- T-shirts;
- Sun visors;
- Door hangers;
- Buttons;
- Bumper stickers;
- Refrigerator magnets;
- CD cases;
- Purse size make-up mirrors;
- Purse size "emergency kits";
- Calculators;
- Refrigerator magnet picture frames;
- Posters;
- Billboards;
- Umbrellas;
- Shoelaces;
- Packaging for crackers and snack food items;
- Photographs; and
- Loose change containers.

WHAT STRATEGIES ARE BEST TO USE?

When attempting to decide which strategies are best to use, one must consider numerous factors. First, one must consider the audience: who are the target individuals that you want to reach. What demographic characteristics comprise this target audience? Demographics to consider will include the average age you want to address, the ethnic make-up, marital status, income level, and occupational make-up of the group and educational levels. The age cohort is important because one would hope that messages may also consider some of the cohort-related issues that the individual may find of specific importance and have relevance over the course of their lifetime (see Chapter 2 for historical landmarks). Ideally, one would not consider targeting messages using the Internet or Internet blogs if the individual is not computer literate.

A second consideration is your message that you want to address using your strategy. Are you interested in pursuing a message to ensure older adults are aware of the benefits of a flu vaccine, perceived susceptibility, perceived seriousness or all of these issues? Do you want to address the subjective norms or beliefs as a part of the strategy? Health behaviors play a critical and vital role in the development of these messages as well.

A number of other considerations, which may be more pragmatic or logistical, are also relevant to consider when developing media strategies. These include such things as time, financial resources, human resources, specific health promotion strategies, and a message to target. Time considerations include how much time is available in order to get the message out. Is the plan to meet a deadline for the next month, to meet some goals established for National Diabetes Awareness month for example, or is there a longer-range plan to develop a health fair six months down the line? Conversely, is one's organization planning for media approaches for the next year, and designing some educational tools to be used monthly for themes? Along with the consideration of time, one must also consider how much time you have available to work on a specific issue, and how much time a specific anticipated strategy will take you to pursue.

Financial resources are another consideration when devising media strategies. Working within a limited budget may also limit the specific type of strategies one could pursue. When limited resources are available, one may consider using public resources such as radio or the local newspapers. Soliciting corporate partners can also be a helpful venue for developing financial support for media efforts. For example, grocery stores often partner with regional or national associations and utilize their grocery bags to showcase specific events, and these can be useful for promotion of a health message or media approach. Depending on one's financial situation, one may also be able to purchase the services of a social marketer to develop a marketing campaign that is more substantial.

Human resources may include the personnel available to develop a marketing campaign, or to promote and market such media. Individuals with expertise may not necessarily be available within a health or human services agency setting. This may be the time to utilize the expertise of a local academic setting such as a community college or a university and tap into a service learning project with the local institution. Human service workers or people with a liberal arts background may have the expertise to manage resources or conduct case management functions; however, these same individuals may lack a theoretical background to convey health promotion messages or use health behavior frameworks in the design of media strategies. Conversely, experts with this expertise may not be familiar with the specific nature of aging issues and the content, so partnerships bridging these human resources are very important.

USING MEDIA ADVOCACY FOR POLICY
DEVELOPMENT AND PROGRAM PLANNING

The use of media as an advocacy tool in the fields of public health and human services/aging does not have a long-standing tradition (Tappe & Galer-Unti, 2001). In public health, the use of media has sometimes been coined as "social marketing." However, this approach has been used primarily for targeting health interventions and has addressed the individual at the initial stages of readiness for change (precontemplation and contemplation). A further discussion on how these stages fit into the health behavior repertoire was discussed in the Chapter 10. In contrast to a social marketing approach, media advocacy can be effectively carried out using artifacts that send a simple take-home message. There are several benefits to incorporating media advocacy into a repertoire of skills for advocacy development. First, it is quick and can be inexpensive. Second, it helps assure that one's message is known and by using a variety of strategies with the media, one may be able to amplify the impact. Last, other fields and occupations take advantage of using media strategies to promote their message. Hence, there is no reason we need to be left behind, as advocates within the field of aging (Baker, Leitner, & McAuley, 2001).

SUMMARY

This chapter has reviewed a number of specific media advocacy strategies and provided some innovative approach to sending a message. These strategies can be used as stand-alone methods, or in combination with each other. Media artifacts can also be a creative way to get one's message out to the general public in a simple manner in areas that can be highly technical. These strategies build on understanding one's health and help-seeking behavior, and enable advocates to influence a wide number and array of people with limited resources and energy.

USEFUL WEB SITES

American Public Health Association (APHA), Advocacy Tips, Top Ten Rules for Advocacy: http://www.apha.org/advocacy/tips
    This Web site provides the reader with APHA's top 10 rules for advocacy efforts. The site also provides links for the reader to advocacy activities, policy statements, advocacy priorities, reports and fact sheets, and ideas for taking action. Links are also available to how-to sites related

to advocacy efforts to influence policy makers, public meetings, and letter writing.

Centers for Disease Control and Prevention, Health Marketing Basics: http://www.cdc.gov/healthmarketing/basics.htm
    This site provides helpful tips related to health marketing, beginning with an introduction to the concept, identifying a "market mix" and developing a marketing plan. It also provides some insight into market exchange and target markets.

The AGS Foundation for Health in Aging Advocacy Center: http://www. healthinaging.org/
    This site, hosted by the American Geriatrics Society, offers tools for advocacy on issues that are important for the health and well-being of older adults. It provides links to sites with state-of-the-art information on the diseases and disorders of older adults, physician referral services, and aging stories.

A Journalist's Guide to the Internet: http://reporter.umd.edu
    This site, developed by a journalist (Dr. Christopher Callahan, Dean, Walter Cronkite School of Journalism and Mass Communication) provides a step-by-step guide and links to advocacy efforts from a journalist's perspective. Links include maps, sources, directors, listservs, search tools, online newspapers, newsgroups, federal and state government links, and much more.

The Gerontological Society of America, Expert Referral Service: http://www/geron.org/referrals.htm
    This site provides the reader with links to experts in virtually any area in the field of aging. These can be helpful for the advocate seeking expert testimony on a specific topic within the field of aging.

Health Literacy Consulting: http://www.healthliteracy.com/tips/asp
    This site helps organizations communicate effectively to their target audience. Developed by a private consultant, it provides resources on health literacy, ideas for writing and editing effectively, and links to resources that can be used to promote health literacy through advocacy.

NASW Advocacy: http://www.naswdc.org/advocacy/default/.asp
    This Web site provides the reader with a range of tips for effective advocacy from a social work perspective. It provides links for grassroots advocacy, a legislative advocacy network, legislative issues, congressional testimony, letters and comments, and a tool kit for effective lobby action. The site also provides links to enable one to look up legislative bills and provides a link to useful publications that have been utilized in recent advocacy efforts.

REFERENCES

American Public Health Association (APHA). (n.d.). *APHA media advocacy manual.* Washington, DC: American Public Health Association.

Baker, P., Leitner, J., & McAuley, W. J. (2001). Preparing future aging advocacy advocates: The Oklahoma Aging Advocacy Leadership Academy. *The Gerontologist, 41,* 394–400.

Bernhardt, J. M. (2004). Communication at the core of effective public health. *American Journal of Public Health, 94* (12), 2051–2053.

Cavill, N., & Bauman, A. (2004). Changing the way people think about health enhancing physical activity: Do mass media campaigns have a role? *Journal of Sports Sciences, 22* (8), 771–790.

Coalition of National Health Education Organization Partners. (n.d.) Making your advocacy efforts count. Retrieved July 12, 2006, from http://www.healtheducationadvocate.org

Dorfman, L. (2005). More than a message: Framing public health advocacy to change corporate practices. *Health Education and Behavior, 32*(3), 320–336.

Freimuth, V. S., & Quinn, S. C. (2004). The contribution of health communication to eliminating health disparities. *American Journal of Public Health, 94*(12), 2053–2058.

Hudson, R. B. (2004, Spring). Advocacy and policy success in aging. *Generations,* 17–24.

Moore, J. K. (2004). Photography as a tool for advocacy and policy change: Successes from CARE and photosensitive's HIV positive campaign. *International Conference on AIDS,* July 11–16: abstract no. MoPeE4172.

Mueller, M., Page, C., & Kuerbis, B. (2004). Civil society and the shaping of communication-information policy: Four decades of advocacy. *The Information Society, 20* (3), 169–185.

Randolph, W., & Viswanth, K. (2004). Lessons learned from public health mass media campaigns: Marketing health in a crowded media world. *Annual Review of Public Health, 25,* 419–437.

Tappe, M. K., & Galer-Unti, R. A. (2001). The health educators' role in promoting health literacy and advocacy for the 21st century. *Journal of School Health, 71*(10), 477–482.

Coalitions and Coalition Building for Advocacy and Policy Development

WHY ADVOCACY?

Many disciplines have advocacy embedded at the heart of the activities they aspire to carry out. In addition, several disciplines, such as social work, include advocacy within their own code of ethics, and major activities for the profession. While advocacy takes on a host of different definitions, at the heart of all definitions is the act of speaking in favor of another's cause or speaking or writing in support of something (Webster's Dictionary, 2001). While many professions seek to challenge injustices within communities, increasingly, the act of advocacy is being built into the range of activities that professionals engage in. Advocacy is the bridge between what is seen as a social, health, or community need, and the outcome, such as policy development or program-/practice-related activities.

In many profession, such as social work, one of the core values is to advocate for social justice. The National Association of Social Workers (NASW) Code of Ethics notes that through the value of social justice, social workers are called to challenge social injustice. According to the NASW Code of Ethics (1999):

> Social workers pursue social change, particularly with and on behalf of vulnerable and oppressed individuals and groups of people. Social workers' social change efforts are focused primarily on issues of poverty, unemployment, discrimination, and other forms of social injustice. These

activities seek to promote sensitivity to and knowledge about oppression and cultural and ethnic diversity. Social workers strive to ensure access to needed information, services, and resources; equality of opportunity; and meaningful participation in decision making for all people.

Professions such as social work have a responsibility to a broader society through their commitment to social welfare. In essence, social workers strive to promote the general welfare of society, from local to global levels. They try to promote the development of human resources, communities, and environments. The NASW Code of Ethics also challenges social workers to advocate for some basic living conditions that respect human dignity and that promote human needs and foster human, economic, social, political, and cultural values of the core population. When translated to an aging population, social workers, as an example, strive to develop information and resources that will encourage and foster the dignity and worth of older adults and their families. This includes the process of advocacy for standards and living conditions that are consistent with the lifestyle and values that an older adult has been exposed to during their lifetime.

Within our service delivery systems there are a number of unresolved issues and areas for program development that will require advocacy. Gaps in service delivery are prime reasons why we would want to engage in advocacy efforts. Gaps in policy development are also major areas and reasons that require advocacy efforts on our part as health professionals and social workers. Examples include the need for oral health screening and prevention services available through Medicare and falls prevention education available through Medicare.

STRATEGIES FOR ADVOCACY: COALITION BUILDING

A number of strategies are available that can be used to develop initiatives that can impact one's advocacy efforts. These strategies can be used to promote the development of new programs and services and can include the use of and/or development of coalitions, the use of media and media advocacy, and the use of consumer advocates.

The following section will address each of these strategies in greater depth.

What Are Coalitions?

Coalitions can be defined as temporary alliances or factions that can be used for the benefit of a political strategy or goal. Essentially a coalition includes an organized group of people in a community who set out to work towards a common goal. The coalition can have individual, group, institutional, community and public policy goals.

What Are Some Reasons for Developing Coalitions?

A number of reasons exist for why coalition building would be an effective strategy for the development of resources, policies, or programs. These include issues or concerns such as:

- Conducting needs assessments;
- Addressing lack of resources;
- Data collection strategies;
- Action/evaluations;
- Advocacy;
- Roadmaps/blueprints/vision; and
- Evidence-based approaches.

PARTNERS FOR COALITION ENTITIES

A number of community-based partners can serve to build effective partnerships in the coalition-building process. These partners, whether traditional or nontraditional in the sense of being vested in community efforts, can all contribute to the welfare of a community in an effort to incorporate older adults within the community and build on existing programs and services. Such partners include the following diverse interest groups, also illustrated in Table 12.1.

- Academia;
- Public health;
- Human service providers;
- Faith-based communities;
- Law and safety enforcement;
- Medical/education;
- Volunteer associations; and
- Sports and recreations entities.

Academia

Academia can prove to be an effective and helpful partner in the process of building coalitions for advocacy development in several ways. Their expertise lies in scholarship and training. Experts may provide scope insofar as the latest developments in the literature and ideas about the

TABLE 12.1   Partnerships for Coalitions

Partner	Private or public entity
Post-secondary institutions	Public and private
Public health	Public
Human service providers	Public and/or private
Faith-based communities	Private
Law and safety enforcement	Public
Media/education	Public and/or private
Volunteer associations	Private
Sports and recreation entities	Public and/or private

specific innovations within the field. They are usually also abreast of seminal documents such as task force reports and so on. In addition to this academic expertise that is provided, these experts can also provide student manpower, and provide student input into the development of student projects, focus groups, or other mechanisms that can enhance the process for academic expertise.

Public Health Expertise

Public health expertise within a coalition can be an asset in several important ways (Minnex & Readman, 2002). First, staff from public health departments can easily understand and interpret data such as vital statistics and epidemiological data, which can contribute to the rationale for program or policy changes. Second, public health has a strong advocacy arm and a tradition of building coalitions, which can also benefit the process.

Human Service Providers

Human service providers can provide some insight into three specific areas, which can be helpful in the coalition-building process. First, they can provide service statistics on the kinds of service needs seen within a specific geographic community and identify gaps in services. Second, they can provide staff who are knowledgeable about the needs and gaps in services within specific designated community areas. Last, they can provide some background into a consumer's perspective through the invitation and inclusion of consumers or their families as target groups, and involve these individuals on coalition forces.

Faith-Based Communities

Faith-based communities can also be key partners in coalitions, since the leaders of faith-based communities have an active linkage with many people within their midst. Church leaders have the capacity to reach many people within their congregations, which can be helpful for community-based advocacy campaigns. Congregations may also be sought to provide expertise to community coalition efforts, and members can write to local, state, and federal legislators to promote the passage of specific legislation (such as seen in the process of passing Medicare Part D or the Americans with Disabilities Act). Lastly, many faith-based communities also have social action committees, which can be used to help promote the work of coalitions, or provide perspectives that can be helpful for the development of a coalition's work.

Law and Safety Enforcement

Law and safety enforcement entities can be helpful in the work of coalitions, especially in aging-related issues, since they are active in communities protecting and serving the needs of elders. They are often the first line of attack when there are needs and issues to be considered related to community safety; however, they can also offer a perspective on the needs and issues that older people will face related to public safety and victimization. They can also, in many cases, be called upon to share some degree of expertise related to the implementation of specific policies and programs.

Media/Education

The media can be an effective coalition partner because they can provide publicity and create public awareness about issues and concerns that the coalition is publicly involved in. The media can also be used to effectively persuade the public and community about specific initiatives that may impact older adults or their family members. Public radio and television stations can also be instrumental in developing and delivering messages that can further the work of a coalition's efforts. They can also be used to develop special educational segments that can showcase an issue or concern that the coalition is attempting to build awareness around, and bridge resources for. An excellent example of the use of the media can be seen in Jackson County, Illinois where a public television network (WSIU—affiliated with Southern Illinois University Carbondale) created awareness of culture change within nursing homes known as the *Pioneering Movement*. Legislative efforts had been underway to develop a bill within the Illinois legislature to facilitate some efforts and expectations within nursing facilities to improve the culture within the nursing facilities of the state.

Volunteer Associations

Volunteer associations can also serve as effective partners in the coalition team. Volunteer associations often take on community service projects, which can be community-oriented and provide partnership to coalitions with person power, and members who have expertise that can be used pro-bono. Lawyers or accountants who may be members of voluntary associations are good examples of expertise that can be tapped into for the purpose of furthering a coalition's issue. Once again, voluntary associations can also be used through membership bases to leverage access to organizational membership. This is especially true now as we move towards an electronic age and the use of the Internet can be a powerful tool for information exchange. Voluntary groups such as local chapters of AARP can also be helpful in leveraging person-power to write letters or make telephone calls to one's local representatives and senators.

Sports and Recreation Entities

Many retired people frequent facilities such as sports and recreation centers. These active seniors can also be a source of consumer group energy, which can be helpful on a coalition group. Workers from these entities are often also in touch with a number of senior citizens, so they also can be an excellent source of contact or connection with older adults.

In summary, a number of partners can serve as effective members within a coalition, and resources that are often overlooked within communities can actually be available to provide intellectual, human, and promotional resources (Gallagher, Stanely, Shearer, & Klerman, 2006).

HOW DO WE BUILD COALITIONS?

Building coalitions can be an art form (built on some science), although some people may argue that one need only to invite people to the table. Successful coalitions actually build some strategy and process into their design, which may in fact help the coalition to meet success. Effective coalition leadership involves the use of strategic processes and mapping of resources to be sure that the necessary ingredients for a successful coalition are in place (Sipe, 2005).

The first step in developing effective coalitions is to develop an issue-based approach to participation. Within this approach, an organizer or facilitator must consider what expertise is required and what is the common goal for all. This requires communication skills, and once community partners are identified, it may be useful to develop one meeting dedicated to building a common vision or purpose. One tool that can be exceedingly helpful is the use of an approach known as the nominal group technique.

COMMUNICATION SKILLS FOR EFFECTIVE COMMUNITY NEGOTIATIONS

There are several communication skills that are essential in order to ensure effective community negotiations. These communication skills include: active listening; conflict management, and an awareness of verbal and nonverbal messages, which are sent through specific roles stakeholder and community members play.

Active listening ensures each participant or stakeholder is heard. This may include the use of techniques such as Nominal Group Techniques (NGT) or DELPHI. In the NGT process, each member is presented with three by five (3X5) inch note cards and asked to present a written statement that reflects their contribution to the issue at hand. People are usually solicited for two or three statements, in response to the facilitator's question. These are then collected and listed for all to view (e.g., using flip-chart paper, or a similar approach). Items are ranked by the number of times they are identified by membership, and then voted on in order of priority for the group. This process ensures that all stakeholders and members of the group are given the opportunity to present their perspective and opinions, including the quieter and less vocal group members. The NGT process also enables the group to develop consensus on items of priority and moves toward the development of a community planning agenda.

The integration and use of consensus means that there is agreement on the general direction. However, ensuring that there is total agreement on every issue is not realistic when we have a range of divergent viewpoints and perspectives, but it is realistic to arrive at consensus where there is agreement on a range of issues at hand. One member may give on one item, and then gain their voice in another area. In order to arrive at this point, it is important to understand sources of conflict.

Sources of Conflict

Several sources of conflict can be expected to arise when working with divergent personalities and differences in professional background, training, experiences, and personal agendas. Often conflict is perceived as negative and to be avoided. It can, however, provide the catalyst for effective and creative problem solving, since conflict resolution and relationship building are closely connected. Effective mastery of conflict in order to move toward creative problem solving begins with understanding sources of conflict. These sources of conflict can include differences in the interpretation of data; relationship conflict; structural conflicts; value conflicts, and interest conflicts.

Conflicts may arise due to differences in perception and interpretation of data. An example to illustrate this may be differences in the interpretation of balance sheets, financial information, or epidemiological data. Data related to incidence and prevalence may not hold the same meaning for a social worker as for a physician. Conversely, one's interpretation of issues related to psychiatry or psychiatric diagnosis may be interpreted in one way (based upon fear and stigma) for a community resident, and quite differently by a member of a treatment team. Thus, these issues may cause conflicts among various members of your coalition. However, an effective resolution is possible (Ospina & Saz-Carranza, 2005).

Roles of Coalition Members

As a planner, one may want to be cognizant of the various roles that members will play within the coalition-building process. If these have not naturally evolved, it may be helpful to assure that there is representation from these various roles within the group, in an effort to assure that there is a skill set readily available to the group. These roles will include initiator, negotiator, advocate, spokesperson, organizer, mediator, and consultant. These roles will be used in the coalition as several ways to foster the development of the coalition. Table 12.2 provides an overview of these roles.

Initiator

Initiators call attention to an issue such as a problem existing in the community, an unmet need, or a situation to be improved. They play a key role in getting the coalition going.

Negotiator

The negotiator represents an organization or group trying to gain something from another group. This individual seeks win-win situations and a middle ground that both sides can accept. They are vital when a range of factions exist at the coalition level.

Advocate

The advocate decides what the client is entitled to and what is keeping the client from receiving what they need. Effective advocacy requires that the advocate has the capacity to assess various stakeholder or coalition member strengths and weakness.

TABLE 12.2   Roles of Group Members

Roles	Types of Roles
Initiator	Task oriented
Contributor	Task oriented
Information seeker	Task oriented
Opinion seeker	Task oriented
Information giver	Task oriented
Opinion giver	Task oriented
Evaluator-critic	Task oriented
Energizer	Task oriented
Procedural technician	Task oriented
Distractor	Individual oriented
Blocker	Individual oriented
Recognition seeker	Individual oriented
Self-confessor	Individual oriented
Playboy	Individual oriented
Encourager	Group/process oriented
Harmonizer	Group/process oriented
Compromiser	Group/process oriented
Gatekeeper	Group/process oriented
Expediter	Group/process oriented
Standard Setter	Group/process oriented
Ego ideal	Group/process oriented
Group observer	Group/process oriented
Follower	Group/process oriented

Spokesperson

The spokesperson presents an organization's views to others without coloring them with his or her opinions. Their role is critical in showcasing the issues and strategies or promoting the outcomes found by the group.

Organizer

The organizer creates groups of people who share a similar concern. The organizer's tasks include developing the leadership potential of others, stimulating others to act, and identifying targets for change.

Mediator

The mediator role helps two sides work out a compromise. The individual who plays the role of the mediator is neutral, not siding with either party. One major task for the mediator will also be to ensure that both sides understand the other's positions and help these two side arrive at a consensus with each other. The mediator will also be responsible for helping to arrive at priorities and build consensus within the group.

Consultant

The consultant provides advice, suggestions, or ideas to another person, group, or organization. Two characteristics are important for the consultant: (1) knowing more than the group that is being initiated as a coalition; and (2) the ability to see his or her advice ignored without getting personally involved or hurt.

Individual Roles and Perspectives

In addition to the specific roles that are important to be represented within the group, it is also important for the coalition leadership to have a grasp on specific personality dynamics. Personality dynamics are such that membership will affiliate with either a task-oriented relationship, a process-oriented relationship, or the role of a distracter. Distracters tend to divert one away from the goal while the former two help move toward goals, either through accomplishing tasks or building relationships.

Understanding the Roles Participants Will Take On

Group members take on a variety of roles, which can either contribute to or hinder the development of a healthy group process. There are essentially three main types of roles group members fall into. These roles are helpful in understanding the group process and include group task roles, group building and maintenance roles, and individual roles. An understanding of each of these roles can lead to the development of understanding how each of these roles can either facilitate the process of task development, or impair the process.

Group Task Roles

The roles of group tasks include the initiator, contributor, information seeker, opinion seeker, information giver, opinion giver, elaborator, coordinator, orientor, evaluator-critic, energizer, and procedural technician. The initiator/contributor tries to find new ways to meet a group goal. The information seeker seeks facts and clarification from facts and asks if these are adequate. The opinion seeker asks for facts and clarification from those making suggestions. The elaborator spells out suggestions and ideas to deduce how an activity will work if adopted by the group. The coordinator pulls ideas and suggestions together and coordinates activities. The orientor summarizes the past, points to where the group departs from goals, and charts future direction. The evaluator-critic subjects the group to standards, questions the group, and plays devil's advocate. The energizer pushers for higher quality activity. The procedural technician contributes to the logistics of the group and distributes materials. The recorder writes suggestions, records group decisions, and serves as the group memory.

Group Building and Maintenance Roles

Group building and maintenance roles have been identified as the encourager, harmonizer, compromiser, gatekeeper, expediter, standard setter or ego ideal, group observer/commentator, and follower. These roles are designed to strengthen the process of group building, develop a stronger bond between the group members, and serve as the glue that binds the process.

The encourager praises and shares warmth with the group. The harmonizer reconciles and mediates, relieves tension. The compromiser meets others half-way. The gatekeeper keeps communication channels open. The standard setter sets standards for the group. The group observer records group process and contributes the same. The follower goes along with the movements of the group.

Individual or Distractor Roles

There are several roles that lead to individual rather than group gain. These roles include the aggressor, the blocker, the recognition seeker, the self-confessor, and the playboy. The aggressor deflates the status and esteem of others, disapproves values of others, attacks efforts for change, and shows envy. The blocker is negative and stubbornly resistant, opposes without reason, and returns to settled or rejected issues. The recognition seeker calls attention to oneself and away from the project at hand through boasting about one's personal achievements. The self-confessor, on the other hand, is known for their input about their shortfalls. The playboy can be cynical, nonchalant, or out of the field.

What Influences These Roles Within Coalitions?

There are a number of factors that will influence these roles among members who are involved in coalitions. These factors include individual members' needs and resources, the situation of the group, and the culture and environment of the group. In addition, human factors can lead to barriers such as mutual trust, negotiation skills, communication skills, appropriate leaders, clear goals, and unified commitment will also affect the group as a whole, and as individual members.

Thus far, this chapter has outlined a variety of issues related to coalitions, group development, and coalition building for aging policies and programs. The next segment will provide examples of coalitions that have been effective in the aging arena.

MODEL COALITIONS AND THEIR OUTCOMES

The National Coalition on Mental Health and Aging (NCMHA)

The National Coalition on Mental Health and Aging has 47 partners to date in the United States and serves as a forum for information sharing among state and local coalitions. Information sharing can relate to a number of issues including best practices, grant opportunities, and national initiatives. It also serves as a vehicle for older adult consumers to share their perspectives at a national level on issues related to mental health and substance abuse. The coalition has also provided a voice in Washington, DC, and in 1995 provided representation and testimony to the White House Conference on Aging. The coalition has been in existence since 1991 and has grown to reach nearly all of the states in the United States over the past 15 years.

The Ontario Healthy Communities Coalition

The Ontario Healthy Communities Coalition, established in 1992, works to promote the ability for communities to strengthen their social, environmental, and economic well-being. They are a direct result of the Health Communities Initiative but have spread throughout Ontario through the use of local and regional coalitions. One of the secrets to their success has been the collective vision of membership, despite the roles and agendas that may be brought to monthly meetings. The coalition has broadened its span and made training materials and its model available to other communities and countries, including in the United States.

Quad Counties Mental Health and Aging Coalition

The Quad Counties Coalition is a collection of service providers who joined forces from four counties in southern Illinois, as a result of a demonstration project implemented by the Office of Mental Health, State of Illinois. This demonstration project was in response to the Surgeon General's report on Mental Health (USDHHS, 1999), which called attention to an intervention to address system integration issues. The coalition has made use of partnerships with service providers, public health aging, mental health, faith-based, and media communities to improve the point-of-service access for older adults, and to improve public awareness of aging and mental health issues. In 2006 the group was recognized for their innovation and success by the American Media Association.

While these three examples merely provide a thumbnail sketch for coalitions, their success has embodied the principles outlined in this chapter.

SUMMARY

In summary, coalition building is not an easy venture, nor is it reasonable to expect the novice program or policy advocate to have the leadership skills necessary to successfully build coalitions. The art and science of effective coalition building lies in understanding both group dynamics and providing leadership to work towards a common agenda and goal. This chapter has reviewed some of the salient ingredients for effective coalition building.

USEFUL WEB SITES

Coalition Building Tool Kit: http://www.ctb.ku.edu/tools/en/sub_section_tools_1057.htm

This Web site links one to a section on coalition building, which is a part of a Community Toolbox series, developed through the University of Kansas. It provides examples, related topics, tools, and checklists for effective coalition building.

Wisconsin Clearing House for Prevention Resources: http://wch.uhs.wisc.edu/01-Prevention/01-prev-Coalition-tools.htm

This Web site provides an excellent source of prevention resources, but in particular, offers tools for coalitions. Included on the site are worksheets to assess coalition effectiveness, coalition job descriptions, coalition recruitment sheets, ideas for leadership, and sample bylaws for coalitions.

National Coalition Building Institute: http://www.ncbi.org/home/index/cfm

This Web site serves as the home page for the National Coalition Building Institute, an international, nonprofit, leadership training organization. They provide training on coalition building, as well as a manual for leaders and activists for building coalitions.

The Partnership Self-Assessment Tool: http://www.partnershiptool.net

This assessment tool enables coalitions to assess how well their collaboration is doing in the areas of leadership, administration, and resources. It provides insight into how to improve the process and helps the group showcase its strengths to potential funders. This Web-based resource from the Center for the Advancement of Collaborative Health originated from the New York Academy of Medicine.

Coalition Sustainability: Long Term Successes and Lessons Learned: http://www.joe.org/joe/2002february/a2.html

This site provides an article that examines the impact of a coalition and its impact 10 years following the inception and development. It reviews lessons learned from the longevity of the project and provide guidance for other programs and coalitions.

REFERENCES

Gallagher, K., Stanely, A., Shearer, D., & Klerman, L. (2006). Challenges in data collection, analysis, and distribution of information in community coalition projects. *Journal of Adolescent Health, 37*(3), S53–S60.

Minnex, W. L., & Readman, C. H. (2002). Health care coalition building. *American Medical Directors Association, 3*(6), 397–399.

National Association of Social Workers. (1999). *NASW code of ethics.* Retrieved April 18, 2007, from http://www.naswdc.org

Ospina, S., & Saz-Carranza, A. (2005, August 5). *Paradox and collaboration in coalition work.* A paper presentation for the 2005 Annual Meeting of the Academy of Management, Honolulu, HI.

Sipe, C. (2005, September-October). Building an active aging coalition. *The Journal on Active Aging,* 60–67.

United States Department of Health and Human Services (USDHHS). (1999). *Mental health: A report of the surgeon general—executive summary.* Rockville, MD: U.S. Department of Health and Human Services, Substance Abuse and Mental Health Services Administration, Center for Mental Health Services, National Institutes of Health, National Institute of Mental Health.

CHAPTER 13

Needs Assessment Tools

NEEDS ASSESSMENTS: AN OVERVIEW

Broadly defined, a needs assessment is a systematic process or activities that are conducted in order to help an individual or system set priorities and make decisions about a program, make decisions about ways to improve an organization, or identify ways to allocate resources. Priorities can be based upon identified needs. Needs assessments can be used for a number of different purposes; however, the main role can be seen as estimating the extent of demand for a specific service or program (Kirst-Ashman & Hall, 2002). Many successful health education and promotion programs have been designed through the use of innovative and comprehensive needs assessment approaches (Bibbs & Mary, 2001; Calderon, 2000; Campbell & Weist, 2001; Fouad, 2004; Fuller, 2001; Jordan, 2002).

Needs are usually identified as the difference between what is or the present state of the way things are, and what should be or a desired state of affairs. Hence, needs assessments try to identify what is, determine the discrepancies, look at the reason for these differences, and build resources to meet these gaps (Witkin & Altschuld, 1995). Needs assessments are very important for the process of developing new resources or deciding if there are new trends in needs at individual or community levels. The impact of bioterrorism on resources for communities caring for older adults is one such example (Shadel, 2002). A needs assessment can also help to identify a gap in resources within a community level that resulted from policy changes (Thompson, 2001). Needs for new programs or needs for policy revisions can also be identified through needs assessments as well. Ideally, this is the first step when building a case to rationalize the need for a new program or service.

WHO IS RESPONSIBLE FOR CARRYING OUT NEEDS ASSESSMENTS?

Needs assessments can be carried out by a wide cast of people. Social workers, public health workers, as well as city planners can carry out needs assessments, as can government organizations. Local citizens or groups of people can also be responsible for carrying out a needs assessment. These groups have been known to band together and work as a citizen's action group. Many groups can actually carry out needs assessments, such as city or governmental planning groups (to identify community needs or needs for resources), local Area Agencies on Aging (for the purpose of identifying programmatic needs), faith-based organizations, and local charity groups.

WHY WOULD INDIVIDUALS, GROUPS, OR ORGANIZATIONS BE INTERESTED IN CONDUCTING A NEEDS ASSESSMENT?

Regardless of the size, individuals, groups, communities, or organizations would be interested in carrying out a needs assessment as a strategy to make sure that resources are in place to help meet the needs of all members of a specific constituency group or community. We often think of the planning process in a casework situation as one mechanism that a caseworker may use to develop a profile of individual needs. Similarly, peer support groups for older adults would assess the needs prior to the onset of a group to decide upon what to focus on within the group intervention. Communities or organizations will conduct needs assessments to help define to what extent a given population may be subject to a specific issue or phenomena.

A prime example of a community needs assessment is the area plan, which is conducted on a regular basis by local Area Agencies on Aging to help develop a profile, state-wide, of needs or areas to focus upon as services or resources are built, revised, or developed. The use of a needs assessment is also really very vital in the development of new programs and services or revision or development of new policies or legislative efforts. Without an accurate picture of the current strengths and resources within a community, it becomes difficult to accurately develop in a rational and comprehensive manner realistic and strategic resources.

CORE CONCEPTS OR BUILDING BLOCKS THAT SERVE AS A FOUNDATION FOR NEEDS ASSESSMENTS

A number of core concepts exist to serve as building blocks, or serve as the foundation for needs assessments. Some of these terms include concepts such as need, target groups, systems, outcome, plan of evidence, and evidence base. In this section, each of these concepts will be examined and showcased.

Need

Need is defined as a gap in programs or services where some form of support or resources are required.

Target Groups

Target groups refer to the specific group who will be the beneficiary of action or for whom we are intending to lobby for change. Usually target groups are identified in the process in order to develop a blueprint for action. Specifically, older adults may be targeted into specific age groups (60+ pre-retirement, 65+ retired, young old, middle old, frail elderly are examples of target groups).

Systems

Systems generally include three specific systems defined as micro, meso, and macro systems. Micro refers to the most basic of systems and considers the individual or issues that impact the individual person. If we consider the individual level we are working to examine the person and their specific needs.

Meso or the Meso system refers to the group or two or more people within a system. A family may be considered a meso system, as well as a group work intervention.

Macro refers to a community or broader system, which takes in the bigger picture. Policy decisions or governmental legislation usually affect the macro level.

Stakeholders refer to people who have a specific interest in a policy, program, or interest group. They are generally people who may be affected by a new policy, practice, or lack of resources.

Outcomes

Outcomes are the end product of some specific action or intervention. Outcomes can occur at the micro-, meso-, or macropractice levels. Outcomes can also be thought of as one's expectations, or what one would like to accomplish as a result of a program, policy, or intervention.

Plan of Action

A plan of action can be thought of as a blueprint or road map to describe a series of activities, who is responsible, and due dates. This plan of action can relate to the implementation of a needs assessment, program, or evaluation of a program, or policy initiative.

Evidence Base

Evidence base refers to the process of using empirical data to justify a program or service. It makes use of factual data rather than opinion or interest group initiatives. It also provides an objective perspective to the issue at hand. A number of secondary data sources are often used in the process of objective assessment, and these have been outlined in chapter 4.

STRATEGIES FOR DEVELOPING A NEEDS ASSESSMENT

Several strategies can be used in the process of developing this inventory of community resources and gaps in the resources. Kirst-Ashman and Hall (2002) identifies five specific strategies that can be used. These include social indicators, key informants, community forum, a survey, and agency-related data. Each is important and can make a significant contribution in part or in combination with other methods in order to create a composite sketch of a community's needs.

Social Indicators

Social indicators include demographic indicators that provide a profile of the community or specific geographic area. Such indicators can be extracted from census data or vital statistics and provide an overview of the context of a community. These indicators can also provide some comparative context comparing a community with a state, regional, national picture or comparative contexts among different countries. A number of Web Sites can be used to gain access to this information, including the United States Census (http://www.census.gov), local area health departments (linked via the individual state Departments of Public Health Homepages and APEX-PH sites, http://www.astho.org/index.php?template=regional_links.php), local Area Agencies on Aging Web Sites, state-based departments on aging, local Centers for Disease Control and Prevention (http://www.cdc.gov), the data warehouse on aging (http://www.cdc.gov/nchs/agingact.htm) and the National Association of Planning Councils Social Indicators (http://www.socialindicators.com/).

A number of variables can be used as social indicators to provide profiles of a specific community. Some of the specific social indicators that could be useful in the planning process include the following variables:

- Population profile (number of people in five-year increments, used to create a population pyramid, or the rate of people/percentage of people over 65 years of age);
- Population pyramid (male and female);
- Education level;
- Housing;
- Employment profiles;
- Ethnicity;
- Marital status;
- Literacy rates;
- Unemployment and poverty rates;
- Number of people affected with mobility limitations;
- Number of people affected with specific health conditions;
- Morbidity rates; and
- Mortality rates.

These select variables provide a sampling of potential variables that can be used to present a demographic profile of the community to be served. These variables can develop a composite sketch of a community and provide a profile to make the case for needed services, programs, or policies. Table 13.1 provides some useful sources of information that can provide social indicator data.

Key Informants

Key informants are people who can give you an idea about what is happening from their perspective within a specific community of interest. The key informant approach asks especially knowledgeable individuals about the needs of a given community who are sought out to share their opinions about needs in a particular area (Kirst-Ashmann & Hall, 2002). Key informants can be individuals who are well connected with the communities for which they serve. Key informants can run the gamut from being the mayor, precinct captain, representatives from aging-related services, or local elders in the community who are well connected with people or resources within a given community or region. Key informants can provide much insight into community resources, strengths, activities, individuals, and groups.

TABLE 13.1   Data Sources for Needs Assessments

Source	Web Site/Homepage
United States Census	(www.census.gov) Local area health departments (vital statistics)
Local area agencies on aging Web sites (Eldercare locator)	http://www.eldercare.gov/Eldercare/Public/Home.asp State based departments on aging (contact available in Table 13.3)
The Centers for Disease Control and Prevention	(www.cdc.gov)
The Data Warehouse on Aging	(http://www.cdc.gov/nchs/agingact.htm)
National Association of Planning Councils Social Indicators	(http://www.socialindicators.com/)

Typically we tend to think of key informants as individuals who are formal leaders in the community; however, Kretzmann and McKnight (1993) suggest that key informants can be drawn from all walks of life within the community and suggest that those individuals well connected through social ties can also provide much insight into the natural resources and assets within a community. Their workbook entitled *Building Communities From the Inside Out: A Path Toward Finding and Mobilizing a Community's Assets* provides a step-by-step approach to utilizing and mobilizing disenfranchised groups to better understand the community and their assets available. They also make the argument that the most effective key informants are people who have had long-standing consumer roots within communities and can provide a perspective on some of the hidden talents and resources within community settings. Older adults, especially retirees, can often fit into this realm and provide skills, expertise, and consultation on a range of issues, often at low or no cost. Hence, this pool of key stakeholders should not be discounted or ignored.

Community Forum

A community forum is designed to hear a variety of voices from the community. Public notice is given and people from the community attend to share their perspective. This approach assumes that the general public has some awareness of a community's needs. Usually there are widely advertised meetings within communities, which are held in community settings in order to bring together a cross section of people. Community forums held within senior centers or senior nutrition sites are generally well accepted by older adults who make use of these settings and are an excellent way to seek input from seniors about their perceptions of community-based needs for older adults. This approach is commonly used by area agencies on aging, when deciding upon priorities for a community's area plan.

The steps to conducting an area plan are not complex and are generally relatively inexpensive to carry out. A facilitator identifies a specific date, time, and setting for a community forum to take place. Once identified, local advertising can take place, which can be followed up with public service announcements, or announcements within a local meal site. During the actual "speak out" or community forum, people are given an opportunity to present ideas in front of a group through the use of a microphone. The facilitators or assessment team will be available to transcribe these ideas, and provide transcripts of the meeting. If resources permit, these can also be taped, or videotaped, and transcribed. Participants may also provide written testimony to the facilitation team, which can be incorporated into the assessment plan.

Field Study and Survey Data

In this approach, information is collected in order to identify issues and trends related to a specific topic area. Academic partners or university entities are often very helpful in this process. In this approach, the needs assessment is based upon gathering data in the community through focus group sessions, and through a completed survey instrument, with pre-identified questions. Methodologists would refer to the survey questionnaire as a quantitative approach to data collection, since the responses developed within the survey instrument are usually closed ended and have been predetermined.

Rates Under Treatment or Agency Service Data

Rates under treatment uses a specific count of people who are currently receiving services (e.g., home health care) to estimate the actual need for services within a given community. These service statistics relate to the numbers of clients who use a specific service. Once it is clear what issues or programs/services that one would like to explore, a specific set of variables can be identified, and service statistics used to develop a profile of these variables of concern. Service statistics can include the number of home-delivered meals provided, case management and screening, transportation services provided, and in-home counseling of recipients to name a few. Table 13.2 provides an overview of some service statistics for services provided via a local area agency on aging.

One may want to contact their state department on aging office for an overview of state, regional, and area-based service statistics. A contact listing is provided in Table 13.3.

TABLE 13.2 A Sample Overview of Service Statistics

	Persons served	Units of service	Areas served
Access services			
Case management [1]	3,250	6,100	13 counties
Information & assistance[1]	9,000	14,000	13 counties
Outreach[1]	5,500	5,500	13 counties
Transportation[1]	650	19,066	10 counties [2]
In-home services			
Home-delivered meals	2,000	320,000	13 counties
Residential repair (home modifications [1])	40	40	13 counties
Community services			
Congregate meals	2,400	230,000	13 counties
Legal assistance[1]	650	9,000	13 counties
Routine health screening	2,500	1,350	13 counties
Health promotion	600	225	6 counties
Physical fitness & group exercise	60	180	3 counties
Medication management	600	200	13 counties
Gerontological counseling (can be provided in-home)	25	285	13 counties
Ombudsman	3,910	4,110	13 counties

Family caregivers support program (for family caregivers and grandparents raising grandchildren)	Persons served		Units of service		Areas served
	Caregivers	Grandparents	Caregivers	Grandparents	
Information	2,400	10	4,000	10	13 counties
Outreach	1,400	2	1,400	2	13 counties
Case management	550	15	800	50	13 counties
Counseling for family caregivers	35	3	225	60	13 counties
Seminars, workshops, & education	115	20	90	4	13 counties
Respite care (in-home & adult day service)	150	1	8,000	25	13 counties
Supplemental "gap-filling" services	15	15	15	15	13 counties
Legal assistance	40	4	300	50	13 counties

Notes: [1]These services are a priority for receiving Supportive Service funds.

[2]Every county has transportation services, but some counties rely on other funding sources to provide rides to senior adults.

TABLE 13.3 Departments on Aging Contact List in the United States

States/Agency Names	Director	Address	Telephone #	E-mail/Web Site Address
Alabama				
Alabama Department Senior Services	Irene B. Collins	RSA Plaza, Suite 470 770 Washington Avenue Montgomery, AL 36130-1851	(334) 242-5743 (800) 243-5463	ageline@adss.state.al.us www.adss.state.al.us/
Alaska				
Alaska Commission on Aging	Linda Gohl	Division of Senior Services Department of Administration P.O. Box 110209 Juneau, AK 99811-0209	(907) 465-3250 (800) 478-6065	dsdsmedicareinfo@health. state.ak.us www.alaskaaging.org/
Arizona				
Aging and Adult Administration	Rex Critchfield	Department of Economic Security 1789 West Jefferson Street #950A Phoenix, AZ 85007	(602) 542-4446	amflores@azdes.gov www.de.state.az.us/aaa/
Arkansas				
Division Aging and	John M. Selig	Arkansas Dept. of Human Services	(501) 682-2441	www.arkansas.gov/dhhs/aging/
Adult Services		P.O. Box 1437, Slot S-530 1417 Donaghey Plaza South Little Rock, AR 72203-1437		

California				
California Department of Aging	Lora Connolly	1600 K Street Sacramento, CA 95814	(916) 322-5290 (800) 735-2929	pwheeler@aging.ca.gov www.aging.state.ca.us/
Colorado				
Aging and Adult Services	Marva Livingston Hammons	Colorado Dept of Human Services 1575 Sherman Street, Ground Floor Denver, CO 80203	(303) 866-2800	liz.mcdonough@state.co.us www.cdhs.state.co.us/
Connecticut				
Division of Elderly Services	Pamela Giannini	25 Sigourney Street, 10th Floor Hartford, CT 06106-5033	(860) 424-5298 (800) 842-1508	pgr.dss@po.state.ct.us www.ct.gov/dss/site/default.asp
Delaware				
Delaware Division of Services for Aging	Allan R. Zaback	Dept. of Health and Social Services 1901 North DuPont Highway New Castle, DE 19720	(302) 255-9390 (302) 577-4791	DSAAPDinfo@state.de.us www.dhss.delaware.gov/dhss/dsaapd/index.html

(continued)

TABLE 13.3 Departments on Aging Contact List in the United States (Continued)

States/Agency Names	Director	Address	Telephone #	E-mail/Web Site Address
District of Columbia				
District of Columbia Office of Aging	E. Veronica Pace	One Judiciary Square - 9th Floor 441 Fourth Street, N.W. Washington, DC 20001	(202) 724-5626 (202) 724-5622	dcoa@dc.gov www.dcoa.dc.gov/dcoa/site/ default.asp
Florida				
Department of Elder Affairs	Carole Green	Building B-Suite 152 4040 Esplanade Way Tallahassee, FL 32399-7000	(850) 414-2000	information@elderaffairs.org http://elderaffairs.state.fl.us/
Georgia				
Division of Aging Services	Maria Greene	Department of Human Resources 2 Peachtree Street N.E. 36th Floor Atlanta, GA 30303-3176	(404) 657-5258	www.aging.dhr.georgia.gov/ portal/site/DHR-DAS/
Hawaii				
Hawaii Executive Office on Aging	Pat Sasaki	250 South Hotel Street, Suite 109 Honolulu, HI 96813-2831	(808) 586-0100	eoa@health.state.hi.us http://www4.hawaii.gov/eoa/

Idaho

Idaho Commission on Aging	Sarah Scott	P.O. Box 83720 Boise, ID 83720-0007	(208) 334-3833	sscott@aging.idaho.gov www.idahoaging.com/ abouticoa/index.htm

Illinois

| Illinois Department on Aging | Charles D. Johnson | 421 East Capitol Avenue, Suite 100 Springfield, IL 62701-1789 | (217) 785-3356
(312) 814-2630 | www.state.il.us/aging/ |

Indiana

| Bureau of Aging In-Home Services Division of Disability, Aging and Rehabilitative Services | Stephen A. Smith | Family and Social Services Admin. 402 W. Washington Street, #W454 P.O. Box 7083 Indianapolis, IN 46207-7083 | (317) 232-7123
(317) 232-7020 | Wpoindexter@fss.state.in.us
www.state.in.us/fssa/elderly/
aging/about.html |

Iowa

| Iowa Department of Elder Affairs | Mark A. Haverland | Clemens Building, 3rd Floor 200 Tenth Street Des Moines, IA 50309-3609 | (515) 242-3333 | Sherry.James@iowa.gov
www.state.ia.us/elderaffairs/ |

Kansas

| Department on Aging | Kathy Greenlee | New England Building 503 S. Kansas Ave. Topeka, KS 66603-3404 | (785) 296-4986
(800) 432-3535 | wwwmail@aging.state.ks.us
www.agingkansas.org/index.htm |

(continued)

TABLE 13.3 Departments on Aging Contact List in the United States (Continued)

States/Agency Names	Director	Address	Telephone #	E-mail/Web Site Address
Kentucky				
Office of Aging Services Cabinet for Families and Children	Pamela Johnson-Betts	Division of Aging Services 275 East Main Street 3W-F Frankfort, KY 40621	(502) 564-6930	www.chfs.kh.gov/
Louisiana				
Governor's Office of Elderly Affairs	Godfry P. White	P.O. Box 80374 Baton Rouge, LA 70898-0374	(225) 342-7100	elderlyaffairs@goea.state.la.us www.louisiana.gov/elderly affairs/
Maine				
Bureau of Elder and Adult Services	Diane Scully	Department of Human Services 35 Anthony Avenue State House-Station #11 Augusta, ME 04333	(800) 262-2232	www.maine.gov/dhhs/beas/
Maryland				
Maryland Department of Aging	Jean W. Roesser	State Office Building, Room 1007 301 West Preston Street Baltimore, MD 21201-2374	(410) 767-1100 (800) 243-3425	www.mdoa.state.md.us/

Massachusetts				
Massachusetts Executive Office of Elder Affairs	Gene Williams	One Ashburton Place, 5th Floor Boston, MA 02108	(617) 727-7750 (800) 243-4636	Annette.V.Peele@state.ma.us www.mass.gov/
Michigan				
Michigan Office of Services to the Aging	Sharon L. Gire	611 W. Ottawa, N. Ottawa Tower 3rd Floor P.O. Box 30676 Lansing, MI 48909	(517) 373-8230	OSADirector@michigan.gov www.miseniors.net/
Minnesota				
Minnesota Board on Aging	Jim Varpness	444 Lafayette Road St. Paul, MN 55155-3843	(651) 431-2500	mba@state.mn.us www.mnaging.org/
Mississippi				
Division of Aging and Adult Services	Dr. Marion Dunn-Tutor	750 N. State Street Jackson, MS 39202	(601) 359-4925 (800) 345-6347	www.mdhs.stat.ms.us/aas.htm
Missouri				
Division of Senior Services	Julie M. Eckstein	Dept of Health and Senior Services P.O. Box 1337 615 Howerton Court Jefferson City, MO 65102-1337	(573) 751-3082	info@dhss.mo.gov www.dhss.mo.gov/

(continued)

TABLE 13.3 Departments on Aging Contact List in the United States (Continued)

States/Agency Names	Director	Address	Telephone #	E-mail/Web Site Address
Montana				
Senior and Long Term Care Division	Joan Miles	Dept. of Public Health & Human Services P.O. Box 4210 111 Sanders, Room 211 Helena, MT 59620	(406) 444-4077	www.dphhs.mt.gov/sltc/
Nebraska				
Department of Health and Human Services	Victor Walker	Division on Aging P.O. Box 95044 1343 M Street Lincoln, NE 68509-5044	(402) 471-2307	vic.walker@hhss.ne.gov www.hhs.state.ne.us/ags/ agsindex.htm
Nevada				
Nevada Division for Aging Services	Michael J. Willden	Department of Human Resources State Mail Room Complex 3416 Goni Road, Building D-132 Carson City, NV 89706	(775) 687-4210	www.nvaging.net/
New Hampshire				
Division of Elderly and Adult Services	Douglas P. McNutt	State Office Park South 129 Pleasant Street, Brown Bldg. #1 Concord, NH 03301	(603) 271-4680	www.dhhs.state.nh.us/

New Jersey

| Department of Health and Senior Services | Patricia Polanski | New Jersey Division of Senior Affairs, P.O Box 807, Trenton, New Jersey 08625-0807 | (609) 943-3436 | www.state.nj.us/health/senior/index.shtml |

New Mexico

| State Agency on Aging | Lynne Anker-Unnever | La Villa Rivera Building 228 East Palace Avenue Ground Floor Santa Fe, NM 87501 | (505) 827-7640 | www.nmaging.state.nm/us |

New York

| New York State Office for The Aging | Neal E. Lane | 2 Empire State Plaza Albany, NY 12223-1251 | (518) 474-5731 (800) 342-9871 | www.aging.state.ny.us/index.htm |

North Carolina

| Department of Health and Human Services | Dennis Streets | Division of Aging 2101 Mail Service Center Raleigh, NC 27699-2101 | (919) 733-3983 | dennis.streets@ncmail.net www.dhhs.state.nc.us/aging/ |

North Dakota

| Department of Human Services | Linda Wright | Aging Services Division 600 South 2nd Street, Suite 1C Bismarck, ND 58504 | (701) 328-4601 (800) 451-8693 | dhsaging@nd.gov http://www.nd.gov/human services/ |

(continued)

TABLE 13.3 Departments on Aging Contact List in the United States (Continued)

States/Agency Names	Director	Address	Telephone #	E-mail/Web Site Address
Ohio				
Ohio Department of Aging	Merle Grace Kearns	50 West Broad Street-9th Floor Columbus, OH 43215-5928	(614) 466-5500	www.goldenbuckey.com
Oklahoma				
Aging Services Division	Carey Garland	Department of Human Services P.O. Box 25352 312 N.E. 28th Street Oklahoma City, OK 73125	(405) 521-2281	www.okdhs.org
Oregon				
Senior and Disabled Services Division	Bruce Goldberg	500 Summer Street, N.E. 3rd Floor Salem, OR 97301-1073	(503) 945-5811 (800) 282-8096	spd.web@state.or.us www.oregon.gov/DHS/index. shtml
Pennsylvania				
Pennsylvania Department of Aging	Nora Dowd Eisenhower	Commonwealth of Pennsylvania Forum Place 555 Walnut Street, 5th floor Harrisburg, PA 17101-1919	(717) 783-1550	aging@state.pa.us www.aging.state.pa.us/aging

Rhode Island				
Department of Elderly Affairs	Corinne Calise Russo	160 Pine Street Providence, RI 02903-3708	(401) 462-0501 (401) 462-3000	larry@dea.state.ri.us www.dea.state.ri.us/
South Carolina				
Office of Senior and Long Term Care Services	Robert M. Kerr	Dept. of Health and Human Services P.O. Box 8206 Columbia, SC 29202-8206	(803) 898-2501	info@dhhs.state.sc.us. www.dhhs.state.sc.us/
South Dakota				
Office of Adult Services and Aging	Gail Ferris	Richard F. Kneip Building 700 Governors Drive Pierre, SD 57501-2291	(605) 773-3656	DDSInfo@state.sd.us www.state.sd.us/social/asa/index.htm
Tennessee				
Commission on Aging and Disability	Nancy Peace	Andrew Jackson Building 9th floor 500 Deaderick Street Nashville, Tennessee 37243-0860	(615) 741-2056 ext. 134	nancy.peace@state.tn.us www.state.tn.us/comaging/
Texas				
Texas Department of Aging and Disability Services	Adelaide Horn	4900 North Lamar, 4th Floor Austin, TX 78751 - 2316	(800) 252-9240	mail@dads.state.tx.us www.dads.state.tx.us/

(continued)

TABLE 13.3 Departments on Aging Contact List in the United States (Continued)

States/Agency Names	Director	Address	Telephone #	E-mail/Web Site Address
Utah				
Division of Aging & Adult Services	Alan Ormsby	Box 45500, 120 North 200 West Salt Lake City, UT 84145-0500	(801) 538-3910 (877) 424-4640	DAAS@utah.gov www.hsdaas.utah.gov/
Vermont				
Vermont Department of Aging and Disabilities	Patrick Flood	Waterbury Complex 103 South Main Street Waterbury, VT 05671 - 2301	(802) 241-2400	patrick.flood@dail.state.vt.us www.dad.state.vt.us/
Virginia				
Virginia Department for the Aging	Julie Christopher	1600 Forest Avenue, Suite 102 Richmond, VA 23229	(804) 662-9333 (800) 552-3402	aging@vda.virginia.gov www.aging.state.va.us/
Washington				
Aging and Adult Services Administration	Shelly Willis	Department of Social & Health Services P.O. Box 45050 Olympia, WA 98504-5050	(360) 725-2310	OlympiaParentEd@aol.com www.aasa.dshs.wa.gov/

West Virginia

West Virginia Bureau of Senior Services	Sandra K. Vanin, Ed.D	Holly Grove-Building 10 1900 Kanawha Boulevard East Charleston, WV 25305	(304) 558-3317	svanin@boss.state.wv.us www.state.wv.us/senior services/

Wisconsin

Bureau of Aging and Long Term Care Resources	Donna Mc-Dowell	Department of Health and Family Services 1 West Wilson Street Room 450 Madison, WI 53707-7850	(608) 266-2536	rosnefp@dhfs.state.wi.us www.dhfs.wisconsin.gov/

Wyoming

Division on Aging	Beverly Morrow	Wyoming Department of Health 6101 Yellowstone Road, Suite 259B Cheyenne, WY 82002-0710	(307) 777-7986	wyaging@state.wy.us http://dfsweb.stat.wy.us/

Focus Groups

The focus group approach takes advantage of a specific, select group of individuals who can share their insights on a particular phenomena or situation. This approach can be useful to identify gaps in services, or identify potential and innovative solutions, and help with the construction of new survey instruments that can be used in the quantitative approach to data collection. Methodologists would identify the focus group approach as a qualitative method of data collection.

A focus group relies upon a small group of individuals, who are well informed on a specific issue. Generally, it is best to select a manageable number—6 to 12 participants works best. These people are invited to meet at a predesignated time and are selected because of the perspective that they can bring to the table on specific concerns and issues. Subjects are recruited through the use of an invitational letter, asking them to attend a focus group on a specific night. Best results occur when the written invitation is followed up with a verbal invitation. Prior to the meeting, a series of open-ended questions is drafted by the facilitators. Although not necessary, preparing these questions and placing each question on a color-coded sheet of paper, or 3 by 5 inch index card can be a real organizational asset during the focus group. A nominal group technique (NGT) process (Dunham, 1998) can also be used to discuss answers among the group members.

Since there are always people within a group who are more vocal, and who will dominate a conversation, this approach assures that each member of a group will have the opportunity to contribute their thoughts and perspectives. Once all questions have been reviewed, and the participants have had an opportunity to respond in writing, the facilitator generates a discussion, to solicit feedback from the participants on their responses. This can be handled by reviewing each question, one by one, and allowing participants to share responses and highlights from their index cards. This discussion can be tape-recorded, and transcribed following the group discussion. Both the response cards and transcribed notes from the discussion can be used in the process of content analysis. The end results will be a set of transcriptions that then will be used to articulate main themes or issues from the focus group approach. Figure 13.1 provides an example of focus group questions, and an index card prepared in advance of coordinating a focus group.

Environmental Scans

An environment scan is an analysis and evaluation of internal conditions and external data and factors that affect the organization (Government

Cairo Senior Center's Focus Group Questions

1. Please list as many services that you are aware of for seniors (people 60 years of age and older) in Cairo and/or other areas of Alexander county.

2. Happy Days is a Senior Center for Seniors in the community who are over the age of 60 and a resource center for caregivers of older adults. Can you list some reasons why people do and do not use the services?
   Do use   Do not use

3. How can the community be more involved with the Senior Center?

4. What resources or programs would you like to see for seniors in Cairo and Alexander County?

5. What could make this senior center a more vital resource for the community?

6. How do we get the word out to seniors about the Senior Centers and the services they offer?

7. Who are community people not here at this table that we should be talking to about senior services?

8. Is there anything else that you think is important that we should be aware of to help us strengthen these resources for seniors?

FIGURE 13.1   Sample focus group questions.

of Saskatchewan, 2006). The process of an environmental scan makes use of identifying an understanding of the current environment in a particular field or subject area through the identification of key components of the "SWOT" analysis (strengths, weaknesses, opportunities, and threats), using key informants and other resources. The major aim of an environmental scan is to identify trends, gaps, and issues as a basis for future planning.

A SWOT analysis makes use of a process that provides an overview of a community area or organizational network. This SWOT process makes use of a small group discussion process among key stakeholders, who are divided into four specific groups. Each group examines the entities strengths, weaknesses, opportunities, and threats. Once compiled, each of these arenas can be arranged into one complete picture to illustrate your culture or community.

The National Council on Aging in collaboration with three other aging-related organizations—the Center for Healthy Aging, the Home Safety Council, and the Archstone Foundation, created an environmental scan to examine the issue of falls. Their document entitled *Falls Free: Promoting a National Falls Prevention Action Plan* examined the strengths, weaknesses, opportunities, and threats (SWOT) to demonstrate how these selected organizations and agencies were addressing falls prevention in older adults.

Once each of these areas is identified by your key constituents, some of the same basic strategies identified within this chapter can be put into use as strategies to identify the component parts of this needs assessment. Some examples of how these strategies have been incorporated can be found in areas such as chronic care and community-based resources (Branch, 2000); health visiting (Cowley, 2003, 2004) and community health education (Cowley, 2000)

A MODEL FOR NEEDS ASSESSMENT

Key questions or issues to consider in the process of needs assessment can be placed in a model to help conceptualize and organize information. This model includes an examination of some of the questions raised in Figure 13.2.

Step 1: Identify what is the problem.

Step 2: Develop a definition of the problem so you and each stakeholder have a specific and clear understanding of what your terms mean.

Step 3: Identify the extent of the problem through the use of existing and secondary data sources such as vital statistics and service statistics.

Step 4: Identify what key stakeholders tell us about the problem and their perception of the same.

Step 5: Identify what community members perceive about the 'problem" through community forums.

Step 6: Analyze the various perspectives and look for agreement and areas of difference between perspectives.

Step 7: Develop an inventory of what resources are available within the community to deal with the problem and enable resolution.

Step 8: Identify what resources are still necessary in order to bring the issue or problem/concern to resolution.

SUMMARY

A community needs assessment can be an ideal venue to enable the program planner or policy analyst the opportunity to assess the needs of the community, size up the strengths and weaknesses, and identify strategies for moving forward and building resources. This chapter has provided an

- What is the problem?

- What is the extent of the problem?

- What do we know from existing data, such as vital statistics, secondary data and service statistics?

- How is the problem defined?

- What do key stakeholders tell us about the problem?

- What do community forums reveal about the problem?

- Who agrees and who disagrees—stakeholder perspectives.

- What resources are available within the community to deal with the problem or enable resolution?

- What resources are still needed to meet the gap in needs?

FIGURE 13.2   Sample framework for needs assessment.

overview of strategies to build upon to develop a needs assessment. When used in combination with a health behavior framework, one can decide upon needs of a community and attempt to build community support for this resource or policy change through media advocacy and coalition building.

USEFUL WEB SITES

Community Tool Box: http://ctb.ku.edu/tools/en/section_1042.htm
   This Web Site links to a section on conducting needs assessment surveys, which is a part of a Community Toolbox series, developed through the University of Kansas. It provides examples, related topics, tools, and checklists.

NOAA Coastal Services Center: http://www/csc.noaa.gov/needs/
   This Web Site provides an overview of how to develop assessment instruments and questionnaires, enables an understanding of where needs assessments fit in the project development process, and provides some basic steps to the novice on conducting needs assessments.

Handbook for needs assessment in Ohio's Aging Network: http://www.goldenbuckeye.com/infocenter/publications/needsassess.html
This Web Site links the reader to a handbook for needs assessments, which was developed by Ohio's Aging Network. It also provides some sample needs assessment surveys.

Conducting Environmental Scans: http://www.horizen.unc.edu/courses/papers/enviroscan
This Web Site provides a primer for environmental scanning. The text was initially seen as a chapter in a primer for new researchers. It provides the novice with some basic skills in conducting environmental scans.

REFERENCES

Bibb, S. C., & Mary, J. (2001). Nielubowicz essay award. Population-based needs assessment in the design of patient education programs. *Military Medicine, 166*(4), 297–300.

Branch, L. G. (2000). Assessment of chronic care need and use. *Gerontologist, 40*(4), 390–396.

Calderon, J. L. (2000). Focus groups: A qualitative method complementing quantitative research for studying culturally diverse groups. *Education Health, 13*(1), 91–105.

Campbell, S., & Weist, M. D. (2001). Collaboration among the education, mental health, and public health systems to promote youth mental health. *Psychiatry Service, 52*(10), 1348–51.

Cowley, S. (2000). A taxonomy of needs assessment, elicited from a multiple case study of community nursing education and practice. *Journal of Advanced Nursing, 31*(1), 126–134.

Cowley, S. (2003). A structured health needs assessment tool: Acceptability and effectiveness for health visiting. *Journal of Advanced Nursing, 43*(1), 82–92.

Cowley, S. (2004). Structuring health needs assessments: The medicalisation of health visiting. *Social Health Illness, 26*(5), 503–526.

Dunham, D. (1998). *Nominal group technique: A user's guide.* Retrieved August 25, 2005, from http://instruction.bus.wisc.edu/obdemo/readings/ngt/html

Fouad, M. N. (2004). The development of a community action plan to reduce breast and cervical cancer disparities between African-American and White women. *Ethnicity and Disease, 14*(3), 53–60.

Fuller, J. (2001). Use of community health needs assessment for regional planning in country South Australia. *Australian Journal of Rural Health, 9*(1), 12–27.

Government of Saskatchewan. (2006). *Making life better.* Retrieved October 17, 2006, from http://www.gov.sk.ca/finance/accountability/2006/keyterms.htm

Jordan, J. (2002). Health needs assessment and needs-led health service change: a survey of projects involving public health doctors. *Journal of Health Services Research and Policy, 7*(2), 71–80.

Kirst-Ashman, K., & Hall, G. (2002). *Understanding generalist practice.* Pacific Grove, CA: Brooks/Cole Publishers.

Kretzmann, J. P., & McKnight, J. (1993). *Building communities from the inside out: A path toward finding and mobilizing a community's assets.* Evanston, IL: Center for Urban Affairs and Policy Research.

Shadel, B. N. (2002). Bioterrorism risk perceptions and educational needs of public health professionals before and after September 11, 2001: A national needs assessment survey. *Journal of Public Health Management Practice, 10*(4), 282–289.

Thompson, A. H. (2001). A social problem index for Canada. *Canadian Journal of Psychiatry, 46*(1), 45–51.

Witkin, B. R., & Altschuld, J. W. (1995). *Planning and conducting needs assessments: A practical guide.* Thousand Oaks, CA: Sage Publications.

CHAPTER 14

From Tools to Vision

USING TOOLS AND STRATEGIES TO REACH YOUR VISION

At this point, we have introduced a number of tools and strategies. It seems prudent to consider how to use these tools to reach one's vision: a vision for policy development or a vision for program development. The purpose of this chapter is to review the various tools and strategies, along with policies that have been addressed thus far, and integrate these issues and skills with one's vision for either program planning or policy development.

Although some of the concepts presented may have been familiar to the reader, there may be issues or concepts that are completely new. The key becomes how to use these skills and integrate them into one's repertoire of skills for policy development, policy analysis, or program planning/development. What mechanisms can one realistically develop, in an effort to showcase gaps within the current existing public policy, or existing programs and services. How would we use these measures to develop a policy brief, a white paper, or a position paper, or media artifacts to showcase an issue? How do we use these strategies to bring our vision to fruition?

First, when considering a white paper, or when considering writing testimony of any sort, it is very important to consider who the audience will be, and within this context, examine the philosophical paradigms of each of these individuals. It may be helpful to map this out on paper, as part of a strategy. Once the key players have been mapped out, identify what you will anticipate each of these key players' philosophical paradigm may in fact be, and prepare yourself to ask for support for your position. Once you have a clear picture of their perspective, prepare yourself with data to address their concerns.

Second, build a case for the need for revision of an existing policy or program/service. Earlier in this book we discussed evidence-based policy development and presented several sources of data. These sources can provide a useful backdrop to support renewed initiatives.

Third, know how existing legislation or program guidelines actually work, and what has been signed into legislation. This is very helpful when you are attempting to showcase the need for changes.

Last, build a short presentation addressing your concerns that can be used when you meet with a legislator or program director. This can be in the form of a brief, or one-page fact sheet. It can be based upon a white paper or legislative analysis that you have developed previously. Samples of media artifacts to fulfill this purpose are presented in Chapter 1.

FROM TOOLS TO POLICY DEVELOPMENT

Policy development is a skill, which improves over time. When engaging in policy development, remember to always befriend your local legislator, regardless of party affiliation. If you are a known entity, you are more likely to reap success than if you are a one-time caller. Once you have established a relationship, then you have some inroads, which will make the process much more smooth when you actually have an issue of concern, or policy revisions that you would like to see implemented.

When building support for a particular bill introduced into the legislature, use both your skills from needs assessment and coalition building to garner support. The needs assessment data will be helpful when arguing for a need or service. Building a coalition pursues the issue with a unified and stronger voice from a range of stakeholders.

FROM TOOLS TO PROGRAM DEVELOPMENT

When considering program development, all that has been previously stated related to policy development still holds true. Some additional strategies or tools to use at this juncture include the health behavior models. Keeping in mind the stages of change, and which stage a person/ community may be attuned with, will provide a multitude of results. In addition, these tools will enable the program planner to target the intervention so that resources are maximized, and to enable minimal inputs.

SUMMARY

This chapter has attempted to integrate the theories and concepts presented up to this point in the book.

PART IV

Program and Services: Realities and Visions

This last part of the text outlines specific programmatic areas that flow from aging policies, and specific components that flow from federally mandated policies. Each chapter will be written with the same basic outline: a current profile of the issues (incidence and prevalence), an overview of the programs, specific features and strengths of the programs, gaps and areas for development, model programs, challenges for the future, and useful Web sites. The tools and concepts presented earlier will be integrated and woven throughout each of the chapters.

CHAPTER 15

Long-Term Care and Home- and Community-Based Care

A CURRENT PROFILE OF LONG-TERM CARE AND COMMUNITY-BASED CARE NEEDS

A continuum of services exists within the long-term care and community care settings. Within each of these settings, the standards of care may differ, the expectations of consumer functional status differs, and payment schemes may differ. In this chapter we will discuss community-based care options such as home health, seniors congregate living, assisted living options, skilled nursing facilities, and long-term care facilities. Although differences may exist from state to state relative to who qualifies for these options, and when they qualify, these will be discussed in some detail specifically providing an overview of these as options for care management of older adults.

A common misconception about nursing home care is that the majority of older people will end up living in a nursing home. In fact, only about 5% of older adults actually reside in a nursing home setting. In addition, the rate of individuals residing in nursing homes between 1985 and 1999 is on the decline overall (54 per 1,000 in 1985 as compared to 43 per 1,000 in 1999). The oldest old, people 85 years of age and older, have also dramatically decreased in terms of nursing home census. In 1985, 220 per 1,000 people of this age group resided in nursing homes, while in 1999, this same figure dropped to 183 per 1,000. Figure 15.1 provides an overview of these data and a comparison between age groups and between 1985 and 1999 (CDC, NCHS, 2004).

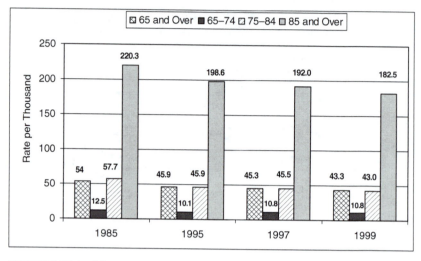

FIGURE 15.1   Nursing home utilization.
Notes: Data refer to rate per 1,000 of nursing home residence, age 65 and older, by age group, 1985, 1995, 1997, and 1999. Data refer to individuals living in long-term care facilities, rather than personal care, foster care or domiciliary care homes.
Source: Centers for Disease Control and Prevention, National Center for Health Statistics, National Nursing Home Survey

It is anticipated that one of the main reasons people seek residential care in nursing home settings is because they can no longer handle tasks such as activities of daily living. As illustrated in Table 15.1, nursing home residents over a 15-year time period have become progressively more functionally impaired. One can compare males in 1985 to males living in nursing home settings in 1999. In 1985, 63% of the males living in nursing homes required assistance with four to six activities of daily living. In 1999, this figure jumped to 74% for males. Females, in comparison, were more functionally impaired than males, and in 1985, 71% of women in nursing home settings required assistance with four to six activities of daily living, as compared to 78% in 1999. The population currently living in nursing homes with one to three activity of daily living needs has also decreased both for men and women by nearly 5% over the past 15 years (i.e., 29% in 1985 for men as compared to 21% in 1999; and 25% for women in 1985 and 20% in 1999).

While fewer than 5% of Medicare enrollees age 65 and older lived in long-term care settings (as of 2003), as people age they are more inclined to live in long-term care facilities and less likely to remain in

TABLE 15.1   Need for Help With Activities of Daily Living Within Care Facilities

Year	Gender	No ADLs	1–3 ADLs	4–6 ADLs
1985	Male	8.8	28.8	62.5
	Female	3.8	25.3	70.9
1995	Male	3.0	25	72
	Female	3.8	25.3	70.9
1997	Male	5.0	25.7	74.4
	Female	1.8	20.4	77.8
1999	Male	5.0	20.7	74.3
	Female	2.4	19.6	78.0

Notes: Numbers represent percentages. The six activities of daily living (ADLs) included are bathing, dressing, eating, toileting, and transferring in and out of bed or chairs. Requiring assistance refers to assistance from nursing home facility staff. Help received from family members or friends is not included. Data refer to individuals living in long-term care facilities, rather than personal care, foster care or domiciliary care homes.
Source: Centers for Disease Control and Prevention, National Center for Health Statistics, National Nursing Home Survey

traditional community-based settings. According to the Medicare Beneficiary Survey (2003) nearly all adults 65 to 74 years of age (98%) still remained active in traditional community settings; however, 93% remained in traditional community settings between ages 75 and 84 years of age. Conversely, the oldest old, 85 years of age or older, have more health care needs, and only 75% remain in traditional community settings, while 8% remain in community housing with services and 17% reside in long-term care facilities. This is a dramatic difference since we see 17% of the oldest old living in long-term care facilities as compared to 5% of people in the 75–84 age group category. Table 15.2 provides an illustration of these trends.

Despite the fact that older adults today have greater care needs, more people with needs for help with instrumental activities of daily living or activities of daily living are remaining in the community with supports. Although it appears that community-based, residential options may be cost-effective (Hebert et al., 1999; Levine, 1999), many of these options have also led to an industry geared towards assistive care and home health supports (Albrecht, 1992; Callahan, 1998; Coughlin, 1999; Gottlieb & Caro, 1999; Kane, 1999). These supports can include home health care (Bishop, 1999). Although only 59% of older adults, who have no activity

TABLE 15.2   Medicare Enrollees Living in Residential Services

Type of facility	Age group			
	65 and over	65–74 yrs	75–84 yrs	85 and over
Long term care facility	4.4	1.0	4.5	17
Community housing	2.5	.9	2.6	8
Traditional community	93.1	98.1	92.9	75

Notes: Numbers are reported as percentages. Community housing with services applies to respondents who reported they lived in retirement communities or apartments, senior citizen housing, continuing care retirement facilities, assisted living facilities, staged living communities, board and care facilities/home and other similar situations AND who reported that they had access to one or more of the following services through their place of residence; meal preparation, cleaning or housekeeping services, laundry services, and help with medications. Respondents were asked about access to these services but not whether they actually used the services. Long-term care facilities were defined as those that were certified by Medicare or Medicaid; or has 3 or more beds, and is licensed as a nursing home or other long term care facility and will provide at least one personal care service, or 24 hour, 7 day per week supervision by a caregiver. Data refer to Medicare enrollees.
Sources: Centers for Medicare and Medicaid Services & Medicare Current Beneficiary Survey

limitations, currently reside in the community, the remaining 41% reside in the community with some sort of supports including 9% with three or more ADL limitations, 18% with 1–2 limitations, and 13% with an IADL limitation only. Fewer than one-third of people who remain in their homes with some housing services have no problems with activities of daily living or instrumental activities of daily living. Fewer than a quarter of all people living in a community-based setting (22%) have problems with IADLs only, and 28% have problems with one-two ADL functions who live in the community with supports. Despite impairment, 19% of people with three or more ADL limitations still live in the community with some supports. Figure 15.2 illustrates residential services and showcases that individuals living in long-term care facilities are the most debilitated with two-thirds (66%) having three or more ADL limitations. Hence, it should be noted that people with activity limitations are remaining in the community longer, and home-health supports have been instrumental in enabling people to remain in the community.

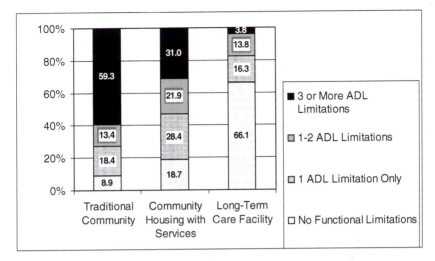

FIGURE 15.2   Percentage of people with functional limitations by residential setting.

Notes: Activities for Daily Living (ADL)'s refer to difficulty performing or inability to perform bathing, dressing, eating, getting in/out of chairs, walking or using the toilet. Instrumental Activities of Daily Living (IADLs) refer to doing light or heavy housework, using the telephone, meal preparation, shopping and managing money.

Community housing with services applies to respondents who reported they lived in retirement communities or apartments, senior citizen housing, continuing care retirement facilities, assisted living facilities, staged living communities, board and care facilities/home and other similar situations AND who reported that they had access to one or more of the following services through their place of residence; meal preparation, cleaning or housekeeping services, laundry services, and help with medications. Respondents were asked about access to these services but not whether they actually used the services. Long-term care facilities were defined as those that were certified by Medicare or Medicaid; or has 3 or more beds, and is licensed as a nursing home or other long term care facility and will provide at least one personal care service, or 24 hour, 7 day per week supervision by a caregiver.

Target population: Medicare enrollees

Source: Centers for Medicaid Services, Medicare Current Beneficiary Survey

Figure 15.3 illustrates the nature of people who remain in the community. Between 1984 and 1999 there has been a slight decrease in the number of Medicare recipients needing informal care only (69% as compared to 66%). The number of people requiring formal care only has doubled from 5% to 9% between 1984 and 1999. Given that many people require supports to remain in their homes, it seems essential to examine what supports are available federally through the Older Americans Act, and what services are available through state-based sources. In addition, it also seems prudent to examine what options are available for housing.

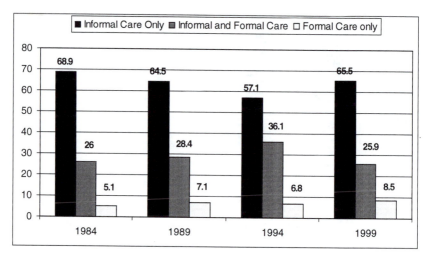

FIGURE 15.3   Caregiving and assistive device use.

Notes: Refers to the distribution of Medicare enrollees age 65 and over receiving personal care for a chronic disability, by type of care, 1984, 1989, 1994, and 1999. Informal care refers to unpaid help that is provided to a person with a chronic disability living in the community. Formal care refers to paid help or assistance.

Target population: Refers to Medicare enrollees living in the community who report that they receive personal care from a paid or unpaid assistant for a chronic disability.

Source: National Long Term Care Survey

Thus, although as a society, we are living longer and placing demands on the community by remaining in the community, it becomes apparent that there is a current need to ensure that programs are available within communities to meet the housing needs of older adults. In addition, it is imperative to understand the current opportunities and options for community-based living. This next section outlines some specific options for community-based living, which include part of the continuum of care.

AN OVERVIEW OF THE PROGRAMS TO MEET HOUSING NEEDS OF OLDER ADULTS

Senior Apartments

Senior apartments are a good choice for older adults who can take care of themselves. Usually, these apartments are developed like standard apartments but differ in that they have an age restriction. Some apartments are also equipped with assistive technology such as hand rails and pull cords.

Overall these apartments are great if one needs a community of elderly neighbors without the hassles of a larger home to manage.

Senior apartments are found in many communities; some are under federal housing guidelines and will only accept low-income seniors, but most are privately owned. They can vary in terms of services but typically offer apartment living and services designed specifically for independent active seniors 55 and older. Since many of these residences are designed for active seniors, most do not offer meal service, housekeeping, or medical assistance.

Senior apartment complexes are usually located near senior centers, parks, shopping malls, golf courses, and public transportation. Many offer van services along with monthly road trips to shows and casinos. Many senior apartment complexes are subsidized by the Dept. of Housing Urban Development (HUD).

Senior age-restricted apartments are usually for those 55 or 62+ and follow HUD regulations that allow for such "age discrimination." If restrictions are 55+, at least one person in the apartment must be at least 55 and the apartment community must have no more than 20% of all residents under the age of 55. If they are 62+, then *all* residents must be at least 62. Exceptions are made by HUD regulations for renters who are under the minimum age, if they are handicapped.

Categories of Senior Apartments

The three pricing categories of apartments (although all may not be available in any one market) are:

- market rate
- above market rate, luxury rentals
- affordable

Market rate units are just that. They offer unit size and numbers of bedrooms and baths as non-age-restricted rentals in the area at a competitive monthly rate, or occasionally 10–15% under general occupancy market-rate rents. The senior orientation of the age-restricted community may, however, offer different amenities and other advantages geared to the needs and preferences of seniors.

Above market rate, luxury rentals are a relatively new phenomenon for the age-restricted market. We see them appealing to the affluent senior wanting a home in a second city, or wanting to be free of maintenance without giving up luxuries. Some high-end age-restricted properties definitely offer "snob" appeal.

Affordable apartments for seniors (sometimes 55+, more often 62+) are in high demand and short supply. Social, cultural, and medical changes have certainly contributed to the need. Contributing factors are:

- predominance of women among the 65+ population and their lower retirement income
- high divorce rates among women now 55 to 80
- women outliving husbands resulting in lowered retirement income
- unplanned longevity leading to outliving one's financial resources

Affordable apartments have been created by government programs since the 1930s. What is defined as affordable in one community may not match the definition of affordable in another community. Housing is "affordable" if one pays no more than 30% of their monthly income for rent and utilities. The government relates affordability to the county median income.

Programs that provide opportunities for affordable housing are structured or defined by regulations from federal, county, or city government legislation.

- "Vouchers" enable a qualified recipient to rent a market-rate home or apartment and the voucher assures the landlord that the renter will pay 30% of his or her monthly income toward the rent and the difference between that portion and the market-rate rent will come from the government entity granting the voucher.
- Bonds may be through city or county redevelopment programs, and use the money raised from the bond sale to fund and subsidize specific development of housing for lower-income people. Bonds may specify what percent of the median income someone must have to qualify to rent in their building. A person may be restricted to making no more than 50% of the median income in the county. Perhaps the funding of the complex specifies that a person can make no more than 120% of median income. The funding is specifically tied to the complex, or specific units that are "affordable."
- Funding can also come from grants that are community, government, or federally based. The grant money functions similarly to bond money, designating percent of county median income at the time of the grant.
- Tax credits are another way that the federal government may encourage development of affordable housing, by awarding tax

credits (money deducted from a company's federal tax obligation) in exchange for developing apartments within restrictive guidelines. Recently properties have been developed to offer affordable apartments that combine tax credits, grants, and bond measures.

The most commonly-known rental vouchers are Section 8 vouchers, which can provide benefits to a qualified renter. They provide rent subsidies so tenants who hold them do not pay more than 30% of their adjusted gross income for rent.

Congregate Housing and multi-level campuses offer what they call independent living. They offer services for those in their own apartments. These services may be optional and charged separately above rent. Shared meals, transportation, and housekeeping are among the most common services provided. This housing type differs from the conventional notion of an apartment and therefore is defined separately as congregate housing or assisted living since that is the one common element for multi-level offerings. The independent living offering is most appropriate for those not able or willing to continue living alone. Recently senior apartment buildings have added services to retain their frail and aging residents.

Assisted Living

Assisted living is an industry term for multifamily housing with congregate and personal care services. Assisted living goes by many names, including personal care, residential care, congregate care, and, in some areas, board and care. The services offered vary widely but frequently include as core services meals, housekeeping, transportation, and often some assistance with laundry, grooming, medications management, and other functions of daily living (Jurkowski, Kemp & Patterson, 2004). Special care units in some facilities care for individuals with cognitive impairment and respiratory assistance needs. Unless an assisted living facility is a component of a continuing care or "life-care" community, it does not offer the health care services of a nursing facility. For safety reasons most states require residents to self-evacuate their personal living quarters (with or without ambulatory equipment) in the event of an emergency.

The federal government does not establish standards for assisted living as it does for nursing homes, which participate in the federal Medicare program. Most states license and regulate assisted living residences and an increasing number of states place Medicaid-eligible adults in assisted living residences as an alternative to traditional placement in a nursing home. This trend leads many to speculate that the federal government will become increasingly involved in setting minimum standards of care in residences electing to participate in the federal–state Medicaid program. National associations representing selective areas of the industry have increased self-regulation efforts, motivated in part to delay federal oversight and regulation. The number of older adults living in assisted living is estimated to be between 600,000 and 1 million, with as many as 50,000 receiving Medicaid support, compared with 1.6 million older adults in nursing home beds including 1 million with Medicaid assistance.

Board and Care

Board and care homes are smaller in scale than assisted living facilities. They provide a room, meals, and help with daily activities. Some states will allow some nursing services to be provided, but these homes are not medical facilities. These homes may be unlicensed, and even licensed homes are infrequently monitored by the state.

Board and care is offered in a homelike setting with medical care for 2 to 10 residents. Some are converted/adapted single-family homes. The number of residents is a function of zoning regulations, which limit the number of unrelated occupants that can live in a single residence.

Foster Care

Foster care is sometimes limited to only two residents. Most designated converted homes offering care are allowed only five or six residents. Those that appear to be converted homes, but offer more beds, are usually licensed as assisted living residences.

A Comparison Between Board and Care, Residential Care, and Foster Care

A Board and care, residential care, or foster care home may be able to provide residents the services found in an assisted living facility, a skilled nursing home, or, in some cases, an Alzheimer's facility, depending on the goal and licensing of the individual facility. Many board and care facilities have their own specialty or emphasis, and the intensity or type of care needed by residents within a home may be similar. For instance, some specialize in care of seniors in the middle stages of Alzheimer's. Another may only take early-stage Alzheimer's residents. Another home may only be licensed to accept those mildly impaired mentally, or needing "custodial" help (reminding, meal service, laundry, housekeeping help, and driving services). In many states they would need to be licensed to hand out medications, assist with bathing, or care for a patient who cannot turn themselves in bed. Since there are so many board and care homes, hundreds in a populated county, it is also unrealistic to think that licensing can monitor them all.

Continuing Care Retirement Community

A continuing care retirement community is a gate-secured campus offering residential services ranging from independent living and assisted living to nursing home care, all on one campus. It usually provides a written contract between the resident and the community, which offers a continuum of housing, services, and health care services, commonly all on one campus. CCRC residents enjoy an independent lifestyle with the knowledge that if they become sick or frail, their needs will continue to be met. In general, residents are expected to move into the community while they are still independent and able to take care of themselves.

Continuing Care Accreditation Commission is the Consumer's Report of the CCRC world. They rate CCRC facilities based on their excellence, integrity, volunteerism, credibility, innovation, and independence.

Some states support legislation for older adults who wish to stay in their homes by restructuring the delivery of services to include home-based services as well as institutional care. Such restructuring impacts all aspects of service, including the provision of housing, health, financial, and supportive services for older people, and can include a nursing home conversion program established by state departments of Public Health and Public Aid. This program approach would reduce reliance on nursing homes by Medicaid, the federal-state program that pays the health care costs for the poor. Savings from this effort could then be reallocated to a broader array of options for home-based or community-based services to older adults (Albrecht, 1992; Sutton & Dejong, 1998; Wheatley, DeJong, & Sutton, 1996).

STRATEGIES FOR REMAINING IN ONE'S HOME

Home Equity Conversion

Reverse mortgages are a type of home equity conversion involving payments to, rather than from, the homeowner. This special type of loan guarantees older homeowners monthly cash advances or occasional lump sums that do not require repayment until the homeowner sells the home, moves away, or dies.

Sale Leaseback

Sale leaseback is when the home is sold to a third party (often the adult child of the homeowner) who immediately leases it back to the seller (older homeowner) under an agreement of life tenancy. (*Note:* Anyone considering Home equity conversion should discuss their intentions with trusted advisors who are knowledgeable about these programs.)

MAINTENANCE PROGRAMS

Home Maintenance and Repair

Programs are designed to help older persons to remain in their own homes or apartments by making repairs to the home at little or no cost to the residents. "Repairs" can include yard work, painting, electrical or plumbing repairs, repairs to steps or porches, or the addition of adaptive devices for persons with disabilities. Some of these programs are supported by federal subsidies; others are private initiatives.

Illinois Home Weatherization Assistance Program

This program is designed to help low-income residents have more energy-efficient homes. Typical kinds of weatherization include sealing cracks with weather-stripping and caulk, insulating attics and walls, and repairing windows and doors. Furnace work may also be provided. Weatherization services are free to households that are eligible for the Low Income Home Energy Assistance Program (LIHEAP); to those who have an occupant receiving Supplemental Security Income (SSI), Temporary Assistance for Needy Families (TANF), or Aid to Aged, Blind and Disabled (AABD), or to those with specified annual incomes. Renters may be assisted if they are eligible, but a 50% landlord contribution for weatherization work is required.

ISSUES FACING LONG-TERM AND COMMUNITY-BASED CARE FOR OLDER ADULTS

A growing number of issues face long-term and community-based care facilities for older adults. These issues will be discussed in brief in the next few pages. Although they address shortcomings in long-term care facilities, skilled nursing care facilities, and additional community settings, the issues are by no means exhaustive, and probably only scratch the surface of issues to be faced. Such choices are vital for the healthy and productive functioning of older adults (Greenwald, 1999).

Long-Term Care Facilities

Long-term care facilities within the next decade will face challenges related to the level of care required for facilities to provide to individual residents. As the population of individuals who enter into care within these facilities grows more frail and more needy in terms of care due to the increased nature of functional debilitation, facilities will both need to be better equipped to meet these needs and be prepared to work within a system of financing that may compromise care. Increasingly, these facilities will also see more cases that will require specialized dementia care units and Alzheimer's care units to support the care needs of their residents. Long-term care facilities will also be challenged with culture change issues that will push them to move towards a home-based environment rather than an institutional setting. These culture changes may also include a culture that will need to accommodate for people that have habitually embraced a substance-use culture (i.e., older adults who were a product of the 1960s drug subculture). Movements are afoot within nursing homes across the country to build a so-called homelike and comfortable atmosphere for residents.

Finally, the long-term care movement may be also subjected to care for people who have been discharged from penal systems, or who have served life sentences but are now frail and elderly. Although many states currently have laws on their books that deny or defer admission to these individuals, shrinking resources in the future may challenge the current system of long-term care facilities.

Assisted Living Facilities

Assisted living facilities will be on the rise over the next decade, and without any oversight through accreditation bodies, may run the risk of providing uneven quality of care. Moreover, it appears that an aim of the assisted living movement could be to capitalize on older adults who have resources and can afford to pay for care; hence the marketplace and business community may be dictating how these facilities are operated as opposed to a long-term care system.

Community-Based Care

Community-based care options will be called to expand and challenge traditional strategies for doing business. An increased emphasis on home modifications and repair programs will also take place, as more people want to remain in their own homes with some help in home maintenance. A second challenge will be to locate and train home health workers to meet the growing needs of older adults, especially seniors living in rural communities. Training for home health aides will also become critical since these workers are virtually the eyes and ears for care coordinators and family members. In the future, we can expect that we will see an expansion of training opportunities for the home-health or home support worker. These training opportunities will ultimately be helpful and beneficial to the older adult, since home-health workers will hopefully be more astute and attuned to medical and social issues that older adults present and will be prepared to more clearly articulate these issues in behavioral terms.

Consumer-Directed Home Help and Care Options

Consumer-directed home help and care options will be in greater demand over the next decade. In order to meet baby boomers' demand for these options, state departments on aging will need to look at new strategies or ways to finance and build options within their continuing care programs to meet these needs. Consumer-directed care options will also span not only older adults but will also be sought after by people with disabilities (Sutton & DeJong, 1998).

People With Disabilities Requiring Community-Based Care

Increasingly, people with disabilities will challenge the institutional model paradigm traditionally exercised by long-term care facilities. The independent living paradigm (DeJong, 1979) set the stage for people with disabilities to be functional within the least restricted environment. The cash and counseling models of consumer directed care will become a model sought after by people with disabilities who want to have control of their care and be empowered by their ability to manage their own care.

OPPRESSED GROUPS AND VISIBLE MINORITIES

Oppressed groups and visible minorities will pose demands upon the current systems to be culturally relevant and to assure that policies are in place within facilities to meet the needs of individuals requiring care. Examples will include the gay/lesbian groups of elders who may request opportunities for intimate expression within long-term care settings, within environments that may not necessarily be comfortable with addressing sexual orientations other than their own. A second example may include addressing the cultural needs of ethnically diverse populations, whether that may be via religion, cuisine, or meeting rooms to meet the family needs of these groups. Last, community care options to meet the needs of people with disabilities will also need to be considered, as an alternative to the traditional placements in nursing home care.

SUMMARY

In summary, this chapter has examined the current status of the long-term care system, sought to provide different residential models of care for people as they require community-based settings or settings with supports, and examined issues that will face the long-term and community-based care settings in the future.

REFERENCES

Albrecht, G. L. (1992). *The disability business: Rehabilitation in America.* CA: Sage.

Bishop, C. (1999). Efficiency of home care: Notes from an economic approach to resource allocation. *Journal of Aging and Health, 11*(3), 341–359.

Callahan, J. J. (1998). Social policy in the age of the market. *The Public Policy and Ageing Report, 9*(2), 13–15.

Centers for Disease Control and Prevention, National Center for Health Statistics. (2004). *National nursing home study.* Bethesda, MD: Government Printing Office.

Coughlin, J. F. (1999). Setting a national policy agenda for technology and healthy ageing. *The Public Policy and Ageing Report, 10*(1), 1–6.

De Jong, G. (1979). Independent living: From social movements to analytic paradigm. *Archives of Physical Medicine and Rehabilitation, 60,* 435–446.

Greenwald, J. (1999, August 30). Elder care: Making the right choice. *Time,* 52–56.

Gottlieb, A., & Caro, F. (1999). Extending the effectiveness of home-care through low-cost adaptive equipment. *The Public Policy and Aging Report, 10*(1), 13–15.

Hebert, R., Dubuc, N., Buteau, M., Derosiers, J., Bravo, G., Trottier, L., et al. (1999). *Resources and costs associated with disability of elderly people living at home and in the institutions.* Presented at the American Health Services Research 16th Annual Meeting, Chicago, IL.

Jurkowski, E., Kemp, M., & Patterson, S. (2004). Assisted living, social work practice & the elderly. In M. Holosko & M. Feit (Eds.), *Social work practice and the elderly* (364–387). Toronto: Canadian Scholar's Press.

Kane, M. D. (1999) Examining the efficiency of home care. *Journal of Aging and Health, 11*(3), 322–340.

Levine, C. (1999). Home sweet hospital: The nature and limits of private responsibilities for home care. *Journal of Aging and Health, 11*(3), 341–359.

Sutton, J., & DeJong, G. (1998). Managed care and people with disabilities: Framing the issues. *Archives of Physical Medicine and Rehabilitation, 79,* 1312–1316.

Wheatley, B., DeJong, G., & Sutton, J. (1996). How managed care is transforming American health care: A survey of rehabilitation providers in leading markets. *The Georgetown Public Policy Review, 1*(2), 134–147.

United States Department of Health and Human Services, Centers for Medicare and Medicaid Services. (2003). *Medicare beneficiary survey, 2003.* Retrieved June 15, 2007, from www.cms.hhs.gov/center/hha.asp

Mental Health and Substance Abuse Programs: Services and Issues

A CURRENT MENTAL HEALTH PROFILE OF OLDER ADULTS IN THE UNITED STATES

It is predicted that disability due to mental illness in individuals over 65 will become a major public health problem in the near future due to demographic changes (USDHHS, 1999). This problem is magnified in rural communities because of the various barriers that play a role in accessing care for rural residents. (New Freedom Commission on Mental Health, 2004). Consequently, the solution to the burgeoning issue may not rest with professionals, but the voice of the consumers themselves, older adults.

WHAT IS MENTAL HEALTH?

According to the former U.S. Surgeon General, David Satcher, mental health is "[t]he successful performance of mental functions and the ability to be productive in one's life, to have positive relationships, to have the ability to deal with adversity; and to be flexible in a changing environment" (USDHHS, 1999). Hence, if this definition is considered, the notion of mental health and aging will take into consideration how people adapt to the changes in their life and the tasks of late life. Mental health intervention should focus on recognition that people are somewhere on the continuum and need assistance to move forward. Successful interventions will require the partnership of the older adult, physician, and/or social service provider.

Despite the thought that all older adults have the same needs, several researchers and social scientists have made the distinction between the young old, middle old, and old old. The needs and issues may not be similar for the three different categories of older adults. Bernice Neugarten, a well-known developmental psychologist argued (1984) that the young old are vigorous and competent, while the old old suffer from physical, mental, or social losses and require a range of supportive and restorative health services. Neugarten also argued that ageist attitudes prevail in the mental health system and cause a challenge in providing adequate services. Given these premises, what are the perspectives towards mental health services, older adults and physicians/providers of services?

Mental Health, Older Adults, and Physicians

Sarkisian, Hays, Berry, and Mangione (2001) studied expectations regarding aging among older adults and physicians who cared for older adults. They found that physicians perceived that their domains of concern were physical function, cognitive function, social function, pain, and sexual function. In contrast, they found that older adults differed in their expectations and areas of concern. The older adults were concerned about issues related to mental health such as anxiety, emotional well-being, happiness, sleep, and their own mortality.

Kaplan, Adamek, and Martin (2001) studied the knowledge and attitude of physicians related to assessing mental health issues for older adults. Their findings suggest that the physician's own confidence in assessing depression was the strongest predictor in whether assessment, diagnosis, and treatment would occur. Hence, the older adult who may be feeling depressed may or may not receive treatment, despite their requests, and treatment would be largely determined by the physician's own comfort level.

The attitudes, knowledge, and behavior of family physicians regarding depression in older adults was studied by Gallo, Ryan, and Ford (1999). They found that physicians recognized the value of treatment for older adults; however, they also found that physicians' intervention of choice was medication-based. Physicians did not see the value of psychotherapy or "talk therapy." These authors also found a need for stronger collaboration between the physician and practitioner and older adult in treatment.

The goals of caregivers and clinicians were examined by Bogardus (2001) to determine if there was a difference in the goal related to mental health (MH) treatment by each group. They found that there were clear differences in goals between caregivers and physicians. Caregivers were interested in behavioral and emotional health, while physicians were interested in day-to-day physical functioning of the caregiver or patient.

Mackenzie, Gekoski, and Knox (1999) examined whether family physicians treated mental disorders in older patients differently than in their younger patients. The findings suggested that there were differences that may contribute to lower use of mental health services by older adults. Findings also suggest that physicians reported being less prepared to deal with older adults.

Patterns of care for depressed older adults in a large HMO were studied by Unutzer et al. (1996). They found older adults were less likely than younger adults to receive more than two primary care visits for depression. Their findings also suggest that older adults were less likely to receive specialty mental health care following antidepressant medications.

Other findings that suggest barriers to treatment for older adults have been identified by several researchers. Older adults are more likely to seek treatment from physicians than mental health agencies due to the labels and stigma. Older adults are under-represented in treatment for mental health issues (Bane, 1997). Rural communities face additional barriers to treatment, which include stigma, lack of trained professionals, and barriers of availability and accessibility (Bane, 1997).

Mental Health, Older Adults, and Social Services

The differences in service use between urban and rural services for memory-related problems in older adults were studied by Chumbler, Cody, Booth, and Beck (2001). This group of researchers found that rural residents were more likely to seek treatment from their primary care physician and these same rural residents were less likely to seek help from mental health specialists. Interestingly, travel difficulties and lack of providers seem to account for the differences.

Bane (1997) examined issues of case management in rural settings for older adults. In his work, he found that older adults are underrepresented as recipients of mental health services. In addition, he found that barriers such as stigma and lack of access could be broken down by case managers. Finally, Bane concluded that a key role for case managers included outreach and education in order to break down these barriers.

Mickus, Colenda, and Hogan (2000) examined the general awareness of mental health services of the older adult population. They found that people over 65 would initially seek treatment from the primary care provider. In addition, their findings corroborated with the work of Chumbler et al. (2001) and Bane (1997). They found that older adults in rural communities were not likely to seek care from mental health providers, nor seek counseling or educational care.

THE EPIDEMIOLOGY OF MENTAL HEALTH ISSUES OF OLDER ADULTS

How prevalent are mental health conditions for older adults? Is there cause for concern? Actually, over 40% of older adults may suffer from some form of psychiatric condition, as reported in the U.S. Surgeon General's Report on Mental Health (USDHHS, 1999). These may take the form of any anxiety disorder (11%), simple phobias (7.3%), severe cognitive impairments (6.6%), any mood disorder (4.4%), a major depressive episode (3.8%), or agoraphobia (4.1%) (USDHHS, 1999).

The incidence and prevalence of psychiatric disorders is similar between urban and rural centers (Kessler et al, 1994); however, people residing in rural communities have much more limited access to services (IRHA, 2006; USDHHS, 2000; Lambert, 1995). Furthermore, rural residents are less likely to have financial or insured benefits to access mental health services (Mueller, Kashinath, & Ullrich, 1997). In addition, programs to specifically train and promote the placement of rural mental health professionals are not available, and those that do exist are often not located in rural areas (Bird, Dempsey, & Hartley, 2001).

Depression in Older Adults

Despite the popular perception that mental health is not a major issue within both urban and rural communities, it is not clear that we have an accurate reading on the full extent of depression and other symptoms of psychopathology among adults in our aging population. According to the Centers for Disease Control (CDC)'s Trends in Health and Aging, only 2.8% of the population of people 65 years of age and older visited a mental health professional in the year preceding 2004. When this figure was age adjusted, it was reported that 3% sought help from a mental health professional in the 65–74 age group, as compared to 2.9% in the 75 and older age group. Females were more likely to seek treatment than males. These data are amplified by the data found in the Health and Retirement study, which utilized the Center for Epidemiologic Study Depression Scale (C-ESD) to screen for depression within an elderly population. These data found that 17.8% of women, and 10.9% men were screened with clinically relevant depressive symptoms. When age adjusted, it was found that the 65–69 year-old age group showed 15.6% women and 9.7% men to be displaying symptoms; within 70–74 year-olds, 17.6% women as compared to 9.6% men; within the 75–79 year-olds 18.2% women as compared to 9.9% men; within the 80–84 year-olds, 18.1% women as compared to 15% men and within the 85 year-old and over age group 21.9% women as compared to 14.9% men. Figure 16.1 illustrates and compares these prevalence rates.

Ironically, a problem with diagnosis is that diagnosis usually is conducted through the *Diagnostic and Statistical Manual of Mental Disorders* (DSM-IVR) (American Psychiatric Association, 2000), symptoms of major depression, and an individual would have to have at least four of the eight behavioral criteria for a sustained period of time (at least 2 months) in order to be diagnosed with a major depression. Since individuals who are older adults often do not meet the full criteria for major depression, a new diagnostic entity of minor depression has been proposed to in order to characterize some of these patients. "Minor depression," a component form of depression, has not yet recognized as an official disorder, and the architects of the DSM-IVR propose further research on it prior to its official recommendation.

According to some studies (Alexopoulos, 1997; Gallo & Lebowitz, 1999) this form of minor depression is much more common than major depression and anywhere from 8%–20% of the older adult population

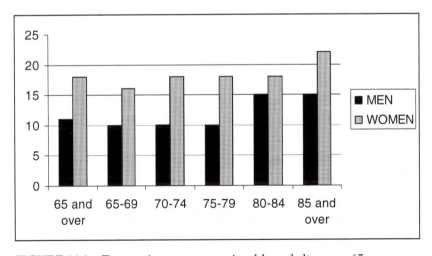

FIGURE 16.1   Depressive symptoms in older adults, ages 65+.
Notes: This reflects the percentage of people age 65 years and older with depression with clinically relevant symptoms, 2002.
The definition of "clinically relevant depressive symptoms" is four or more symptoms out of a list of eight depressive symptoms from an abbreviated version of the Center for Epidemiological Studies Depression scale (CES-D), adapted by the Health and Retirement study. The CES-D scale is a screening tool for depression.
Source: Health and Retirement Study

living in the community can be found with some form of minor depression. The Surgeon General's Report on Mental Health (USDHHS, 1999) suggests that given depression is more difficult to assess and detect in older adults, more research is needed to define the clinical features that might help identify older adults at increased risk for sustained depressive symptoms and suicide.

Late-Onset Depression

According to the Surgeon General's Report on Mental Health (USDHHS, 1999, p. 347), "Major or minor depression diagnosed with first onset later than age 60 has been termed *late-onset depression.*" Patients with late-onset depression display greater apathy (Krishnan, Hays, Tupler, George, & Blazer, 1995) and less lifetime personality dysfunction (Abrams, Rosendahl, Card, & Alexopoulos, 1994). Cognitive deficits may be more prominent, with more impaired executive and memory functioning (Salloway et al., 1996) and greater medial temporal lobe abnormalities on magnetic resonance imaging, similar to those seen in dementia (Greenwald et al., 1997) It has also been predicted that one is more likely to suffer from a reoccurrence of depression once there has been depression after the age of 60 (Reynolds, 1998).

Some known risk factors that have been identified for late-onset depression include widowhood (Bruce, Kim, Leaf, & Jacobs, 1990; Harlow, Goldberg, and Comstock, 1991; Mendes de Leon, et al., 1994; Zisook & Shuchter, 1991), physical illness (Bachman et al., 1992; Cadoret & Widmer, 1988; Harlow et al., 1991), high school or less education (Wallace & O'Hara, 1992; Gallo, Royall, & Anthony, 1993), problems with one's activities of daily living (Bruce & Hoff, 1994), and the use of alcohol (Saunders et al., 1991).

Alzheimer's Disease

Prevalence and Incidence

Alzheimer's disease is a recognized disorder associated with aging and has become more of a concern in the press following the recent passing of Ronald Reagan. Approximately 8% to 15% of people over age 65 have Alzheimer's disease (Ritchie & Kildea, 1995). It is also anticipated that the prevalence of dementia (most of which is accounted for by Alzheimer's disease) nearly doubles with every 5 years of age after age 60 (Jorm, Korten, & Henderson, 1987). Apparently, more women than men are diagnosed with Alzheimer's disease (that is, the *prevalence* of the disease appears to be higher among women), but this may be an artifact of the reality that women have a longer life span than men. (Lebowitz, Pearson, & Cohen, 1998). Incidence studies also reveal age-related increases in Alzheimer's disease (Aevarsson & Skoog, 1996; Breteler, Claus, van Duijn, Launer, & Hofman, 1992; Hebert et al., 1995; Johansson & Zarit, 1995; Paykel et al., 1994). It is anticipated that 1% of those age 60 to 64 are affected with dementia; 2% of those age 65 to 69; 4% of those age 70 to 74; 8% of those 75 to 79; 16% of those age 80 to 84; and 30% to 45% of those age 85 and older (Jorm et al., 1987; Evans et al., 1989).

The "graying of America" is likely to result in an increase in the number of individuals with Alzheimer's disease, yet shifts in the composition of the affected population also are anticipated. Increased education is correlated with a lower frequency of Alzheimer's disease (Hill et al., 1993; Katzman, 1993; Stern et al., 1994), and future cohorts are expected to have attained greater levels of education. For example, the portion of those currently 75 years of age and older—those most vulnerable to Alzheimer's disease—with at least a high school education is 58.7%. Of those currently age 60 to 64 who will enter the period of maximum vulnerability by the year 2010, 75.5% have at least a high school education. A higher educational level among the at-risk cohort may delay the onset of Alzheimer's disease and thereby decrease the overall frequency of Alzheimer's disease (by decreasing the number of individuals who live long enough to enter their period of maximum vulnerability). However, this trend may be counterbalanced or overtaken by greater longevity and longer survival of affected individuals. Specifically, improvements in general health and health care may lengthen the survival of dementia patients, increase the number of severely affected patients, and raise overall levels of comorbidity. Similarly, through dissemination of information to patients and clinicians, better detection, especially of early-stage patients, is expected. Some authors suggest that the increased use of protective agents, such as vitamin E, also may increase the number of patients in the middle phases of the illness (Cummings & Jeste, 1999).

Anxiety Disorders

Prevalence of Anxiety

Anxiety symptoms and syndromes are important but understudied conditions in older adults. It has been estimated that in the community, about 11.4% of adults aged 55 years and older meet criteria for an anxiety disorder in 1 year (Flint, 1994). Phobic anxiety disorders are among the most common mental disturbances in late life according to the Epidemiological Catchments Area (ECA) study. Prevalence studies of panic disorder (0.5%) and obsessive-compulsive disorder (1.5%) in older samples reveal low rates. (Bland, Newman, and Orn, 1988; Copeland et al., 1987a; Copeland et al., 1987b; Lindesay, Briggs, & Murphy, 1989). Although the National Comorbidity Study did not cover this age range, and the ECA did not include this disorder, other studies showed a prevalence of generalized anxiety disorder in older adults ranging from 1.1% to 17.3% higher than that reported for panic disorder or obsessive-compulsive disorder (Copeland et al., 1987a; Skoog, 1993). Worry or "nervous tension," rather than specific anxiety syndromes, may be more important in older people. Since many of the symptoms of anxiety mirror symptoms of heart-related disease, anxiety is often underdiagnosed or misdiagnosed within an older adult cohort group.

Schizophrenia in Late Life

Although schizophrenia is commonly thought of as an illness of young adulthood, it can both extend into and first appear in later life. Diagnostic criteria for schizophrenia are the same across the life span, and DSM-IV places no restrictions on age of onset for a diagnosis to be made. Symptoms include delusions, hallucinations, disorganized speech, disorganized or catatonic behavior, as well as affective flattening. Symptoms must cause significant social or occupational dysfunction, must not be accompanied by prominent mood symptoms, and must not be uniquely associated with substance use.

Prevalence and Cost

One-year prevalence of schizophrenia among those 65 years or older is reportedly only around 0.6%, about one-half the one-year prevalence of the 1.3% that is estimated for the population aged 18 to 54 (USDHHS, 1999).

Alcohol and Substance Abuse Disorders

Alcohol Abuse and Dependence

Although we may carry a stereotype of an older adult as being white or gray haired, jovial, meek, or frail, we seldom think of older adults as substance abusers, out-of-control drinkers, or at risk for these conditions. Recent analyses of data examining alcohol consumption practices in older men and women drawn from sources such as the National Health Interview Survey (NHIS 2000; NHIS, 2004), the Behavioral Risk Factor Surveillance System (BRFSS, 2001; USDHHS, NCHS, 2001; USDHHS, NCHS, 2004) and the National Household Survey on Drug Abuse (NHSDA, 2000) have recently shed light on the prevalence of alcohol consumption among older adults. In fact, these data suggest that older adults in the 65 and older age category found 56.8% of the population at risk for drinking in the past 30 days, when surveyed. On the days these same older adults report that they drink, 32.1% say they have two or more drinks (NHIS, 2004). Brelow, Faden, and Smothers (2003) found in their secondary analyses of these data that about one third of the U.S. elderly population consume alcohol, regardless of risk. These authors concluded that as we see our population "graying" over the upcoming decades, practitioners and public health officials will need to be more aware of dealing with this segment of the population.

The prevalence of heavy drinking (12 to 21 drinks per week) in older adults is estimated at 3% to 9% (Liberto, Oslin, & Ruskin, 1992). One-month prevalence estimates of alcohol abuse and dependence in this group are much lower, ranging from 0.9% to 2.2% (Regier et al., 1988). Alcohol abuse and dependence are approximately four times more common among men than women (1.2% vs. 0.3%) ages 65 and older (Grant, Harford, Dawson, Chou, & Pickering, 1994). Although lifetime prevalence rates for alcoholism are higher for white men and women between ages 18 and 29, African American men and women had higher rates among those 65 years and older. For Hispanics, men had rates between those of whites and African Americans. Hispanic females had a much lower rate than that for whites and African Americans (Helzer, Burnam, & McEvoy, 1991). Although longitudinal studies suggest variously that alcohol consumption decreases with age (Adams, Garry, Rhyne, Hunt, & Goodwin, 1990; Temple & Leino, 1989), we can anticipate that alcohol abuse or dependence will increase as the baby boomers age, since that cohort has a greater history of alcohol consumption than current cohorts of older adults.

Misuse of Prescription and Over-the-Counter Medications

We have to date a limited amount of information about the actual misuse of prescription drugs among older adults. A Special Committee on Aging (1987) reported that the use of prescription drugs among older adults was approximately three times as frequent as in the general population. In addition, Kofoed (1984) found that the use of over-the-counter medications by this group was even more extensive. Annual estimated expenditures on prescription drugs by older adults in the United States are $15 billion annually, a fourfold greater per capita expenditure on medications compared with that of younger individuals (Anderson, Kerluke, Pulcins, Hertzman, & Barer, 1993; Jeste & Palmer, 1998). It should be no surprise that problems with misuse and abuse of substances among our older adult population may be attributed to problems related to aging—failing eyesight or misunderstanding the directions. Thus underuse, overuse, or erratic use can be attributable in part to a lack of health literacy, failing eyesight, or problems such as cataracts. In extreme instances, these problems then result in drug and substance abuse.

Mental health issues and substance abuse disorders often co-occur for both adults and children (Regier et al., 1990). Despite this awareness, and evidence-based practices that have been established for treating these co-occurring disorders (Drake et al., 2001) a limited amount of work and research has been done to examine both the etiology and treatment of these disorders either individually or as co-occurring within rural areas. The field appears to lack an understanding of both the need and method to tailor evidence-based approaches to treat people with co-occurring disorders in rural areas (USDHHS, 2004).

Although older adults may be at increased risk or vulnerability to experiencing mental health-related problems, they often do not seek or are not successful at linking with the necessary mental health services (USDHHS, 1999). A variety of factors can account for this outcome including stigma of mental illness; ageism; complexity and fragmentation of services; lack of coordination between medical, mental health, and aging systems of care; lack of professional staff trained in geriatric mental health; and inadequacy of health insurance coverage (USDHHS, 1999). Symptoms of depression existing and undetected within the older adult population have been noted in the literature (Bland, et al., 1988; Blazer, 1999; Dorfman et al, 1995; Proctor, Morrow-Howell, Rubin, & Ringenberg, 1999; Rogers & Barusch, 2000). Consequently a poorly coordinated system of care and lack of integration between systems (especially aging, mental health, and primary care) contributes to this problem (USDHHS, 1999). This problem becomes magnified when layered with the issues of substance use and abuse for older adults, whether the use is via prescription or over the counter.

Schonfeld (1993) examined prevalence estimates of alcohol use and misuse among older adults through surveying staff providing services to older adults. He found few staff had received in-service training on substance abuse issues, but conversely saw these topics as issues of high priority in their day-to-day work. Although this study is dated, and occurred primarily in urban areas, are there differences or have these issues changed by the present day?

This issue is further illustrated by the work of Hanson and Guthiel (2004), who made the case for brief motivational interviewing as a successful intervention when working with older adults. They argue that social workers and other health professionals do not adequately address problem drinking with older adults. These authors suggest that issues such as inadequate knowledge about addictive behaviors, limited development in assessment tools, and limited evidence-based treatment options account for social work practitioners' limitations when dealing with these issues. These findings build on the work of Klein and Jess (2002) who found that staff training and education issues were identified as limited, despite a clear awareness that alcohol posed a problem for people who were residing in intermediate care facilities. They interviewed 111 directors of intermediate care facilities in the United States to learn that although alcohol use was common in facilities, comfort level on the part of the staff related to alcohol use among older adults was limited.

Emlet, Hawks, and Callahan (2001) in their retrospective chart study of 148 community-dwelling older adults found that functional status was not a predictor for alcohol use and abuse among older persons. Males were three times more likely to drink than females. Moreover, the authors illuminate the growing problem of substance abuse/use among older adults and articulate the need for intervention with this target population. Although they did not specifically examine older adults in rural areas, we can anticipate the issues are similar.

Memmet (2003) argues that older adults in general are at risk for the development of polydrug problems due to interactive effects of alcohol and prescription or over-the-counter medications. The importance of screening elderly clients for substance abuse is a critical factor in the detection and treatment of substance use issues among the elderly.

Although minimal research has been conducted in rural areas, Musnick, Blazer, and Hays (2000) examined a sample of elderly people affiliated with the Baptist religion, living in rural areas of central North Carolina. They found a strong relationship between religiosity (being Baptist) and the non-use of alcohol. They also found that among Baptists that did not attend services regularly, there was a relationship between symptoms of depression and alcohol use.

It has been found that older adults are at risk of alcohol abuse and has been argued that treatment for older adults should be differentiated from that of other age groups. However LaGreca, Akers, and Dwyer (1988) found in the sample of 1,410 older adults (60+) living in retirement communities that problem drinking was not linked to members of the communities or life transitions. Conversely, social support networks did not serve as mediators for the impact of life events on alcohol use. Their work extends the work of Alexander and Duff (1988) who discovered after surveying three retirement communities that drinking was an integral part of the leisure subculture.

Although Brody (1982) suggested that developing an understanding of alcohol-related issues with older adults was critical, especially in the areas related to detection and treatment, little progress in the area appears to have been made over 20 years. This seems to also have been argued by several of the preceding studies. Moreover, a dearth of studies exist to examine the prevalence of alcohol use among older adults in rural communities, issues that providers face, and barriers to solutions/ interventions within a rural context. As our population grays, baby boomers age, and more older adults migrate to rural areas in pursuit of escaping the expense and challenges of urban lifestyles, answers to these questions will quickly become more critical.

Mental Health and Older Adults

Depressive symptoms are an important indicator of general well-being and mental health among older adults. People who report many depressive symptoms often experience higher rates of physical illness, greater functional disability, and higher health care utilization (Mehta, Yaffe & Covinsky, 2002; Wells et al., 1989). Mental health issues and substance abuse disorders often co-occur for both adults and children (Regier et al., 1990). Although older adults may be at increased risk or vulnerability to experiencing mental health-related problems, they often do not seek or are not successful at linking with the necessary mental health services (USDHHS, 1999). A variety of factors can account for this outcome including stigma of mental illness, ageism, complexity and fragmentation of services, lack of coordination between medical, mental health, and aging systems of care, lack of professional staff trained in geriatric mental health, and inadequacy of health insurance coverage (USDHHS, 1999). Consequently, there is a poorly coordinated system of care and lack of integration between systems (especially aging, mental health and primary health care).

While most older people prefer to live in the community, mental disorders have been implicated as one of the major risk factors to institutionalization (Katz & Parmelee, 1977; USDHHS, 1999). Despite this, community-based services to meet the needs of older adults in community care settings have largely been provided through the general medical sector since the mental health organizations have focused primarily on persons with severe persistent mental health disorders. However, the focus of primary care is often medical and acute care; thus, mental health issues are often overlooked (George, 1992; USDHHS, 1999). Home health agencies provide limited short-term care (Meeks & Murrell, 1997; Meeks et al., 1997; Robinson, 1990).

Mental Health in Rural Communities vs. Urban Communities

The realities that specialty mental health services for older adults have been underutilized is identified in the literature (Burns & Taube, 1990; NIA, 2000; Proctor et al., 1999; Proctor et al., 2003). In addition, general health has served in fact as the mental health system of care for older adults

(Regier, Goldberg, & Taube, 1978). Social services have in fact been under-utilized by older adults who are in need of mental health services (Proctor et al., 1999); however, older adults with physical care needs and co-morbid medical conditions were more likely to be in need of mental health services (Proctor et al., 2003). Patients living in rural areas were less likely to use certain mental health services than their urban counterparts; however, the need was documented to be similar in nature across both locations.

SOCIAL WORK, MENTAL HEALTH, AGING, AND SERVICE UTILIZATION

Despite the dearth of research and efficacy studies on the benefits of various treatment modalities for mental health issues and older adults, *Mental Health: The Report of the Surgeon General* (USDHHS, 1999) argues for a range of services that can be an adjunct to the formal treatment setting and supports the concept of health education and health promotion strategies to create an awareness of the aging process and mental health functioning within the aging process. A range of interventions that have largely not been evaluated can be used to help improve the mental health of older adults living in the community. These may include peer support, wellness programs, life reviews, bereavement groups, health promotion, and health education programs (Cohen, 1995; Haight, Michel, & Hendrix, 1998; Rowe & Kahn, 1997; Scott-Lennox & George, 1996; Waters, 1995). Social workers can play a major role in this educative process if they understand mental health and older adults, as well as the role that health disparities can play in the continuum of mental health functioning. The intersection between disability, chronic physical conditions, and depression is not well understood or underscored often by social workers working in community-care settings. These issues may be compounded with the location of one's residence and socio-economic status. This study will begin to address these issues conceptually and lay the foundation for pilot data that can be utilized to better prepare social workers working in community-care and home-health settings.

From our previous studies, we can see that we are in need of programming to meet the mental health needs of older adults. The next section will address programs available to meet the mental health care needs of older adults.

PROGRAMS AVAILABLE TO MEET THE MENTAL HEALTH CARE NEEDS OF OLDER ADULTS

Medicare

Medicare has a small provision for mental health care in its original plan. Under the original plan, Medicare Part A, some expenses related to mental health care given in a hospital are covered, which include one's room, meals, nursing care, and other related services and/or supplies. Medicare Part A has a cap on the number of days one is able to have paid while in an inpatient psychiatric facility, during one's lifetime. Although there is no lifetime limit for inpatient care provided through a general hospital, Medicare will only cover up to 190 days of inpatient psychiatric hospital services care during one's lifetime.

Medicare Part B will help pay for mental health services generally given outside a hospital, including visits with a doctor, clinical psychologist, clinical social worker, clinical nurse specialist, nurse practitioner, and/or physician's assistant and lab tests. These services, however, are only paid for by Medicare when provided for by a health professional who has been approved to accept Medicare reimbursement.

Medicare Part B also helps pay for outpatient mental health services or services provided for through an outpatient or mental health clinic, physician's office, therapist's office, or outpatient hospital department. In addition, services such as individual and group therapies approved by one's local state are covered, family counseling in relation to the older adult's treatment plan is covered, lab work and psychological assessments, occupational therapy related to one's treatment plan, individual patient training, and education and diagnostic tests are covered.

A number of services are not covered within the Medicare plan. Some of these services that are not covered include any meals and transportation to or from mental health treatment, support groups that are offered in non-medical settings for peer support, and any testing/job training that has not been a part of the prescribed mental health plan.

Partial hospitalization programs are also funded through Medicare Part B. This type of therapeutic program provides intensive psychiatric care through active treatment but differs from counseling or outpatient care in its intensity, duration, and depth of treatment available from one's physician or therapist. Partial hospitalization treatment offers day treatment and does not require any inpatient overnight stays. Generally these partial hospitalization programs are provided through either hospital outpatient departments or local community mental health centers. Medicare can pay for partial hospitalization programs on the condition one's physician can make the case that without such a program, the consumer would require an inpatient stay for treatment. In addition, the physician and partial hospitalization program need to be provided by a recognized Medicare provider in order to receive reimbursement.

Medicare is a program available to individuals who have worked up to 40 quarters and contributed through payroll tax into a plan. In the event that one does not have this plan to qualify for, or lives below a specific income level, mental health services are still available under the Medicaid program.

Medicaid

Generally one can qualify for resources through Medicaid or public aid mental health services if one's resources or monthly income are less than $1,464 for a couple or $1,097 for an individual, and total bank accounts, stocks, bonds, or other resources are worth less than $6,000 for a couple or $4,000 for an individual. *Note:* These are 2007 income amounts and may change on January 1 of each succeeding year. Alaska and Hawaii also have slightly higher income limits. Generally speaking, therapists working with older adults and receiving state public aid or Medicaid funding may be required to provide therapeutic treatment based upon an evidence-based best practice model. These are intervention strategies that have been approved by the Substance Abuse and Mental Health Services Administration (SAMHSA) and National Institute of Mental Health (NIMH) as being interventions guided by successful clinical trials and an evidenced-based approach to treatment. Not all state public aid/Medicaid sources require these intervention approaches, and some states such as Illinois currently allow for the therapist to utilize their professional judgment as to which intervention strategies work best for a specific diagnosis and patient.

Area Agencies on Aging

Under the Older Americans Act of 2000, some funding was available to area agencies for short-term supportive counseling for mental health needs. However, these funds did not cover the areas of screening and assessment for older adults adequately and were designated for pilot initiatives rather than long-term programs. The Older Americans Act Amendments of 2006 (PL 109-365) will expand the delivery of mental health services. Mental health services or mental health screening will replace the terms health screening or health services in the act, including Section 306. The amendments of 2006 also propose new Mental Health Multidisciplinary Centers under Title IV. The House bill amends section 419 by adding new language requiring centers to collect information on best practices in long-term care service delivery, housing, and transportation. It also will require mental health multidisciplinary centers to provide training and technical assistance to support community-based mental health services to older people. The Senate bill S. 3570 amended Section 419 by authorizing new grants to states on a competitive basis for the development and delivery of systems for mental health screening and treatment services for older individuals. Such grants will support programs that will: (1) increase public awareness related to benefits of prevention and treatment of mental health conditions faced by people 60 years of age and older; (2) target stigma associated with mental disorders and other barriers that impact the diagnosis and treatment of mental health disorders. If state agencies receive such funds they will be required to allocate the funds through area agencies on aging to carry out the programs.

SERVICE DELIVERY SETTINGS FOR MENTAL HEALTH CARE FOR OLDER ADULTS

Traditionally services for mental health care for older adults have been constrained and limited to settings designed for chronically mentally ill adults and specialized services for treating the older adult has been limited. The *Surgeon General's Report on Mental Health* (USDHHS, 1999) provided an overview of settings within which mental health treatment occurs. They suggest that mental health services for older adults within communities occurs within homes, group homes, retirement communities, primary care and general medical care sectors, outpatient therapy, board and care homes, assisted living facilities, and community mental health centers. Institutional settings for mental health treatment of older adults occurs within nursing homes, general hospitals with psychiatric units, general hospitals without psychiatric units, state mental hospitals, and Veterans Affairs hospitals.

Unfortunately these settings have tailored interventions to meet the needs of an adult population rather than offering any specializations for an older adult population. In addition, when state funds are limited or budgets are in need of retrenchment, the first target group to be dismissed are older adults who do not fit into the category of chronically mentally ill. This calls into question the need to look at alternative treatment modalities and policies that embrace the older adults and build in their unique needs and therapeutic approaches. These models will undoubtedly be possible with the 2006 amendments to the Older Americans Act.

Increasingly, primary care settings are also beginning to address mental health needs of older adults, through screening, assessment, and educational approaches. Several model programs have incorporated social work staff to provide screening and assessment services to patients, during their wait for the primary care physician (Gask, Sibbald, & Creed, 1997; Katon et al., 1996, 1997; Schulberg et al., 1995; Stolee, Kessler, & Le Clair, 1996). While these approaches are still in their infancy, and primary care still requires being addressed before physicians will adequately deal with the older adults' mental health needs adequately, these intervention schemes hold great promise. Such approaches minimize the potential for stigma and prejudice both on the part of the provider and the patient. Overall, models that consider the integration of mental health treatment into primary care were designed to meet the needs of people with depression, but other disorders may also be targeted within primary care settings. A set of recommendations for appropriate referrals to specialty mental health care is available through the American Association for Geriatric Psychiatry (AAGP, 1997).

ISSUES FACING OLDER ADULTS AND MENTAL HEALTH CARE NEEDS

A number of issues currently face older adults residing in the community with mental health care needs. These include the financing of mental health care for older adults, community-based care, prevention services, screening and detection, and medication management. This section will review some of these specific issues and showcase areas for further development.

Financing Mental Health Care for Older Adults

Up until the Older Americans Act Amendments of 2006, financing mental health care for older adults was an issue that led to a battleground between divisions of aging and mental health and substance abuse arenas. Each group perceived that mental health care for older adults was not their mandate, and funding for services and resources was limited if existent. Departments on Aging perceived mental health issues and services to be the role of Departments/divisions for Mental Health (DMH). Conversely, divisions of mental health perceived their role to be one of intervention for people with chronic mental illness rather than acute, short-term issues. DMHs also perceived that issues related to service delivery for older adults was the mandate of the aging directorates, regardless of specialty area need. Consequently, financing (or lack of financing) is and remains an issue for older adult service delivery settings.

Financing also plays a critical role when delivering services, either assessment or intervention. Ultimately, one must work with an older adult with a different set of approaches than one would take when working with children, teenagers, or younger adults. Older adults may require a longer time period within which to complete assessments due to the need for a slower-paced interview, and a longer period of time to develop rapport or engage the individual in the therapeutic relationship. This becomes difficult for caseworkers who may be reimbursed per session as opposed to per case. Effective models of financing assessments may revert to using a block-funded approach to service delivery rather than a case-by-case approach.

Community-Based Care

Community-based care for mental health concerns has largely been delivered through local community mental health centers. The centers were originally developed to meet the needs of the deinstitutionalized long-term psychiatric patients, who moved into local communities following the passage of the Community Mental Health Centers Act of 1966 (PL 88-164). These settings have aged along with their constituents, and now many of the young adults with chronic mental health problems have also aged and are in the older adult (60+) target group. Unfortunately, the funding schemes and the modus operandi are very much focused on providing community-based services to stabilize individuals with chronic mental health needs, rather than older adults with acute and short-term care needs. Conversely, the settings are often stigmatizing, and unfavorable to older adults with short-term mental health needs. Treatment groups available through partial hospitalization programs often target the younger patient, and older adults often feel out of place. These issues become compounded when considering a smaller rural community setting, where privacy is limited, and one would not be able to maintain their anonymity when confronted with visiting a community mental health center.

Models for Gero-Psychiatry

A number of models are beginning to develop around the United States for gero-psychiatry. These model demonstration projects hold promise for innovative ways to provide screening, detection, education, and intervention services for older adults. Such approaches will be imperative for the effective treatment of older adults. These models will also hopefully provide for a nonstigmatized approach to dealing with older adults and will also improve the specialty areas for intervention services from older adults. These model approaches will also require some legislative base and intervention to provide a legislative mandate for individual states to create these services. A sample piece of legislation is available at http://www.ilga.gov/legislation/publicacts/pubact91/acts/91-0799.html

Prevention Services

Currently, federal legislation does not have any provisions for prevention-oriented services. The legislative base behind Medicare and the Older Americans Act (2000 amendments) do not provide for preventative services. Individual states and funded initiatives through NIMH, National Institute on Aging (NIA), and SAMHSA have provided funds to develop evidence-based prevention interventions; however, these approaches are often not funded federally; once deemed effective, individual states may introduce them into their systems for their constituents. It is hoped that the 2006 amendments to the Older Americans Act will facilitate some prevention-oriented approaches particularly to target the onset of depression in older adults or target substance use issues for older adults. SAMHSA's Action Plan for Older Adults, Fiscal Years 2006 and 2007 begins to address these needs and is available in Appendix B.

Screening and Detection

The ideal venue for an older adult to be assessed for mental health needs (e.g., depression, cognitive impairment, or substance use/misuse) would be during an initial assessment for home health services or within primary care settings. Currently, not all community-care settings screen for these mental health issues during their initial assessments or follow-ups. In addition, not all home health caseworkers are trained to understand the behavioral symptoms associated with the DSM-IV diagnostic groups. Without training of caseworkers or primary care health providers, many signs of mental disorders may go undetected or untreated. The screening and assessment tools also used for this population group are limited and require further development. Last, many of the tools for screening and assessment were normed and developed using a nursing home and institutionalized population, while the same tools are currently needed for a community-dwelling, noninstitutionalized population.

Medications

Medications for the treatment of psychiatric disorders are often tested within clinical trials on a younger adult population; hence, there is limited information about how these metabolize within an older adult's system. It is quite common for people over the age of 60 to require several attempts with different medications prior to finding the one that will best work within one's body and among the other drugs one may be taking. One may be required to pursue a variety of medications prior to finding one that will work effectively. Challenges are that we have a limited understanding of clinical trials that can be used with an older adult population. Second, with Medicare Part D enrollment periods only once per year, one may have greater out-of-pocket expenses than anticipated due to different medication prescriptions. required to stabilize an acute mental health condition.

People With Chronic Mental Health Needs Who Are Aging

There is an important distinction that needs to be made between the needs of individuals with chronic mental illness who are older adults and older adults with acute mental health needs. People with chronic mental health needs who are aging have multiple health and mental health issues that result in the use of institutionalized services as compared to older adults with brief periods of instability.

Oppressed Groups and Visible Minorities

The seminal work articulated in *Mental Health: Culture, Race, and Ethnicity: A Supplement to Mental Health: A Report of the Surgeon General* (USDHHS, 2001) points out the fact that culture, race, and ethnicity are not addressed adequately at all within mental health service delivery settings in the United States. If one adds an additional variable of age into the equation, it becomes relatively clear very quickly that older adults who are visible minorities, or from traditionally oppressed groups may be less likely to have access to culturally sensitive and relevant services. Clinical trials need to include individuals who are older adults and representative of minority groups, when considering the development of new medications. Approaches to evidence-based treatment require the inclusion of people who are minorities and older adults. Effective treatment interventions could also be expanded through a more concrete understanding of the role culture plays in one's health behaviors and help-seeking behavior. People from minority groups also need to be able to assure language access, and investigation is required to better understand the role that culture and ethnicity play in relation to shame, stigma, and discrimination. The area of understanding cultural minorities and mental health care is an area that can present opportunity for development.

MODEL PROGRAMS AND BEST PRACTICE APPROACHES TO MENTAL HEALTH SERVICE DELIVERY

Although a range of behavioral health approaches exist to meet the mental health and substance misuse needs of older adults, the concept of evidence-based interventions is becoming widely prescribed by behavioral health service providers. Levkoff, Chen, Fisher, and McIntyre (2006) have developed a guide to the implementation of such programs. In the section to follow, some specific programs, recognized by the Substance Abuse and Mental Health Services Administration (SAMHSA), are presented for potential intervention strategies and best practice models for mental health service delivery.

Mental Health and Aging Systems Integration Initiative

This gero-psych initiative began in 2001 as an initiative from the Division of Mental Health, State of Illinois. In its original conception, and proposal, the Mental Health and Aging Systems Integration Initiative (MHASI) project proposed that each gero-pysch specialist would be engaged in activities to include systems integration (30%), screening and assessment (40%), and education/training (30%) (Request for Proposals (RFP), USDHSSIL, 2000). Initial pilot data from the first 9 months of operation suggest that most of the activities have been focused within the systems integration component. This unique partnership has brought together key stakeholders from the aging, mental health, and academic arenas in an attempt to bridge the systems of care for older adults who may be at risk for gero-psychiatric concerns. Central features of this approach includes coalitions of providers, media advocacy using fact sheets, local public television and radio, educational initiatives through senior nutrition sites and health fairs, caregiver support, peer support groups, and individualized screening/assessment approaches for older adults. The specialists also offer consultation to aging, mental health, and substance abuse providers to assure that each of these groups are comfortable with treatment and intervention services for older adults (USDHHS, 2006a).

The Center for Older Adult Recovery at Hanley Center

In 1998, the Hanley Center in West Palm Beach, Florida opened its pioneering Center for Older Adult Recovery, after developing an age-responsive model of treatment of alcohol and chemical addictions. Hanley's outcomes suggest that the older adult target group can be the most successful with recovery rates when compared to any other age group. The program offers prevention for late onset addiction as well. Situated in lush tropical enclaves, Hanley Center offers its older adult consumers a Serenity Fountain and Garden and a homey, comfortable residence. Hanley's holistic treatment model addresses patients' physical and mental status as well as the values of this generation.

After an initial thorough evaluation, individualized treatment takes on a slower pace, due to the normal aging process, as well as chronic medical conditions, cognitive impairment, and possible dual diagnosis. Hanley's interdisciplinary team of highly skilled professionals provides holistic treatment in the areas of medicine, psychiatry, psychology, and counseling, wellness, spirituality, and expressive arts. Continuing care plans are put into place prior to patients' discharge and are specific to the individual's special needs (USDHHS, 2006b).

The Gatekeeper Program

The Gatekeeper model seeks at-risk older adults who typically do not come to the attention of the formal mental health, substance abuse, and aging service delivery systems. This volunteer program was developed in 1978 by the late Raymond Raschko, MSW, at Elder Services Mental Health, Spokane,

Washington. The program recruits and trains community businesses and organizations to identify high-risk older adults who may be exhibiting signs and symptoms that indicate they need assistance. Gatekeepers may include meter readers, bank tellers, postal carriers, first responders, utility workers, and many others. Following a referral, a geriatric mental health specialist makes a home visit to conduct a comprehensive assessment and evaluation. Appropriate linkages are made to mental health, substance abuse, aging, medical, and other social services. Research has shown the Gatekeeper model to be an effective outreach model for identifying socially isolated older adults who show signs of psychiatric symptoms (USDHHS, 2005).

MENTAL HEALTH CARE CHALLENGES FOR THE FUTURE

Mental health challenges for the future are many, and although this chapter has touched upon several, this section will definitely not be exhaustive. The biggest challenge will probably be the very nature of financing to meet the community-based noninstitutionalized population. Prevention, screening, detection, and intervention strategies to meet the needs of baby boomers as they age will be another challenge. Models of service delivery that are innovative, preventative in nature, and nonstigmatizing will also be an important goal to strive towards. Establishing systems of care that are not fragmented and provide a seamless system of service delivery will also be an important goal for mental health, health care, and public health service delivery systems.

SUMMARY

This chapter has taken us through a journey to examine the current status of mental health and older adults, with a particular emphasis on depression, cognitive disorders, anxiety, and schizophrenia. Programs and services have been reviewed and issues still outstanding within the mental health arena have been discussed. This chapter has concluded with laying out some challenges for the future in the area of mental health and older adults.

USEFUL WEB SITES

Mental Health America: http//:www.nmha.org
   This Web site provides consumer-oriented information on a range of mental health topics by audience, issue, disorders, treatments, and

medications. It also provides links to a range of policy issues and mental health topics.

Suicide and Depression Fact Sheets: http//:www.nimh.gov/publicat/ elderlydepsuicide.cfm
This site provides an excellent set of fact sheets on older adults, depression, and suicide. It is written on a level that enables the reader to glean some behavioral signs and symptoms about suicide, and identify if they or a loved one are at risk. The fact sheets are a product of the National Institute of Mental Health.

National Institute of Mental Health: http://www.nimh.nih.gov
This Web site provides up-to-date health information on a range of disorders including anxiety disorders, PTST, depression, and eating disorders with some vantage points for older adults.

Substance Abuse and Mental Health Services Administration (SAMHSA): http://www/samhsa.gov
This Web site provides a matrix of services for older adults. It includes information and linkages to the Older Americans Substance Abuse and Mental Health Technical Assistance Center, and campaigns for public awareness. Current campaigns at the time of the writing of this book include a "Do the Right Dose" campaign and an "as you age" campaign. The site also provides links to professional resources that can be useful in gleaning current knowledge in the area, and developing resources for professional development and public education.

Senior Health online Depression information: http://nihseniorhealth.gov/ depression/toc.html
This site provides an overview of numerous health topics of interest, including depression in older adults. Since approximately two million Americans age 65 or older suffer from major depression, and another five million suffer from less severe forms, a collaborative effort between the National Institute on Aging (NIA) and the National Library of Medicine (NLM) worked conjointly to develop this senior-friendly medical Web site.

SAMHSA Fact Sheets on drugs of interest: http://www.oas.samhsa.gov/ drugs.cfm
This Web site provides fact sheets on various drugs, with up-to-date medical background information.

Older Adult Technical Assistance Network: http://www.samhsa.gov/ OlderAdultsTAC/
Through work with national experts and researchers, federal agencies and national aging organizations, the Older Americans Substance Abuse

and Mental Health Technical Assistance Center is collecting, reviewing, and assessing the best available knowledge, research, and programmatic efforts around substance abuse and mental health science for older adults.

REFERENCES

Abrams, R. C., Rosendahl, E., Card, C., & Alexopoulos, G. S. (1994). Personality disorder correlates of late and early onset depression. *Journal of the American Geriatrics Society, 42,* 727–731.

Adams, W. L., Garry, P. J., Rhyne, R., Hunt, W. C., & Goodwin, J. S. (1990). Alcohol intake in the healthy elderly. Changes with age in a cross-sectional and longitudinal study. *Journal of the American Geriatrics Society, 38,* 211–216.

Aevarsson, O., & Skoog, I. (1996). A population-based study on the incidence of dementia disorders between 85 and 88 years of age. *Journal of the American Geriatrics Society, 44,* 1455–1460.

Alexander, F., & Duff, R. W. (1988). Social interaction and alcohol use in retirement communities. *The Gerontologist, 28*(5), 632–636.

Alexopoulos, G. S. (1997, November 6). *Epidemiology, nosology and treatment of geriatric depression.* Paper presented at Exploring Opportunities to Advance Mental Health Care for an Aging Population, meeting sponsored by the John A. Hartford Foundation, Rockville, MD.

American Association for Geriatric Psychiatry (AAGP). (1997). *Recommendations from primary care physicians: When to refer depressed elderly patients to a geriatric psychiatrist* Bethesda, MD: Author.

American Psychiatric Association. (2000). *Diagnostic statistical manual of psychiatric disorders IV-revised (DSMIV-R).* Washington, DC: Author.

Anderson, G. M., Kerluke, K. J., Pulcins, I. R., Hertzman, C., & Barer, M. L. (1993). Trends and determinants of prescription drug expenditures in the elderly: Data from the British Columbia Pharmacare Program. *Inquiry, 30,* 199–207.

Bachman, D. L., Wolf, P. A., Linn, R., Knoefel, J. E., Cobb, J., Belanger, A., et al. (1992). Prevalence of dementia and probable senile dementia of the Alzheimer type in the Framingham Study. *Neurology, 42,* 115–119.

Bane, S. D. (1997). Rural mental health and aging: Implication for case management. *Journal of Case Management, 6*(4), 158–161.

Behavioral Risk Factor Surveillance System (BFRSS). (2001). Retrieved August 25, 2005, from http://www.cdc.gov/brfss/

Bird, D. C., Dempsey, P., & Hartley, D. (2001). *Addressing mental health workforce needs in underserved rural areas: Accomplishments and challenges.* Portland, ME: Maine Rural Health Research Center, Muskie Institute, University of Southern Maine.

Bland, R. C., Newman, S. C., & Orn, H. (1988). Prevalence of psychiatric disorders in the elderly in Edmonton. *Acta Psychiatrica Scandinavica Supplement, 338,* 57–63.

Blazer, D. (1999). Depression in the elderly. *New England Journal of Medicine, 320,* 164–166.

Bogardus, S. T. (2001). Goals for the care of frail older adults: Do caregivers and clinicians agree? *The American Journal of Medicine, 110*(2), 97–102.

Brelow, R. A., Faden, V. B., & Smothers, B. (2003). Alcohol consumption by elderly Americans. *Journal of Studies on Alcohol, 64*(6), 884–892.

Breteler, M. M., Claus, J. J., van Duijn, C. M., Launer, L. J., & Hofman, A. (1992). Epidemiology of Alzheimer's disease. *Epidemiology Review, 14,* 59–82.

Brody, J. A. (1982). Aging and alcohol use. *Journal of American Geriatrics Society, 30*(2), 123–126.

Bruce, M. L., & Hoff, R. A. (1994). Social and physical health risk factors for first-onset major depressive disorder in a community sample. *Social Psychiatry and Psychiatric Epidemiology, 29,* 165–171.

Bruce, M. L., Kim, K., Leaf, P. J., & Jacobs, S. (1990). Depressive episodes and dysphoria resulting from conjugal bereavement in a prospective community sample. *American Journal of Psychiatry, 147,* 608–611.

Burns, B., & Taube, C. A., (1990). New directions in research on assertive community treatment. *Hospital & Community Psychiatry, 41,* 642–647.

Cadoret, R. J., & Widmer, R. B. (1988). The development of depressive symptoms in elderly following onset of severe physical illness. *Journal of Family Practice, 27,* 71–76.

Centers for Disease Control and Prevention. (2006). *Trends in health and aging.* Washington, DC: Government Printing Office.

Chumbler, N. R., Cody, M., Booth, B. M., & Beck, C. K. (2001). Rural-urban difference in service use for memory-related problems in older adults. *Journal-Behavior Health-Services and Research, 28*(2), 212–221.

Cohen, G. D. (1995). Mental health promotion in later life: The case for social portfolio. *American Journal of Geriatric Psychiatry, 3,* 277–279.

Copeland, J. R., Dewey, M. E., Wood, N., Searle, R., Davidson, I. A., & McWilliam, C. (1987a). Range of mental illness among the elderly in the community: Prevalence in Liverpool using the GMS-AGECAT package. *British Journal of Psychiatry, 150,* 815–823.

Copeland, J. R., Gurland, B. J., Dewey, M. E., Kelleher, M. J., Smith, A.M., & Davidson, I. A. (1987b). Is there more dementia, depression and neurosis in New York? A comparative study of the elderly in New York and London using the computer diagnosis AGECAT. *British Journal of Psychiatry, 151,* 466–473.

Cummings, J., & Jeste, D. (1999). Alzheimer's disease and its management in the year 2010. *Psychiatric Services, 50,* 1173–1177.

Dorfman, R. A., Lubben, J. E., Mayer-Oakes, A., Atchison, K., Schweitzer, S. O., DeJong, F. J., et al. (1995). Screening for depression among a well elderly population. *Social Work, 40*(3), 295–304.

Drake, R. E., Essock, S. M., Shanner, A., Carey, K. B., Minkoff, K., Kola, L., et al. (2001). Implementing dual diagnosis services for clients with severe mental illness. *Psychiatric Services, 52,* 469–476.

Emlet, C., Hawks, H., & Callahan, J. (2001). Alcohol use and abuse in a population of community dwelling, frail older adults. *Journal of Gerontological Social Work, 35*(4), 21–33.

Evans, D. A., Funkenstein, H. H., Albert, M. S., Scherr, P. A., Cook, N. R., Chown, M. J., et al. (1989). Prevalence of Alzheimer's disease in a community population of older persons. Higher than previously reported. *Journal of the American Medical Association, 262,* 2551–2556.

Flint, A. J. (1994). Epidemiology and comorbidity of anxiety disorders in the elderly. *American Journal of Psychiatry, 151,* 640–649.

Gallo, J. J., & Lebowitz, B. D. (1999). The epidemiology of common late-life mental disorders in the community: Themes for the new century. *Psychiatric Services, 50,* 1158–1166.

Gallo, J. J., Ryan, S. D., & Ford, D. (1999). Attitudes, knowledge, and behavior of family physicians regarding depression in late life. *Archives of Family Medicine, 8*(3), 249–255.

Gallo, J. J., Royall, D. R., & Anthony, J. C. (1993). Risk factors for the onset of depression in middle age and later life. *Social Psychiatry and Psychiatric Epidemiology, 28,* 101–108.

Gask, L., Sibbald, B., & Creed, F. (1997). Evaluating models of working at the interface between mental health services and primary care. *British Journal of Psychiatry, 170,* 6–11.

George, L. K. (1992). Community and home care for mentally ill older adults. In J. E. Birren, R. B. Sloane, G. D. Cohen, N. R. Hooyman, B. D. Lebowitz, & M. I. Wykle (Eds.), *Handbook of mental health and aging* (2nd ed., pp. 793–813). San Diego, CA: Academic Press.

Grant, B. F., Harford, T. C., Dawson, D. A., Chou, P. S., & Pickering, R. P. (1994). Prevalence of DSM-IV alcohol abuse and dependence: United States, 1992. *Alcohol Health and Research World, 18,* 243.

Greenwald, B. S., Kramer-Ginsberg, E., Bogerts, B., Ashtari, M., Aupperle, P., Wu, H., et al. (1997). Qualitative magnetic resonance imaging findings in geriatric depression. Possible link between later-onset depression and Alzheimer's disease? *Psychological Medicine, 27,* 421–431.

Haight, B. K., Michel, Y., & Hendrix, S. (1998). Life review: Preventing despair in newly relocated nursing home residents' short- and long-term effects. *International Journal of Aging and Human Development, 47,* 119–142.

Hanson, M., & Guthiel, L. A. (2004). Motivational strategies with alcohol involved older adults: Implications for social work practice. *Social Work, 49*(3), 364–372.

Harlow, S. D., Goldberg, E. L., & Comstock, G. W. (1991). A longitudinal study of risk factors for depressive symptomatology in elderly widowed and married women. *American Journal of Epidemiology, 134,* 526–538.

Hebert, L. E., Scherr, P. A., Beckett, L. A., Albert, M. S., Pilgrim, D. M., Chown, M. J., et al. (1995). Age-specific incidence of Alzheimer's disease in a community population. *Journal of the American Medical Association, 273,* 1354–1359.

Helzer, J. E., Burnam, A., & McEvoy, L. T. (1991). Alcohol abuse and dependence. In L. N. Robins & D. A. Regier (Eds.), *Psychiatric disorders in America: The Epidemiologic Catchment Area study* (pp. 81–115). New York: Free Press.

Hill, L. R., Klauber, M. R., Salmon, D. P., Yu, E. S., Liu, W. T., Zhang, M., et al. (1993). Functional status, education, and the diagnosis of dementia in the Shanghai survey. *Neurology, 43,* 138–145.

Illinois Rural Health Association (IRHA). (2006). *Mental health in rural Illinois: Recovery is the goal: An analysis of mental health care in rural Illinois.* Springfield, IL: Author.

Jeste, D. V., & Palmer, B. (1998). Secondary psychoses: An overview. *Seminars in Clinical Neuro Psychiatry, 3,* 2–3.

Johansson, B., & Zarit, S. H. (1995). Prevalence and incidence of dementia in the oldest-old: A longitudinal study of a population-based sample of 84–90 year olds in Sweden. *International Journal of Geriatric Psychiatry, 10,* 359–366.

Jorm, A. F., Korten, A. E., & Henderson, A. S. (1987). The prevalence of dementia: A quantitative integration of the literature. *Acta Psychiatrica Scandinavica, 76,* 465–479.

Kaplan, M. S., Adamek, M. E., & Martin, J. L. (2001). Confidence of primary care physicians in assessing the suicidality of geriatric patients. *International Journal of Geriatric Psychiatry, 16*(7), 728–734.

Katon, W. J., Robinson, P., Von Korff, M., Lin, E., Bush, T., Ludman, E., et al. (1996). A multifaceted intervention to improve treatment of depression in primary care. *Archives of General Psychiatry, 53,* 924–932.

Katon, W., Von Korff, M., Lin, E., Unutzer, J., Simon, G., Walker, E., et al. (1997). Population-based care of depression: Effective disease management strategies to decrease prevalence. *General Hospital Psychiatry, 19,* 169–178.

Katz, I. R., & Parmelee, P. A. (1997). Overview. In R. L. Rubinstein & M. Lawton (Eds.), *Depression in long term and residential care* (pp. 1–28). New York: Springer.

Katzman, R. (1993). Education and the prevalence of dementia and Alzheimer's disease. *Neurology, 43,* 13–20.

Kessler, R. C., McGonagle, K. A., Zhao, S., Nelson, C. B., Hughs, M., Ehleman, S., et al. (1994). Lifetime and 12-month prevalence rates of DSM-III-R psychiatric disorders in the United States. *Archives of General Psychiatry, 51,* 8–19.

Klein, W. C., & Jess, C. (2002). One last pleasure? Alcohol use among elderly people in nursing homes. *Health and Social Work, 27*(3), 193–203.

Kofoed, L. L. (1984). Abuse and misuse of over-the-counter drugs by the elderly. In R. M. Atkinson (Ed.), *Alcohol and drug abuse in old age* (pp. 49–59). Washington, DC: American Psychiatric Press.

Krishnan, K. R., Hays, J. C., Tupler, L. A., George, L. K., & Blazer, D. G. (1995). Clinical and phenomenological comparisons of late-onset and early-onset depression. *American Journal of Psychiatry, 152*, 785–788.

LaGreca, A. J., Akers, R. L., & Dwyer, J. W. (1988). Life events and alcohol behavior among older adults. *The Gerontologist, 28*(4), 552–558.

Lambert, D. (1995). Access of rural AFDC Medicaid beneficiaries to mental health services. *Health Care Financing Review, 17*, 133–145.

Lebowitz, B. D., Pearson, J. L., & Cohen, G. D. (1998). *Clinical geriatric psychopharmacology.* Baltimore: Williams & Wilkins.

Levkoff, S. E., Chen, H., Fisher, J. E., & McIntyre, J. S. (2006). *Evidence-based behavioral health practices for older adults: A guide to implementation.* New York: Springer.

Liberto, J. G., Oslin, D. W., & Ruskin, P. E. (1992). Alcoholism in older persons: A review of the literature. *Hospital and Community Psychiatry, 43*, 975–984.

Lindesay, J., Briggs, K., & Murphy, E. (1989). The guy's/age concern survey: Prevalence rates of cognitive impairment, depression and anxiety in an urban elderly community. *British Journal of Psychiatry, 155*, 317–329.

Mackenzie, C. S., Gekoski, W. L., & Knox, V. J. (1999). Do family physicians treat older patients with mental disorders differently from younger patients? *Canadian Family Physician, 45*, 124–129.

Meeks, S., Carstensen, L. L., Stafford, P. B., Brenner, L. L., Weathers, F., Welch, R., et al. (1997). Mental health needs of the chronically mentally ill elderly. *Psychology and Aging, 5*, 163–171.

Meeks, S., & Murrell, S. A. (1997). Mental illness in late life: Socioeconomic conditions, psychiatric symptoms, and adjustment of long-term sufferers. *Psychology and Aging, 12*, 296–308.

Mehta, K. M., Yaffe, K., & Covinsky, K. E. (2002). Cognitive impairment, depressive symptoms, and functional decline in older people. *Journal of the American Geriatrics Society, 50*(6) 1045–1050.

Memmet, J. L. (2003). Alcohol consumption by elderly Americans. *Journal of Studies on Alcohol, 64*(6), 884–892.

Mendes de Leon, C. F., Kasl, S. V., & Jacobs, S. (1994). A prospective study of widowhood and changes in symptoms of depression in a community sample of the elderly. *Psychological Medicine, 24*, 613–624.

Mickus, M., Colenda, C., & Hogan, A. (2000). Knowledge of mental health benefits and preferences for type of mental health providers among the general public. *Psychiatric Services, 51*(2), 199–202.

Mueller, K., Kashinath, P., & Ullrich, F. (1997). Lengthening spells of "uninsurance" and their consequences. *Journal of Rural Health, 13*(1), 29–37.

Musnick, M. A., Blazer, D. G. & Hays, J. C. (2000). Religious activity, alcohol use, and depression in a sample of elderly Baptists. *Research on Aging, 22*(2), 91–116.

National Health Interview Survey (NHIS). (2000). Retrieved August 25, 2005, from http://www.cdc.gov/nchs/about/major/nhis/quest_data_related_1997_forward.htm

National Household Survey on Drug Abuse (NHSDA). (2000). Retrieved August 25, 2005, from http://www.health.org/govstudy/bkd405/

National Institute on Aging (NIA). (2000). *Senior health facts.* Retrieved May 20, 2007, from www.seniorhealth.gov

Neugarten, B. L. (1984). Psychological aspects of aging and illness. *Psychosomatics,* 25(2), 123–125.

New Freedom Commission on Mental Health. (2004). *Subcommittee on rural issues: Background paper.* DHHS Pub. No. SMA-04–3890. Rockville, MD.

Paykel, E. S., Brayne, C., Huppert, F. A., Gill, C., Barkley, C., Gehlhaar, E., et al. (1994). Incidence of dementia in a population older than 75 years in the United Kingdom. *Archives of General Psychiatry, 51,* 325–332.

Proctor, E., Morrow-Howell, N., Doré, P., Wentz, J., Rubin, E., Thompson, S., et al. (2003). Co-morbid medical conditions among depressed elderly patients discharged home after acute psychiatric care. *The American Journal of Geriatric Psychiatry, 11*(3), 329–338.

Proctor, E. K., Morrow-Howell, N., Rubin, E., & Ringenberg, M. (1999). Service use by elderly patients after psychiatric hospitalization. *Psychiatric Services, 50*(4), 553–555.

Regier, D. A., Goldberg, I. D., & Taube, C. A. (1978). The defacto U.S. mental health service system: A public health perspective, *Archives of General Psychiatry, 35*(6), 85–93.

Regier, D. A., Farmer, M. E., Rae, D. S., Locke, B. Z., Keith, S. J., Judd, L. L., et al. (1990). Comorbidity of mental disorders with alcohol and other drug abuse. *Journal of the American Medical Association, 264,* 2511–2518.

Regier, D. A., Boyd, J. H., Burke, J. D. Jr., Rae, D. S., Myers, J. K., Kramer, M., et al. (1988). One-month prevalence of mental disorders in the United States. Based on five epidemiologic catchment area sites. *Archives of General Psychiatry, 45,* 977–986.

Reynolds, C. F., III. (1998, March 8–11). *The challenge of treatment in 70+ year olds with recurrent major depression: Excellent short-term but brittle long-term response.* Annual meeting of the American Association for Geriatric Psychiatry, San Diego, CA.

Ritchie, K., & Kildea, D. (1995). Is senile dementia "age-related" or "ageing-related"? Evidence from meta-analysis of dementia prevalence in the oldest old. *Lancet, 346,* 931–934.

Robinson, G. K. (1990). The psychiatric component of long-term care models. In B. S. Fogel, G. L. Gottlieb, & A. Furino (Eds.), *Mental health policy for older Americans: Protecting minds at risk* (pp. 157–178). Washington, DC: American Psychiatric Press.

Rogers, A., & Barusch, A. (2000). Mental health service utilization among frail, low income elders: Perceptions of home service providers and elders in the community. *Gerontological Social Work, 34*(2), 23–38.

Rowe, J. W., & Kahn, R. L. (1997). Successful aging. *Gerontologist, 37,* 433–440.

Salloway, S., Malloy, P., Kohn, R., Gillard, E., Duffy, J., Rogg, J., et al. (1996). MRI and neuropsychological differences in early- and late-life-onset geriatric depression. *Neurology, 46,* 1567–1574.

Sarkisian, C. A., Hays, R. D., Berry, S. H., & Mangione, C. M. (2001). Expectations regarding aging among older adults and physicians who care for older adults. *Medical-Care, 39*(9), 1025–1036.

Saunders, P. A., Copeland, J. R., Dewey, M. E., Davidson, I. A., McWilliam, C., Sharma, V., et al. (1991). Heavy drinking as a risk factor for depression and dementia in elderly men. Findings from the Liverpool longitudinal community study. *British Journal of Psychiatry, 159,* 213–216.

Schonfeld, L. (1993). Behavioral treatment of addictions. *Addictive Behaviors, 18*(2), 105–106.

Schulberg, H. C., Madonia, M. J., Block, M. R., Coulehan, J. L., Scott, C. P., Rodriguez, E., et al. (1995). Major depression in primary care practice: Clinical characteristics and treatment implications. *Psychosomatics, 36,* 129–137.

Skoog, I. (1993). The prevalence of psychotic, depressive, and anxiety syndromes in demented and non-demented 85-year olds. *International Journal of Geriatric Psychiatry, 8,* 247–253.

Scott-Lennox, J. A., & George, L. (1996). Epidemiology of psychiatric disorders and mental health services use among older Americans. In B. L. Levin & J. Petrila (Eds.), *Mental health services: A public health perspective* (pp. 253–289). New York: Oxford University Press.

Special Committee on Aging. (1987). *Medicare prescription drug issues: Report to the Chairman, Special Committee on Aging.* Washington, DC: General Accounting Office.

Stolee, P., Kessler, L., & Le Clair, J. K. (1996). A community development and outreach program in geriatric mental health: Four years' experience. *Journal of the American Geriatrics Society, 44*, 314–320.

Stern, Y., Gurland, B., Tatemichi, T. K., Tang, M. X., Wilder, D., & Mayeux, R. (1994). Influence of education and occupation on the incidence of Alzheimer's disease. *Journal of the American Medical Association, 271*, 1004–1010.

Temple, M. T., & Leino, E. V. (1989). Long-term outcomes of drinking: A 20-year longitudinal study of men. *British Journal of Addiction, 84*, 889–899.

United States Department of Health and Human Services (USDHHS). (1999). *Mental health and older adults. Chapter five appearing in report of the surgeon general on mental health needs.* Bethesda, MD: U.S. Government Printing Office.

United States Department of Health and Human Services (USDHHS). (2000). *NIA's strategic plan to address health disparities in aging: Fiscal Years 2000–2005.* Bethesda, MD: U.S. Government Printing Office.

United States Department of Health and Human Services (USDHHS). (2001). *Mental health: Culture, race and ethnicity, A supplement to mental health: A report to the Surgeon General.* Rockville, MD: U.S. Department of Health and Human Services, Public Health Service, Office of the Surgeon General.

United States Department of Health and Human Services, Centers for Disease Control and prevention, National Center for Health Statistics. National Health Interview Survey (NHIS). (2004). Hyattsville, MD: National Center for Health Statistics, Centers for Disease Control and Prevention.

United States Department of Health and Human Services (USDHHS). (2005). Featured program: The Gatekeeper model, *e-Communication, 1*(2). Retrieved November 12, 2006, from http://www.samhsa.gov/OlderAdultsTAC/

United States Department of Health and Human Services (USDHHS). (2006a). Featured Program: The Mental Health and Aging Systems Integration Initiative, *e-Communication, 2*(1). Retrieved November 12, 2006, from http://www.samhsa.gov/Older AdultsTAC/

United States Department of Health and Human Services. (2006b). Featured Program: The Recovery Center, *e-Communication, 2*(1). Retrieved November 12, 2006, from http://www.samhsa.gov/OlderAdultsTAC/

United States Department of Health and Human Services, National Center for Health Statistics (USDHHS, NCHS). (2001). *Behavioral risk factor surveillance system (BFRSS).* Bethesda, MD: Government Printing Office.

United States Department of Health and Human Services, National Center for Health Statistics (USDHHS, NCHS). (2004). *Behavioral risk factor surveillance system (BFRSS).* Bethesda, MD: Government Printing Office.

Unutzer, J., Katon, W. J., Simon, G., Walker, E. A., Grembowski, D., & Patrick, D. (1996). Depression, quality of life, and use of health services in primary care patients over 65: A 4-year prospective study. *Psychosomatics, 37*, 35.

Wallace, J., & O'Hara, M. W. (1992). Increases in depressive symptomatology in the rural elderly: Results from a cross-sectional and longitudinal study. *Journal of Abnormal Psychology, 101*, 398–404.

Waters, E. (1995). Let's not wait till it's broke: Interventions to maintain and enhance mental health in late life. In M. Gatz (Ed.), *Emerging issues in the mental health and aging* (pp. 183–209). Washington, DC: American Psychological Association.

Wells, K. B., Stewart, A., Hays, R. D., Burnam, M. A., Rogers, W., Daniels, M., et al. (1989). The functioning and well-being of depressed patients: Results from the Medical Outcomes Study. *Journal of the American Medical Association, 262,* 914–919.

Zisook, S., & Shuchter, S. R. (1991). Depression through the first year after the death of a spouse. *American Journal of Psychiatry, 148,* 1346–1352.

CHAPTER 17

Health Programs, Services, and Issues

Older adults are living longer today than they were a hundred years ago, and many of the changes in life span can be attributed to technology, changes in living conditions, and an understanding and attentiveness to health. This being said, the health status of older Americans (and aging populations in most industrialized countries in the world) is a glaring concern for health policy and program planners due to the economic costs of care and need to ensure that people who grow old are also healthy. Julie L. Gerberding, director, Centers for Disease Control and Prevention, has suggested that "The aging of the population is one of the major public health challenges of the 21st century. With more than 70 million baby boomers in the United States poised to join the ranks of those aged 65 or over, the prevention of diseases and injuries is one of the few tools available to reduce the expected growth of health care and long-term care costs" (Gerberding, 2006).

At the turn of the century (1900), over 100 years ago, only 3 million people (4%) in the United States were over the age of 65. In 2006, more than 36 million Americans are found within this same age group, and it is predicted that this number is expected to grow by 2030 to over 70 million people as our current population ages. In addition to the increased numbers of older adults, we will also see an increase in racially and ethnically diverse older adults.

A CURRENT HEALTH PROFILE OF OLDER ADULTS IN THE UNITED STATES

The aging of America is triggering a higher demand for health care and social services. Currently, about 80% of older adults have at least one chronic condition, and 50% have at least two. These chronic conditions include diagnostic categories such as heart disease, stroke, diabetes, cancer, and Alzheimer's disease. These chronic conditions impact older adults severely to the point that they cannot perform basic activities of daily living such as bathing, shopping, dressing, and eating. As a consequence the quality of life can be impacted and caregivers can also be affected by the additional burden of care required.

Along with increased longevity for older adults, it is predicted (CDC, 2006) that health care costs will also increase 25% by 2030. Consequently, the prevention of morbidity is a critical way to reduce health care costs. In addition, the prevention of disease and injury will also help older adults remain independent for as long as possible, which will result in improved quality of life and defer the need for costly long-term care. Figure 17.1 provides an overview of the types of chronic diseases that affect older adults. Figure 17.2 provides the data to support these percentages based on 2003 statistics.

As Figure 17.3 indicates, diseases of the heart have witnessed the most dramatic decrease over time, while other diseases have changed slightly. Alzheimer's disease has witnessed the most dramatic increase in prevalence over the past 20 years, as showcased in Figure 17.2.

Chronic Health Conditions

Chronic health conditions affect older adults (65+) and impact their overall health status. Over half of the population interviewed through the National Health Interview Survey (CDC NHIS, 2006) reported having arthritis. NHIS is a panel study, administered to a representative sample of the U.S. population. Leading chronic health conditions for women in 2003 were arthritis (55%), hypertension (54.7%), and heart disease (27.7%). Leading causes of chronic diseases for men were hypertension (48.1%), arthritis (42.9%) and heart disease (37.2%). It is interesting to note that women reported higher rates of arthritis, hypertension, and asthma as compared to men, while men surpassed women in the areas of heart disease, stroke, emphysema, chronic bronchitis, and diabetes.

PROGRAMS AVAILABLE TO MEET THE HEALTH CARE NEEDS OF OLDER ADULTS

In response to health care needs a number of programs are available for older adults to utilize to maintain their health status or promote their health care. These programs include Medicare, Medicaid, the Centers for Disease Control and Prevention, and the Area Agencies on Aging. This section will discuss each of these programs.

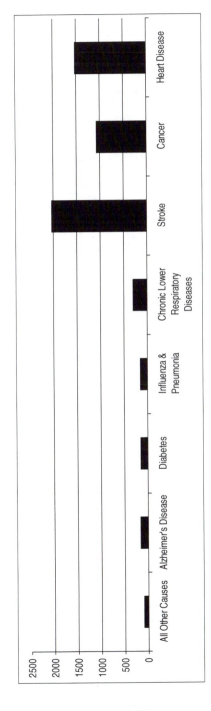

FIGURE 17.1 Causes of death among U.S. adults, 65+, 2001.

Notes: These are reported as rates per 100,000 by the Centers for Disease Control and Prevention, 2003. Heart disease is reported as 1,524 per 100,000 as compared to cancer (1,073 per 100,000); influenza and pneumonia (154.8 per 100,000); diabetes (150.7 per 100,000) and HIV (1.5 per 100,000).

Source: www.agingstats.gov

273

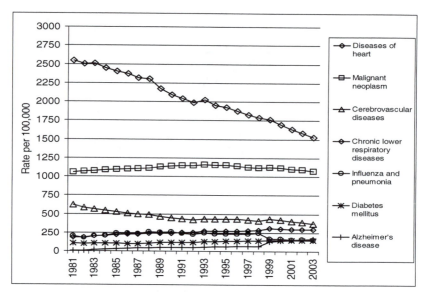

FIGURE 17.2   Mortality among people 65+ years

Notes: Data is reported as a rate per 100,000. Data is based upon ICD9 codes.

Source: CDC, National Center for Health Statistics, National Vital Statistics Report, 2002.

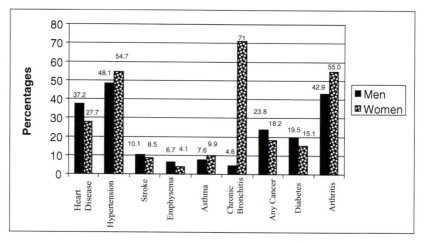

FIGURE 17.3   Chronic health conditions.

Notes: Data is based upon a 2-year average from 2003–2004. The question used to ascertain arthritis was "Have you EVER been told by a doctor or other health professional that you have some form of arthritis, rheumatoid arthritis, gout, lupus, or fibromyalgia"? Data also refer to a civilian, noninstitutionalized population.

Source: Centers for Disease Control and Prevention, National Center for Health Statistics, National Health Interview Survey.

274

Medicare

Robert Butler, in his book titled *Why Survive? Growing Old in America*, suggests that most Americans could breathe a sigh of relief when Medicare was signed into law in 1965 that their basic health care needs would be taken care of as they grew into old age. Unfortunately, this expectation was far from reality. Despite the fact that health care expenses account for 12% of the average senior's household spending, Medicare only covers about 57% of the total health care costs for older adults, and the balance of the costs are left to the individual (Vierck & Hodges, 2003).

Essentially services covered through Medicare are services that are "medically reasonable and necessary for the diagnosis and treatment of illness or injury or to improve the functioning of a malformed body member" (Social Security Act, 1965). As described earlier in this text, Medicare consists of four parts: A, B, C and D. However, the services described in this section will deal with Parts A and B.

Services covered by Medicare Part A include inpatient hospital care, skilled nursing facility care (up to 100 days following hospitalization), home health visits, and some hospice care. Home health care can include services such as skilled nursing care on a part-time or intermittent basis by a licensed/registered nurse and help with medical activities such as changing bandages, IV therapy, and so on. This program also includes services from a certified home health aide on a part-time or intermittent basis to help with personal care if one is in receipt of another medical service to include physical therapy (includes exercise to regain movement and strength), speech therapy (includes exercises to regain and strengthen speech skills), medical social services (help with social and emotional concerns related to the illness), and occupational therapy (helps patient regain ability to do usual daily activities by themselves).

Medicare Part A does not cover services such as acupuncture, dental care and dentures, cosmetic surgery, custodial care, health care while traveling outside the United States, hearing aids, orthopedic shoes, outpatient prescription drugs, routine or yearly physical exams, routine care of one's feet, routine care of one's eyes, screening tests, and immunizations.

Medicare Part B does provide for some of the screening and preventative services not available through part A; however, in order to qualify for these services, individuals must voluntarily opt into Medicare Part B, and pay a monthly premium. Services available through Medicare Part B include consultations, and home, office, and institutional visits. Medical and health services including laboratory and diagnostic tests, x-ray and radiation therapy, outpatient hospital services, rural health clinic services, durable medical equipment, home dialysis supplies and equipment, artificial devices, physical and speech therapy, and ambulance services. Preventative services include an annual screening mammography, screening Pap smear and screening pelvic exam once every 3 years, diabetes self-management training services, bone mass measurement, and prostrate cancer screening. Although there are guidelines for how often one may receive these screening services, if a person is deemed to be at risk of developing medical conditions such as glaucoma, diabetes, or cancer, screenings can be approved to be conducted at more frequent intervals. Drugs and vaccines such as flu shots, certain cancer drugs, and hepatitis B vaccines are covered also under Medicare Plan B. A wider array of prescription drugs, however, are covered under Medicare Part D.

In November 2004, Medicare Part D was signed into legislation as an amendment to the current Medicare plan. Although it was not implemented until late 2005 and early 2006, its overall intent was to assist older adults with their prescription drug expenses. The registration process takes place through the use of an online program and can range in the number of providers available, depending upon the state within which one resides. Although the process of using an online mechanism was intended to be efficient and reduce paperwork, the barriers to using this service had not been anticipated by Congress. People considered older adults (65 and older in this instance) may not be as computer literate as anticipated, and people residing in rural communities may have limited access to computer network systems. In addition, the literacy levels of a proportion of old-old has also posed challenges to using this program as effectively as envisioned by the architects.

Medicaid

Medicaid is a health care program designed to meet the needs of the poorest people (across the life span, including adults who are 65 years of age and older) and is a program that is jointly funded between individual states and the federal government. Medicaid, as we saw earlier, was a program that became law in 1965 under Title XIX if the Social Security Act. Since each state establishes its own eligibility standards, as well as determines the type, amount, duration, and scope of services, it may be difficult to identify the specific services one can receive from this program. Each state sets the rate of payment for services and administers its own program; thus, eligibility as well as services may vary from state to state.

Despite the variation across states for Medicaid coverage, the federal government contributes between 50% and 88% of the costs of each state Medicaid program. Some of the services covered include inpatient and outpatient hospital services, laboratory and x-ray services, skilled nursing home services, physicians' services, physical therapy, hospice care, and rehabilitative services.

Medicaid can provide services to medically needy older adults and can work with Medicare to assure health care coverage for low-income older adults. In addition to providing coverage for poor older adults, it also provides health care coverage for the poor and disabled.

The Centers for Disease Control and Prevention

CDC is committed to ensuring that all people, especially those at greater risk for health disparities, will achieve their optimal life span with the best possible quality of health in every stage of life. With new health protection goals that support healthy people in healthy places across all life stages, CDC is setting the agenda to enable people to enjoy a healthy life by delaying death and the onset of illness and disability by accelerating improvements in public health.

Within CDC's National Center for Chronic Disease Prevention and Health Promotion, the Healthy Aging Program serves as the focal point for older adult health. The Healthy Aging Program is engaged in many activities designed to provide a comprehensive approach to health promotion and disease prevention for older adults. It also has developed five ways to implement this approach, often in collaboration with other CDC programs, such as injury prevention and adult immunization.

1. Providing high-quality health information. CDC provides reliable, science-based, high-quality information on the health of seniors for policy makers, public health and aging professionals, the media, and consumers through publications, conferences, training sessions, and Web sites/listservs. The Healthy Aging Web site (http://www.cdc.gov/aging) also provides valuable information and is regularly updated. Working with the American Society on Aging, the Healthy Aging Program engages journalists across the country on issues such as arthritis, immunizations, and fall prevention.

2. Facilitating the prevention efforts of health care providers and others who serve older adults. Medicare pays for many critical preventive services, yet fewer than 1 in 10 adults aged 65 years or older receive all recommended screenings and immunizations. CDC's Healthy Aging Program supports a model program called SPARC (Sickness Prevention Achieved through Regional Collaboration), which has shown significant success in broadening the use of preventive services. SPARC works to promote public access to services, help medical practices provide preventive services, and strengthen local accountability for service delivery. SPARC currently operates in counties in Connecticut, Massachusetts,

and New York, where it serves as a local bridge between public health, aging services, and the health care system. Among its successes is doubling the use of mammography screening among targeted populations in these states.

3. Integrating public health prevention expertise with the reach of the aging services network. As described in the Older Americans Act, CDC has an advisory role to the aging services network, which reaches seniors in virtually every U.S. community. To take full advantage of opportunities to improve the health of older adults, the Healthy Aging Program strives to integrate public health's expertise in research, health tracking, and programs with the experience and reach of the aging services network. CDC and the Administration on Aging (AOA), in collaboration with the Chronic Disease Directors and the National Association of State Units on Aging, funded 35 grants to promote partnerships between state health departments and state units on aging during fiscal years 2003–2005. In fiscal year 2006, CDC and AOA will continue using these State-based Examples of Network Innovation, Opportunity, and Replication (SENIOR) grants to support evidence-based programs at state and local levels.

4. Identifying and putting into practice what works in prevention. Research shows that if seniors maintain just three healthy habits—moderate physical activity, good nutrition, and no smoking—they can delay disability by as much as 10 years. The benefits of such research, however, will never be realized unless this knowledge is applied to programs in communities. The Healthy Aging Program supports the Healthy Aging Research Network, a subset of CDC's Prevention Research Centers, to implement a prevention research agenda for older adult health. Current work includes an evidence-based review of interventions for depression and development of a tool that communities can use to assess environmental barriers, resources, and opportunities for physical activity.

5. Monitoring changes in the health of older Americans. CDC is the lead national agency responsible for collecting data and monitoring changes over time in the health of older Americans. This information helps strengthen efforts to prevent disease, disability, and injury, and it identifies health-related disparities among different groups of older adults. In 2004, CDC released *The State of Aging and Health in America 2004*, which was developed with the Merck Institute of Aging & Health and The Gerontological Society of America. This report provides national and state data on 15 key indicators related to older adult health and rates the nation and the states on how well they are meeting national Healthy People 2000 targets. In addition, the report includes examples of

successful strategies for improving the health and quality of life of older adults. (CDC, 2006)

Area Agencies on Aging

Local Area Agencies on Aging fund local service providers or provide health-related services as outlined in the Older Americans Act. Some programs and services related to health care issues include health promotion activities. Health promotion provides programs and activities relating to chronic disabling conditions, the prevention and reduction of effects of disease, reduction of alcohol and substance abuse, smoking cessation, weight loss and control, and stress management. Information is provided to older people, usually at senior centers, on chronic disabling conditions such as osteoporosis and cardiovascular disease. Also, information is provided on diagnosis, prevention, treatment, and rehabilitation of age-related diseases and disabling chronic conditions, such as Alzheimer's disease and other related dementia disorders. Other health promotion topics include home safety, safety as drivers and as pedestrians, safe use of medications, alternative/complementary medicine health fraud and cons, healthy lifestyles, healthy hearts, self-protection, and crime prevention.

Health screenings are also conducted within senior nutrition sites or as a service for older adults, spearheaded by local area agencies on aging. These routine health screenings enable older adults to improve their own awareness and understanding of their health issues and encourage them to obtain the necessary health and medical treatment. In most instances, the main focus of this health screening program is to identify, evaluate, and link health conditions to the appropriate health care service necessary. Health screenings include monthly blood pressure checks, occasional blood sugar screening, testing for glaucoma, cholesterol, diabetes, hearing, vision, and so on. Generally there is no charge for screenings, however individual Area Agencies on Aging or their designees may charge a nominal fee, depending on the cost to administer such services.

ISSUES FACING OLDER ADULTS AND HEALTH CARE NEEDS

Financing Health Care for Older Adults

As can be expected, a major issue that will be faced in the United States will relate to financing of health care services for older adults, especially through the Medicare program. The number of days spent in hospitals or skilled nursing facilities has increased steadily over the past decade. In 2002, while the average number of days per patient visit to the hospital had seen a decline to 5.8 days (FIFARS, 2006) from 8.3 days in 1992, the use of health care services in terms of Medicare-covered stays per 1,000 people actually saw an increase from 1992 but stabilized between 1999 and 2002. The number of skilled nursing home stays also increased over the decade from 28 per 1,000 in 1992 to 72 days per 1,000 in 2002 (CMMS, 2003). Figure 17.4 illustrates this point for recipients of Medicare.

The use of home health services has seen a sharp decline since the implementation of the Balanced Budget Act of 1997, while physician visits and consultations have been on the increase for Medicare enrollees since this period, and increased from 11,359 in 1992 to 13, 685 in 2002 (CMMS, 2003). Physician visits and consultations along with home health visits were much more common among people over the age of 65 than hospitalization or admission into a skilled nursing facility. Home health care visits decreased from 8,376 in 1996 to 2, 358 in 2002 (CMMS, 2003). Figure 17.5 provides an illustration of the use of health care services.

While the number of physician consultations has increased, this may be due in part to the decrease in Medigap and increases in HMO coverage

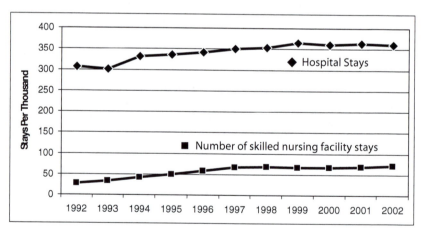

FIGURE 17.4   Hospital and nursing facility stays.
Notes: Data for Medicare enrollees in fee-for-service only. Managed care enrollees were excluded from the denominator effective 1994.
Source: Centers for Medicare and Medicaid Services, Medicare claims and enrollment data.

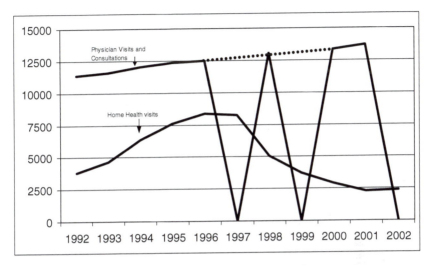

FIGURE 17.5   Physician and home health care visits.

Notes: Physicians visits and consultations refer to settings including physician offices, hospitals, emergency rooms, and nursing homes. Data are for Medicare enrollees in fee-for-service only. Visits are represented per 1,000 Medicare enrollees. No data is available for physician visits for 1997, 1999 and 2000. In these cases this period represented with a dotted line

Source: Centers for Medicare and Medicaid Services claims and enrollment data.

(purchased as a supplement such as Medicare Part C). Medicaid coverage increased slightly between 1999 and 2003. Figure 17.6 illustrates the sources of health insurance used.

A comparison of health care expenditures for Medicare enrollees over a decade (1992 as compared to 2003) is important, and although the amount of money expended may be greater in some areas, the amount as a percent of the total is actually lower. For example, the data suggest that there was a decrease in inpatient hospital expenditure from 32% in 1992 to 26% in 2003, an increase in physician/outpatient hospitalizations from 32% in 1992 to 35% in 2003, and a dramatic decrease in funds expended for nursing home/long-term care (20% in 1992 as compared to 14% in 2003). Expenditures for health care dramatically increased from 8% in 1992 to 14% in 2003 (Centers for Medicare and Medicaid Services, 2003). Table 17.1 illustrates health care expenditures comparing 1992 to 2003. The rising expenditures for prescription drug coverage led to the development of Medicare Part D prescription drug coverage.

Health care costs increase as one ages (see Figures 17.7 and 17.8), and it has been cited that the largest amount of health care expenditures

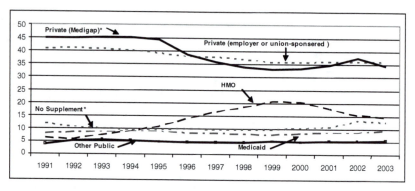

FIGURE 17.6   Sources of health insurance.
Notes: Estimates are based upon enrollees' status in the fall of each year.
*Includes people with supplements where the sponsor is not known.
Source: Centers for Medicare and Medicaid Services, Medicare Current Beneficiary Survey.

occur during the last year of one's life. Figure 17.7 illustrates health care expenditures over a 10-year period, with the 85-year-old and older group of Medicare enrollees utilizing the highest amount of Medicare funds. In 2003, payments for health care services were expended for key components identified within the Medicare Act, but as Table 17.2 illustrates, Medicaid, out-of-pocket expenses, and other sources also make up some of the payer sources for services. Medicare supported 100% of hospice care expenses in 2003, 88% of inpatient hospital expenses, 83% of home health care expenses, and 80% of short-term institution stays. Physician/

TABLE 17.1   Health Care Expenditures

Type of Facility	1992	2003
Inpatient hospital	32	26
Physician/outpatient hospital	32	35
Nursing home/long-term institution	20	14
Home health care	4	3
Prescription drugs	8	14
Other(short-term hospitalization/dental)	4	8

Figures are reported as percentages.
Notes: Refers to the average annual cost of health care for Medicare enrollees age 65 and over, in 2003 U.S. dollars, by age group, 1992–2003. Data include both out-of-pocket costs and costs covered by insurance. Dollars are inflation adjusted to 2003 using the Consumer Price Index.
Target population: Data refer to Medicare enrollees.
Source: Centers for Medicare and Medicaid Services, Medicare Current Beneficiary Survey

medical expenditures accounted for 66% of Medicare expenditures, and 63% of expenditures expended on outpatient hospitalizations. Less than 1% was expended on dental care and 3% of Medicare enrollees utilized payments for prescription medications (FIFARS, 2006). Despite the fact that oral health care mirrors the body and is a predictor of heart disease, cardiovascular problems, and oral cancers (USDHHS, 1999), virtually no expenditures occurred within the Medicare plan for dental care or oral health.

Auditory and Vision Care

Findings from the National Health Interview Survey (CDC NCHS, 2004) revealed that nearly one-third of all women over the age of 65 (34%) reported that they had some trouble hearing, as compared to nearly half of the men surveyed (48%). This disparity may be due to occupational-related injuries acquired by males. Men would be more prone than women to acquire such injuries. This is illustrated in Figure 17.9.

The outcomes for sight are far better for people over 65 years of age. Only 19% of women reported having trouble seeing, as compared to 14% of their male counterparts (NHIS, 2004). This is illustrated in Figure 17.9.

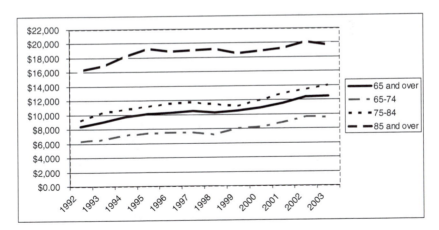

FIGURE 17.7   Annual health care costs, persons 65+ years, 1992–2003.
Notes: Data include both out-of-pocket costs and costs covered by insurance. Dollars are inflation adjusted to 2003 using the Consumer Price Index.
Target population: Data refer to Medicare enrollees.
Source: Centers for Medicare and Medicaid Services, Medicare Current Beneficiary Survey.

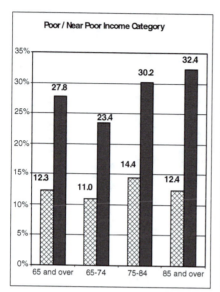
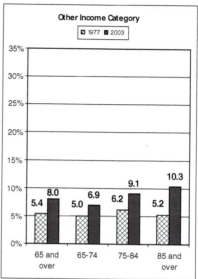

FIGURE 17.8   Out-of-pocket health care expenditures—Medicare enrollees.

Notes: Out-of-pocket health care expenditures exclude personal spending for health insurance premiums. Including expenditures for out-of-pocket premiums in the estimates of out-of-pocket spending would increase the percentage of household income spent on health care in all years. People are categorized into the "poor/near poor" income category if their household income is below 125% of the poverty level; otherwise, people are categorized into the "other" income category level. The poverty level was calculated according to the U.S. Census Bureau guidelines for the corresponding year.

Source: Agency for Healthcare Research and Quality. Medical Expenditure Panel Survey (MEPS) and MEPS predecessor surveys

Oral Health Care

Nearly one quarter of all individuals reported in 2004 having lost all of their natural teeth. Women were slightly more likely to have lost their natural teeth (27%) as compared to men (24%). This alarming statistic is illustrated in Figure 17.9.

Prevention Services

One aspect of prevention intervention includes immunizations, especially for influenza and pneumococcal disease. Over a 15-year period (1989–2004) there has been a steady increase in the number of people over 65 years of age who have had immunizations; however, non-Hispanic whites are the most likely to pursue such prevention strategies, followed by Hispanics, while the least likely are non-Hispanic blacks (CDC NCHS, 2004).

TABLE 17.2   Sources of Payment for Health Care Services

Health care service	Medicare	Medicaid	Out-of-Pocket	Other
Hospice	100	0	0	0
Inpatient hospital	88	1	3	8
Home health care	83	1	10	6
Short-term institution	80	3	7	10
Physician/medical	66	2	16	17
Outpatient hospital	63	2	10	25
Prescription drugs	3	10	33	56
Dental	1	0	75	25
Nursing home/long-term care	1	48	45	6
Other	53	9	19	19

Notes: Data are reported as percentages. Data refer to sources of payment for health care services for Medicare enrollees age 65 and older, by type and service, 2003. The "other" category refers to private insurance, Department of Veterans Affairs, and other public programs.
Target population: Data refer to Medicare enrollees.
Source: Centers for Medicare and Medicaid, Medicare Current Beneficiary Survey.

Diet

While the only health care program that addresses nutrition is found in the Older Americans Act (nutrition sites), older adults (65+ years of age) have better diets generally when compared to a younger age group (45–64 years of age). Nearly 20% of the older age group reported a good diet as compared to 12% of 45–64 year olds. When comparing the population below poverty level, only 9% reported a good diet as compared to 21% from the above poverty age group (CDC NCHS, 2000; Saffel-Shrier & Catinella, 2002). While senior meal sites were developed to provide for a healthy diet among older adults (60+) at risk and living below the poverty level, people living below the poverty level reported that they perceived their diet to be poor at the same rate as people above the poverty level (14%). Figure 17.10 illustrates these findings.

Screening and Detection

Over the past 15 years there has been a dramatic increase in screening for breast cancer through the use of mammographies (Haas et al., 2005). In 1987, nearly 15% of Hispanic and black women sought mammograms, as compared to nearly 25% of the non-Hispanic white population of

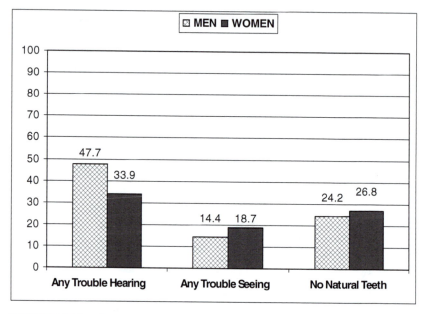

FIGURE 17.9   Sensory impairments and oral health needs.

Notes: Data refer to the percentage of people age 65 and over who reported having any trouble hearing, any trouble seeing, or no natural teeth, by sex, 2004. Respondents were asked "Which statement best describes your hearing without a hearing aid: good, a little trouble, a lot of trouble, deaf?" for the purpose of hearing. Regarding vision, respondents were asked "Do you have any trouble seeing, even when wearing glasses or contact lenses?" Last, respondents were asked, in one question, "Have you lost all your upper and lower natural (permanent) teeth?"

Target population: Data refer to the civilian noninstitutionalized population.

Source: Centers for Disease Control and Prevention, National Center for Health Statistics, National Health Interview Survey.

women over the age of 65. By 2003, all three groups of women have been seeking screening services at a rate of nearly 70% of the population, as illustrated in Figure 17.11. This dramatic increase can be due to public awareness and health promotion efforts to improve the prevalence of women who seek early screening and detection services.

Medications

Prescription drug costs by far have been paid by people 65 years of age and older from out-of-pocket sources. Although public programs over a 10-year period have paid out the least amount of money for prescription drug coverage, the amount paid has nearly tripled over a decade (Figure 17.12). The average number of prescriptions filled by Medicare enrollees has also

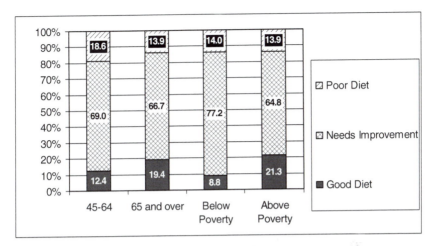

FIGURE 17.10   Perceptions of dietary quality—people 65+ years.

Notes: Refers to dietary quality ratings of people age 45 and over, as measured by the Healthy Eating Index, by age group and poverty status, 1999–2000. Dietary quality was measured using the Healthy Eating Index (HEI), which consists of 10 components, each representing a different aspect of a healthful diet based on the U.S. Department of Agriculture's Food Guide Pyramid and the Dietary Guidelines for Americans. An HEI score above 80 indicates a good diet, an HEI score between 51 and 80 signals a diet that needs improvement, and an HEI score below 51 indicates a poor diet. The maximum score is 100 on the HEI scale.

Target population: Data refer to a noninstitutionalized civilian population.

Source: Centers for Disease Control and Prevention, National Center for Health Statistics, National Health and Nutrition Survey.

nearly doubled from an average of 18 prescriptions per year in 1992 to 32 filled per person in 2002. Figure 17.13 illustrates these facts.

People With Disabilities Who Are Aging

Health promotion efforts over the past two decades may have actually had some impact for the health and functional status of Americans. When examining the age-adjusted percentage of Medicare enrollees age 65 and over who are chronically disabled, Figure 17.14 illustrates that over the 15-year period between 1984 and 1999, the noninstitutionalized population has actually improved in their functional status by 5%.

Women are also more apt to experience physical limitations than men and are nearly twice as likely to have problems with stooping/kneeling (18% for women as compared to 9% for men). While nearly 24% of female Medicare enrollees over the age of 65 had problems with walking two to three blocks, only 14% of men in the same cohort experienced these

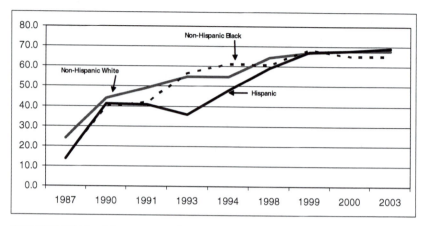

FIGURE 17.11   Mammography screening.

Notes: Refers to the percentage of women, age 65 and over, who had a mammogram in the past 2 years, by race and Hispanic origin, selected years, 1987–2003. Estimates for 2000 have been revised and may differ from what was reported in the *Older Americans 2004*.

Target population: Data refer to a noninstitutionalized civilian population.

Sources: Centers for Disease Control and Prevention, National Center for Health Statistics, National Health Interview Survey.

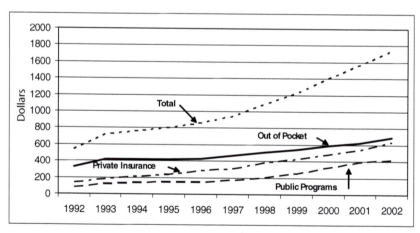

FIGURE 17.12   Prescription drug costs—noninstitutionalized Medicare enrollees.

Notes: Refers to the average annual prescription drug costs and sources of payment among noninstitutionalized Medicare enrollees age 65 and over, in 2002 dollars, 1992–2002. Dollars have been inflation-adjusted to 2002 using the Consumer Price Index. Public programs include Medicare, Medicaid, Department of Veterans Affairs, and other state and federal programs.

Target population: Data refer to Medicare enrollees.

Source: Centers for Medicare and Medicaid Services, Medicare Current Beneficiary Survey.

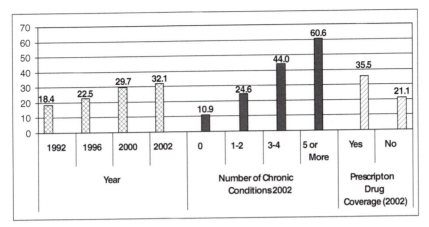

FIGURE 17.13   Average number of filled prescriptions by chronic conditions.

Notes: Refers to the average annual number of filled prescriptions among non-institutionalized Medicare] enrollees age 65 and over, by selected characteristics. Chronic conditions include cancer (other than skin cancer), stroke, diabetes, heart disease, hypertension, arthritis, and respiratory conditions (emphysema, asthma, chronic pulmonary disease). Prescription drug coverage includes people with partial-year coverage. The number of filled prescriptions counts each refill separately.

Target population: Data refer to Medicare enrollees.

Source: Centers for Medicare and Medicaid Services, Medicare Current Beneficiary Survey.

problems. While 15% of women in the Medicare enrollee category had trouble with lifting 10 pounds, only 7% of men within the same category experienced these same problems. This is one of the few times where we see larger disparities for women when compared to men in health status. Figure 17.15 illustrates that these data are for Medicare enrollees only and have been taken from the Centers for Medicare and Medicaid Services, Medicare Current Beneficiary Survey.

Oppressed Groups and Visible Minorities

The health care status of people who are living below the poverty line and visible minorities who are 65 years of age or older consistently have poorer health outcomes than those who are white non-Hispanics. Health promotion efforts need to be targeted towards meeting the health needs of minorities and oppressed groups in efforts to improve their overall health status. Although some gains have been made by people in poverty, continued intervention in terms of policy development and program planning is necessary. The need to examine strategies that meet the needs of minorities in efforts to reduce health disparities has become a crucial

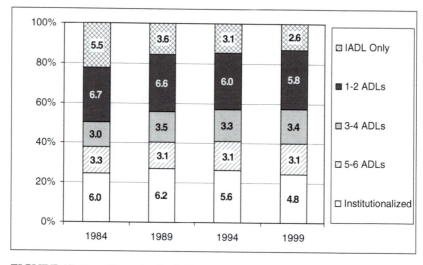

FIGURE 17.14   Chronic disability.
Notes: Refers to age-adjusted percentage of Medicare enrollees age 65 and over who are chronically disabled, by level of category of disability, 1984, 1989, 1994 and 1999. Disabilities are grouped into two categories; one with limitations in activities of daily living (ADLs) and limitations in instrumental activities of daily living (IADLs). Individuals are considered to have an ADL disability if they report using equipment to perform the activity, or not performing the activity at all because of their health or disability. Individuals are considered to be chronically disabled if they have at least one ADL or one IADL limitation that is expected to last 90 days or longer, or they are institutionalized. Data for 1989 do not sum to the total because of the rounding.
Target population: Data refer to Medicare enrollees.
Source: National Long Term Care Survey.

issue in the health care arena. Health disparities for people of color, visible minorities, and oppressed groups were well documented in *Healthy People 2010* (USDHHS, 2000), and continues to be documented in the literature (Choi, 2003; Min, Elliott, Wenger & Saliba, 2006; Moody-Ayers, Stewart, Convinsky, & Inouye, 2005; O'Rand & Hamil-Luker, 2005). Intervention strategies to target the specific needs of these groups will be paramount in the future.

MODEL PROGRAMS AND BEST PRACTICE APPROACHES TO HEALTH CARE DELIVERY

Several programs show promise for model programs to lead to best practice approaches in the health care delivery system. In this section, a few programs are showcased that offer promise to build upon the health outcomes for older adults over the age of 60 or 65.

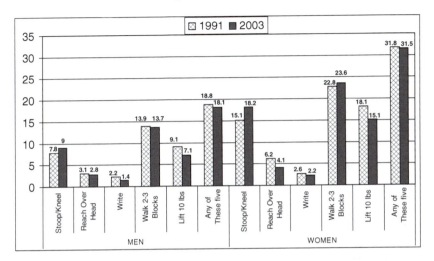

FIGURE 17.15   Disability, ability to perform functions, comparison 1993, 2003.

Notes: Data refer to the percentage of Medicare enrollees age 65 and over who are unable to perform certain physical functions, by sex, 1991 and 2003. Rates for 1991 are age-adjusted to the 2003 population.

Target population: Data refer to Medicare enrollees.

Source: Centers for Medicare and Medicaid Services, Medicare Current Beneficiary Survey.

It has been noted that African Americans have poorer health outcomes than Hispanics and non-Hispanic whites. Marks, Nesteruk, Swanson, Garrison, and Davis (2005) explored the relationship between religion and health among African Americans to learn how religion can be used to either predict or facilitate health outcomes. This team sought to learn why highly religious African Americans live significantly longer. They took a purposive sample of highly religious African American adults from the New Orleans area and interviewed this sample using an in-depth, qualitative approach to examine the religion–health–longevity interface. This team found six themes that related to their research question, which included: active faith involvement and the aged, avoiding negative coping, evading violence, the absence of hope, social support, and the power of prayer.

In an attempt to reduce nursing home admissions and improve overall functional ability, Vass, Avlund, Lauridsen, and Hendriksen (2005) developed an intervention of ongoing education, administered by the primary care physicians and preventative health care professionals. This brief, educational program for primary care professionals was found to help preserve older people's functional ability. In addition, education improved functional ability. There were no differences in mortality rates for people over the age of 80 after 3 years following the program's inception and intervention. Subjects over the age of 80 benefited from this intervention program and were able to stay in their homes longer and remain active with a greater ability to handle their activities of daily living.

Vaccinations for older adults, particularly vaccination for influenza, is important for the promotion of health outcomes among an older adult population. Despite this, many older adults are dubious about seeking vaccinations. Tabbarah et al. (2005) examined the correlates of repeat influenza vaccination to determine what influences decision making to seek vaccinations. This investigative team studied 250 people who were 50 years of age and older, from two community health centers in Pittsburgh, Pennsylvania. Essentially this investigative team found that one's health beliefs and subjective norms played a central role in determining if one would pursue a vaccination. In addition, they recommend an educational intervention that targets older adults and helps identify one's perceived health beliefs and cultural norms as a first step in deciding when and why to seek the intervention.

HEALTH CARE CHALLENGES FOR THE FUTURE

A number of health care challenges exist, which will need address and development in order to meet the challenges posed by an older adult population. These include the following challenges:

- Develop strategies to collect and utilize data that provide an overview of both the health status and health behaviors of older adults. Within this data collection process, target an emphasis on health disparities to build on our understanding of the differences in health outcomes.
- Identify (in partnership with interested stakeholder groups) and build upon additional data surveillance measures that will address gaps in data on health issues for older adults. These measures may include data on the health status, health needs, and quality of life at the end of life and racial/ethnic and urban/rural differences in health care utilization and needs.
- Expand policy and program development research efforts to foster the development of evidence-based health promotion programs and strategies available for community practice, particularly in the areas of lower-income and rural communities.

- Develop opportunities for professionals to become more knowledgeable about and skilled at using data for action, implementing evidence-based health promotion interventions, and communicating the importance of healthy lifestyles and advance care planning to older adults within both health policy and programs.
- Develop health education and health promotion programs that target healthy lifestyles, early detection of diseases, immunizations, injury prevention, and self-management techniques for older adults.
- Increase the number of programs that target health behavior that are rooted in health behavior models and utilize health behavior strategies to guide the development of health behavior interventions.

Perhaps the greatest challenge to be faced related to health care will be the cost of health care and rising health care expenditures. Despite the fact that our population is growing older, and living longer, health care will also be an expensive commodity. The challenges outlined only address a fraction of the concerns—hence a broader concern will be how these initiatives will be financed.

SUMMARY

This chapter has explored the health status of older adults, outlined some programs and services available to older adults, examined health care issues faced by older adults, and explored some model programs and interventions that can be helpful in facilitating the health status of older adults. Health care is clearly a commodity of value as one ages, and a number of challenges exist in the development and maintenance of a healthy older adult population.

USEFUL WEB SITES

The American Association of Retired People (AARP) Health Site: http://www.aarp.org/health/
This Web site published by the AARP provides a consumer guide to effective and affordable drugs, tips for easing caregiver stress, health security information, and a host of other health-related topics for the consumer to assure healthy living.

The Centers for Disease Control and Prevention (CDC), Healthy Aging for Older Adults: http://www.cdc.gov/aging
This Web site provides a background to healthy aging and prevention

of chronic diseases, sponsored by the Division of Health Promotion, CDC. The site provides a range of links including links to health information for older adults, statistics/research, publications related to healthy aging and older adults, public health and aging listservs, and links to organizations. In addition, the site provides links to CDC-funded organizations that deal with information related to healthy aging for older adults.

American Society on Aging (ASA) Healthcare and Aging Network: http://www.asaging.org/networks/index.cfm?cg=HAN

This Web site provides a background and links to the Healthcare and Aging Network (HAN), an ASA constituent group. The Healthcare and Aging Network is a professional community of individuals and organizations working to promote innovative, high-quality approaches to meeting the health care needs of older adults.

Aging and Seniors, Public Health Agency of Canada, Health Canada: http://www.phac-aspc.gc.ca/seniors-aines/index_pages/whatsnew_e.htm

This Web site provides insight into health and aging issues in Canada. The site, sponsored by Health Canada, managed by the Division of Aging and Seniors, provides leadership on health issues related to aging and seniors. The site also provides a host of links to sites related to aging and health, within the Canadian context. The site is interesting, since Canada offers socialized health care to its residents across the life span.

MedlinePlus: http://www/nlm.nih.gov/medlineplus/seniorshealthissues.html

This Web site, a service developed in collaboration between the National Institute of Health and the U.S. National Library, provides an up-to-date reference on senior health issues, from A to Z. The Web site provides access to a range of recent articles as well.

National Institutes of Health (NIH) Senior Health Guidelines: http://www.nihseniorhealth.gov/

This site was developed for older adults conjointly between the National Institute on Aging, and the National Library of Medicine (both of which are part of the National Institutes of Health). The site provides up-to-date information on a variety of health topics listed from A to Z. The information includes state-of-the-art techniques and data.

REFERENCES

Centers for Disease Control and Prevention, National Center for Health Statistics (CDC NCHS). (2000). *Summary health statistics for the U.S. population, The National Health Nutrition and Environment Survey, 2000.* Hyattsville, MD: U.S. Department of Health and Human Services.

Centers for Disease Control and Prevention, National Center for Health Statistics (CDC NCHS) (2003). *Summary health statistics for the U.S. population, The National Health Interview Survey, 2003*. Hyattsville, MD: U.S. Department of Health and Human Services.

Centers for Disease Control and Prevention, National Center for Health Statistics (CDC NCHS) (2004). *Summary health statistics for the U.S. population, The National Health Interview Survey, 2004*. Hyattsville, MD: U.S. Department of Health and Human Services.

Centers for Disease Control and Prevention, National Center for Health Statistics (CDC NCHS) (2006). *Summary health statistics for the U.S. population, The National Health Interview Survey, 2006*. Hyattsville, MD: U.S. Department of Health and Human Services.

Centers for Disease Control and Prevention (CDC). (2006). Retrieved October 23, 2006, from http://www.cdc.gov/nccdphp/publications/aag/aging.htm

Centers for Medicare and Medicaid Services (CMMS). (2003) *Research, statistics, data and systems*. Retrieved October 23, 2006, from www.cms.hhs.gov/home/rsds.asp

Choi, N. G. (2003). Determinants of self-perceived changes in health status among pre-and early-retirement populations. *International Journal of Aging and Human Development, 56*(3), 197–222.

Federal Interagency Forum on Aging-Related Statistics (FIFARS). (2006). *Older Americans Update 2006: Key Indicators of Well-Being. Federal Interagency Forum on Aging-Related Statistics*, Washington, DC: U.S. Government Printing Office.

Gerberding, J. L. (2006). Healthy aging: Preserving function and improving quality of life among older Americans. Retrieved April 27, 2007, from: http://www.cdc.gov/nccdphp/publications/aag/aging.htm

Haas, J. S., Kaplan, C. P., Des Jarlais, G., Gildengoing, V., Perez-Stable, E. J., & Kerlikowski, K. (2005). Perceived risk of breast cancer among women at average and increased risk. *Journal of Women's Health, 14,* 845–851.

Marks, L., Nesteruk, O., Swanson, M., Garrison, B., & Davis, T. (2005). Religion and health among African Americans: A qualitative examination. *Research on Aging, 27*(4), 447–474.

Min, L. C., Elliott, M. N., Wenger, N. S., & Saliba, D. (2006). Higher vulnerable elders survey scores predict death and functional decline in vulnerable older people. *Journal of the American Geriatrics Society, 54*(3), 507–511.

Moody–Ayers, S. Y., Stewart, A. L., Covinsky, K. E., and Inouye, S. K. (2005). Prevalence and correlates of perceived societal racism in older African American adults with type 2 diabetes mellitus. *Journal of the American Geriatrics Society, 53*(12), 2202–2208.

O'Rand, A. M., & Hamil-Luker, J. (2005). Process of cumulative adversity: Childhood disadvantage and increased risk of heart attack across the life course. *Journals of Gerontology: Series B: Psychological Services and Social Sciences, 60,* 117–124.

Saffel-Shrier, S., & Catinella, A. P. (2002). Functional approach to nutrition screening among ambulatory older persons. *Journal of Nutrition for the Elderly, 22*(2), 71–82.

Tabbarah, M., Zimmerman, R. K., Richard, K., Nowalk, M. P., Janosky, J. E., Troy, J. A., et al. (2005). What predicts influenza vaccination status in older Americans over several years? *Journal of the American Geriatrics Society, 53*(8), 1354–1359.

United States Department of Health and Human Services (USDHHS). (1999). *The Surgeon General's report on oral health*. Washington, DC: Government Printing Office.

United States Department of Health and Human Services (USDHHS). (2000). *Healthy people 2010: Health objectives for the nation* (2nd ed., Vol. 1). Washington, DC: Government Printing Office.

Vass, M., Avlund, K., Lauridsen, J., & Hendriksen, C. (2005). Feasible model for prevention of functional decline in older people: Municipality-randomized, controlled trial. *Journal of the American Geriatrics Society, 53*(4), 563–568.

Vierck, E., & Hodges, K. (2003). *Aging, demographics, health and health services.* New York: Greenhaven Press.

CHAPTER 18

Grandparents Raising Grandchildren

A CURRENT PROFILE OF GRANDPARENTS RAISING GRANDCHILDREN IN THE UNITED STATES

For generations grandparents have played a definitive role in the raising of grandchildren. The role of a grandparent is an esteemed accomplishment—a right of passage. The parent role of disciplinarian, provider, taxi, and sounding board for children has dwindled and the fruit of their labor is becoming a grandparent. To many older adults, this right of passage is an exciting time and a spectacular event that can be savored and enjoyed without feeling the strain of responsibility that raising children produces.

Unfortunately, for many older adults, this right of passage is met with many cumbersome details and unexpected twists and turns. These twists and turns include the movement into a role of grandparents raising grandchildren. According to the U.S. Census Bureau (Bryson & Casper, 2000), 5,771,671 grandparents reported living in a household with one of more of their own grandchildren under 18 years of age. Of this number, 42% were solely responsible for their grandchildren. Within this framework, African American children were the most prevalent (13.2%), followed by Native American or Pacific Islander children (10.6%), Hispanic children (7.8%), and white children (4.2%). According to AARP, the national demographic breakdown of grandparents raising grandchildren is: 29% are African American, 17% are Hispanic/Latino, 2% are American Indian or Alaskan Native, 3% are Asian, and 47% are white (AARP, 2006a).

Where are these grandparents who are raising their grandchildren? According to the U.S. Census (2000), the top 10 states include: California

(625,934), Texas (448,439), New York (297,239), Florida (258,952), Illinois (213,465), Georgia (164,423), Pennsylvania (164,354), Ohio (157,298), Michigan (143,523), and North Carolina (135,158).

In the United States 4.5 million children are living in a grandparent-headed household. According to AARP this statistic represents a 30% increase from the years 1990 to 2000. In Illinois alone, there are 213,465 children living in grandparent-headed households. This number represents almost 7% of the children in the state of Illinois. Of the children living in a grandparent-headed household, 119,676 are there with no parent present (AARP, 2006a).

Grandparents raising grandchildren face a broad range of issues that come with this responsibility. Some of the issues are financial, legal, health (physical and mental health, insurance), housing, education, respite care, supportive services, child rearing (special needs of grandchildren), social isolation, and access to information/education (AARP, 2006b). The research from an AARP study and others, learned that agencies' outreach services have not adequately provided opportunity for education and services for this target population. Grandparents tend to be highly uninformed about existing supports and services, and all too often are misinformed by the professionals or primary care providers who seek to help them (AARP, 2006b; Holliamn, Giddings & Closson, 2001; Smith, Beltran, Butts, & Kingson, 2001; Wallace, 2001).

More than 1 in 10 grandparents (10.9%) at some point raise a grandchild for at least 6 months, and usually for far longer periods of time. The median age of grandparent caregivers is 59.3 and over half are aged 60 and above (Fuller-Thomson, Minkler, & Driver, 1997). Now that we have a profile of our grandparent caregivers, why is this phenomenon on the increase?

REASONS FOR THE INCREASE IN RELATIVE CAREGIVING

What turn of events or circumstances have led to the increases in relative caregiving? A part of the increase in kinship care beginning in the 1980s is attributed to legal mandates and changes in child welfare reimbursement policies and practices that encouraged placement with relatives over non-relative foster care. Federal and state laws and policies promoting formal kinship care, however, do not explain the sizable concomitant growth in the number of children who informally have been "going to Grandma's"— to stay (Cox, 1999). It has also been suggested that during the last decade, for every one grandchild in the formal foster care system, another six were informally being raised by relatives (Harden, Clark, & McGuire, 1997).

According to the Administration on Aging (USDHHS AoA, 2002), key among the social factors contributing to the increase in this phenomena of grandparents raising grandchildren include alcohol and drug abuse, unemployment, child abuse and/or neglect, incarceration, abandonment, divorce, teenage pregnancy, mental health problems, family violence, death of a parent, HIV/AIDS, and poverty.

Substance abuse, one of the leading contributing factor to grandparents raising grandchildren, has included the cocaine epidemic (Burnette, 1997) and most recently, the methamphetamine epidemic. The facts that an estimated 15% of women aged 15–44 are substance abusers, and that almost 40% of these women have children living with them (USDHHS NIDA, 1997), suggest that drug and alcohol abuse are likely to remain important contributing factors. It has been more recently identified that drug and substance abuse as one of the leading factors for grandparents to raise their grandchildren (USDHHS AoA, 2002).

Divorce, teen pregnancy, and the rapid growth in single-parent households also are major factors responsible for the rise in intergenerational households headed by grandparents. Such trends have contributed to the dramatic drop in the number of children living in two-parent households (from over 86% in 1950 to about 70% by the mid-1990s)—a factor that appears to increase the likelihood of children entering relative care (Harden et al., 1997).

The HIV/AIDS epidemic is also considered another growing contributor to the phenomenon of grandparent caregiving. The leading cause of death among African Americans aged 25–44, HIV/AIDS had claimed the lives of the mothers of an estimated 125,000 to 150,000 American children and youth by the year 2000. Despite limited data on custody, available information suggests that grandmothers typically are the sole or primary caregivers to children whose primary parent is living with, or has died as a result of, AIDS (Joslin & Harrison, 1998). More recently, figures suggest that HIV/AIDS has been on the rise in African American women (CDC, 2006), which often leads to grandparent-headed households once the parent is no longer able to care for their children due to advanced stages of HIV illness or death.

Grandparents also are primary caregivers to well over half of the children of imprisoned mothers in the United States. Dramatic increases in the number of incarcerated women, which grew six-fold over the last decade and a half (Glass & Huneycut, 2002; USDHHS AoA, 2002), suggest that this trend will likely continue to contribute to the growth of intergenerational households headed by grandparents.

ISSUES FACING GRANDPARENTS RAISING GRANDCHILDREN

A number of issues face grandparents raising grandchildren, including financial burdens or poverty, role expectations and realities, changes in social support, and health conditions. This next section will explore these issues in greater detail.

Poverty

First, many of the factors discussed in the previous section are tied in fundamental ways to the continued problem of poverty in our nation, which itself remains a significant vulnerability factor for grandparent caregiving (Burnette, 1997; Minkler, 1999). Grandparent-headed households are more likely to be raising their grandchildren in poverty, and over 20% of households were living in poverty in at least 18 states in the United States according to the U.S. Census Bureau (2000), while in at least 33 of the states at least 15% of their grandparents were raising grandchildren living in poverty. According to the Children's Defense fund, children in kinship foster placements are more likely to live with a family that must spend half of its income on rent, has difficulty with getting adequate food, and does not own a car (USDHHS AoA, 2006). For older working relatives, the assumption of caregiving frequently means quitting a job, cutting back on hours, or making other job-related sacrifices that may put their own future economic well-being in jeopardy. Retired or nonemployed caregivers also frequently suffer financially and sometimes report spending their life savings, selling the car, or cashing in life insurance to cope financially with the new role (Minkler, Driver, Roe, and Bedein, 1993).

Social/Role Issues

A number of social/role issues also challenge grandparents in their role as caregivers. In a qualitative study of 26 grandparent caregivers, a number of themes emerged related to the grandparents' perception of their roles. These included the grandparent caregiver role being off-time or unexpected, role conflict, and role ambiguity (USDHHS AoA, 2002). In terms of role timing, grandparents felt that parenting skills were not as much as an issue as attempting to raise a child within contemporary society—that is the timing of the parenting role did not fit with their life stage, and they had lost touch with the current trends, music, and expectations of an up and coming generation. Role conflicts were expressed by grandparents who struggle between wanting to be the grandparent but were slid into the role of the parent attempting to provide discipline and establish clear boundaries (Gerard, Landry-Meyer, & Guzell-Roe, 2006).

Socialization

An online assessment of grandmothers raising their grandchildren (McGowen, Ladd, & Strom, 2006) revealed that grandmothers' health played a role in their ability to care for their grandchildren. Many stated that they tired more easily, were not physically capable of doing some of the activities that they would like with their grandchildren, and felt an impact on their private time. Private time and social relationships with their spouses and friends were impacted by their caregiving role. In addition, the focus for grandmothers also changed from homemaking and careers to caregiving.

These issues have also been found previously by researchers and have been documented in the literature. Decreased socialization with friends and/or family, and an inability to continue participation in senior centers and church activities as a consequence of caregiving responsibilities has been widely reported among caregiving grandparents (Burton, 1992; Hayslip, Shore, Henderson, & Lambert, 1998; Hayslip & Patrick, 2003; Jendrek, 1994; Minkler et al., 1993; Shore and Hayslip, 1994). Reduction in marital satisfaction also has been noted (Jendrek, 1994).

Health Care

High rates of depression, poor self-rated health, and/or the frequent presence of multiple chronic health problems have been reported in both national and smaller-scale studies of grandparents raising grandchildren (Burton, 1992; Dowdell, 1995; Minkler et al., 1993; Minkler, Fuller-Thomson, Miller, & Driver, 1997; Grinstead, Leder, Jensen, & Bond, 2003). Such problems appear particularly prevalent among caregiving grandmothers. One national study found that 32% of caregiving grandmothers met the clinical criteria for depression, compared to 19% of noncaregiving grandmothers. Similarly, grandmothers raising grandchildren were significantly more likely to have limitations in activities of daily living (ADLs) such as caring for personal needs, climbing a flight of stairs, or walking six blocks, with fully 56% reporting at least one ADL limitation (Fuller-Thomson and Minkler, 2000).

In addition to the grandparents having health problems, children also share in a host of health issues and problems, although Solomon and Marx (1995) found that children in relative-headed households may have better health overall than children living with a single parent. Some of the significant health and health-associated problems that have been observed, particularly among those children who came into the grandparents' care, include prenatal exposure to drugs or alcohol, and/or parental abuse or neglect. High rates of asthma and other respiratory problems, weakened immune systems, poor eating and sleeping patterns, physical disabilities, and attention deficit hyperactivity disorder (ADHD) are among the problems grandchildren have experienced, which in turn may impact the caregiver's physical and mental health (Dowdell, 1995; Minkler & Roe, 1996; Shore & Hayslip, 1994).

Several studies have documented the tendency for caregivers to delay or fail to seek formal help for themselves, particularly with mental or emotional health problems (Burnette, 1999; Minkler, Driver, Roe, & Bedein, 1993; Shore and Hayslip, 1994). Coping strategies had been greatly impacted by the acceptance of responsibility, confrontive coping, self-control, positive reappraisal, and distancing from specific issues for which limited coping strategies are available (Ross & Aday, 2006). Strategies to improve coping, identified by 50 African American grandparents (mean age = 63.12) included seeking social support and developing a series of adaptive coping strategies, particularly when confronted with a difficult child, or parents who were dysfunctional. Length of time as a grandparent raising a grandchild also led to a variety of adaptation techniques and improved coping strategies (Harper & Hardesty, 2001; Henderson & Cook, 2005). These adaptation techniques are important over the long term for grandparents. Table 18.1 provides an overview of the length of time grandparents were responsible for grandchildren.

Policy and Legislation

The policies that dictate how programs and services for grandparents raising grandchildren will be developed and delivered fall under the Older Americans Act (OAA). The OAA originated in 1965 and contains different titles that address aging issues. The act created the Administration on Aging. It also "authorizes grants to states for community planning and services, programs, as well as for research, demonstration and training projects in the field of aging" (PL 89-73). Under Title IV grants are available for discretionary programs for the aging population. This is where many of the services for grandparents raising grandchildren are covered.

Another policy affecting grandparents raising grandchildren falls under the National Family Caregiver Support Program. Under this program "state agencies on aging work with area agencies on aging and community

TABLE 18.1   Length of Time Grandparents Were Responsible for Raising Grandchildren

Length of time	30–59 yrs of age	60 yrs and older
Not responsible for grandchild	50%	69%
Less than 1 year	13%	5%
1–2 years	13%	5%
3–4 years	8%	4%
Responsible for 5 years or more	16%	17%

Source: U.S. Bureau of the Census, 2001.

service provider organizations to provide support services including information and assistance to caregivers, counseling, support groups, respite and other home and community based services to families" (USDHHS AoA, 2006). The Illinois Family Caregiver Support Program, for example, offers services to older adults who are 60 and over. This program contains supplemental services that aim to address caregiver emergencies, such as providing school supplies and other assistance where there are gaps in services (IDoA, 2007).

PROGRAMS AVAILABLE TO MEET THE NEEDS OF GRANDPARENTS RAISING GRANDCHILDREN

Medicare

Medicare does not provide any services for individual grandparents raising grandchildren. However, some limited support is available for mental health counseling for people who may benefit from supportive counseling to buffer the stress of "parenting" as a grandparent.

Medicaid

Medicaid in most states supports health care coverage for grandchildren, who otherwise may not have health insurance. The Children's Health Insurance Program (CHIP), although federally mandated, operates at a state level, with different eligibility criteria for each state. Health insurance can be a tremendous asset for families where health care coverage would be prohibitive due to the cost factor. Many insurance companies refuse to allow grandparents to include grandchildren as dependents on their insurance policies unless the children are in legal custody of the policy holder. In 1996, one in three children in grandparent-headed households were without health insurance, compared to one in seven in the overall child population (Casper & Bryson, 1998).

Area Agencies on Aging

According to PL 109-365, the Older Americans Act Amendments of 2006, Title IV, there is an allotment for funding in the planning of activities to prepare communities for the aging of the population, which includes grandparents who are 55 years of age and older and are raising children. Previously the cut off was 60 years of age. This can include those caring for a child by blood, marriage, or adoption.

Child Welfare

Child welfare authorities can provide a wealth of information to grandparents raising grandchildren on a range of issues from child care/ day care to custody and legal issues. Custody options can range from physical custody, legal custody, and private guardianship to kinship foster care and finally adoption. Each one of these categories provides a different level of responsibility and legal mandate, which can be identified on a state-by-state level through the state's child welfare programs. Support programs for special needs children and adoption assistance is also available within most states to grandparents raising grandchildren.

Finally, at the current time assistance to grandparents serving as foster care parents is available through some states. Grandparents raising grandchildren can qualify as foster parents and may be able to access funds for after school programs, respite care, day care, and assistance with board and care.

MODEL PROGRAMS AND PROACTIVE APPROACHES TO ADDRESSING THE NEEDS OF GRANDPARENTS RAISING GRANDCHILDREN

A number of programs and interventions have shown promise to be helpful to grandparents raising grandchildren. This section will outline some of these programs, including strengths-based case management, a satellite video program, a let's talk tape series program, and a cooperative extension program.

Whitely, White, and Yorke (1999) explored the use of a strengths-based case management approach with grandparents raising grandchildren through a project known as "Project Healthy Grandparents." This strengths-based case management method embraced the strengths of individuals and utilized these strengths as a strategy to build resilience and resolve current problems and issues. Although there is a lack of empirical evidence on the impact of using a strengths-based approach to case management, it is clear that this approach garners the resources of the individual, enables a positive approach to problem solving, and makes a qualitative difference in the lives of grandparents raising grandchildren. Success was also measured through the expanded choices and opportunities that the grandparents believed that they had acquired, and the measure of empowerment and control reported by grandparents.

In the hopes of raising awareness of the issues related to grandparents raising grandchildren, a national satellite video program was developed and broadcast to a national audience in January of 1999 (Targ & Brintnall-Peterson, 2001). The video conference, known as "Grandparents

Raising Grandchildren: Implications for Professionals and Agencies," was designed to provide information, skills, resources, and supports to better serve the population of grandparents raising grandchildren. Although nationally based, each site had a local facilitator who was able to tailor the information and intervention to meet local needs and concerns. Activities immediately before and after the video conference broadcast series was designed to encourage local agencies and organizations to share information and identify service gaps and barriers within their home-based communities in efforts to promote issues of grandparents raising. Outcomes suggested that this approach has provided communities with a better understanding of the issues, programs, and resources, and facilitated the expansion of services within organizations. The video conference also served as a springboard to start local support groups, address local needs, and expand services within individual organizations. A follow-up to this session indicated that the video conference approach also improved awareness, encouraged the need for support groups, encouraged new groups to join forces with existing coalitions to develop resources for grandparents raising grandchildren (67% increase), and encouraged the development and/or expansion of new groups (61% expansion). In addition to the actual improvement in knowledge, skills, and awareness, this approach also facilitated an awareness of the benefits of a distance education approach to skills development with grandparents raising grandchildren (Targ & Brintnall-Peterson, 2001).

The "Let's Talk" tape series is an audiotape series of eight tapes that deals with a different topic valued by grandparents (Kropf and Wilks, 2003). The tapes are presented in an easy listening format that provides a conversation between a grandparent and commentator, in a question and answer format, and runs in length between 11 and 23 minutes. The topics attempt to bridge the needs for materials related to parenting/ grandparenting, and caregiver stress, and have been designed for busy people so that they can be inserted into a tape player during convenient times of day, and listened to during those spare moments. Topics include (1) taking care of your health; (2) being involved in relationships with family and friends; (3) addressing your legal questions and concerns related to custody, guardianship, and wills; (4) community resources; (5) building relationships with one's grandchildren; (6) raising one's grandchildren, joys and challenges; (7) taking care of oneself; and (8) making the most of the experience and taking care of oneself again. Each tape follows a set structure; grandparents review basic information about a topic, identify risk situations, and make a behavioral plan. The series was evaluated with a pre–post test design on 60 grandparents using a variety of instruments such as the Grandparent Burden and Satisfaction Questionnaire, the General Health Questionnaire, CESD-Depression scale, Ways of Coping, and Parental Locus of Control index. The intent behind this series is to minimize potential crises that one may experience as a grandparent, help in raising a grandchild, enhance coping strategies, reduce behavioral issues on the part of the child, and avert any negative or adverse situations.

Cooperative Extension programs have built a network of resources throughout at least 10 states throughout the country known as the Relatives as Parents Program (RAPP). While the Cooperative Extension program is the lead organizer, they have created partnerships with other agency entities such as area agencies on aging, AARP, Health Start, Tribal Partners, and others to create programs and resources that are helpful to grandparents raising grandchildren (Crocell, 2004). With these programs, grandparents learn about resources within their community and can take advantage of local support groups and other supportive services, and agencies can become part of a statewide network of service providers.

CHALLENGES FOR GRANDPARENTS RAISING GRANDCHILDREN IN THE FUTURE

A number of challenges face, and will continue to face grandparents raising grandchildren. The rate and number of grandparents raising grandchildren will continue to grow in the future, especially within smaller and rural communities. Grandparents will also face the same review and audit by child welfare agencies licensed for foster parenting. This interface with the child welfare system will pose its own unique challenges for both the aging and child welfare systems.

Grandparents under 60 raising grandchildren will also face their own set of challenges, since resources mandated for grandparents through the Older Americans Act exclude grandparents under the age of 60. Thus, these individuals will be left to deal with an existing limit to resources, through a resource-poor child welfare system. Dealing with the child welfare system, kinship and guardianship rights will also present its own myriad of challenges for grandparents, regardless of age.

Another challenge worth noting is the interruption of one's life stage, and the boomerang back to an earlier stage of development, which many grandparents have long passed. This challenges both the roles of the individuals raising and being raised. Challenges also result from generational differences and generation gaps both in communication and in socializing a child from a different age cohort.

Grandparents over the age of 60 also face challenges when dealing with rules and regulations facing housing, finances, and so on. Many senior housing settings do not allow children to live or stay for prolonged periods of time on the premises. For some grandparents, this has meant moving to a family friendly setting, in order to accommodate their grandchildren.

Finally, a major challenge is health and associated health issues. Stressors related to the burden of caregiving can contribute adversely to one's health situation, and this is something that requires both consideration and address by local programs and respite services for grandparents raising grandchildren.

SUMMARY

This chapter has provided an overview of the current status of grandparents raising grandchildren. It has also provided some background into the literature and provided an awareness of issues that grandparents face as primary caregivers. A literature review examined some of the current issues and services needed. Resources and services designed to meet the needs of grandparents raising grandchildren were discussed, and programmatic responses identified through the national resources. Finally, some best practice interventions were outlined for review.

USEFUL WEB SITES

Grandparenting: http://www.aarp.org/families/grandparents/
    The AARP grandparents' resource center provides the grandparent with useful information ranging from parenting skills, and caregiver stress, to legal advice. The site also provides for fact sheets that are state-specific and provide state-based information.

Grandparents Raising Grandchildren: Aging Internet Information Notes: http://www.aoa.gov/prof/notes/Docs/Grandparents_Raising_Grand children.pdf
    This site provides a range of helpful information spanning statistics to best practice resources.

Grandparents Raising Grandchildren: Benefits and Assistance: http://www.firstgov.gov/Topics/Grandparents.shtml
    This government Web site provides a range of topics of interest to grandparent caregivers including benefits and assistance, health and safety information, reports and publications, and state-based contacts for grandparents to locate resources within their own state.

REFERENCES

AARP. (2006a). *Intergeneration relationships: Grandparents raising grandchildren.* Washington, DC: Author.

AARP. (2006b). *AARP Illinois state fact sheet: A resource for grandparents and other relatives raising children.* Retrieved April 28, 2007, from http://www.giclocalsupport. org/doc/kinship_care_2006_il.pdf

Burnette, D. (1997). Grandparents raising grandchildren in the inner city. *Families in Society, 78,* 489–499.

Burnette, D. (1999). Physical and emotional well-being of custodial grandparents in Latino families. *American Journal of Orthopsychiatry, 69,* 305–318.

Burton, L. M. (1992). Black grandparents rearing grandchildren of drug addicted parents: Stressors, outcomes and social service needs. *Gerontologist, 32,* 744–751.

Bryson, K. & Casper, L. (2000). *Coresident grandparents and grandchildren. Current population reports, special studies, P23-198.* Washington, DC: U.S. Census Bureau.

Casper, L. M., & Bryson, K. R. (1998). *Co-resident grandparents and their grandchildren: Grandparent maintained families.* (Working Paper No. 26). Washington, DC: U.S. Bureau of the Census, Population Division. Retrieved May 20, 2006, from http:// www.census.gov/population/www/documentation/twps0026.html

Centers for Disease Control and Prevention (CDC). (2007). *HIV/AIDS among women.* Retrieved May 20, 2007, from http://www.cdc.gov/hiv/topics/women/resources/fact sheets/pdf/women.pdf

Cox, C. B. (1999). *Group leaders: Springer series on lifestyles and issues in aging.* New York: Springer.

Crocoll, C. E. (2004). Grandparents raising grandchildren: Help from cooperative extension. *Journal of Family and Consumer Sciences, 96*(4), 59–60.

Dowdell, E. (1995). Caregiver burden: Grandmothers raising their high risk grandchildren. *Journal of Psychosocial Nursing Mental Health Services, 33*(3), 27–30.

Fuller-Thomson, E., & Minkler, M. (2000). African American grandparents raising grandchildren: A national profile of demographic and health characteristics. *Health & Social Work, 25*(2), 109.

Fuller-Thomson, E., Minkler, M., & Driver, D. (1997). A profile of grandparents raising grandchildren in the United States. *Gerontologist, 37,* 406–411.

Gerard, J. M., Landry-Meyer, L., & Guzell Roe, J. (2006). Grandparents raising grandchildren: The role of social support in coping with caregiving challenges. *International Journal of Aging & Human Development, 62*(4), 359–383.

Glass, J. C., & Huneycut, T. L. (2002). Grandparents raising grandchildren: The courts, custody, and educational implications. *Educational Gerontology, 28*(3), 237–251.

Grinstead, L. N., Leder, S., Jensen, S., & Bond, L. (2003). Integrative literature reviews and meta-analyses: Review of research on the health of caregiving grandparents. *Journal of Advanced Nursing, 44*(3), 318–326.

Harden, A. W., Clark, R., & Maguire, K. (1997). *Formal and informal kinship care* (Report for the Office of the Assistant Secretary for Planning and Evaluation, Task Order HHS 100-95-0021). Washington, DC: U.S. Department of Health and Human Services. Retrieved May 10, 2006, from http://aspe.hhs.gov/hsp/cyp/xskincar.htm

Harper, W. J., & Hardesty, P. H. (2001). Differentiating characteristics and needs of minority grandparent caregivers. *Journal of Ethnic & Cultural Diversity in Social Work, 9*(3/4), 133–150.

Hayslip, B., & Patrick, J. H. (2003). *Working with custodial grandparents.* New York: Springer Publishing Co.

Hayslip, B., Shore, R. J., Henderson, C. E., & Lambert, P. L. (1998). Custodial grandparenting and the impact of grandchildren with problems on role satisfaction and role meaning. *Journals of Gerontology, 53,* S164–S173.

Henderson, T. L., & Cook, J. L. (2005). Grandma's hands: Black grandmothers speak about their experience rearing grandchildren on TANF. *International Journal of Aging & Human Development, 61*(1), 1–19.

Holliamn, D. C., Giddings, M. M., & Closson, S. (2001). Beyond the myth of collaboration: Creating genuine partnerships to support grandparents raising grandchildren. *Reflections, 88–97.*

Illinois Department on Aging (IDoA). (2007). *Older Adult Services Act: 2007 report to the General Assembly.* Retrieved May 20, 2007, from http://www.state.il.us/aging/1news_pubs/publications/oasa_anreprt2007.pdf

Jendrenk, M .P. (1994). Policy concerns of white grandparents who provide regular care to their grandchildren. *Journal of Gerontological Social Work, 23*(1/2), 175–199.

Joslin, D., & Harrison, R. (1998). The hidden patient: Older relatives raising children orphaned by AIDS. *Journal of the American Medical Women's Association, 53*(2), 65–71.

Kropf, N. P., & Wilks, S. (2003). Grandparents raising grandchildren. In B. Berkman & L. Harootyan (Eds.), *Social work and health care in an aging society* (pp. 177–200). New York: Springer.

McGowen, M. R., Ladd, L., & Strom, R. D. (2006). On-line assessment of grandmother experience in raising grandchildren. *Educational Gerontology, 32*(8), 669–684.

Minkler, M. (1999). Intergenerational households headed by grandparents: Contexts, realities, and implications for policy. *Journal of Aging Studies, 13*(2), 199–218.

Minkler, M., Driver, D., Roe, K. M., & Bedein, K. (1993). Community interventions to support grandparent caregivers. *The Gerontologist, 33*(6), 807–811.

Minkler, M., Fuller-Thomson, E., Miller, D., & Driver, D. (1997). Depression in grandparents raising grandchildren: Results of a national longitudinal study. *Archives of Family Medicine, 6,* 445–452.

Minkler, M., & Roe, K. M.(1996). *Grandmothers as caregivers: Raising children of the crack-cocaine epidemic.* Newbury Park, CA: Sage Publications.

Ross, M., & Aday, L. (2006). Stress and coping in African American grandparents who are raising their grandchildren. *Journal of Family Issues, 27*(7), 912–932.

Shore, R. J., & Hayslip, B. (1994). Custodial grandparenting: Implications for children's development. In A. E. Gottfried (Ed.), *Redefining families: Implications for children's development* (pp. 171–218). New York: Plenum Press.

Smith, C. J., Beltran, A., Butts, D. M., & Kingson, E. R. (2001). Grandparents raising grandchildren: Emerging program and policy issues for the 21st century. *Journal of Gerontological Social Work, 35*(1), 33–45.

Solomon, J. C., and Marx, J. (1995). "To my grandmother's house we go": Health and school adjustment of children raised solely by grandparents. *The Gerontologist, 35,* 386–394.

Targ, D. B., & Brintnall-Peterson, M. (2001). Grandparents raising grandchildren: Impact of a national satellite video program. *Journal of Family Issues, 22*(5), 579–593.

U.S. Bureau of the Census. (2003). *Household relationships and living arrangements of children under 18 years of age.* Retrieved April 28, 2006, from http://www.census.gov/prod/2003pubs/c2kbr-31.pdf

U.S. Department of Health and Human Services, Administration on Aging (USDHHS AoA). (2002). *Grandparents and other relatives raising children: Challenges of caring for the second family.* Washington, DC: Author.

United States Department of Health and Human Services, Administration on Aging (US-DHHS AoA). (2006). Grandparents raising grandchildren. Retrieved May 21, 2007, from www.aoa.gov/press/grand/gpd.asp

United States Department of Health and Human Services, National Institute of Drug Abuse (USDHHS NIDA) (1997). *Trends in drug and other substance use.* Rockville, MD: U.S. Government Printing Office.

Wallace, G. (2001). Grandparent caregivers: Emerging issues in elder law and social work practice. *Journal of Gerontological Social Work, 34*(3) 127–136.

Whitley, K. R., White, S. J., & Yorke, B. (1999). Strengths-based case management: Application to grandparents raising grandchildren. *Families in Society, 80*(2), 110–119.

CHAPTER 19

Elder Abuse and Neglect

A CURRENT PROFILE OF ELDER ABUSE FACING OLDER ADULTS IN THE UNITED STATES

Is elder abuse a grave issue in the United States? Do we have a profile of the prevalence of elder abuse in the United States? According to a study conducted in 2004 by the Survey of State Adult Protective Services (APS), findings show that there was an increase of 19.7% in the combined total of reports of elder and vulnerable adult abuse and neglect reports and an increase of 15.6% in substantiated cases since the reports were conducted in the year 2000. In 2003, APS reported that their agencies nationwide had received 565,747 reports of suspected elder and vulnerable adult abuse as compared with 482,913 reports identified in the 2000 study.

Within the APS survey, nationwide, 253,426 incidents were reported. These included a low of 85 reports in Guam to a high of 66,805 in California. On average, this resulted in 8.3 reports of abuse per 1,000 older Americans (NCEA, 2006).

The 2004 survey of APS resources found that older women were far more likely than older men to suffer from abuse or neglect. In fact, it was found that nearly two out of every three victims (65.7%) of elder abuse were women. Abused victims were also older, and nearly half of victims (42.8%) were age 80 or older (NCEA, 2006). Although victims are represented by some diversity, the majority of victims (77.1%) were white.

Although each state is mandated to host an adult protective services registry, not all respond to the reporting of their data. Hence, according to the National Center of Elder Abuse Protection's recent survey (NCEA, 2006), not all states reported to survey calls for information regarding elder abuse statistics. Thus, although we have some profile of alleged perpetrators, it is somewhat incomplete. What we do know, however, is that more than half of the alleged perpetrators of elder abuse or neglect were female (52.7%) and nearly three quarters of the alleged offenders (75.1%) were less than 60 years of age. The majority of perpetrators in 2003 were adult children (32.6%) or other family members (21.5%). Only 11.3% of perpetrators were identified as spouses or intimate partners (NCEA, 2006).

At the current time, less than half of the states in the United States maintain an abuse registry or database that identifies alleged perpetrators. This makes it difficult to glean a clear picture of the abuse profile. At the current time, 40.4% of the states (21 states) maintain an abuse registry, while 31 states/territories or 59.6% do not maintain a registry.

When examining types of specific maltreatment that has been substantiated, it appears that self-neglect occurs most frequently (37.2%), followed by caregiver neglect (20.4%), financial exploitation (14.7%), emotional/psychological/verbal abuse (14.8%), physical abuse (10.7%), sexual abuse (1%), and other (1.2%). Despite these statistics, it is estimated that only 10% of all cases of neglect or abuse are ever reported, and an even smaller percentage of substantiated reports are available.

WHO REPORTS ELDER ABUSE?

In the final analysis, who do we find that reports abuse? Although there are a variety of sources, the most common source of reports of elder abuse and neglect allegations appeared to be first family members (17% of cases), followed by human and social service workers (10.6%) and followed by friends and neighbors (8%). Although these data are reported from only 11 states, when compared to some specific states such as Illinois, it appears to be an average (NCEA, 2006; IDoA, 2007).

PROGRAMS AND SERVICES AVAILABLE TO ADDRESS ISSUES OF ELDER ABUSE

Medicare

Although Medicare does not have any specific mandate for Elder Abuse services, funds are available for counseling resulting from the trauma related to abuse, through the mental health provisions (see Chapter 15 on Mental Health). Providers can use ICD-10 codes for "elder abuse" to denote that the hospitalization or treatment was as a result of abuse. However, since these codes are not used as often as they should; thus it is difficult to decide to what extent elder abuse is represented in Medicare claims cases (Wood, 2006).

State-Based Services Offered Through Departments on Aging

Each state, through the Older Americans Act and Administration on Aging, is mandated to provide adult protective services (APS), for people over the age of 60 years of age. Adult protective services oversees cases of complaints related to financial, emotional, sexual, and physical exploitation, and neglect. Most states have a confidential reporting hotline, which allows those concerned to confidentially report cases of concern, which are then followed up by APS workers for substantiation and potential charges. While APS concerns itself for the most part with adults over the age of 60 years of age living in the community, people who are living within long-term care settings are followed by a state based ombudsman program.

The Centers for Disease Control and Prevention (CDC)

The Centers for Disease Control and Prevention do not offer specific services to address abuse and neglect; however, they do sponsor several data collection systems that have variables that address issues of abuse, neglect, and violence. Some of these specific databases include the following:

- National Home and Hospice Survey (NHHS): Questions are asked regarding recognizing elder abuse.
- National Electronic Injury Surveillance System (NEISS-AIP): Contains information on the assaults of elders. Perpetrator data is not always noted in the medical record and not coded.
- Chronic Disease Behavioral Risk Factor Surveillance System (BRFSS): Has some questions on elder abuse in the caregiver survey being implemented as part of BFRSS.

Area Agencies on Aging

A program designed to protect the rights of older persons who live in long-term care facilities is overseen through local Area Agencies on Aging. It received its mandate through the Older Americans Act, known as the

Long Term Care Ombudsman Program. It protects and promotes the rights and quality of life for people who reside in long-term care facilities (nursing homes). This is done through regional ombudsmen who have hands-on working relationships with the residents and staff of the facilities within their program areas.

The Long Term Care Ombudsman program works in conjunction with long-term care facilities to assure that residents and their families are aware of their rights, to resolve complaints, to provide information on residents' needs and concerns to their families, facility staff, and communities, and to advocate for quality institutionalized care. Although the program is limited to facility residents over the age of 60, the program does provide for current residents, prospective residents, or former residents of a long-term care facility. The program generally will act upon resident or family concerns or long-term care facility staff members and administrators with resident-related concerns. The program is also responsive to individuals and families who are considering nursing home placement as a long-term care option, the community at large, and other interested groups concerned about the welfare of residents of long-term care facilities.

Essentially, the ombudsman listens to resident and family concerns, through a confidential approach. They will generally involve the resident and/or family in the investigation and resolution plan and try to resolve problems within the facility, prior to seeking outside counsel. The Long Term Care Ombudsman Program can be of assistance to individual residents or prospective residents, and/or family members when these parties are seeking information about long-term care facilities, or answers about issues such as facility services or standards, medical coverage, resident rights, and/or transfer or discharge.

Although concern about elder abuse and neglect is mandated in the Older Americans Act, state departments on aging choose how they will administer this type of community program. The latest amendments to the Older Americans Act (PL 109-365) incorporates self-neglect into the definitions associated with elder abuse and neglect. In addition, Title VII expands elder abuse prevention to include financial literacy, grants to expand best practices, and data collection efforts. The new act amends Section 721 authorizing the use of Title VII funds to carry out public education and outreach to promote financial literacy and prevent identity theft and financial exploitation of older individuals. It also amends Section 721 authorizing the use of Title VII funds to carry out public education and outreach to promote financial literacy and prevent identity theft and financial exploitation of older individuals. Other innovations in these amendments include the creation of a new Section 752, entitled "State and Tribal Grants To Strengthen Long-Term Care And Provide Assistance

For Elder Justice Programs." This authorizes grants to states and Indian tribes to strengthen long-term care and provide assistance for elder justice programs. It also provides for the use of funds for a number of elder justice activities including: elder abuse prevention and detection, safe haven models, case review and assistance, volunteer programs, multidisciplinary elder justice activities, programs to address underserved populations of elders, and others. The amendment also creates new Section 753, authorizing grants to improve, streamline, and promote the uniform collection of national data on elder abuse, neglect, and exploitation.

TYPES OF ELDER ABUSE AND NEGLECT

According to the Administration on Aging (AoA, 2004) elder abuse is an umbrella term referring to any knowing, intentional, or negligent act by a caregiver or any other person that causes harm or a serious risk of harm to a vulnerable adult. They also have provided definitions of specific types of abuse and neglect as follows:

- Physical abuse is inflicting, or threatening to inflict, physical pain or injury on a vulnerable elder, or depriving them of a basic need.
- Sexual abuse is the infliction of nonconsensual sexual contact of any kind.
- Emotional or psychological abuse is the infliction of mental or emotional anguish or distress on an elder person through verbal or nonverbal acts.
- Financial or material exploitation is the illegal taking, misuse, or concealment of funds, property, or assets of a vulnerable elder.
- Neglect is the refusal or failure by those responsible to provide food, shelter, health care, or protection for a vulnerable elder.
- Self-neglect is characterized as the behavior of an elderly person that threatens his/her own health or safety.
- Abandonment is the desertion of a vulnerable elder by anyone who has assumed the responsibility for care or custody of that person. (AoA, 2004).

MODEL PROGRAMS AND BEST PRACTICE APPROACHES TO ADDRESSING THE LEGAL NEEDS OF OLDER ADULTS

Some model programs do exist within communities, which attempt to address issues of abuse and neglect. While the examples showcased are not exhaustive, they do provide for some guidance for innovative interventions for the future. It should be noted that the programs showcased have been identified as best practice programs by the Administration on Aging.

Breaking the Silence—Media Campaign (Illinois Department on Aging)

The Illinois Department on Aging's Office of Elder Rights offers an Elder Abuse Awareness Campaign Tool Kit to elder abuse provider agencies and area agencies on aging throughout the State of Illinois in their attempt to educate providers on elder abuse and promote prevention efforts. The kit include news releases that can be used with television stations, radio station news editors, and local newspapers to promote events or provide some background to the issue of elder abuse.

The B*SAFE Program

B*SAFE is an acronym for *Bankers and Seniors Against Financial Exploitation*. This program was developed through support from the Illinois Department on Aging. The B*SAFE program is a partnership that helps train bank personnel on the detection, prevention, and reporting of financial exploitation. The program is supported by:

- Illinois Department on Aging
- Illinois Bankers Association
- Illinois Community Bankers Association
- Office of the Attorney General
- TRIAD, an organization comprised of law enforcement, government entities, and advocacy groups committed to the prevention of crimes against the elderly

This program was developed in 2001 through a collaboration of law enforcement and state agencies, to address the growing problem of financial exploitation. B*SAFE is a public education program that targets bank personnel as the first line of defense against financial exploitation. A senior often sees the same teller who routinely handles their financial transactions each time they visit the banking facility. That teller is in a prime position to be able to detect any changes from the senior's normal transactions.

The B*SAFE program educates the teller on potential signs of financial exploitation. The program also encourages networking between the bank, local law enforcement, and the elder abuse provider agency (EAPA). The teller training is handled through the EAPA agency. Each EAPA has a staff member that has been through the B*SAFE train-the-trainer program, who will be able to provide training to bank personnel.

In 2005, the Illinois Department on Aging received a grant from the Illinois Criminal Justice Information Authority (ICJIA) to develop and print inserts to be distributed to bank customers via their monthly bank statements. The grant also included the development and printing of a financial exploitation brochure targeted at senior customers, to be made available at banking facilities, as well as posters that financial institutions can display in their lobbies. The materials are available in English and Spanish. Publications are available on the Web site for the Illinois Department on Aging.

CHALLENGES FOR ELDER ABUSE AND NEGLECT PROGRAMS IN THE FUTURE

Cultural values, beliefs, and traditions significantly affect family life. They dictate family members' roles and responsibilities toward one another, how family members relate to one another, how decisions are made within families, how resources are distributed, and how problems are defined (Kosberg & Garcia, 1995; Tatara, 1999). Culture further influences how families cope with stress and determines if and when families will seek help from outsiders. Understanding these factors can significantly increase professionals' effectiveness. Colleagues, coworkers, clients themselves, and members of the community members are workers' most valuable resource in understanding the role of culture. Although it is not possible to achieve an understanding of all the diverse cultures workers are likely to encounter, learning the questions and framing the role of culture and elder abuse using the health belief model set the stage as a critical first step to understand this dilemma. Questions to consider include:

- What role do seniors play in the family? In the community?
- Who, within the family, is expected to provide care to frail members? What happens when they fail to do so?
- Who makes decisions about how family resources are expended? About other aspects of family life?
- Who, within the family, do members turn to in times of conflict or strife?
- What conduct is considered abusive? Is it considered abusive to use an elder's resources for the benefit of other family members? To ignore a family member?
- (With immigrant seniors), when did they come to the United States and under what circumstances? Did they come alone or

with family members? Did other family members sponsor them and, if so, what resources did those family members agree to provide? What is their legal status?

- What religious beliefs, past experiences, attitudes about social service agencies or law enforcement, or social stigmas may affect community members' decisions to accept or refuse help from outsiders?
- Under what circumstances will families seek help from outsiders? To whom will they turn for help (e.g., members of the extended family, respected members of the community, religious leaders, physicians)?
- What are the trusted sources of information in the community? What television and radio stations, shows, and personalities are considered reliable? What newspapers and magazines do people read?
- How do persons with limited English speaking or reading skills get their information about resources?

The answers to these questions can provide guidance to professionals in working with members of diverse ethnic and cultural communities. They will help workers understand expectations and dynamics within families and determine what services will be most appropriate and acceptable. They will help workers identify trusted persons who can be called upon for help. Finally, they can provide insight into promising approaches and vehicles for spreading the word about available services.

CHALLENGES FOR LEGAL ISSUES IN AGING FOR THE FUTURE

A number of challenges are apparent within the field of elder abuse. These include some of the following:

- There needs to be consistent definitions and measures for reporting that are used across every state to assure that elder abuse trends can be tracked and studied nationwide (Dulop, Rothman, Condon, & Martinez, 2000).
- Data is currently not consistently reported on the race and ethnicity of both the victims and alleged perpetrators. This is an important dimension as we attempt to understand how ethnic variation plays a role in the face of the perpetrators and victims of elder abuse. Some states do collect this data routinely, while others do not (National Committee on the Prevention of Elder Abuse, n.d.).
- There needs to be training in the detection and reporting of elder abuse for nontraditional "gatekeepers" in the community that

are in contact with older adults. These gatekeepers include the postal service workers, bank employees, and utility workers who may witness signs of elder abuse but not know how to report or what to report (Anetzberger et al., 2000).

- Outcome data that documents substantiation of cases following reports are not consistently collected by state-based agencies. This would be extremely helpful in developing an understanding of the process of the investigation, and barriers that impede any further investigation or intervention.
- State Adult Protective Services and Ombudsman programs are largely underfunded, which makes it difficult to follow up on cases or substantiate abuse within cases reported.
- Older adults themselves may feel vulnerable or at risk for being abused; however, they may not feel like there are options available to them for recourse should they report or want to assure that their family members do not continue to abuse them. This may be an impediment for resolving cases effectively and efficiently.
- The concept of self-neglect will become increasingly important and controversial. Many professional groups and their codes of ethics for practice may value self-determinism and autonomy; however, the concept of self -neglect may receive more attention as larger cities face building code and fire regulation violations due to individual self-neglect and hoarding. Dealing with the balancing act between community safety, public health concerns, and individual rights will be a challenge in the future.

SUMMARY

The incidence and prevalence of elder abuse is probably largely under-reported. While efforts are being made to understand the magnitude of the problem, limited resources hamper progress. The Older Americans Act has some resources in place to deal with the education of providers and screening/detection of individuals who have been at risk of abuse; however, Adult Protective Services plays a key role here in this intervention process. The role of one's cultural beliefs and help-seeking behavior also plays a significant role. Challenges in uncovering this silent epidemic face the health care provider, programs, and services.

USEFUL WEB SITES

The International Network for the Prevention of Elder Abuse (INPEA): http://www.inpea.net/

INPEA has produced the *Community Guide to Raise World Awareness on Adult Abuse Tool Kit.* The Tool kit provides sample ideas and templates for activities and examples of materials, resources, proclamations, and messages. The Tool kit is available for free download at the Web site above.

The National Center on Elder Abuse: http://elderabusecenter.org
This Web site provides data, fact sheets, and other information on elder abuse, neglect, and exploitation in the United States.

The National Clearinghouse on Abuse in Later Life: http://www.ncall.us/
This clearinghouse is responsible for information on coordinating elder abuse prevention efforts with domestic violence and sexual assault programs.

Eldercare Locator: http://www.eldercare.gov
This site enables one to contact a local area agency on aging about volunteering to call or visit an isolated senior.

The National Committee for the Prevention of Elder Abuse: http://www.preventelderabuse.org
This site provides researchers, practitioners, educators, and advocates dedicated to protecting the safety, security, and dignity of America's most vulnerable citizens. The committee was established in 1988 to achieve a clearer understanding of abuse and provide direction and leadership to prevent it. The committee is one of six partners that make up the National Center on Elder Abuse, which is funded by Congress to serve as the nation's clearinghouse on information and materials on abuse and neglect.

REFERENCES

Anetzberger, G. J., Palmisano, B. R., Sanders, M., Bass, D., Dayton, C., Eckert, S., et al. (2000). A model intervention for elder abuse and dementia. *The Gerontologist, 40,* 492–497.

Administration on Aging. (2004). Elder Abuse and Neglect. Retrieved June 15, 2007 from http://www/prof/notes/docs/elderabuseneglect.pdf

Dulop, B. D., Rothman, M. B., Condon, K. M., & Martinez, I. L. (2000). Elder abuse: risk factors and use of case data to improve policy and practice. *Journal of Elder Abuse & Neglect, 12,* 3–4, 95–122.

Illinois Department on Aging (IDoA). (2007). *Older Adult Services Act: 2007 report to the General Assembly.* Retrieved May 20, 2007, from http://www.state.il.us/aging/1news_pubs/publications/oasa_anreprt2007.pdf

Kosberg, J. I., & Garcia, J. L. (Eds.). (1995). *Elder abuse: International and cross-cultural perspectives.* Binghamton, NY: Haworth Press.

National Center for Elder Abuse (NCEA). (2006). *Statistics on elder abuse.* Retrieved May 28, 2007 from http://www.ncea.org

National Committee for the Prevention of Elder Abuse. (n.d.). *The role of culture in elder abuse.* Retrieved May 18, 2007, from http://www.preventelderabuse.org/issues/culture.html

Tatara, T. (1999). *Understanding elder abuse in minority populations.* Philadelphia: Taylor & Francis.

Understanding and combating elder abuse in minority communities. (1997). Proceedings of a 1997 conference sponsored by the National Center on Elder Abuse (NCEA). Washington, DC.

Wood, E. (2006). *The availability and utility of interdisciplinary data on elder abuse: A white paper for the National Center on Elder Abuse.* Washington, DC: National Center on Elder Abuse.

CHAPTER 20

Legal Issues

LEGAL ISSUES AND OLDER ADULTS

The United States has been touted by some experts to be one of the most litigious countries in the world. It should come as no surprise that families, long-term care facilities, and nursing homes are riddled with anxieties with respect to legal issues and the aging segment of our population (Kapp, 2003). One can hardly be admitted into a hospital at the current time without some aspect of legal issues cropping up—especially related to one's living will or health care advanced directive. These issues cover issues of respecting one's choices through informed consent and decision-making capacity and also include life-sustaining treatment concerns. Major items of concern with life-sustaining treatments include do-not-resuscitate orders, withdrawing treatment, tube feeding, active euthanasia, and assisted suicide.

Legal issues, especially issues related to informed decision making, generally identified through documents such as a power of attorney or medical power of attorney, are important and critical documents to assure that one's wishes are carried out in business and personal transactions. This first segment of this chapter addresses legal issues with a special emphasis on the concept of a power of attorney.

POWER OF ATTORNEY

A power of attorney is a legal instrument that is used to delegate legal authority to another. The person who signs (executes) a power of attorney is called the principal. The power of attorney gives legal authority to another person (called an agent or attorney-in-fact) to make property, financial, and other legal decisions for the principal.

A principal can give an agent broad legal authority, or very limited authority. The power of attorney is frequently used to help in the event of a principal's illness or disability, or in legal transactions where the principal cannot be present to sign necessary legal documents.

Types of Powers of Attorney

Several types of powers of attorney are in existence, regardless of the state within which one resides. These three types include nondurable, durable, and springing powers of attorney.

A nondurable power of attorney takes effect immediately. It remains in effect until it is revoked by the principal, or until the principal becomes mentally incompetent or dies. A nondurable power of attorney is often used for a specific transaction, like the closing on the sale of residence, or the handling of the principal's financial affairs while the principal is traveling outside of the country.

Durable power of attorney enables the agent to act for the principal even after the principal is not mentally competent or physically able to make decisions. The durable power of attorney may be used immediately and is effective until it is revoked by the principal, or until the principal's death.

Springing power of attorney becomes effective at a future time. That is, it "springs up" upon the happenings of a specific event chosen by the power of attorney. Often that event is the illness or disability of the principal. Springing power of attorney will frequently provide that the principal's physician will determine whether the principal is competent to handle his or her financial affairs. A springing power of attorney remains in effect until the principal's death, or until revoked by a court.

Durable and springing powers of attorney are frequently used to plan for a principal's future incapacity or disability and loss of competence resulting, for example, from Alzheimer's disease or a catastrophic accident. By appointing an agent under a durable or springing power of attorney, the principal is setting up a procedure for the management of his or her financial affairs in the event of incompetence or disability.

A nondurable power of attorney enables a principal to decide in advance who will make important financial and business decisions in the future. It is also helpful in avoiding the expense of having a court appoint a guardian to handle the principal's affairs in the event of incompetence or disability.

Legal Authority Granted via a Power of Attorney

Whether nondurable, durable, or springing, a power of attorney can be used to grant any, or all, of the following legal powers to an agent:

- Buy or sell one's real estate;
- Manage one's property;

- Conduct one's banking transactions;
- Invest, or not invest, one's money;
- Make legal claims and conduct litigation;
- Attend to tax and retirement matters; and
- Make gifts on the principal's behalf.

Selecting an Agent for a Power of Attorney

One should choose a trusted family member, a proven friend, or a professional with an outstanding reputation for honesty. Signing a power of attorney that grants broad authority to an agent is very much like signing a blank check. Certainly, one should never give a power of attorney to someone they do not trust fully, nor should anyone be forced into signing a power of attorney.

Multiple agents may also be appointed. If two or more agents are appointed, the principal must decide whether they must act together in making decisions involving one's affairs, or whether each can act separately. There are advantages and disadvantages to both forms of appointment. Requiring one's agents to act jointly can safeguard the soundness of their decisions. On the other hand, requiring agreement of all agents can result in delay or inaction in the event of a disagreement among them, or the unavailability of one of them to sign legal documents.

Allowing agents to act separately may ensure that an agent is always available to act for the best interests of one's affairs. However, it may also result in confusion and disagreements if the agents do not communicate with one another, or if one of them believes that the other is not acting in your best interests.

In some states, a statutory short-form power of attorney provides space to appoint an alternate or substitute agent. A substitute agent can act if the first agent is unable or unwilling to act for the benefit of the principal. It is generally a good idea to appoint a substitute agent.

Powers of attorney are only as good as the agents who are appointed. Appointing a trustworthy person as an agent is critical. Without a trustworthy agent, a power of attorney becomes a dangerous legal instrument, and a threat to the principal's best interests (Georgas, 1998).

A common concern for individuals, especially older adults, is that once a power of attorney is signed, is it possible for the principal to make legal and financial decisions for oneself? An agent named in a power of attorney is only a representative, not one's boss. As long as an individual has the legal capacity to make decisions, they can direct their agent to do only those things that they want done.

Obligations of an Agent

The agent is obligated to act in the best interests of the principal, and to avoid any "self-dealing." Self-dealing is acting to further the selfish interests of the agent, rather than the best interest of the principal.

An agent appointed in a power of attorney is a fiduciary, with strict standards of honesty, loyalty, and candor to the principal. An agent must safeguard the principal's property, and keep it separate from the agent's personal property. Money should be kept in a separate bank account for the benefit of the principal. Agents must also keep accurate financial records of their activities, and provide complete and periodic accountings for all money and property coming into their possession.

It should be made clear to one's agent that an accurate accounting of records of all transactions completed is expected, and periodic accountings are also expected. An agent can also be directed to provide an accounting to a third party—a member of one's family or trusted friend—in the event that the principal is unable to review the accounting for themselves.

Potential Abuses by Agents

A power of attorney can be abused, and dishonest agents have used powers of attorney to transfer the principal's assets to themselves and others. Hence, it is important to appoint an agent who is completely trustworthy, and to require the agent to provide complete and periodic accountings to you or to a third party.

Transfer of Assets

Another common concern that may face older adults, their children, or people with chronic disabilities relates to the transfer of assets, and weighing out if the transfer of a principal's assets to other people is positive and advantageous. A principal may want to authorize transfers or gifts of property for estate planning and other valid purposes. In some states, it is possible for powers of attorney to permit agents to make gifts to members of the principal's family, if the principal so authorizes in the power of attorney. The principal can also customize a power of attorney to permit the agent to make gifts to non-family members.

Monitoring and Oversight

There is no official or government monitoring of agents acting pursuant to power of attorney. That is the responsibility of the principal. It is therefore important to insist that an agent keep accurate records of all transactions completed, and provide periodic accountings. Should a principal, a member of the principal's family, or a friend have grounds to believe that an agent is misusing a power of attorney, the suspected abuse should be reported to the police or other law enforcement authority to protect the principal from the loss of his or her property. Consider asking a lawyer for help and advice.

The power of attorney may be revoked at any time. This revocation should be in writing, and the principal should inform their agent that their powers are being revoked, and a request made to return all copies of their power of attorney. In addition, one should notify their bank or other financial institution where one's agent has used the power of attorney that it has been revoked. A copy of the revocation should also be filed with the county clerk if your power of attorney has been filed in the clerk's office. Generally speaking, if one should decide to revoke a power of attorney, it is probably in their best interests to consult a lawyer and arrange to have a new power of attorney executed.

A power of attorney is not necessarily filed within a specific government office, unless it is used in a real estate transaction. In that case, it must be filed in the county clerk's office. And when it is filed in the county clerk's office, the power of attorney is a public record open to inspection by the public. A writing that revokes a filed power of attorney should also be filed in the county clerk's office.

If one should file a power of attorney in the county clerk's office, generally they should be able to get additional certified copies from the county clerk for a small fee. A certified copy is legally equivalent to the original document. It is often convenient to have certified copies of one's power of attorney on hand. One's signature on the power of attorney must be witnessed by a notary public. Although one is not required to hire a lawyer in order to prepare a power of attorney, since a power of attorney is such an important legal instrument, the careful consumer will consult a lawyer who can:

- Provide legal and other advice about the powers that are appropriate to be delegated;
- Provide counsel on the choice of an agent;
- Outline the agent's legal and fiduciary obligations while acting under a power of attorney; and
- Ensure that the power of attorney is properly executed and meets all legal requirements.

The typical fee for preparing a power of attorney is modest. Before engaging a lawyer to prepare a power of attorney, one should inquire about the fee and feel free to get prices from other lawyers and law firms. Local Area Agencies on Aging often fund legal clinics or resources that handle legal documents such as powers of attorney for seniors 60 years of age and older.

HEALTH CARE POWER OF ATTORNEY

A health care power of attorney grants an agent the power to make medical decisions for the principal when the principal cannot make that decision for themselves. This might occur when the principal slips into a coma after a motor vehicle accident, for example. With a properly drafted health care power of attorney, the agent has authority to consult with the principal's physician, evaluate the risks of certain medical procedures, and give or withhold consent for the physician to perform the procedure. The health care power of attorney only becomes effective when the principal is unable to make medical decisions for himself or herself because of mental incapacity.

Living Wills and Advanced Directives

A living will, which is also known as an advanced health care directive, is a signed document that instructs an attending physician not to keep one alive with artificial measures if they become permanently unconscious. In other words, if one suffers from a terminal illness or catastrophic physical trauma that permanently reduces brain activity to a vegetative state, with no possibility of recovery, the living will expresses one's desire not to be kept alive under such circumstances.

Although these documents are called living "wills" they have nothing to do with a person's last will and testament. The last will and testament is for passing of one's property to the people chosen after one's death. The living will, on the other hand, expresses one's desires about their medical care near the end of their life (Carter, 1998).

PROGRAMS AND SERVICES AVAILABLE TO ADDRESS LEGAL ISSUES FOR OLDER ADULTS

Medicare

While Medicare does not offer legal assistance per se, a dimension of Medicare that does impact legal issues is the whole arena of fraud. Over-billing, and charges for services that may have never been performed, are often issues that can be cause for legal concern.

State-Based Departments on Aging

Departments on Aging in every state have a legal assistance developer. The role of this individual is to provide leadership and technical assistance in the development and enhancement of quality legal and advocacy assistance for older persons in greatest economic or social need. Developers often have other roles and responsibilities, including coordinating their states' elder rights efforts and promoting alternative legal assistance delivery systems. Legal assistance developers often refer persons in need of assistance to the appropriate legal providers for the elderly, and help with outreach and public education. In addition, their role leads them to direct the design and implementation of programmatic systems to improve the quality and quantity of legal assistance for the elderly in their individual states.

The Older Americans Act and Area Agencies on Aging

The Older Americans Act (Sec. 306(a)(15)(A-E): & Sec 731 (a) (b)) incorporates language that provides funding for legal services through local area agencies on aging. These financial provisions are found in Title III and VII of the Older American's Act. Some of the specific services that can be provided include:

- Last will and testament;
- Durable power of attorney;
- Health care power of attorney;
- Assistance with securing public benefits;
- Social Security, SSI, Medicare, Medicaid, and veteran's benefits;
- Family law: divorce and related matters;
- Consumer problems: dishonest vendors, fraud;
- Guardianship for those no longer able to care for self or property;
- Public and educational forums for senior citizens on legal issues; and
- Elder abuse and related issues.

Despite this long list of services, there are some types of services not provided, which include:

- Legal services for criminal cases;
- Representation in the probate of estates;
- Commercial or business matters; and
- Contingency fee cases.

Although each state can set the requirements for compensation for services, generally the services are without costs to the clients. Filing fees and services fees may be required in some cases, or required, if the client is able to afford the payments. No clients will be refused services for lack of financial means in the majority of states.

MODEL PROGRAMS AND BEST PRACTICE APPROACHES TO ADDRESSING THE LEGAL NEEDS OF OLDER ADULTS

American Association of Retired Persons

The American Association of Retired Persons (AARP) has developed a range of resources on end of life, living wills, and dying and death, which are very helpful. These were developed following the Terri Schiavo tragedy, in the hopes that people will have a resource on making decisions for themselves and their family, related to end of life issues. In addition, to these resources, materials have also been developed and are available for distribution to members on dealing with managed care organizations and the end-of life issues (Fox, 1999).

American Society on Aging

The American Society on Aging (ASA) provides a comprehensive Web seminar on the legal and ethical issues of aging. The seminars provide continuing education credits and are available to professionals 24 hours per day. Topics include "Liability and Risk Management Issues in Aging Services," and "Legal and Ethical Aspects of Decision Making by and for Older Persons, Part I and II."

CHALLENGES FOR LEGAL ISSUES IN THE AGING ARENA FOR THE FUTURE

A number of challenges will continue to grow in the future with regard to power of attorney, health care power of attorney, and legal issues in general. One of the most significant will be the importance of choosing and preparing agents to truly act on one's behalf. The future may hold some planning venues or "individualized legal action plans" developed by the principal in order to provide a guide for agents. This can be more critical in cases where the principal sees a decline in their overall health and cognitive function.

A second challenge is to enable individuals to plan for their future while they are of sound mind and cognitively intact, especially in cases where people will lose their cognitive function over time. Issues related to capacity, decision making, and informed consent will also be paramount as we move into the future. Kapp (2001, 2002) raises these issues very eloquently and makes the case that planning by individuals and with individuals prior to diminished capacity is essential as a step to preserving the rights of individuals as they grow older.

A third challenge will include the availability of hospice and end-of-life care experts who are culturally competent. Duffy, Jackson, Schim, Ronis, and Fowler (2006) showcase the differences in racial/ethnic preferences in end-of-life care between Whites and Blacks. In addition, they suggest that there are gender preferences that will illuminate the need for specific intervention options for men and women as well as strategies that take into account one's racial and ethnic background.

The health care market will also drive medical or health care power of attorney decisions in the future. The notion of purchasing services for one's health care in light of diminished cognitive capacity and the ethics associated with the same has been raised eloquently by Kapp (1999). In addition, skyrocketing health care costs, and declines in the overall availability of medical resources for the increasingly graying population, could call attention to the need to consider a process to "ration" resources for older adults. This rationing concept can lead to situations within which assisted suicide becomes an option for people that is legal in the majority of states. Currently, Oregon is the only state in the United States for which physician-assisted suicide is a legal option (State of Oregon, n.d.), but debates on either side of this issue, especially econometric debates, may lead to the legalization of physician assisted suicide options.

Finally, the debates around end-of-life care, physician assisted suicide, and right to life will continue to be challenges that will face us, especially as we move into a "booming" graying society. This discussion may require input from bio-ethicists, and members of various religious communities, in concert with older adults, and is the scope of a more extensive discussion. Foley and Hendin (2002) and Quill and Battin (2004) have prepared a series of debates that provide a comprehensive perspective on both sides of this camp, which are well worth informed discussion and deliberation.

SUMMARY

This chapter has explored several legal issues that face older adults. Power of attorney, both durable and nondurable, were also addressed in this chapter, and a differentiation made between these types of power of attorney and the health care power of attorney. In addition, legal services provided to older adults as a result of the Older Americans

Act were explored, and challenges within the realm of legal issues outlined.

USEFUL WEB SITES

American Association of Retired Persons (AARP): http://www.aarp.org/families
This site provides a host of resources to individuals and their families on end-of life issues, estate planning, living wills, powers of attorney, and self-help guides for the creation of these materials.

Administration on Aging (AoA), Legal Assistance Developers: http://www.aoa.gov/eldfam/Elder_Rights/Legal_Assistance/LSD%20newlist.pdf
This site provides a listing of individuals who are available through the state departments on aging to provide oversight for legal assistance through the Older Americans Act. The site provides a registry of experts for each state in the United States. Every state has a legal assistance developer who provides leadership and technical assistance in the development and enhancement of quality legal and advocacy assistance for older persons in greatest economic or social need. Developers often have other roles and responsibilities, including coordinating their states' elder rights efforts and promoting alternative legal assistance delivery systems.

American Geriatrics Society Legal Resources: http://www.healthinaging.org/AGINGINTHEKNOW/chapters_ch_trial.asp?ch=4
This site provides a plethora of information for the reader on issues that relate to legal concerns of older adults. They include segments to enable individuals to assess competency and informed consent, as well as a host of legal issues for consideration.

American Society on Aging Web Seminar on Legal Issues for Older Adults: http://www.asaging.org/webseminars/websem.cfm?EventID=4439
This site provides Web seminars 24 hours per day on legal and ethical issues for older adults, which can also be used for continuing education credits. Three specific seminars are available through this site: Liability and Risk Management in Aging Services, and Legal and Ethical Aspects of Decision Making by and for Older Persons Parts I and II.

State of Oregon, Death with Dignity Act: http://www.oregon.gov/DHS/ph/pas/index.shtml
This site provides an overview of links related to Oregon's Death with Dignity Act. At the time of this writing, Oregon was the only state to legalize a physician-assisted suicide option for residents of its state. This site provides an overview of the protocol, statistics, and responses to frequently asked questions.

REFERENCES

Carter, T. (1998). *Your personal directive: More than a living will. Self-counsel legal series.* Bellingham, WA: Self-counsel Series.

Duffy, S., Jackson, F. C., Schim, S. M., Ronis D. L., & Fowler, K. E. (2006). Racial/ethnic preferences, sex preferences, and perceived discrimination related to end-of-life care. *Journal of the American Geriatrics Society, 54*(1), 150–157.

Foley, K., & Hendin, H. (2002). *The case against assisted suicide for the right to end-of-life care.* Baltimore, MD: Johns Hopkins University Press.

Fox, P. (1999). *End of life in managed care organizations.* Washington, DC: AARP.

Georgas, S. (1998). *Power of Attorney Kit: A do it yourself kit. Self-counsel legal series.* Bellingham, WA: Self-counsel Series.

Kapp, M. (1999). From medical patients to health care consumers: Decisional capacity and choices to purchase coverage and services. *Aging and Mental Health, 3*(4), 294–300.

Kapp, M. (2001). Legal interventions for persons with dementia in the USA: Ethical, policy and practical aspects. *Aging and Mental Health, 4,* 312–315.

Kapp, M. (2002). Decisional capacity in theory and practice: Legal process versus "bumbling through." *Aging and Mental Health, 6*(4), 413–417.

Kapp, M. (2003). Legal anxieties and end-of-life care in nursing homes. *Issues in Law and Medicine, 19*(2), 111–134.

Quill, T. E., & Battin, M. P. (2004). *Physician assisted dying: The case of palliative care and patient choice.* Baltimore, MD: Johns Hopkins University Press.

State of Oregon. (n.d.). *Death with Dignity Act.* Retrieved November 4, 2006, from http://www.oregon.gov/DHS/ph/pas/index.shtml

CHAPTER 21

Challenges for the Future: Realities and Visions

The preceding chapters have addressed a number of areas that will affect the lives of people as they age or people who are older adults. Philosophical paradigms, statistics, evidence-based approaches, dealing with the media, making people aware of new technologies, and preparing for communities to best deal with issues of aging are all major issues to be concerned about. A range of issues has been presented; however, this chapter provides an overview of the most significant issues to be addressed or to require intervention. Hence, the most challenging of issues for the future are framed in a "top 10 list."

THE TOP 10 LIST OF CHALLENGES FOR THE FUTURE

The top 10 list of challenges for the future will include the following. Each will be described in detail to follow:

1. Designing paradigms to meet the demographic and social needs of our graying population through evidence-based approaches
2. Social Security—boom or bust?
3. Medicare: Will there be a pot at the end of the rainbow for preventative services?
4. Understanding health behavior and planning with this understanding in mind
5. Using the media, advocacy, and coalitions for social change
6. Home- and community-based care
7. Mental health programs, services, and issues

8. Health programs, services, and issues
9. Long-term care
10. Diversity and special populations

1. Designing Paradigms to Meet The Demographic and Social Needs of Our Graying Population Through Evidence-Based Approaches

Reality

The evolving needs identified by our graying boomer population will create an increased demand upon our public and private systems for resources and services. The financial resources available through public sources will see an increased demand for funding of services and resources at community, regional, and state levels. These demands will be experienced by both the public sector and private sources such as philanthropic or faith-based organizations. Consequently, an increased need to showcase how the donor investment has been utilized will be paramount. Evidence and best practices will guide program development for the future while needs assessments and data will transform both the development of programs and the mounting of program evaluations.

Vision

A vision for the future to meet the demand from this "top 10" list will include the increased need for accountability and evidence to support a specific program or service. Agency programs and services will become increasingly savvy with the use of statistics or data to provide a basis for program development and program design, and to document the efficacy and impact of interventions. In addition, these programs and services will become more interested in using quantitative and qualitative outcomes to market programs to consumers, since there may be a feeling that consumers from the upcoming boomer era will be driven to decision making based upon empirical findings and evidence. The bottom line—considering that the upcoming boomer population has prided itself on decision making through consumer reports and the like, this perspective will also be an important dimension in the development of services and resources both for accountability and marketing.

2. Social Security

Reality

A major reality facing the Social Security program in the United States is whether to privatize the program or enable the program to remain as a public resource or program for all to benefit from. Debate will continue to ensue regarding the privatization of the Social Security retirement fund in order to maintain solvency into the Social Security trust fund. In reality, though, if such a measure were to occur, the system risks being thrust back into a situation of instability that led to the very development of the Social Security program—a stock market crash. While private interests may be to privatize, it may well be that the interests at heart for privatization are fueled by an innate desire to assure that investors have funds available for investment. Hence, individuals with marginal resources, the working poor, and the vast majority of people living and working within the United States today could conceivably retire with limited funds available to them both at the time of their retirement and long into their retirement years. This may result in cost shifting, since many of these same individuals, with limited funds available for retirement, will in effect require some assets for income. These assets could result in an increased flux of individuals funded through Medicaid or public aid resources and an increase in the elderly poor.

The changing demographics and increased numbers of people who have experienced multiple marriages, divorce agreements, and settlements resulting in pension splitting will skyrocket over the next few decades, resulting in more people than ever in situations where their current pension resources cannot adequately meet their needs. Consequently, the end result will be that some financial intervention will be required to meet the economic and social security needs of people into their retirement years.

Another reality worth considering is the reality that the Social Security Act does not merely cover retirement benefits for people who have retired, but also includes numerous other titles that fund a large number of need-based programs such as children's health insurance programs, maternal and child health programs, and so on. A reality for the future is that some of these programs may need to be revised in order to assure costs and funds are available through the Social Security Trust Fund. Since many individual state revenues depend upon these federal funds in order to remain solvent, it is unlikely that these programs will quickly receive support to dismantle.

Retirement ages currently have shifted and people who previously could have retired without penalty at 64 years of age are now being forced to work longer and into their late 60s (at least 67 years of age for people born after 1954). While reality is that people will need to work longer in order for the fund to remain solvent, the reality is that many of the jobs will change, and technical skills required by specific jobs will also change. The challenge thus for the workforce will be to assure that workers maintain their skills in order to help businesses remain competitive in the future, and that small business also enable their workforce to upgrade skills in an effort to remain competitive.

A third challenge to the Social Security system will be the very retirement and pension systems paid by employers to employees. Increasingly, corporate entities have dismantled or dissolved company pension systems, with no ethical concern for how this may affect older workers. Thus, this leaves individuals to rely upon the Social Security retirement system for support. This creates a challenge to the current Social Security fund, forcing many people to become dependent upon federal and public sources of funds for a financial safety net into their retirement.

Finally, a challenge for the future will be to keep the Social Security fund solvent and available for financial resources to support older adults as they leave the workforce. Unlike other countries in the world, the United States opted to construct a "pay as you go" system, in which current revenues invested are used to finance current pension needs. Thus, a challenge may be to examine alternative forms of revenue investment in order to assure that there the fund retains the "pay as you go" features, but also accommodates needs for the future.

Vision

The vision for the Social Security fund for the future may include some options that are not popular views. The first unpopular view may include taxation for corporate entities to support individuals who provided backbone and essential labor services such as farmers and the working class. Since many of the same entities would be impacted in some way, and many may be active participants in the elite power structure, they may not be willing to quickly seek being singled out to share their portion of corporate funding to a Social Security fund through additional corporate taxation.

A second vision for the future will be developing "Social Security passport accounts" for people entering into the workforce under the age of 30. These accounts will support individuals through investments for an individual cohort fund but will also address the needs of retirees of the present day. A portion of the funds will be invested into a "pay as you go" plan, and a second portion will go into a fund, designed to be invested and used at a later date (similar to the Social Security plan in Germany).

The third vision for Social Security will be that the plan provide an option for those beyond a specific income level to be able to privately invest their funds. Thus, a safety net will still prevail for the working class, but the option for those with incomes of $100,000 or more to invest a portion of their Social Security/retirement funds will also be a possibility.

3. Medicare

Reality

Medicare, a health insurance program for older adults who have worked 40 quarters during their vocational lifetime, and contributed to the program, will also face serious financial distress in the future. While the program currently funds a range of services through four component parts: Medicare Part A, Medicare Part B, Medicare Part C, and Medicare Part D, the reality is that these specific component parts may become increasingly stressed financially as time moves on.

A second reality is that currently there is much duplication of services per procedure by medical practitioners, who want to assure that they have taken the best care possible. Strategies to reduce the duplication of services will be necessary in efforts to reduce costs to the overall Medicare program. Consistent with the notion of reducing costs will also be the need to reduce long-term care costs through an increased emphasis on prevention services.

Vision

Consideration of the challenges that will be faced by the health care system and Medicare funding leads to several visions. An overall focus on holistic care for older adults to include prevention and screening services would greatly enhance the overall program, and address some of the costly long-term health care costs that are faced by individuals who do not have their health care problems detected early enough. In line with these prevention services the vision will include oral health screening services regardless of whether one has their natural teeth or are edentulous. In addition, we will also include services for the maintenance of one's natural teeth. A second area for prevention services will include physical activity, strength training, and falls prevention services/education.

Although Medicare is based upon a micro-system program (services to individuals), another vision for the future will include opportunities for state Departments on Aging in collaboration with Departments of Public Health to apply for Medicare funds to assure the funding of specific community health initiatives targeting prevention messages. This vision directly leads into the next on the "top 10" item.

4. Understanding Health Behavior and Planning with This Understanding in Mind

Reality

Currently few health promotion programs are utilized as a venue for modifying health behavior, but they are on the increase. The challenge will be to continue to assure that these models are utilized. Planning for health care resources making use of such notions as the health beliefs of specific target groups, their perceived seriousness, perceived susceptibility, and perceived barriers can greatly improve the efficacy of specific resources. Using health behavior models to understand health behavior and plan for resources can be a tremendous asset for resource development, but also in preparation for meeting the needs of specific target groups. In addition, the use of health behavior models can greatly enhance the applicability of specific resources to specific target groups, regional variations, and age cohort groups and differences.

Vision

Hence the vision is that all programs that target health behavior will utilize health behavior models to better describe and understand health behavior. Interventions will be developed with a theoretical framework to guide the actual intervention. Limited resources will encourage agencies and resources to move towards the development of resources and services that assure the greatest impact for investment.

5. Using the Media, Advocacy, and Coalitions for Social Change

Reality

In the second chapter of this book, the lack of advances within the aging arena as compared to other areas was stark, and noteworthy. Limited energy can be devoted to the development of policies and programs to promote the field of aging. With this reality, it is paramount to develop and utilize strategies that will promote the development of programs and services for older adults. Since energies are finite, it becomes important to use the media, advocacy, and coalitions for social change efforts.

Policy development efforts can realize more progress when efforts are pooled together through the use of coalitions. Change efforts often require an interface of various resources and services. Successful efforts to lobby and advocate for policy changes to congresspeople and senators have been effectively enacted through joint efforts from multiple forces. The Americans with Disabilities Act is a solid example of this type of coalition effort, where resources were pooled together with the end result being the passage of the ADA. Coalitions also enable communication across lines and lead to improved program and service utilization.

Coalitions bring broad-based public support to an issue and can be used to leverage political support. Such advocacy efforts can help facilitate broad-based social change at policy and programmatic levels.

The media can be an incredibly valuable asset in this process. They can showcase the issues and help facilitate awareness of the need and strategies for action through a number of venues. In addition the media can be used to showcase the need for health education and public education on issues that will impact older adults and potentially the boomer generation.

Vision

Coalitions will be used to help develop broad-based community support for initiatives and programs. The media will be used to help inform the public of issues and resources. Innovative approaches to the use of media such as media artifacts, fact sheets, and advertisement campaigns will also be used as strategies to improve broad-based community support for programs and initiatives.

6. Home- and Community-Based Care

Reality

Currently, most American people want to remain in their homes as long as possible. This growing phenomenon has led to the need for and importance of increased resources to deliver home- and community-based support and care. While this may be possible within urban areas and larger centers, rural areas and communities with small population bases will be a challenge in the future.

Although the Older Americans Act has focused on home-based supports to assure one's activities of daily living (ADLs) can be carried out, limited attention has been paid to resources that will allow for work or home-based support around one's home, and resources to carry out handyperson work and/or home repairs. This will be a growing issue as the community census of older adults increases and the numbers of natural social supports that people have available to help the elders in the community decreases.

The concept of autonomy, personal choice, and empowerment are also concepts that play a critical role within community-based settings. Although older adults would prefer to make decisions on who will provide in-home care, at the present time, only a select number of states can provide this degree of autonomy. Community-based care and voucher systems are only available in specific states at the current time. These voucher systems enable family members to provide care or be considered a paid caregiver to an elder or disabled person requiring care within their home. The "cash and carry" systems need to be expanded to additional states and provide a broader range of potential users.

Rural communities may not have the same resources for older adults simply because the resources and service providers may not be available. Rural communities also face the dilemma that there are often more people per capita requiring resources, but fewer services or resources available. Transportation also poses a challenge for older adults and their need for services. Providers are often limited in the degree of service which they can provide due to the costs and increasing costs of travel to deliver services. In some ways, people who have been well connected to their peers and community will continue to have connections with people within their network to provide home-based supports. Unfortunately, those who have been perceived as deviant within communities will continue to be ostracized into old age and may be the most in need.

Home- and community-based care are not available to all people in the community, and the program is a needs-assessed program. Thus, there is a wide pool of people who do not have access to services by virtue of the fact that their economic status is slightly above the eligibility requirements; however, these individuals are not financially well off and could not necessarily afford to pay for the home- and community-based services required to maximize their independence.

Another reality to consider is the number of older adults who are in need of nutrition and food programs. An expansion of home-delivered meal programs is going to be necessary to meet the needs of people who are frail and would like to remain in their own homes, and also be nutritionally sound.

Although a number of amendments to the Older Americans Act (2006) were proposed that would impact home and community-based services, this legislative mandate does not come with funding for improved services. Individual state authorities on aging (State Departments on Aging services) can take advantage of expansion of services if the funds are available. However, if funds are not available through state-based treasuries, such expansion will be unrealistic to be expected.

Vision

Some ideal strategies to meet the needs of home- and community-based services will include an expansion of the voucher system available to an increased number of states.

Home-based supports can be expanded to include home maintenance and home repairs for people who would like to remain in their homes. In addition, improved training for home health aids should occur in the future, since these individuals are often a vital link between family and the older adults. These home health workers often serve as the eyes and ears for families to their beloved elders. However, home health workers are often ill-advised of behaviors and actions that can be symptomatic of issues that can foster greater concern or potential for life-threatening conditions, or signs of abuse and neglect. Enhanced training may also help bolster the workers' ability to recognize signs that can prevent further deterioration of health and provide some preventative approaches to care.

Cooperatives available as an alternative to home care system programs would enable people from a range of income levels to be cared for and will also become in vogue as the future unfolds. Since there will be a growing population of people whose income will exceed the eligibility criteria for home-based services, this group will need some form of home-based supports. Cooperatives, which were fashionable especially in the 1960s, will be redeveloped by up and coming aging boomers to provide for the necessary home-based services to meet the needs of this group in efforts to remain at home. In addition, the same constituents that creatively develop these cooperatives will also develop policies and lobby for legislation that will provide incentives for such initiatives both fiscally and socially.

7. Mental Health Programs, Services, and Issues

Reality

Mental health has been viewed as a step-child to medicine, and in a stigmatizing manner for older adults. Although there is some provision for counseling in the Older Americans Act, it has not been sufficient, nor has it provided for the degree necessary to meet the needs of older adults. Services provide for a minimum of counseling or support services to people in need of acute services. The current mental health programs are based upon policies for long-term chronic mentally ill, and do not avail themselves to people who are afflicted with the normal issues of aging. Screening and assessment programs to reach older adults are not consistent across designated regions within state boundaries, let alone across states. The quality of these programs to meet the mental health needs of older adults is inadequate, and early detection programs are practically nonexistent. Peer support programs for older adults to discuss mental health issues are needed and greatly lacking both in number and quality. Educational interventions to make people aware of services and supports to best understand the realities of aging are also necessary and needed.

Vision

Some visions for the future includes the Positive Aging Act, which attempts to enhance mental vitality among older adults, rather than let people remain under- or undiagnosed. The Ronald Reagan Alzheimer's Act will hopefully bring conversation and attention to the need for improved treatment, education, and intervention to individuals and families affected with Alzheimer's disease. The most recent amendments to the Older Americans Act (2006) impacting the mental health of older adults will enable the development of resources, including Centers for Mental Health Intervention and Centers for excellence. Finally, programs that target the promotion of mental vitality will replace the intervention programs for mental health.

8. Health Programs, Services, and Issues

Reality

In the United States, health care is seen as a commodity, rather than a right. Attached to this commodity is a service or resource that is rising in cost, and those costs will continue to skyrocket as time moves on. Hence, a challenge to deal with these rising costs will be to find solutions, one of which may be rationing of health services such as seen in Oregon.

A second challenge to the health care system is the need for an increased focus on prevention—prevention programs for chronic health diseases, and for diseases that may lead to more serious and costly health care issues.

A third challenge to the health care system will be the focus on holistic care rather than disease-specific care. Oral health care is one such specific example, which can have an impact more intensely than merely the oral cavity. Since the mouth is a mirror of the rest of the body (Older Americans Act, 2006), the need is real for services and programs to examine oral health care within the continuum of health care services. The challenge will also include the expansion of current Medicare policy to include oral health care, since it is a myth that all older adults are edentulous.

In Oregon, one option available to people, especially people diagnosed with a chronic health problem, is the option of assisted suicide. This dilemma will pose challenges to state government and health authorities, since in the long run, individual choices to avoid the high cost of treatment for the inevitable, may push or lobby for these options within the realm available to older adults. This assisted suicide option may be perceived as one solution to the high costs of health care; however, such an option will be fraught with concern from religious groups and faith-based communities.

The costs of health care will continue to be a challenge in the future, especially costs associated with procedures that can be prevented in older adults. The costs of falls and hip fractures can often be avoided but will be an issue in attempting to curb health care costs.

Vision

Health care services for older adults in the future will include resources for preventative procedures to include dental care and falls prevention approaches. Models where supplemental insurance provides for these services may also be a wave of the future.

In an effort to deal with increasing costs of health care, some states within the United States will use the Oregon model of service delivery as a blueprint for state-based services. This may include some "rationing" of services and a legalized option for assisted suicide. In response to this option, individuals and interest groups will speak in support of the right to life.

9. Long-Term Care

Reality

Although at the current time, only about 5% of older adults utilize long-term care facilities, a challenge still exists that limited resources for long-term care are available. These resources leave a lot to be desired. Older adults struggle with the multiple moves they may need to undergo as they proceed through the continuum of services from assisted living to congregate living, to nursing home and finally hospice care. The number of moves and changes one must endure during this time period is particularly challenging for older adults who have or are developing diminished cognitive capacity.

Vision

A strategy to meet the challenge outlined for long-term care will include the development of campus settings with a range of housing options for older adults. This continuum of services will move people from assisted living through hospice care all on the same campus.

10. Diversity and Special Populations

Reality

Health disparities are rampant when we compare and contrast health outcomes among older adults who are in need of care or resources and who are people of color or members of a traditionally oppressed group. These health disparities only continue to grow as one ages and more health problems or issues evolve. Unfortunately, services and resources are not necessarily developed to meet the unique culture or health beliefs of specific culture groups, nor are programs and policies developed to be culturally sensitive. Health literacy is a venue for promoting health information, but once again, our system is not set up to best deal with educating individuals through the lens of culturally relevant resources.

Vision

The development of culturally relevant resources to narrow the gap found with health disparities could be an important strategy to cultivate. Programs and intervention efforts that target health literacy that are culturally relevant and developed at specific reading levels to accommodate for educational attainment may also be some important strategies to bridge the gap resulting from health disparities.

SUMMARY

Aging is a reality in our society. Whatever we choose, whatever path we follow, we will still age, and policies, programs, and services will need to be in place to address the issues growing old brings to bear. As we prepare to meet the challenges that our society presents, policies for aging will require development and address. Although this chapter has addressed 10 major challenges that the future will bring, in reality, there will be the need for policy advocates to be prepared to address and deal with these challenges through skills and the ability to develop innovative strategies for policy development and policy change.

Policy development and program design to meet the challenges of an aging society are unique challenges that must be addressed. These issues require an understanding of the various players and philosophical paradigms that shape the values and visions within our society. Despite advances that may take place in science and technology, advances in aging policy has sadly lagged behind. Part of this lag may be attributed to the lack of empirical evidence used to justify changes, and the dearth of anecdotal evidence that has prevailed. Evidence-based policy development can be a strategy to help facilitate rationale for policy advocates to pursue. In effect, revised strategies will be necessary for policy advocates in their quest for the challenges that lie ahead.

Traditionally, we have focused upon Social Security and Medicare as policies that most impact older adults in our nation. This text, however, has made the case that other policies also have an impact on the lives of older adults, including the Americans with Disabilities Act, the Older Americans Act, and the Community Mental Health Centers Act. Each of these pieces of legislation will continue to play a key role in the lives of older adults.

Policy and program development advocates in the future will also benefit from using a new set of skills in their pursuit of policy and program development. These skills that will be invaluable in one's "tool kit" will include an understanding of health behavior models, coalition building strategies, needs assessment strategies, and skills for dealing with the media and preparing media artifacts. These skills will be essential in building effective programs and policies for the future.

Finally, programs and services can only hope to benefit, and the challenges for the future can only be slowly addressed with a renewed set of strategies for program planning and policy development. This text has attempted to empower the policy advocate or program planner with some new skills and strategies that can impact programs and services in the future and break down the challenges of today. The future of services to meet the needs of older adults is in our hands. Let us craft these wisely, skillfully and with a renewed vision.

REFERENCES

Older Americans Act. (2006). Public Law No 109-365, Congressional Record, Vol. 152, USC 3001, 2006.

SAMHSA's Action Plan for Older Adults, Fiscal Years 2006 and 2007

PURPOSE	Promote adoption of evidence-based mental health and substance abuse programs for older adults and promote the integration of older adult issues into SAMHSA's other Matrix priority areas.
PERFORMANCE MEASURES	Long Term Measures • Increase the percent of adults aged 65 to 74 with SMI who are served by the State mental health agencies (Baseline: 8%, URS, 2003) • Decrease the percent of adults aged 50 and older who are in need of substance abuse treatment but do not receive it (Baseline: 3%, NSDUH, 2004) • Decrease the percent of adverse drug reaction emergency department visits of adults age 65 and older (Baseline: 29,830 out of 155,006 related ED visit or 19.2%, DAWN, 2003) Annual Measures • Increase the number of candidate programs addressing older adult mental health and substance abuse that apply for review by the National Registry of Evidence-based Programs and Practices (NREPP). (Baseline: In FY 2005, one, inquiry to Older Americans Substance Abuse and Mental Health Technical Assistance Center and NREPP Data, April 2006) • Increase the number of participants who attend training and technical assistance activities sponsored by SAMH

	SA's Older Americans Substance Abuse and Mental Health Technical Assistance Center, which address the mental health and substance abuse needs of older adults. (Baseline: in FY 2005, 40 participants, inquiry to Older Americans Substance Abuse and Mental Health Technical Assistance Center, April 2006)
POLICY AND PROGRAM PARAMETERS— including drivers:	The following are policy and program parameters that are addressed or reflected in the action plan: • Demographics regarding mental health and substance abuse require increased Federal and State focus on older Americans. As many as 17% of older adults knowingly or unknowingly engage in alcohol or medication misuse and abuse. The most prevalent group of mental disorders among older adults, anxiety disorders, affect an estimated 11.4% of the older adult population. Older adults represent 13% of the population; however, account for 18% of all suicide deaths. • Limited resources prohibit SAMHSA from addressing this need solely through programs targeted to older adults. Must use major existing programs as mechanism for change. • Requirement of most grant programs to utilize and/or implement an evidence-based practice or program, as consideration for funding.
KEY ACTIVITIES— FY 06-07:	• Ensure that older adults are a significant population in SAMHSA's four redwood grant programs, as appropriate: Mental Health Systems Transformation SIG, Access to Recovery, Strategic Prevention Framework SIG, and COSIG. (Track State and community grant activities, technical assistance, and outcomes). • Continue collaboration with the Administration on Aging to identify evidence-based practices and promote them in the Aging Services Network, and support and coordinate efforts concerning state planning, including the development of state plans on substance abuse, mental health, health promotion and/or health education for older adults. • Collect and report NOMS for older adults. • Increase the number of candidate programs addressing older adult substance abuse and mental health that apply for review by the National Registry of Evidence-based Programs and Practices (NREPP).

As Matrix Lead, I agree to the incorporation of the concepts, strategies, and goals outlined in this Action Plan into my performance contract.

Submitted by:	Daryl Kade, *Matrix Lead*	Date:	4/14/06
Approved by:	Charles G. Curie, *Administrator*	Date:	5/5/06

Older Prisoners: Is There Life After "Life" Sentencing? A White Paper

Ron Hillerman

NATURE OF THE PROBLEM

Older prisoners defined as over the age of 50 years are the fastest-growing segment of the United States prison population (Ellsworth & Helle, 1994). Even though many Americans hold stereotypes of adult offenders as "aggressive young men," prison administrators have found that "the 'graying' of America is indeed reflected in the prison population" (Petersilia, 2001; Morton, 1992). The past decade has seen a dramatic increase in the number of incarcerated elderly inmates. This has been due to mandatory minimum sentencing, longer sentences, and tighter parole policies. Correction officials recognize that the costs associated with older prisoners is nearly triple than that of other inmates, primarily due to the expense of health care.

Poor living conditions in prison, inadequate medical treatment, and prior lifestyles (which accelerate aging and medical conditions) make older prisoners a unique population with special prerelease considerations (Fazel, O'Donnell, & Jacoby, 2004; Colsher, et al., 1992) When one examines the growing number of older inmates in federal and state prisons we have to determine their health needs; that is, physical, mental, and social health needs. Thus, we must focus on whether accompanying service delivery issues are meeting these needs adequately.

In January of 1995, the National Prison Project of the American Civil Liberties Union reported that 28 states and the District of Columbia were under consent decree or court order to decrease overcrowding either throughout their entire state system or within at least one of their major prison facilities. In the past two decades, prison gangs have established themselves in our correctional system. In the past, aging inmates were afforded a higher status due to their advanced age and experience with crime; however, this has changed. Younger prisoners no longer respect older prisoners; indeed, they appear to disrespect them now (Hunt, Riegal, Morales, & Waldorf, 1993). Thus, in addition to the health-related issues that older prisoners face, they are also being victimized or live in fear of victimization.

Generally, older prisoners do not act out in retaliation to these fears. Prison officials have found these older inmates are less likely to escape, violate prison rules, or receive disciplinary reports. Older prisoners are so well behaved that many prison officials view them as having a stabilizing or calming effect on younger inmates; thus, older prisoners are seen as "good insurance against the future" (Krajick, 1979, p. 98; Watson, 2004). However, this does not apply to all older offenders—some are just "old and ornery." Studies have shown that serious institutional disciplinary problems appear to be linked to the length of the sentence, amount of time already served, and length of time between visits and other external contacts.

POLICY LEGISLATION

The policy legislation necessary for adequate and humane treatment of older prisoners has been clearly defined in the court decision of Estalla v. Gamble (1976). This establishes that all inmates have the right to appropriate medical care. Studies have shown that on average older prisoners suffer from three chronic health problems and 15% to 25% have some form of mental illness. They require highly specialized and expensive medical care. However, most prison hospitals are set up to address the acute care needs of younger inmates. Aday (1994) noted that most states do not have any specific written policies to address aged or infirm inmates. Hence, most states would have to set a written policy by an administrative directive.

Ninety percent of the 600 prison hospitals in the United States fail to "meet basic standards of care established by the medical profession" (Lundstrom, 1994, p.166). The law not only provides for appropriate medical treatment but also rights to: (a) a reasonably safe environment, (b) appropriate treatment, (c) special education, (d) access to programs and resources, and (e) due process (Colsher et al., 2002).

This is the prevailing policy throughout the United States. Correctional officials view the Older Americans Act and the Americans with Disabilities Act as providing sufficient protection for the elderly and the disabled. The departments consider creating specific conditions based on age as contradictory to these laws.

IMPLEMENTATION

The state of Georgia has been the most innovative in new approaches to dealing with the elderly prison population of the state, expected to reach 8,000 by the year 2010 . The state operates a men's prison where 650 elderly prisoners live orderly lives in gymnasium-sized dorms. Inmates at this facility usually require the assistance of a wheelchair or a walker. Other states are accommodating the aged with various methods. Pennsylvania has built a state-of-the-art geriatric facility. About half the states within the United States, at the current time, offer hospice care for the frailest inmates. Angola Prison in Louisiana not only allows hospice care, but also allows prisoners to bury inmates, transporting them by horse and buggy to the prison cemetery. In the interest of preventive heath care, Ohio has created fitness programs for its older prison inmates.

The GRACE Project (Guiding Responsive Action in Corrections at End of life) has compiled a profile of program components that constitute best practices. These include: (1) involvement of inmates as hospice volunteers; (2) increased visitation for families; (3) interdisciplinary teams, including physician, nurse, chaplain, and social worker, at a minimum; (4) comprehensive plan of care; (5) advance care planning; (6) training in pain and symptom management; (7) bereavement services; and (8) adaptation of the environment for comfort.

A separate geriatric facility can be effective in facilitating the release of elderly offenders. Georgia has already released 49 inmates due to health issues. Inmates are harder to ignore when they are segregated in one facility. However, every system can be taken advantage of. This was shown by an inmate who stayed in a wheelchair for 6 months, only to leap up and run away when taken to an outside hospital. He was caught moments later.

AFFECTED POPULATION

The general prison population is greatly affected by the lack of policy for older prisoners. Clear policy initiatives must be defined for segregating older prisoners in geriatric or assisted living correctional facilities, and guidelines must be established for compassionate release programs. This will include a clear definition of what is to be considered an older prisoner.

Most prison systems are operated prisons holding twice the inmates they were built to house. Federal judges have cited some prison health care systems as neglectful and depriving inmates of adequate treatment. If terminally ill offenders were released to more community-based health care systems this would help alleviate the burden. Prison hospitals cannot adequately treat the general population of offenders when the medical staff is consumed with treating inmates who are infirm. Chronic conditions such as cancer, if diagnosed in the early stages for the younger offender, can be properly treated and prevent future costs.

California alone spends 1.1 billion dollars on inmate health care. This has doubled in the past 7 years. At one point, they asked the University of California, which has a very highly regarded medical system, to take over administration of the prison's health care system. They declined, but if the older prisoners with serious conditions were isolated in a geriatric facility, then an outside system such as this might be able to manage it effectively.

When the issue of prison overcrowding is not addressed the results can be disastrous. The state of Idaho went under a federal court order to remove close to 200 inmates from the overcrowded system. Idaho's answer to the problem was to send the inmates out of state. The cost to send 200 inmates out of state for 1 year is roughly 4.5 million dollars. Idaho did send 300 inmates to be confined in Louisiana in 1997. Five of them escaped, including one child molester who was on the loose for 5 years before being recaptured. One hundred inmates, incensed about conditions in a Louisiana prison, rioted and caused $35,000 in damage. Clearly, these inmates were directly affected by Idaho not reviewing alternatives to overcrowding.

INTENDED IMPACT

The underlying reason that in the future we will see more compassionate release programs and correctional geriatric or correctional assisted living facilities is that state legislatures are beginning to realize this will shift some of the health care costs to the federal government. It would free state funds to balance state budgets. Consequently, the money could be used for schools, parks, and highways. Imagine the cost savings of creating minimum-security units for geriatric prisoners and staffing them with fewer, but specially trained corrections officers. Maximum-security institutions represent maximum costs in terms of security for inmates.

A good illustration for the cost saving involved would be to the case of inmate #41465, Helen Loheac, in California. The shrunken 82-year-old wakes up every morning to change into her prison uniform. Then guards must outfit her with ankle chains, belly chains, and handcuffs. Next, she is transported 40 minutes for dialysis. She suffers from chronic renal failure, a condition that she figures costs the state $436,000 a year, not counting the two $24.75-an-hour armed corrections officers who guard her, all five feet and 90 pounds, for up to 8 hours a day three times a week.

Another cost savings will be realized by the states when sick inmates are released who have the potential to tap Medicare, Social Security, or veterans benefits. They can be tracked with a 10-dollar-a-day bracelet system. Systematic release programs have been implemented in Virginia, Maryland, Louisiana, North Carolina, and Michigan, and California is actively considering such a program. These types of programs tend to be embraced by conservatives and liberals alike, primarily because they are low-risk. The recidivism rate for older offenders is very low.

ACTUAL IMPACT

The state legislatures will have to be presented with the facts on older prisoners for them to grasp the magnitude of the problem. They will have to be presented with the facts about the fastest growing segment of the inmate population. They need to know that in some states almost half of the inmates over age 50 are serving life in prison and will eventually die in prison. They need to understand the cost associated with housing a terminally ill offender as opposed to a community-based nursing home. Current comparisons show the terminally ill could be treated in a nursing home for $41,000 a year as compared to $69,000 a year in a prison.

Recidivism rates studied by reputable national studies show a rate of only 2% for those paroled over age 55. The concept of "criminal meno-pause" setting in for the elderly offender, where they grow less impetuous and less prone to violence, needs to be explained.

Lawmakers are going to have to make tough choices in the years ahead. They need to face the reality of the "lock them up and throw away the key" laws. In order to do this they need the problem clearly outlined for them by correction officials and policy advocates. They need to be taken into the state's prisons and view the problem first hand. The problem is many lawmakers will agree that there is a problem. Yet, they will refuse to do anything about it due to public opinion. With public opinion today, a policy maker cannot appear to be soft on crime. This can prevent them from being reelected. Therefore, the actual impact of compassionate release programs will be an outcry from victims' rights organizations.

ALTERNATIVE STRATEGIES OR RECOMMENDATIONS

Finally, to initiate policy change the key concept for elderly offenders is that as inmates age the costs of imprisonment goes way up; at the same time the benefits of imprisonment in terms of public safety go way down. Scott Thornsley (2005), freelance writer for the Allentown, Pennsylvania, *Morning Call,* has suggested a number of recommendations to alleviate some of the population of elderly prisoners and give support to the belief that prison cells should be reserved for those who are currently a serious threat to the community. Based upon Thornsley's work, the following recommendations should be considered in order to address the needs of older prisoners who are serving life sentences, or who have served their time. These recommendations are as follows:

1. Create legislation to allow seriously and terminally ill inmates medical release from prison through the courts. As the law stands now, release is possible only if the state is unable to care for the inmate.
2. Create a governmental inter-agency committee to review the medical release of inmates. This would create another state bureaucracy; however, for a program to be effective it will need oversight.
3. Establish a mental health court in each judicial district to reduce population stress on the correctional system by using an alternative to incarceration for mentally ill offenders when appropriate.
4. Amend the sentencing laws for those convicted in the future of first-degree murder by adding the option for the jury or the judge to consider life with the possibility of parole in cases where the death penalty is not being sought. This would allow those sentenced to 25 years to life to become eligible for parole upon serving 25 years and attaining a minimum age of 50 years.
5. Amend the sentencing law for second-degree murder by adding a provision allowing consideration of a sentence of life imprisonment with the possibility of parole when an inmate reaches 50 years of age and has served 25 years of his sentence.
6. Develop a public media campaign to address fears and apprehensions that may exist on the part of community members when confronted with absorbing older adults who have been incarcerated, and have served their time, or life sentences.

In an effort to establish real solutions to the overcrowded conditions of our prisons and the burdening financial costs to our correctional systems, various aspects of a proposed policy must be outlined. First, all three-strike laws must be reviewed. Many jurisdictions go against public opinion by including strikes for nonviolent and drug-related crimes that "the public does not consider are among the most serious offenses" (Turner, Sundt, Applegate, & Cullen, 1995, p. 179). Consequently, if such laws are to be established, they need to have a mandatory minimum sentence, such as 10 years, in which case access to parole could be granted for those who have aged into a low-risk bracket for recidivism. New policies would also need to take a hard look at determinate sentencing and truth-in-sentencing laws, which do not allow access to parole.

Second, a new policy would reinvent the way parole boards operate. Parole board review laws under a new policy would take into consideration cases where terminal and physically disabling diseases exists. In such cases, when the disease or physical condition renders an inmate harmless to society, this health status could be used as a basis for a parole board's decision for release.

Criteria that older offenders must participate in "meaningful" prison activities should be reviewed. Studies have shown that prison staff tend not to encourage older prisoners to participate in educational or vocational programming. Rather, most of these programs are viewed as more beneficial to younger inmates. Therefore, to include this as parole criteria is age-biased.

The creation of so many lifers in our prison system has caused a new age of institutional dependence. Obviously, when older prisoners are released they find themselves in the middle of receiving Social Security and attempting to obtain meaningful employment. However, they may be eligible for some additional benefits, and this should be reviewed on a case-by-case basis and could remove some of the financial burden from the state treasury. Any type of case management services provided in the community will be more cost effective than actual time served in prison.

Community-based alternatives must be examined when older prisoners are released from prison. The programs that exist for parolees include: day treatment, intensive and regular parole programs, nursing homes, and residential treatment programs. Furthermore, electronic detention exists for those who require more extensive supervision. However, electronic detention makes them ineligible for federal benefits such as Medicare and Social Security. Thus, these policies also require review.

Poverty issues impacting recently released older prisoners will have to be addressed. The Job Training and Partnership Act and the Older Americans Act can provide some assistance to recent parolees, but for these policies to be effective more assistance will be necessary to allow the older parolee access to programs. This type of assistance, while always controversial in public opinion, will be much more cost effective and more humane than the cost of housing older felons in prison.

Considering a new policy in regard to older offenders has provided some real answers. The selective release programs and alternative housing options used in this policy make sense: ethically, financially, legally, medically, and socially. It will require multilevel interventions to achieve the goal. Unfortunately, the political feasibility of sufficiently funding any type of alternative program is always a question. Many politicians will agree these are viable alternatives. Despite this, they will refuse to support such programs. Public opinion forces lawmakers to appear tough on crime if they want to assure political survival. Our sociopolitical motivations must be addressed if we are to have release programs for even low-risk offenders. The alternative is to continue building prisons and pass the burden of these costs on to our community. This reality ignores the fact that funds to support older adults incarcerated for life, or beyond their life sentence, takes funds from vital community services such as education, health care, and other social service.

In summary, older adults who have served life sentences will continue to pose challenges to the penal and aging health care systems. The costs of continued care through the prison system far outweighs the costs of care within a community-based care system. Despite these financial realities, limited community-based service systems are available to individuals upon the completion of their "life" sentence. This paper proposes a series of recommendations for policy and program planning in an effort to meet the needs of older adults who have been incarcerated. The recommendations, however, could also apply to other states around the country. Programs and services need expansion in efforts to meet the medical and health care needs of older adults who have been incarcerated for life sentences. Although these options may be more humane, community stigma and fear may prevail.

ABOUT THE AUTHOR

Mr. Ron Hillerman currently is employed at Menard Correctional Facility, Chester, Illinois. He has served as a correctional officer for 13 years, and has spent the last 4 years as a corrections counselor. His undergraduate work was completed at Western Illinois University, and he is currently pursuing a master's degree in social work at Southern Illinois University, Carbondale, with the hopes of working in the mental health field. In Mr. Hillerman's spare time, he enjoys his family farm, running, horseback riding, fishing, and outdoor activities as well as his two grandchildren.

REFERENCES

Aday, R. H. (1994). Golden years behind bars: Special programs and facilities for older inmates. *Federal Probation, 58*(2), 47–54.

Colsher, P. L., Wallace, R. B., Loeffelholz, P. L., & Sales, M. (1992). Health status of older male prisoners: A comprehensive survey. *American Journal of Public Health, 82*(6), 881–884.

Colsher, P. L., Wallace, R. B., Loeffelholz, P. L., & Sales, M. (2002). American correctional system. *The American Journal of Public Health, 82*(6), 881–884.

Ellsworth, T., & Helle, K. A. (1994). Older offenders on probation. *Federal Probation, 58*(4), 43–50.

Fazel, S., Hope, T., O'Donnell, I., & Jacoby, R. (2004). Unmet treatment needs of older prisoners: A primary care survey. *Age and Ageing, 33*, 396–398.

Hunt, G., Riegal, S., Morales, T., & Waldorf, D. (1993). Changes in prison culture: Prison gangs and the case of the Pepsi generation. *Social Problems, 40*(3), 398–409.

Krajick, J. (1979). Growing old in prison. *Corrections Magazine, 5*, 32–46.

Lundstrom, S. (1994). Dying to get out. *Brigham Young University Journal of Public Law, 9*(1), 155–188.

Morton, J. B. (1992). *Administrative overview of the older inmate.* Washington, DC: National Institute of Corrections.

Petersilia, J. (2001). Prison re-entry: Public safety and reintegration challenges. *The Prison Journal, 81*(3), 360–375.

Thornsley, Scott (2005). Allow medical release for aging, seriously ill inmate. *The Morning Call* (5)1–2. Retrieved December 2, 2005, from http://web.lexis-nexis.com.proxy.lib.siu.edu/universe/document

Turner, M. G., Sundt, J. L., Applegate, B. K., & Cullen, F. T. (1995). "Three strikes and you're out" legislation: A national assessment. *Federal Probation, 59*(3), 16–35.

Watson, R. (2004). Prison health care: A review of the literature. *International Journal of Nursing Studies, 41*(2), 119–128.

Selected Bibliography

AARP. (1993). *Old and alone in rural America.* Washington, DC: AARP.

AARP. (1998). *Global aging report: Aging everywhere.* Washington, DC: AARP.

AARP. (1998). *Reframing the health care system: State profiles, 1997.* Washington, DC: AARP.

AARP. (1999). *Web place.* Retrieved August 19, 2001, from http://www.aarp.org

Abrams, R. C., Rosendahl, E., Card, C., & Alexopoulos, G. S. (1994). Personality disorder correlates of late and early onset depression. *Journal of the American Geriatrics Society, 42,* 727–731.

Adamek, M. E., & Kaplan, M. S. (2000). Caring for depressed and suicidal older patients: A survey of physicians and nurse practitioners. *International Journal of Psychiatry-in-Medicine, 30*(2), 111–125.

Administration on Aging. (2001). *Site index: Including links to major off-site resources.* Retrieved August 31, 2001, from http://www.aoa.gov/Siteindex.html

Administration on Aging. (2001). *Web sites on aging. The Administration on Aging and the Older Americans Act (1965 as Amended).* Retrieved August 31, 2001, from http://www.aoa.gov/Siteindex.html

Administration on Aging (AoA). (2007). *Administration on Aging network for professionals.* Retrieved May 20, 2007, from www.aoa.gov

Ai, A. L., Peterson, C., Rodgers, W., & Tice, T. N. (2005). Effects of faith and secular factors on locus of control in middle-aged and older cardiac patients. *Aging and Mental Health, 9*(5), 470–481.

Ajzen, I. (1980). *Understanding the attitudes and predicting social behavior.* Englewood Cliffs, NJ: Prentice-Hall.

Ajzen, I. (1998). *Attitudes, personality and behavior.* Chicago: Dorsey Press.

Albrecht, G. L. (1992). *The disability business: Rehabilitation in America.* One Thousand Oaks, CA: Sage Publications.

Alessi, C. A., Josephson, K .R., Harker, J. O., Pietruszka, F. M., Hoyl, M. T., & Rubenstein, L. Z. (2003). Yield, reliability, and validity of a postal survey for screening community-dwelling older people. *Journal of the American Geriatrics Society, 51*(2), 194–202.

Alexander, F., & Duff, R. W. (1988). Social interaction and alcohol use in retirement communities. *The Gerontologist, 28*(5), 632–636.

Alexopoulos, G. S. (1997, November 6). *Epidemiology, nosology and treatment of geriatric depression.* Paper presented at Exploring Opportunities to Advance Mental Health Care for an Aging Population, meeting sponsored by the John A. Hartford Foundation, Rockville, MD.

Altman, A., Cooper, P. F., & Cunningham, P. J. (1999). The case of disability in the family: Impact on health care utilization and expenditures for non-disabled members. *Milbank Quarterly, 77*(1), 39–75.

Altpeter, M., Bryant, L., Schneider, E., & Whitelaw, N. (2006). Evidence-based health practice: Knowing and using what works for older adults. *Home Health Services Quarterly, 25*(1/2), 1–11.

American Public Health Association. (n.d.). *APHA media advocacy manual.* Washington, DC: American Public Health Association.

The Americans with Disabilities Act: An Overview. Retrieved October 4, 2005, from http:// janweb.icdi.wvu.edu/kinder/overview.htm

Anderson, G. M., Kerluke, K. J., Pulcins, I. R., Hertzman, C., & Barer, M. L. (1993). Trends and determinants of prescription drug expenditures in the elderly: Data from the British Columbia Pharmacare Program. *Inquiry, 30,* 199–207.

Anetzberger, G. J., Palmisano, B. R., Sanders, M., Bass, D., Dayton, C., Eckert, S., et al. (2000). A model intervention for elder abuse and dementia. *The Gerontologist, 40,* 492–497.

Assessing community healthcare needs: Lessons from Africa. *Nurse Stand, 15*(47), 41–44.

Atchley, R. (2000). *The social forces of aging: An introduction to social gerontology.* Belmont, CA: Wadsworth Publishing.

Bachman, D. L., Wolf, P. A., Linn, R., Knoefel, J. E., Cobb, J., Belanger, A., et al. (1992). Prevalence of dementia and probable senile dementia of the Alzheimer type in the Framingham Study. *Neurology, 42,* 115–119.

Baker, P., Leitner, J., & McAuley, W. J. (2001). Preparing future aging advocacy advocates: The Oklahoma Aging Advocacy Leadership Academy. *The Gerontologist, 41,* 394–400.

Ball, R. M. (1996). Medicare's roots: What Medicare's architects had in mind. *Generations, 20*(2), 13–18.

Bandura, A. (1977). Self-efficacy: Toward a unifying theory of behavior change. *Psychological Review, 84,* 191–215.

Bandura, A. (1982). Self-efficacy mechanism in human agency. *American Psychologist, 37,* 122–147.

Bane, S. D. (1997). Rural mental health and aging: Implication for case management. *Journal of Case Management, 6*(4), 158–161.

Barry, L. C., Gill, T. M., Kerns, R. D., & Reid, M. C. (2005). Identification of pain-reduction strategies used by community-dwelling older persons. *Journals of Gerontology: Series A: Biological Sciences and Medical Sciences, 60A* (12), 1569–1575.

Bartels, S. J., & Colenda, C. C. (1998). Mental health services for Alzheimer's disease. Current trends in reimbursement and public policy, and the future under managed care. *American Journal of Geriatric Psychiatry, 6,* S85–S100.

Bartels, S. J., Horn, S., Sharkey, P., & Levine, K. (1997). Treatment of depression in older primary care patients in health maintenance organizations. *International Journal of Psychiatry in Medicine, 27,* 215–231.

Bartels, S. J., & Levine, K. J. (1998). Meeting the needs of older adults with severe and persistent mental illness: Public policy in an era of managed and long-term reform. *Public Policy and Aging Report, 9,* 1–6.

Bartels, S. J., Levine, K. J., & Shea, D. (1999). Mental health long-term care for older persons with severe and persistent mental disorders in an era of managed care. *Psychiatric Services, 50,* 1190–1197.

Barton, W. E. (1966). Trends in community mental health programs. *Hospital and Community Psychiatry. 17,* 253–258.

Barusch, A. S. (2002). *Foundations of social policy: Social justice, public programs, and the social work profession.* Itasca, IL: Peacock Publishers.

Behavioral Risk Factor Surveillance System (BRFSS). (2001). Retrieved Aug. 25, 2005, from: http://www.cdc.gov/brfss/

Bellelli, G., Lucchi, E., Minicuci, N., Rozzini, L., Bianchetti, A., Padovani, A., et al. (2005). Results of a multi-level therapeutic approach for Alzheimer's disease subjects in the "real world" (CRONOS project): A 36-week follow-up study. *Aging Clinical and Experimental Research, 17*(1), 54–61.

Bergland, B., & Dixon, L. (1988). *Report of the National Action Commission on the Mental Health of Rural America.* Washington, DC: National Mental Health Association.

Berk, D., Hubert, H., & Fries, J. (2006). Associations of changes in exercise level with subsequent disability among seniors: A 16-year longitudinal study. *Journal of Gerontology: Series A: Biological Sciences and Medical Sciences, 61A* (1), 97–102.

Bernhardt, J. M. (2004). Communication at the core of effective public health. *American Journal of Public Health, 94*(12), 2051–2053.

Bibb, S. C., & Mary, J. (2001). Nielubowicz Essay Award. Population-based needs assessment in the design of patient education programs. *Military Medicine, 166*(4), 297–300.

Billek-Sawhney, B., & Gay, J. (2005). Functional reach test: Are 3 trials necessary? *Topics in Geriatric Rehabilitation, 21*(2), 144–148.

Binstock, R. H. (1998). Health care policies and older Americans. In J. S. Steckenrider & T. M. Parrott (Eds.), *New directions in old-age policies* (pp. 13–35), Albany, NY: State University of New York.

Bird, D. C., Dempsey, P., & Hartley, D. (2001). *Addressing mental health workforce needs in underserved rural areas: Accomplishments and challenges.* Portland, ME: Maine Rural Health Research Center, Muskie Institute, University of Southern Maine.

Bishop, C. (1999). Efficiency of home care: Notes from an economic approach to resource allocation. *Journal of Aging and Health, 11*(3), 341–359.

Bland, R. C., Newman, S. C., & Orn, H. (1988). Prevalence of psychiatric disorders in the elderly in Edmonton. *Acta Psychiatrica Scandinavica Supplement, 338,* 57–63.

Blazer, D. (1989). Depression in the elderly. *New England Journal of Medicine, 320,* 164–166.

Boaz, A., Hayden, C., & Bernard, M. (2000). *Research summary: Department of Social Security research report. No. 101: Attitudes and aspirations of older people: A review of the literature. Social Security Research.* Washington, DC: Government Printing Office.

Bogardus, S. T. (2001). Goals for the care of frail older adults: Do caregivers and clinicians agree? *The American Journal of Medicine, 110*(2). 97–102.

Booth, C. (1999, August 30). Taking care of our aging parents. *Time,* 48–51.

Boroug, M., Ozarin, L. D., & Sharfstein, S. S. (1978). The aftermaths of deinstitutionalization: Problems and solutions. *Psychiatric Quarterly, 50,* 128–132.

Bovenberg, L., & Linden, A. (1997, April/May). Pension policies and the aging society. *The OECD Observer, 205,* 20–24.

Branch, L. G. (2000). Assessment of chronic care need and use. *Gerontologist, 40*(4), 390–396.

Brandon, T. (2005). Empowerment, policy levels and service forums. *Journal of Intellectual Disabilities, 9*(4), 321–331.

Brelow, R. A., Faden,V. B., & Smothers, B. (2003). Alcohol consumption by elderly Americans. *Journal of Studies on Alcohol, 64*(6), 884–892.

Brody, J. A. (1982). Aging and alcohol use. *Journal of American Geriatrics Society, 30*(2), 123–126.

Bronstein, L. R., & Admiraal, K. (2005). Implications of an aging population on the delivery of public sector social services. *Families in Society, 86*(1), 47–54.

Brown, R. S., Clement, D. G., Hill, J. W., Retchin, S. M., & Bergeron, J. W. (1993). Do health maintenance organizations work for Medicare? *Health Care Financing Review, 15*(1), 7–23.

Bruce, M. L., Kim, K., Leaf, P. J., & Jacobs, S. (1990). Depressive episodes and dysphoria resulting from conjugal bereavement in a prospective community sample. *American Journal of Psychiatry, 147,* 608–611.

Buchanan, J. A., & Fisher, J. E. (2002). Functional assessment and noncontingent reinforcement in the treatment of disruptive vocalization in elderly dementia patients. *Journal of Applied Behavior Analysis, 35*(1), 99–103.

Buchanan, J. L., Andres, P. L., Haley, S. M., Paddock, S. M., & Zaslavsky, A. M. (2003). Assessment tool translation study. *Health Care Financing Review, 24*(3), 45–60.

Bruggerman, W. G. (1997). *The practice of macro social work.* Chicago: Nelson Hall.

Burkhauser, R., & Quinn, J. (1997). *Pro-work policy proposals for older Americans in the 21st century.* Syracuse, NY: Center for Policy Research, Maxwell School of Citizenship and Public Affairs.

Butterfoss, F. (2004). The coalition technical assistance and training framework: Helping community coalitions help themselves. *Health Promotion Practice, 5*(2), 118–126.

Cadoret, R. J., & Widmer, R. B. (1988). The development of depressive symptoms in elderly following onset of severe physical illness. *Journal of Family Practice, 27,* 71–76.

Calderón, J. L. (2000). Focus groups: A qualitative method complementing quantitative research for studying culturally diverse groups. *Education Health, 13*(1), 91–105.

Callahan, J. J. (1998). Social policy in the age of the market. *The Public Policy and Aging Report, 9,* (2), 13–15.

Campbell, P. (1997). Population projections: States, 1995–2025. *Current Population Reports, 25–113.*

Campbell, S., & Weist, M. D. (2001). Collaboration among the education, mental health, and public health systems to promote youth mental health. *Psychiatry Service, 52*(10), 1348–1351.

Carter, T. (1998). *Your personal directive: More than a living will.* Bellingham, WA: Self-Counsel Press.

Cavill, N., & Bauman, A. (2004). Changing the way people think about health enhancing physical activity: Do mass media campaigns have a role? *Journal of Sports Sciences, 22*(8), 771–790.

Centers for Disease Control and Prevention. (October 20, 2006). *Healthy aging for older adults.* Retrieved October 23, 2006, from http://www.cdc.gov/aging.htm

Centers for Disease Control and Prevention. (2006). *Trends in health and aging.* Washington, DC: Government Printing Office.

Centers for Medicare and Medicaid Services. (2006). *Medicare and you, 2007: Official government handbook.* Baltimore, MD: Government Printing Office.

Centers for Medicare and Medicaid Services. (n.d.). *Key milestones in CMS programs.* Retrieved December 14, 2006, from http://www.cms.hhs.gov/History/Downloads/CMSProgramKeyMilestones.pdf

Chauvin, S. W. (2001). Assessing the professional development needs of public health professionals. *Journal of Public Health Management Practice, 7*(4), 23–37.

Choi, N. G. (2003). Determinants of self-perceived changes in health status among pre- and early-retirement populations. *International Journal of Aging and Human Development, 56*(3), 197–222.

Chumbler, N. R., Cody, M., Booth, B. M., & Beck, C. K. (2001). Rural-urban difference in service use for memory-related problems in older adults. *Journal-Behavior Health-Services and Research, 28*(2), 212–221.

Clark, P. G., Rossi, J. S., Greaney, M. L., Riebe, D. A., Greene, G., Saunders, S. D., et al. (2005). Intervening on exercise and nutrition in older adults: The Rhode Island SENIOR project. *Journal of Aging and Health, 17*(6), 753–778.

Coalition of National Health Education Organization Partners. (n.d.). *Making your advocacy efforts count*. Retrieved April 22, 2007, from http://www.healtheducation advocate.org

Cohen, G. D. (1995). Mental health promotion in later life: The case for social portfolio. *American Journal of Geriatric Psychiatry, 3*, 277–279.

Coleman, J. V., Patrick, D. L., Eagle, J., & Hermalin, J. A. (1979). Collaboration, consultation and referral in an integrated health-mental health program at an HMO. *Social Work in Health Care, 5*(1), 83–96.

Compton, B. R. (1980). *Introduction to social welfare and social work: Structure, function, and process*. Homewood, IL: Dorsey Press.

Copeland, J. R., Dewey, M. E., Wood, N., Searle, R., Davidson, I. A., & McWilliam, C. (1987). Range of mental illness among the elderly in the community: Prevalence in Liverpool using the GMS-AGECAT package. *British Journal of Psychiatry, 150*, 815–823.

Coughlin, J. F. (1999). Setting a national policy agenda for technology and healthy ageing. *The Public Policy and Aging Report, 10*(1), 1–6.

Cowley, S. (2000). A taxonomy of needs assessment, elicited from a multiple case study of community nursing education and practice. *Journal of Advances in Nursing, 31*(1), 126–134.

Cowley, S. (2003). A structured health needs assessment tool: Acceptability and effectiveness for health visiting. *Journal of Advanced Nursing, 43*(1), 82–92.

Cowley, S. (2004). Structuring health needs assessments: The medicalization of health visiting. *Social Health Illness, 26*(5), 503–526.

Crisp, B. R. (2004). Evidence-based practice and the borders of data in the global information era. *Journal of Social Work Education, 40*(1), 73–86.

Crocoll, C. E. (2004). Grandparents raising grandchildren: Help from cooperative extension. *Journal of Family and Consumer Sciences, 96*(4), 59–60.

Cuellar, A. E., & Wiener, J. M. (1999). Implementing universal long-term care insurance in Germany. *The Public Policy and Aging Report, 10*(3), 2–4.

Dannison, L. L., & Smith, A. B. (2003). Custodial grandparent's community support program: Lessons learned. *Children and Schools, 25*(2), 87–96.

Davey, A. (1999). With respect to old age: Findings of the Royal Commission on long-term care in the United Kingdom. *The Public Policy and Aging Report, 10*(3), 22–27.

Davidson, I. A. (1987). Is there more dementia, depression and neurosis in New York? A comparative study of the elderly in New York and London using the computer diagnosis AGECAT. *British Journal of Psychiatry, 151*, 466–473.

Davis, L. A., Hoppes, S., & Chebsbro, S. B. (2005). Cognitive-communicative and independent living skills assessment in individuals with dementia: A pilot study of environmental impact. *Topics in Geriatric Rehabilitation, 21*(2), 136–143.

Day, P. J. (2006). *A new history of social welfare*. Boston: Allyn & Bacon.

DeJong, G. (1979). Independent living: From social movement to analytic paradigm. *Archives of Physical Medicine and Rehabilitation, 60*, 435–446.

Dendukuri, N., McCusker, J., & Belzile, E. (2004). Identification of seniors at risk screening tool: Further evidence of concurrent and predictive validity. *Journal of the American Geriatrics Society, 52*(2), 290–296.

Denton, M. A., Kennp, C. L., French S., Gafni, A., Joshi, A., Rosenthal, C. J., et al. (2004). Reflexive planning for later life. *Canadian Journal on Aging, 23*(S1), S71–S82.

Department of Justice. (1999). *ADA regulations and technical assistance materials*. Retrieved October 7, 2003, from http://www.usdoj.gov/crt/ada/publicat.html

Derickson, A. (2005). *Health security for all: Dreams of universal health care in America*. Baltimore, MD: Johns Hopkins Press.

Derthick, M. (1979). *Policy making for Social Security.* Washington, DC: Brookings Institute.

Devor, M., Wang, A., Renvall, M., Feigal, D., & Ramsdell, J. (1994). Compliance with social and safety recommendations in an outpatient comprehensive geriatric assessment program. *Journal of Gerontology, 49,* M168–M173.

DiClemente, C. C. (1981). Self-efficacy and smoking cessation maintenance: A preliminary report. *Cognitive Therapy and Research, 5,* 175–187.

DiClemente, C. C. (1986). Self-efficacy and the addictive behaviors. *Journal of Social and Clinical Psychology, 4,* 302–315.

DiClemente, C. C., Prochaska, J. O., Fairhurst, S., Velicer, W. F., Rossi, J. S., & Velasquez, M. (1991). The process of smoking cessation: An analysis of precontemplation, contemplation and contemplation/action. *Journal of Consulting and Clinical Psychology, 59,* 295–304.

Dobelstein, A. W. (1996). *Social wefare policy and analysis* (2nd ed.). Chicago: Nelson-Hall.

Domhoff, G. W. (1956). *Who rules America?* Englewood Cliffs, NJ: Prentice-Hall.

Dorfman, L. (2005). More than a message: Framing public health advocacy to change corporate practices. *Health Education and Behavior, 32*(3), 320–336.

Dorfman, R. A., Lubben, J. E., Mayer-Oakes, A., Atchison, K., Schweitzer, S. O., DeJong, F. J., et al. (1995). Screening for depression among a well elderly population. *Social Work, 40*(3), 295–304.

Drake, R.E., Essock, S. M., Shaner, A., Carey, K. B., Minkoff, K., Kola, L., et al. (2001). Implementing dual diagnosis services for clients with severe mental illness. *Psychiatric Services, 52,* 469–476.

Duffy, S., Jackson, F. C., Schim, S. M., Ronis D. L., & Fowler, K. E. (2006). Racial/ethnic preferences, sex preferences, and perceived discrimination related to end-of-life care. *Journal of the American Geriatrics Society, 54*(1), 150–157.

Dulop, B. D., Rothman, M. B., Condon, K. M., & Martinez, I. L. (2000). Elder abuse: Risk factors and use of case data to improve policy and practice. *Journal of Elder Abuse and Neglect, 12*(3–4), 95–122.

Edmond, T., Megivern, D., Williams, C., Rochman, E., & Howard, M. (2006). Integrating evidence-based practice and social work field education. *Journal of Social Work Education, 42*(2), 377–396.

Egyptian Area Agency on Aging. (1999). *Helping older adults in southern Illinois remain independent since 1978.* Retrieved August 19, 1999, from http://www.egyptianaaa.org/Index.htm

Egyptian Area Agency on Aging. (1999). *Planning for the 21st century.* Retrieved August 19, 1999, from http://www.egyptianaaa.org/AreaPlan.htm

Egyptian Area Agency on Aging. (2001). *FY 2000 planning for the 21st century.* Carterville, IL: Egyptian Area Agency on Aging.

Egyptian Area Agency on Aging. (2004). *Area plan summary for FY 2005–2007.* Carterville, IL: Egyptian Area Agency on Aging.

Ekerdt, D. J., De Labry, L. O., Glynn, R. J., & Davis, R. W. (1989). Change in drinking behaviors with retirement: Findings from the normative aging study. *Journal of Studies on Alcohol, 50,* 347–353.

Ellor, J. R., & Kurz, D. J. (1982). Misuse and abuse of prescription and nonprescription drugs by the elderly. *Nursing Clinics of North America, 17,* 319–330.

Emery, C. F., Kiecolt-Glaser, J. K., Glaser, R., Malarkey, W. B., & Frid, D. J. (2005). Exercise accelerates wound healing among healthy older adults: A preliminary investigation. *Journals of Gerontology: Series A: Biological Sciences and Medical Sciences, 60A* (11), 1432–1436.

Emlet, C., Hawks, H., & Callahan, J. (2001). Alcohol use and abuse in a population of community dwelling, frail older adults. *Journal of Gerontological Social Work, 35*(4), 21–33.

Essex-Sorlie, D. (1994). The Americans with Disabilities Act: History, summary, and key components. *Academic Medicine, 68*(7), 519–524.

Fava, J. L., Norman, G. J., Redding, C. A., Keller, S., Robbins, M. L., Maddock, J. E., et al. (1997). *The multidimensional stress management behaviors inventory.* Kingston, RI: Stress Management Working Group, Cancer Prevention Research Center.

Federal Interagency Forum on Aging Related Statistics. (2000). *Older Americans 2000: Key indicators of well being.* Bethesda, MD: National Institutes on Aging.

Federal Interagency Forum on Aging Related Statistics. (2006). *Data sources on older Americans, 2006.* Washington, DC: Government Printing Office.

Federal Interagency Forum on Aging-Related Statistics. (May 2006). *Older Americans update 2006: Key indicators of well-being: Federal interagency forum on aging-related statistics.* Washington, DC: U.S. Government Printing Office.

Fishbein, M. (1996). Behavioral science and public health: A necessary partnership for HIV prevention. *Public Health Reports, 111*(S1), 5–10.

Flint, A. J. (1994). Epidemiology and comorbidity of anxiety disorders in the elderly. *American Journal of Psychiatry, 151,* 640–649.

Foley, H. A., & Sharfstein, S. S. (1983). *Madness and government: Who cares for the mentally ill?* Washington, DC: American Psychiatric Press.

Foley, K., & Hendin, H. (2002). *The case against assisted suicide for the right to end-of-life care.* Baltimore, MD: Johns Hopkins University Press.

Fouad, M. N. (2004).The development of a community action plan to reduce breast and cervical cancer disparities between African-American and White women. *Ethnicity and Disease, 14*(3), 53–60.

Fox, P. (1999). *End of life in managed care organizations.* Washington, DC: AARP.

Francoeur, R. B. (2006). Flexible item to screen for depression in inner-city minorities during palliative care symptom assessment. *Journal of Geriatric Psychiatry, 14*(3), 228–236.

Freeman, I. C. (2004, Spring). Advocacy in aging policy: Working the bills on Capital Hill. *Generations,* 41–47.

Freimuth, V., & Quinn, S. C. (2004). The contributions of health communication in eliminating health disparities. *American Journal of Public Health, 94*(2), 2053–2055.

Fuller-Thomson, E., & Minkler, M. (2000). African American grandparents raising grandchildren: A national profile of demographic and health characteristics. *Health and Social Work, 25*(2), 109.

Fuller, J. (2001).Use of community health needs assessment for regional planning in country south Australia. *Australian Journal of Rural Health, 9*(1), 12–17.

Fuller-Thomson, E. (2005). Canadian first nation's grandparents raising grandchildren: A portrait in resilience. *International Journal of Aging and Human Development, 60*(4), 331–342.

Galbraith, J. K. (1973). *Economics and the public purpose.* Boston, MA: Houghton-Mifflin.

Gallagher, K., Stanely, A., Shearer, D., & Klerman, L. (2006). Challenges in data collection, analysis, and distribution of information in community coalition projects. *Journal of Adolescent Health, 37*(3), S53–S60.

Gallo, J. J., & Lebowitz, B. D. (1999). The epidemiology of common late-life mental disorders in the community: Themes for the new century. *Psychiatric Services, 50,* 1158–1166.

Gallo, J. J., Ryan, S. D., & Ford, D. E. (1999). Attitudes, knowledge, and behavior of family physicians regarding depression in late life. *Archives of Family Medicine, 8*(3), 249–256.

Gambrill, E. (1999). Evidence-based practice: An alternative to authority-based practice. *Families in Society, 80*(4), 341–350.

Gambrill, E. (2001). Social work: An authority-based profession. *Research on Social Work Practice, 11,* 166–175.

GAO. (1997). *Social Security reform: Implications for women's retirement income. Report to the ranking minority member, subcommittee on Social Security, committee on ways and means, House of Representatives.* Washington, DC: U.S. Government Printing Office.

GAO. (1998). *Social Security reform: Raising retirement age improves program solvency but may cause hardship for some. Testimony: Statement by D. Bovbjerg, Associate Director, Income Security Issues, Health Education and Human Services Division.* Washington, DC: U.S. Government Printing Office.

Gask, L., Sibbald, B., & Creed, F. (1997). Evaluating models of working at the interface between mental health services and primary care. *British Journal of Psychiatry, 170,* 6–11.

Geller, J. L. (2000). The last half-century of psychiatric services as reflected in *Psychiatric Services, Psychiatric Services, 51,* 41–67

Georgas, S. (1998). *Power of attorney kit: A do it yourself kit.* Bellingham, WA: Self-Counsel Press Inc.

George, L. K. (1992). Community and home care for mentally ill older adults. In J. E. Birren, R. B. Sloane, G. D. Cohen, N. R. Hooyman, B. D. Lebowitz, & M. I. Wykle (Eds.), *Handbook of mental health and aging* (2nd ed., pp. 793–813). San Diego, CA: Academic Press.

Gerard, J. M., Landry-Meyer, L., & Guzell Roe, J. (2006). Grandparents raising grandchildren: The role of social support in coping with caregiving challenges. *International Journal of Aging and Human Development, 62*(4), 359–383.

Gerberding, J. L. (1999, July). Washington update: Administration's OAA act introduced in Senate and House, reauthorization expected in this congress. *Gerontology News.* Retrieved September 22, 2002, from: http://www.cdc.gov/nccdphp/publications/aag/aging.htm

Gibbs, L., & Gambrill, E. (2002). Evidence-based practice: Counter arguments to objections. *Research on Social Work Practice, 12*(3), 452–476.

Ginn, J. (1998). Older women in Europe: East follows west in the feminization of poverty. *Aging International,* 101–122.

Ginn, S. (1997). *Women are disproportionately affected by poverty.* Carbondale, IL: Southern Illinois University.

Glanz, K., Lewis, F. M., & Rimer, B. K. (Eds.) (1997). *Health behavior and health education: Theory, research and practice.* San Francisco, CA: Jossey-Bass Publications.

Glass Jr., J. C., & Huneycut, T. L. (2002). Grandparents raising grandchildren: The courts, custody, and educational implications. *Educational Gerontology, 28*(3), 237–251.

Glazebrook, R. (2001). Rural and remote Australian general practitioners' educational needs in radiology. *Journal of Continuing Education in the Health Professions, 21*(3), 140–149.

Glennon, L. (1995). *Our times: The illustrated history of the 20th century.* Atlanta, GA: Turner Publishing.

Godin, G., & Kok, G. (1996). The theory of planned behavior: A review of its applications to health-related behaviors. *American Journal of Health Promotion, 11*(2), 87–98.

Gollaher, D. (1995). *Voice for the mad: The life of Dorothea Dix.* New York: Free Press.

Goodman, C. C., & Silverstein, M. (2001). Grandmothers who parent their grandchildren: An exploratory study of close relations across three generations. *Journal of Family Issues, 22*(5), 557–578.

Gordon, T., & Kannel, W. B. (1983). Drinking and its relation to smoking, BP, blood lipids, and uric acid: The Framingham study. *Archives of Internal Medicine, 143,* 1366–1374.

Government of Saskatchewan. (2006). *Making life better.* Retrieved October 17, 2006, from http://www.gov.sk.ca/finance/accountability/2006/keyterms.htm

Grant, B. F., Harford, T. C., Dawson, D. A., Chou, P. S., & Pickering, R. P. (1994). Prevalence of DSM-IV alcohol abuse and dependence: United States, 1992. *Alcohol Health and Research World, 18,* 243.

Greenstein, R. (1997). Examining details of the new budget legislation. *The Public Policy and Aging Report, 8*(4), 35–42.

Greenwald, J. (1999, August 30). Elder care: Making the right choice. *Time,* 52–56.

Grinstead, L. N., Leder, S., Jensen, S., & Bond, L. (2003). Integrative literature reviews and meta-analyses: Review of research on the health of caregiving grandparents. *Journal of Advanced Nursing, 44*(3), 318–326.

Gubrium, J. F., Rittman, M. R., Williams, C., Young, M. E., & Boylstein, C. A. (2003). Benchmarking as everyday functional assessment in stroke recovery. *Journals of Gerontology: Series B: Psychological Sciences and Social Sciences, 58B*(4), S203–S211.

Haas, J. S., Kaplan, C. P., Des Jarlais, G., Gildengoin, V., Perez-Stable, E. J., & Kerlikowske, K. (2005). Perceived risk of breast cancer among women at average and increased risk. *Journal of Women's Health, 14*(9), 845–851.

Haight, B. K., Michel, Y., & Hendrix, S. (1998). Life review: Preventing despair in newly relocated nursing home residents' short- and long-term effects. *International Journal of Aging and Human Development, 47,* 119–142.

Hanson, M., & Guthiel, L. A. (2004). Motivational strategies with alcohol involved older adults:Implications for social work practice. *Social Work, 49*(3), 364–372.

Harlow, S. D., Goldberg, E. L., & Comstock, G. W. (1991). A longitudinal study of risk factors for depressive symptomatology in elderly widowed and married women. *American Journal of Epidemiology, 134,* 526–538.

Harper, W. J., & Hardesty, P. H. (2001). Differentiating characteristics and needs of minority grandparent caregivers. *Journal of Ethnic and Cultural Diversity in Social Work, 9*(3/4), 133–150.

Hayslip, B., & Kaminski, P. L. (2005). Grandparents raising their grandchildren: A review of the literature and suggestions for practice. *Gerontologist, 45*(2), 262.

Health Care Financing Administration. (2005, August). *Your guide to choosing a nursing home.* Washington, DC: Government Printing Office

Hebert, R., Dubuc, N., Buteau, M., Derosiers, J., Bravo, G., Trottier, L., et al. (1999). *Resources and costs associated with disability of elderly people living at home and in the institutions.* Presented at the American Health Services Research 16th Annual Meeting, Chicago, Illinois.

Helzer, J. E., Burnam, A., & McEvoy, L. T. (1991). Alcohol abuse and dependence. In L. N. Robins & D. A. Regier (Eds.), *Psychiatric disorders in America: The Epidemiologic Catchment Area study* (pp. 81–115). New York: Free Press.

Henderson, T. L., & Cook, J. L. (2005). Grandma's hands: Black grandmothers speak about their experience rearing grandchildren on TANF. *International Journal of Aging and Human Development, 61*(1), 1–19.

Hill, L. R., Klauber, M. R., Salmon, D. P., Yu, E. S., Liu, W. T., Zhang, M., et al. (1993). Functional status, education, and the diagnosis of dementia in the Shanghai survey. *Neurology, 43,* 138–145.

Hiller, S., & Barrow, G. (1999). *Aging, the individual and society.* Belmont, CA: Wadsworth Publishing.

Himmelfarb, S., & Murrell, S. A. (1984). The prevalence and correlates of anxiety symptoms in older adults. *Journal of Psychology, 116,* 159–167.

Hinton, L., Franz, C. E., Yeo, G., & Levkoff, S. E. (2005). Conceptions of dementia in a multiethnic sample of family caregivers. *Journal of the American Geriatrics Society, 53*(8), 1405–1410.

Hodgson, L. G., & Cutler, S. J. (2003). Looking for signs of Alzheimer's disease. *International Journal of Aging and Human Development, 56*(4), 323–343.

Holahan, C. K., & Suzuki, R. (2004). Adulthood predictors of health promoting behavior in later aging. *International Journal of Aging and Human Development, 58*(4), 289–313.

Holliamn, D. C., Giddings, M. M., & Closson, S. (2001). Beyond the myth of collaboration: Creating genuine partnerships to support grandparents raising grandchildren. *Reflections,* 88–97.

Holosko, M., & Feit, M. (2004). *Social work practice with the elderly.* Toronto: Canadian Scholar's Press.

Hooyman, N., & Kiyak, H. A. (Eds.). (1999). *Social gerontology: A multi disciplinary approach.* Boston: Alynn & Bacon.

Howard, M., McMillen, C., & Pollio, D. (2003). Teaching evidence-based practice: Toward a new paradigm for social work education. *Research on Social Work Practice, 13*(2), 234–259.

Hudson, R. (1998). Public vs. private: Success and failures. *The Public Policy and Aging Report, 9*(2), 12–15.

Hudson, R. B. (2004, Spring). Advocacy and policy success in aging. *Generations,* 17–24.

Hunt, L. A. (2003). Driving and dementia. *Generations, 27*(2), 34–38.

Illinois Department on Aging. (1999). *Fact sheet on assisted living and shared housing.* Springfield, IL: State of Illinois.

Illinois Department on Aging. (2006). *Choices for care in Illinois.* Springfield: State of Illinois.

Illinois Department on Aging. (2007). *Older Adult Services Act: 2007 report to the general Assembly.* Retrieved May 20, 2007, from http://www.state.il.us/aging/1news_pubs/publications/oasa_anreprt2007.pdf

Illinois Rural Health Association (IRHA). (2006). *Mental health in rural Illinois; Recovery is the goal. An analysis of mental health care in rural Illinois.* Springfield, IL: Author.

Institute of Medicine. (1988). *The future of public health.* Washington, DC: National Academies Press.

Institute of Medicine. (2003). *The future of the public's health in the 21st century.* Washington, DC: National Academies Press.

International Social Security Association. (1998, Spring). The Social Security protection and older women: The hidden issue of the end of the century. *Aging International,* 49–61.

Inzitari, D., & Basile, A. M. (2003). Activities of daily living and global functioning. *International Psychogeriatrics, 15 Suppl. 1,* 225–229.

Iwami, M. (2002). A CLAS act? Community-based organizations, health service decentralization and primary care development in Peru: Local Committees for Health Administration. *Journal of Public Health Medicine, 24*(4), 246–251.

Jendrenk, M. P. (1994). Policy concerns of white grandparents who provide regular care to their grandchildren. *Journal of Gerontological Social Work, 23*(1/2), 175–199.

Jeste, D. V., & Palmer, B. (1998). Secondary psychoses: An overview. *Seminars in Clinical Neuro Psychiatry, 3,* 2–3.

Jewell, C. J., & Glasser, B. E. (2006). Toward a general analytic framework. Organizational settings, policy goals, and street-level behavior. *Administration and Society, 38*(3), 335–364.

Johnson, M., & Austin, M. J. (2006). Evidence-based practice in the social services: Implications for organizational change. *Administration in Social Work, 30*(3), 75–104.

Jordan, J. (2002). Health needs assessment and needs-led health service change: A survey of projects involving public health doctors. *Journal of Health Services Research and Policy, 7*(2), 71–80.

Jorm, A. F., Korten, A. E., & Henderson, A. S. (1987). The prevalence of dementia: A quantitative integration of the literature. *Acta Psychiatrica Scandinavica, 76,* 465–479.

Jurkowski, E. T. (1987). *Leadership and community participation for people with and without disabilities.* Ann Arbor, MI: Dissertation Abstracts International.

Jurkowski, E. (1999, July). *Demographic trends in aging within rural communities.* Poster Presentation, Rural Health and Social Work conference, Silver Spring, MD.

Jurkowski, E. (1999, July). *Demographic trends in aging within rural communities: Implications for health and social service delivery in the 21st century.* Rural Health and Social Work conference, Silver Spring, MD.

Jurkowski, E. (2005, December 14). *Evidence based policy development.* A paper presentation to the American Public Health Association, Philadelphia, PA.

Jurkowski, E., Kemp, M., & Patterson, S. (2004). Assisted living, social work practice and the elderly. In M. Holosko & M. Feit (Eds.), *Social work practice and the elderly.* Toronto: Canadian Scholar's Press.

Jurkowski, E., & Tracy, M. (2001). Public policy dimensions for an aging society. In R. Ogletree & K. Doyle (Eds.), *Health issues in aging.* Eta Sigma Gamma Mongraph. The Health Education Monograph Series, (2), 20–26.

Kaiser Commission on Medicaid and the Uninsured. (2001). In P. R. Lee & C. L. Estes (Eds.), *The nation's health* (pp. 403–407). Boston: Jones and Bartlett Publishers.

Kamel, S. J., Jarrett, P., & MacDonald, E. (2005). Effectiveness of geriatric evaluation and management units in caring for older adults. *Geriatrics Today, 8*(3), 104–109.

Kane, M. D. (1999). Examining the efficiency of home care. *Journal of Aging and Health, 11*(3), 322–340.

Kaplan, M. S., Adamek, M. E., & Martin, J. L. (2001). Confidence of primary care physicians in assessing the suicidality of geriatric patients. *International Journal of Geriatric Psychiatry, 16*(7), 728–734.

Kapp, M. (1999). From medical patients to health care consumers: Decisional capacity and choices to purchase coverage and services. *Aging and Mental Health, 3*(4), 294–300.

Kapp, M. (2001). Legal interventions for persons with dementia in the USA: Ethical, policy and practical aspects. *Aging and Mental Health, 5*(4), 312–315.

Kapp, M. (2002). Decisional capacity in theory and practice: Legal process versus "bumbling through." *Aging and Mental Health, 6*(4), 413–417.

Kapp, M. (2003). Legal anxieties and end-of-life care in nursing homes. *Issues in Law and Medicine, 19*(2), 111–134.

Karger, H. J., & Stoesz, D. (1990). *American social welfare policy: A structural approach.* New York: Oxford University Press.

Katon, W. J., Robinson, P., Von Korff, M., Lin, E., Bush, T., Ludman, E., et al. (1996). A multifaceted intervention to improve treatment of depression in primary care. *Archives of General Psychiatry, 53,* 924–932.

Katon, W., Von Korff, M., Lin, E., Unutzer, J., Simon, G., Walker, E., et al. (1997). Population-based care of depression: Effective disease management strategies to decrease prevalence. *General Hospital Psychiatry, 19,* 169–178.

Katz, I. R., & Parmelee, P. A. (1997). Overview. In R. L. Rubinstein & M. Lawton (Eds.), *Depression in long term and residential care* (pp. 1–28). New York: Springer.

Katzman, R. (1993). Education and the prevalence of dementia and Alzheimer's disease. *Neurology, 43,* 13–20.

Kaufman, A., Scogin, F., Malonbeach, E., Baumhover, L., & McKendree-Smith, N. (2000). Home-delivered mental health services for aged rural home health care recipients. *Journal of Applied Gerontology, 19*(4), 460–475.

Keating, N. L., Norredam, M., Landrum, M. B., Huskamp, H. A., & Meara, E. (2005). Physical and mental health status of older long-term cancer survivors. *Journal of the American Geriatrics Society, 53*(12), 2145–2152.

Kelly, S. J., Yorker, B. C., Whitley, D. M., & Sipe, T. A. (2001). A multimodal intervention for grandparents raising grandchildren: Results of an exploratory study. *Child Welfare, 80*(1), 27–50.

Kemp, C. L., & Denton, M. (2003). The allocation of responsibility for later life: Canadian reflections on the roles of individuals, government, employers and families. *Aging and Society, 23*(6), 737–760.

Kessler, R. C., McGonagle, K. A., Zhao, S., Nelson, C. B., Hughes, M., Eschleman, S., et al., (1994). Lifetime and 12 month prevalence of DSM-III-R psychiatric disorders in the United States: Results from the national comorbidity survey. *Archives of General Psychiatry, 51*, 8–19.

Kingdon, J. W. (1984). *Agendas, alternatives and public policies.* Boston: Little, Brown and Company.

Kinsella, K., & Gist, Y. (1998). Gender and aging. *International Brief, 98–92.*

Kirst-Ashman, K., & Hull, G. H. (2002). *Understanding generalist practice.* Pacific Grove, CA: Brooks Cole.

Klein, W. C., & Jess, C. (2002). One last pleasure? Alcohol use amoung elderly people in nursing homes. *Health and Social Work, 27*(3), 193–203.

Kocken, P. (2001). Intermediates' satisfaction with a loneliness intervention program aimed at older adults: Linkage of program plans and users' needs. *Patient Education Counseling, 43*(2), 189–197.

Kofoed, L. L. (1984). Abuse and misuse of over-the-counter drugs by the elderly. In R. M. Atkinson (Ed.), *Alcohol and drug abuse in old age* (pp. 49–59). Washington, DC: American Psychiatric Press.

Kolomer, S. (2002). Grandparents raising grandchildren. *Journal of Women and Aging, 14*(3/4), 208.

Kosberg, J. I., & Garcia, J. L. (Eds.). (1995). *Elder abuse: International and cross-cultural perspectives.* Binghamton, NY: Haworth Press.

Kovner, A., & Jonas, S. (1999). *Health care delivery in the United States.* New York, NY: Springer Verlag.

Kretzmann, J. P., & McKnight, J. (2003). *Building communities from the inside out: A path toward finding and mobilizing a community's assets.* Evanston, IL: Center for Urban Affairs and Policy Research.

Kronenfeld, J. J. (2000). Social policy and health care: Social policy and the elderly. In J. Midgley, M. B. Tracy, & M. Livermore (Eds.), *The handbook of social policy* (pp. 222–236). Thousand Oaks, CA: Sage Publications.

Kropf, N. P., & Wilks, S. (2003). Grandparents raising grandchildren. In B. Berkman & L. Harootyan (Eds.), *Social work and health care in an aging society* (pp. 177–200). New York: Springer Publishing Co.

LaGreca, A. J., Akers, R. L. & Dwyer, J. W. (1988). Life events and alcohol behavior among older adults. *The Gerontologist, 28*(4), 552–558.

Lai, S. M., Studenski, S., Richards, L., Perera, S., Reker, D., Rigler, S., et al. (2006). Therapeutic exercise and depressive symptoms after stroke. *Journal of the American Geriatrics Society, 54*(2), 240–247.

Landry, L. (1999). Research into action: Recommended intervention strategies for grandparent caregivers. *Family Relations, 48*, 381–390.

Landry-Meyer, L., & Newman, B. M. (2004). An exploration of the grandparent caregiver role. *Journal of Family Issues, 25*(8), 1005–1025.

Lazarus, R. S. (1966). *Psychological stress and the coping process.* New York: McGraw-Hill.

Lazarus, R. S., & Folkman, S. (1984). *Stress, appraisal and coping.* New York: Springer Publishing Co.

Levine, C. (1999). Home sweet hospital: The nature and limits of private responsibilities for home care. *Journal of Aging and Health, 11*(3), 341–359.

Levkoff, S. E., Chen, H., Coakley, E., Herr, E. C., Oslin, D. W., Katz, I., et al. (2006). Design and sample characteristics of the PRISM-E multisite randomized trial to improve behavioral health care for the elderly. *Journal of Aging and Health, 16*(1). 3–27.

LEXIS-NEXIS' Congressional Universe. (2000). *Older Americans Act.* Retrieved October 6, 2001, from http://web.lexis-nexis.com/congcomp/document

Liberto, J. G., Oslin, D. W., & Ruskin, P. E. (1992). Alcoholism in older persons: A review of the literature. *Hospital and Community Psychiatry, 43,* 975–984.

Lindblom, C. E. (1959). The science of muddling through. *Public Administration Review, 19,* 79–88.

Lindesay, J., Briggs, K., & Murphy, E. (1989). The guy's/age concern survey. Prevalence rates of cognitive impairment, depression and anxiety in an urban elderly community. *British Journal of Psychiatry, 155,* 317–329.

Lipsky, M. (1980). *Street-level bureaucrats.* One Thousand Oaks, CA: Sage Publications.

Livaudais, J. C., Kaplan, C. P., Haas, J. S., Perez-Stable, E. J., Stewart, S., & Des Jarlais, G. (2005). Lifestyle behavior counseling for women patients among a sample of California physicians. *Journal of Women's Health, 14*(6), 485–495.

Mackenzie, C. S., Gekoski, W. L., & Knox, V. J. (1999). Do family physicians treat older patients with mental disorders differently from younger patients? *Canadian Family Physician, 45,* 1219–1224.

Mann, G. (1970). *The history of Germany since 1789.* New York: Praeger Publications.

Marks, L., Nesteruk, O., Swanson, M., Garrison, B., & Davis, T. (2005). Religion and health among African Americans: A qualitative examination. *Research on Aging, 27*(4), 447–474.

Martin-Cook, K., Davis, B. A., Hynan, L. S., & Weiner, M. F. (2005). Randomized, controlled study of an Alzheimer's caregiver skills training program. *American Journal of Alzheimer's Disease and Other Dementias, 20*(4), 204–210.

Mayer, M. (2002). Grandparents rearing grandchildren: Circumstances and interventions. *School Psychology International, 23*(4), 371–385.

McCallion, P., Janick, M., Grant-Griffin, L., & Kolomar, S. (2000). Grandparent carers II: Service needs and service provision issues. *Journal of Gerontological Social Work, 33*(3), 57–84.

McGowen, M. R., Ladd, L., & Strom, R. D. (2006). On-line assessment of grandmother experience in raising grandchildren. *Educational Gerontology, 32*(8), 669–684.

McGuire, L. C., Ahluwalia, I. B., & Strine, T. W. (2006). Chronic disease-related behaviors in U.S. older women: Behavioral risk factor surveillance system, 2003. *Journal of Women's Health, 15*(1), 3–7.

McNamera, P. (2003) *Access to mental health services in rural Illinois: Challenges and future prospects. Public Policy Forum event summary.* Springfield, IL: Illinois Rural Health Association.

McNeill, T. (2006). Evidence-based practice in an age of relativism: Toward a model for practice. *Social Work, 51*(2),147–156.

Meeks, S., Carstensen, L. L., Stafford, P. B., Brenner, L. L., Weathers, F., Welch, R., et al. (1997). Mental health needs of the chronically mentally ill elderly. *Psychology and Aging, 5,* 163–171.

Mehta, K. M., Yaffe, K., & Covinsky, K. E. (2002). Cognitive impairment, depressive symptoms, and functional decline in older people. *Journal of the American Geriatrics Society, 50*(6), 1045–1050.

Melvin, K. (2000). Promoting effective practice in secondary care. *Journal of Public Health Medicine, 22* 287–294.

Memmet, J. L. (2003). Alcohol consumption by elderly Americans. *Journal of Studies on Alcohol, 64*(6), 884–892.

Messinger-Rapport, B., Snader, C. E., Blackstone, E. H., Yu, D., & Lauer, M. S. (2003). Value of exercise capacity and heart rate recovery in older people. *Journal of the American Geriatrics Society, 51*(1), 63–68.

Meuller, K., Kashinath, P., & Ullrich, F. (1997). Lengthening spells of "uninsurance" and their consequences. *The Journal of Rural Health, 13*(1), 29–37.

Mickus, M., Colenda, C., & Hogan, A. (2000). Knowledge of mental health benefits and preferences for type of mental health providers among the general public. *Psychiatric Services, 51*(2), 199–202.

Miller, S., Mor, V., Coppola, K. Tero, J., & Laliberte, L. (1998). The Medicare hospice benefit's influence on dying in nursing homes. *Journal of Palliative Medicine, 1*(4), 367–376.

Mills Wright, C. (1956). *The power elite.* New York: Oxford University Press.

Min, L. C., Elliott, M. N., Wenger, N. S., & Saliba, D. (2006). Higher vulnerable elders survey scores predict death and functional decline in vulnerable older people. *Journal of the American Geriatrics Society, 54*(3), 507–511.

Minkler, M., Driver, D., Roe, K. M., & Bedein, K. (1993). Community interventions to support grandparent caregivers. *The Gerontologist, 33*(6), 807–811.

Minnex, W. L., & Readman, C. H. (2002). Health care coalition building. *American Medical Directors Association, 3*(6), 397–399.

Mohatt, D. F. (2000). Access to mental health services in frontier areas. *Journal of the Washington Academy of Sciences, 86*(3), 35–48.

Moody-Ayers, S. Y., Stewart, A. L., Convinsky, K. E., & Inouye, S. K. (2005). Prevalence and correlates of perceived societal racism in older African American adults with type 2 diabetes mellitus. *Journal of the American Geriatrics Society, 53*(12), 2202–2208.

Moon, M., & Gage, B. (1997). Key Medicare provisions in the Balanced Budget Act of 1997. *The Public Policy and Aging Report, 8*(4), 38–46.

Moore, J. K. (2004). Photography as a tool for advocacy and policy change: Successes from CARE and photosensitive HIV positive campaign. *International Conference on Auto Immune Disorders (AIDS),* July 11–16, abstract no MoPeE4172.

Moore, S. T. (1987). The theory of street-level bureaucracy: Positive critique. *Administration and Society, 19*(1), 74–79.

Moore, S. T. (1990). Street-level policymaking: Characteristics of decision and policy in public welfare. *The American Review of Public Administration, 20*(3), 191–209.

Morago, P. (2006). Evidence-based practice: From medicine to social work. *European Journal of Social Work, 9*(4), 461–477.

Mueller, M., Page, C., & Kuerbis, B. (2004). Civil society and the shaping of communication-information policy: Four decades of advocacy. *The Information Society, 20*(3), 169–185.

Murrell, S. A., Himmelfarb, S., & Wright, K. (1983). Prevalence of depression and its correlates in older adults. *American-Journal-of-Epidemiology, 117*(2), 173–185.

Musnick, M. A., Blazer, D. G., & Hays, J. C. (2000). Religious activity, alcohol use, and depression in a sample of elderly Baptists. *Research on Aging, 22*(2), 91–116.

National Academy on an Aging Society. (1999). *Is demography destiny?* Washington, DC: The Gerontological Society of America.

National Academy on an Aging Society. (1999). The public policy and aging report. *The Public Policy and Aging Report, 11*(2), 1–13.

National Association of Social Workers. (1999). *NASW code of ethics.* Retrieved January 21, 2007, from http://www.naswdc.org

National Center for Elder Abuse (NCEA). (2006). *Statistics on elder abuse.* Retrieved May 28, 2007, from http://www.ncea.org

National Committee for the Prevention of Elder Abuse. *The role of culture in elder abuse.* Retrieved July 23, 2006, from http://www.preventelderabuse.org/issues/culture.html

The National Family Caregiver Support Program. (2006). Retrieved January 16, 2006, from http://www/aoa.gov

National Health Interview Survey (NHIS). (2000). Retrieved August 25, 2005, from http://www.cdc.gov/nchs/about/major/nhis/quest_data_related_1997_forward.htm

National Household Survey on Drug Abuse (NHSDA). (2000). Retrieved August 25, 2005, from http://www.health.org/govstudy/bkd405/

National Institute on Aging (NIA). (2000). *Senior health facts*. Retrieved May 20, 2007, from www.seniorhealth.gov

Nerenberg, L. (1995). *To reach beyond our grasp: A community outreach guide for professionals in the field of elder abuse*. San Francisco, CA: Goldman Institute on Aging.

Neugarten, B. L. (1984). Psychological aspects of aging and illness. *Psychosomatics, 25*(2), 123–125.

Neuner, J. M., Binkley, N., Sparapani, R. A., Laud, P. W., & Nattinger, A. B. (2006). Bone density testing in older women and its association with patient age. *Journal of the American Geriatrics Society, 54*(3), 485–489.

New Freedom Commission on Mental Health. (2004). *Subcommittee on Rural Issues: Background Paper*, DHHS Pub. No. SMA-04–3890. Rockville, MD: Government Printing Office.

Ngoh, C. T., Lewis, I. D., & Connolly, P. M. (2005). Outcomes of inpatient geropsychiatric treatment: The value of assessment protocols. *Journal of Gerontological Nursing, 31*(4), 12–18.

N4a. (2006, October 7). *Side by side comparison of House and Senate Older Americans Act Reauthorization bills*. Washington, DC: National Association of Area Agencies on Aging.

Older Americans hostage: *Free the Older Americans Act! NCOA: Home about NCOA Aging Issues Advocacy Programs & Units News*. Retrieved August 22, 1999, from http://www.noca org/oaa_qa.htm

O'Rand, A. M., & Hamil-Luker, J. (2005). Processes of cumulative adversity: Childhood disadvantage and increased risk of heart attack across the life course. *Journals of Gerontology: Series B: Psychological Sciences and Social Sciences, 60B* (2), S117–S124.

Orel, N. A., Spence, M., & Steele, J. (2005). Getting the message out to older adults: Effective HIV health education risk reduction publications. *Journal of Applied Gerontology, 24*(5), 490–508.

Ospina, S., & Saz-Carranza, A. (2005, August 5). *Paradox and collaboration in coalition work*. A paper presentation for the 2005 Annual Meeting of the Academy of Management, Honolulu, HI.

Palermo, T. (2002) Coalitions: Partnerships to promote agricultural health and safety, *Journal of Agriculture Safety and Health, 8*(2),161–174.

Parr, H., & Philo, C. (2003). Rural mental health and social geographies of caring. *Social and Cultural Geography, 4*(4), 471–488.

Patterson, S. (2000). *Nursing home staffing and quality of care*. Carbondale, IL: Southern Illinois University.

Pennsylvania Department of Aging. (n.d). *Manual for implementing elder abuse prevention media campaigns for special audiences*. Harrisburg, PA: Pennsylvania Department on Aging.

Perneczky, R., Wagenpfeil, S., Komossa, K., Grimmer, T., Diehl, J., & Kurz, A. (2006). Mapping scores onto stages: Mini-mental state examination and clinical dementia rating. *American Journal of Geriatrics Psychiatry, 14*(2), 139–144.

Piven, F. F., & Cloward, R. A. (1979). *Poor people's movements: How they succeed and how they fail*. New York: Random House.

Plath, D. (2006). Evidence-based practice: Current issues and future directions. *Australian Social Work, 59*(1), 56–72.

Population Reference Bureau. (1999). *Aging in the United States: An education module.* Washington, DC: Population Reference Bureau.

Pressman, J. L., & Wildovsky, A. (1979). *Implementation.* Los Angeles: University of California Press.

Prochaska, J. O. (1994). Strong and weak principles for progressing from precontemplation to action on the basis of twelve problem behaviors. *Health Psychology, 13,* 47–51.

Prochaska, J. O., & DiClemente, C. C. (1983). Stages and processes of self-change of smoking: Toward an integrative model of change. *Journal of Consulting and Clinical Psychology, 51,* 390–395.

Prochaska, J. O., DiClemente, C. C., & Norcross, J. C. (1992). In search of how people change: Applications to addictive behavior. *American Psychologist, 47,* 1102–1114.

Prochaska, J. O., DiClemente, C. C., Velicer, W. F., Ginpil, S., & Norcross, J. C. (1985). Predicting change in status for self-changers. *Addictive Behaviors, 10,* 395–406.

Prochaska, J. O., & Velicer, W. F. (1997). The transtheoretical model of health behavior change. *American Journal of Health Promotion, 12,* 38–48.

Prochaska, J. O., Velicer, W. F., DiClemente, C. C., & Fava, J. L. (1988). Measuring the processes of change: Applications to the cessation of smoking. *Journal of Consulting and Clinical Psychology, 56,* 520–528.

Proctor, E. K. (2003). Evidence for practice: Challenges, opportunities, and access. *Social Work Research, 27*(4), 195–196.

Proctor, E., Morrow-Howell, N., Dore, P., Wentz, J. Rubin, E., Thompson, S., et al. (2003). Co-morbid medical conditions among depressed elderly patients discharged home after acute psychiatric care. *The American Journal of Geriatric Psychiatry 11*(3), 329–338.

Proctor, E. K., Morrow-Howell, N., Rubin, E., & Ringenberg, M. (1999). Service use by elderly patients after psychiatric hospitalization. *Psychiatric-Services, 50*(4), 553–555.

Public Law 89–73. 90th Congress, H.R. 3708, July 14, 1965.

Pursley, H. G. (2002). A women's health track for internal medicine residents using evidence-based medicine. *Academic Medicine, 77*(7), 743–744.

Quill, T. E., & Battin, M. P. (2004). *Physician assisted dying: The case of palliative care and patient choice.* Baltimore, MD: Johns Hopkins University Press.

Quinn, J. F., & Mitchell, O. S. (1996). Social Security on the table. *American Prospect, 26,* 6–81.

Randolph, W., & Viswanth, K. (2004). Lessons learned from public health mass media campaigns: Marketing health in a crowded media world. *Annual Review of Public Health, 25,* 419–437.

Rasell, E., Bernstein, J., & Tang, K. (1994). The impact of health care financing on family budgets. *International Journal of Health Services, 24*(4), 691–714.

Rathbone-McCuuan, E., & Bane, S. (2003). Rural mental health: A discussion of service capacity building for rural elders. *Journal of Gerontological Social Work, 41*(1–2), 19–35.

Ray, C. G., & Finley, J. K. (1994). Did CMHCs fail or succeed? Analysis of the expectations and outcomes of the community mental health movement. *Administration and Policy in Mental Health, 21,* 283–293.

Regier, D. A., Boyd, J. H., Burke, J. D. Jr, Rae, D. S., Myers, J. K., Kramer, M., et al. (1988). One-month prevalence of mental disorders in the United States. Based on five epidemiologic catchment area sites. *Archives of General Psychiatry, 45,* 977–986.

Regier, D. A., Farmer, M. E., Rae, D. S., Locke, B. Z., Keith, S. J., Judd, L. L., et al. (1990). Comorbidity of mental disorders with alcohol and other drug abuse: Results from the

Epidemiologic Catchment Area Study. *Journal of the American Medical Association, 264,* 2511–2518.

Regier, D. A., Goldberg, I. D., & Taube, C. A. (1978). The defacto U.S. mental health service system: A public health perspective. *Archives of General Psychiatry, 35*(6), 85–93.

Reid, M. C., & Anderson, P. A. (1997). Geriatric substance use disorders. *Medical Clinics of North America, 81,* 999–1016.

Reuben, D. B., Seeman, T. E., Keeler, E., Hayes, R. P., Bowman, L., Sewall, A., et al. (2004). Refining the categorization of physical functional status: The added value of combining self-reported and performance-based measures. *Journals of Gerontology: Series A: Biological Sciences and Medical Sciences, 59A* (10), 1056–1061.

Reynolds, C. F., III. (1998). *The challenge of treatment in 70+ year olds with recurrent major depression: Excellent short-term but brittle long-term response.* Annual meeting of the American Association for Geriatric Psychiatry, San Diego, CA.

Ritchie, K., & Kildea, D. (1995). Is senile dementia "age-related" or "aging-related"? Evidence from meta-analysis of dementia prevalence in the oldest old. *Lancet, 346,* 931–934.

Roberts-DeGennaro, M. (2001). Building coalitions for political advocacy. *Social Work, 31,* 308–311.

Robins, L. N., & Regier, D. A. (1991). *Psychiatric disorders in America: The epidemiologic catchment area study.* New York: Free Press.

Robinson, G. K. (1990). The psychiatric component of long-term care models. In B. S. Fogel, G. L. Gottlieb, & A. Furino (Eds.), *Mental health policy for older Americans: Protecting minds at risk* (pp. 157–178). Washington, DC: American Psychiatric Press.

Rogers, A., & Barusch, A. (2000). Mental health service utilization among frail, low income elders: Perceptions of home service providers and elders in the community. *Gerontological Social Work, 34*(2), 23–38.

Rosen, A. (2003). Evidence-based social work practice: Challenges and promise. *Social Work Research, 27*(4), 197–208.

Rosenstock, I. M., Strecher, V. J., & Becker, M. H. (1988). Social learning theory and the health belief model. *Health Education Quarterly, 15*(2), 175–183.

Ross, M., & Aday, L. (2006). Stress and coping in African American grandparents who are raising their grandchildren. *Journal of Family Issues, 27*(7), 912–932.

Rowe, J. W., & Kahn, R. L. (1997). Successful aging. *Gerontologist, 37,* 433–440.

Rubin, A., & Parrish, D. (2007). Views of evidence-based practice among faculty in Master of Social Work programs: A national study. *Research on Social Work Practice, 17*(1), 110–122.

Ruiz, D. S., & Zhu, C. W. (2004). Families maintained by African American grandmothers: Household composition and childcare experiences. *Western Journal of Black Studies, 28*(3), 415–423.

Ryan, W. (1976). *Blaming the victim.* New York: Random House.

Saffel-Shrier, S., & Catinella, A. P. (2002). Functional approach to nutrition screening among ambulatory older persons. *Journal of Nutrition for the Elderly, 22*(2), 71–82.

Salloway, S., Malloy, P., Kohn, R., Gillard, E., Duffy, J., Rogg, J., et al. (1996). MRI and neuropsychological differences in early- and late-life-onset geriatric depression. *Neurology, 46,* 1567–1574.

Sarkisian, C. A., Hays, R. D., Berry, S. H. Mangione, C. M. (2001). Expectations regarding aging among older adults and physicians who care for older adults. *Medical-Care, 39*(9), 1025–1036.

Schonfeld, L. (1993). Behavioral treatment of addictions. *Addictive Behaviors, 18*(2), 105–106.

Schulberg, H. C., Madonia, M. J., Block, M. R., Coulehan, J. L., Scott, C. P., Rodriguez, E., et al. (1995). Major depression in primary care practice. Clinical characteristics and treatment implications. *Psychosomatics, 36,* 129–137.

Scott-Lennox, J. A., & George, L. (1996). Epidemiology of psychiatric disorders and mental health services use among older Americans. In B. L. Levin & J. Petrila (Eds.), *Mental health services: A public health perspective* (pp. 253–289). New York: Oxford University Press.

Segal, E. A., & Brzuzy, S. (1998). *Social welfare policy, programs, and practice.* Itasca, IL: F. E. Peacock.

Shadel, B. N. (2002). Bioterrorism risk perceptions and educational needs of public health professionals before and after September 11, 2001: A national needs assessment survey. *Journal of Public Health Management Practice, 10*(4), 282–289.

Simon, R., & Andel, R. (2006). Effects of resistance training and walking on functional fitness in advanced old age. *Journal of Aging and Health, 18*(1), 31–105.

Sipe, C. (2005, Sept./Oct.). Building an active aging coalition. *The Journal on Active Aging,* 60–67.

Skoog, I. (1993). The prevalence of psychotic, depressive, and anxiety syndromes in demented and non-demented 85-year olds. *International Journal of Geriatric Psychiatry, 8,* 247–253.

Smith, B. W., Novak, K. J., & Frank, J. (2001). Community policing and the work routines of street-level officers. *Criminal Justice Review, 26*(1), 17–37.

Smith, C. J., Beltran, A., Butts, D. M, & Kingson, E. R. (2001). Grandparents raising grandchildren: Emerging program and policy issues for the 21st century. *Journal of Gerontological Social Work, 35*(1), 33–45.

Smith, J. (1997). *The changing economic circumstances of the elderly: Income, wealth and social security.* Syracuse, NY: Center for Policy Research, Maxwell School of Citizenship and Public Affairs.

Special Committee on Aging. (1987). *Medicare prescription drug issues: Report to the chairman, Special Committee on Aging.* Washington, DC: General Accounting Office.

Staker, L. V. (2003).Teaching performance improvement: An opportunity for continuing medical education. *Journal of Continuing Education Health Profession, 23*(1), 34–52.

State of Oregon. (n.d.). *Death with Dignity Act.* Retrieved November 4, 2006, from http://www.oregon.gov/DHS/ph/pas/index.shtml

Stern, Y., Gurland, B., Tatemichi, T. K., Tang, M. X., Wilder, D., & Mayeux, R. (1994). Influence of education and occupation on the incidence of Alzheimer's disease. *Journal of the American Medical Association, 271,* 1004–1010.

Stolee, P., Kessler, L., & Le Clair, J. K. (1996). A community development and outreach program in geriatric mental health: Four years' experience. *Journal of the American Geriatrics Society, 44,* 314–320.

Strack, R. W. (2004). Engaging youth through photovoice. *Health Promotion Practice, 5*(1), 49–58.

Sutton, J., & DeJong, G. (1998). Managed care and people with disabilities: Framing the issues. *Archives of Physical Medicine and Rehabilitation, 79,* 1312–1316.

Tabbarah, M., Zimmerman, R. K., Richard, K., Nowalk, M. P., Janosky, J. E., Troy, J. A., et al. (2005). What predicts influenza vaccination status in older Americans over several years? *Journal of the American Geriatrics Society, 53*(8), 1354–1359.

Tappe, M. K., & Galer-Unti, R. A. (2001). The health educators' role in promoting health literacy and advocacy for the 21st century. *Journal of School Health, 71*(10), 477–482.

Targ, D. B., & Brintnall-Perterson, M. (2001). Grandparents raising grandchildren: Impact of a national satellite video program. *Journal of Family Issues, 22*(5), 579–593.

Tatara, T. (1999). *Understanding elder abuse in minority populations.* Philadelphia: Taylor and Francis.

Temple, M. T., & Leino, E. V. (1989). Long-term outcomes of drinking: A 20-year longitudinal study of men. *British Journal of Addiction, 84,* 889–899.

Thompson, A. H. (2001). A social problem index for Canada. *Canadian Journal of Psychiatry, 46*(1), 45–51.

Torres, O. H., Munoz, J., Riuz, D, Ris, J., Gich, I., Coma, E., et al. (2004). Outcome predictors of pneumonia in elderly patients: Importance of functional assessment. *Journal of the American Geriatrics Society, 52*(10), 1603–1609.

Torres-Gil, F. M. (1998). Policy, politics, aging: Crossroads in the 1990s. In J. S. Steckenrider & T. M. Parrott (Eds.), *New directions in old-age policies* (pp.75–87). Albany: State University of New York.

Torres-Gil, F. M., & Villa, V. (2000). Social policy and the elderly. In J. Midgley, M. B. Tracy, & M. Livermore (Eds.), *The handbook of social policy* (pp. 209–220). Thousand Oaks, CA: Sage Publications.

Turner, M. J., Killian, T. S., & Cain, R. (2004). Life course transitions and depressive symptoms among women in midlife. *International Journal of Aging and Human Development, 58*(4), 241–265.

Ubel, P. A., & Jankovic, A. (2005). What is perfect health to an 85-year-old? Evidence for scale recalibration in subjective health ratings. *Medical Care, 43*(10), 1054–1057.

Understanding and combating elder abuse in minority communities. (1997). Proceedings of a 1997 conference sponsored by the National Center on Elder Abuse (NCEA).

United States Bureau of the Census. (1997). *Marital status and living arrangements: March 1997 (update) current population reports,* PPL-90. United States Bureau of the Census. Retrieved June 12, 2006, from http://www.census.gov

United States Census Bureau. (1999). *Statistical brief. (1999): Sixty-five plus in the United States.* Retrieved June 12, 2006, from http://www.census.Gov:80/socdeco/www/agebrief.html

United States Census Bureau. (2000). *Statistical abstract of the United States.* Retrieved October, 5, 2001, from http://www.censusgov/prod/www/statistical-abstract-us.htm

United States Census Bureau. (2001). *Census 2000 data for the state of Illinois.* Retrieved August 31, 2001, from http://www.census.gov/Press-Release/www/2001/tables/redist_il.html

United States Department of Health and Human Services, National Center for Health Statistics (USDHHS NCHS). (1995). National Health Interview Survey. Bethesda, MD: Government Printing Office.

United States Department of Health and Human Services. (1999). *Health, United States, 1999 with Health and Aging Chartbook.* Washington, DC: Government Printing Office.

United States Department of Health and Human Services. (1999). *Mental health and older adults: Chapter five appearing in report of the surgeon general on mental health needs.* Bethesda, MD: U.S. Government Printing Office.

United States Department of Health and Human Services (USDHHS). (2000a). *Oral health in America: A report from the Surgeon General.* Washington, DC: US Government Printing Office.

United States Department of Health and Human Services (USDHHS). (2000b). *Healthy People 2010: Health objectives for the nation.* Washington, DC: Government Printing Office.

United States Department of Health and Human Services (USDHHS). (2000c). *NIA's strategic plan to address health disparities in aging: Fiscal years 2000–2005,* Bethesda, MD: U.S. Government Printing Office.

United States Department of Health and Human Services, National Center for Health Statistics (USDHHS NCHS). (2001a). Behavioral risk factor surveillance system, (BFRSS). Bethesda, MD: Government Printing Office.

United States Department of Health and Human Services (USDHHS). (2001b). Mental health: Culture, race and ethnicity: A supplement to mental health: A report to the surgeon general. Bethesda, MD: U.S. Government Printing Office.

United States Department of Health and Human Services, National Center for Health Statistics. (2002). Health, United States, 2002. Hyattsville, MD: Government Printing Office.

United States Department of Health and Human Services, National Center for Health Statistics (USDHHS NCHS). (2004a), Behavioral risk factor surveillance system (BRFSS). Bethesda, MD: Government Printing Office.

United States Department of Health and Human Services, National Center for Health Statistics. (2004b). Health, United States, 2004. Hyattsville, MD: Government Printing Office.

United States Department of Health and Human Services (USDHHS). (2005). Featured program: The gatekeeper model, e-communication, 1(2). Retrieved June 16, 2006, from http://www.samhsa.gov/OlderAdultsTAC/

United States Department of Health and Human Services (USDHHS). (2006a). Featured program: The mental health and aging systems integration initiative, e-communication, 2(1). Retrieved June 16, 2006, from http://www.samhsa.gov/OlderAdultsTAC/

United States Department of Health and Human Services (USDHHS). (2006b). Featured program: The recovery center, e-communication, 2(1). Retrieved June 16, 2006, from http://www.samhsa.gov/OlderAdultsTAC/

United States Department of Health and Human Services. (2006c). Social Security online: The official website of the U.S. Social Security Administration. Retrieved August 14, 2006, from http://www.ssa.gov/

United States Department of Health and Human Services, National Center for Health Statistics. (2007a). Health, United States, 2006. Hyattsville, MD: Government Printing Office.

United States Department of Health and Human Services. (2007b). Retirement planner: Social Security online. Retrieved January 14, 2007, from http://www.ssa.gov/retirechartred.htm

United States Public Health Service Office of the Surgeon General. (2001). Mental health: A report of the surgeon general. Rockville, MD: Department of Health and Human Services.

United States Social Security Administration. (1995). A brief description of the Social Security program. Washington, DC: Social Security Administration.

United States Social Security Administration. (2005). A brief description of the U.S. social security program. Publication No. 61-009.

Unutzer, J. K., Katon, W., Russo, J., Simon, G., Bush, T., Waler, E., et al. (1999). Patterns of care for depressed older adults in a large-staff model HMO. American Journal of Geriatric Psychiatry, 7(3), 235–243.

Unutzer, J., Katon, W. J., Simon, G., Walker, E. A., Grembowski, D., & Patrick, D. (1996). Depression, quality of life, and use of health services in primary care patients over 65: A 4-year prospective study. Psychosomatics, 37, 35.

Van Balen, R., Essink-Bot, M., Steyerberg, E. W., Cools, H. J. M., & Habbema, J. D. F. (2003). Quality of life after hip fracture: A comparison of four health status measures in 208 patients. Disability and Rehabilitation, 25(10), 507–519.

Vass, M., Avlund, K., Lauridsen, J., & Hendriksen, C. (2005). Feasible model for prevention of functional decline in older people: Municipality-randomized, controlled trial. Journal of the American Geriatrics Society, 53(4), 563–568.

Vinzant, J., & Crothers, L. (1996). Street-level leadership rethinking the role of public servants in contemporary governance. *The American Review of Public Administration,* 26(4), 457–476.

Wagenfeld, M. O., Murray, J. D., Mohatt, D. F., & DeBruyn, J. C. (Eds.). (1994). *Mental health and rural America: 1980–1993.* NIH Publication No. 94-3500. Washington, DC: U.S. Government Printing Office.

Wallace, G. (2001). Grandparent caregivers: Emerging issues in elder law and social work practice. *Journal of Gerontological Social Work,* 34(3), 127–136.

Waters, E. (1995). Let's not wait till it's broke: Interventions to maintain and enhance mental health in late life. In M. Gatz (Ed.), *Emerging issues in mental health and aging* (pp. 183–209). Washington, DC: American Psychological Association.

Watkins, J. (2006). Grandparents raising grandchildren: The growing task facing a new generation. *The Journal of Association for Library Service to Children,* 4(1), 12–14.

Waycie, L. (2006). Groups for grandparents raising grandchildren. *The Journal of Association for Library Service to Children,* 4(1), 17–18.

Webster's New World College Dictionary. (2001). *Webster's New World College Dictionary.* (4th ed.) Cleveland, OH: IDG Books Worldwide.

Wells, K., Miranda, J., Bruce, M. L., Alegria, M., & Wallerstein, N. (2004). Bridging community intervention and mental health services research. *American Journal of Psychiatry, 161,* 955–963.

Wells, K. B., Stewart, A., Hays, R. D., Burnam, M. A., Rogers, W., Daniels, M., et al. (1989). The functioning and well-being of depressed patients: Results from the medical outcomes study. *Journal of the American Medical Association, 262,* 914–919.

Wesley, N. (Ed.) (1999). *Urban health update: Urban health in the new millennium: Seven leaders look to the future.* St. Louis, MO: Thomas Land.

Wheatley, B., Dejong, G., & Sutton, J. (1996). How managed care is transforming American health care: A survey of rehabilitation providers in leading markets. *The Georgetown Public Policy Review, 1(2),* 134–147.

Whitley, K. R., White, S. J., & Yorke, B. (1999). Strengths-based case management: Application to grandparents raising grandchildren. *Families in Society, 80(2),* 110–119.

Wilensky, H. L., & Lebeaux, C. N. (1965). *Industrial society and social welfare.* New York: The Free Press.

Witkin, B. R., & Altschuld, J. W. (1995). *Planning and conducting needs assessments: A practical guide.* One Thousand Oaks, CA: Sage Publications.

Witkin, S., & Harrison, D. (2001). Whose evidence and for what purpose? *Social Work,* 46(4), 293–296.

Wood, E. (2006). *The availability and utility of interdisciplinary data on elder abuse: A White Paper for the National Center on Elder Abuse.* Washington, DC: National Center on Elder Abuse.

Wright, K. (2000). Competency development in public health leadership. *American Journal of Public Health, 90(8),* 1202–1207.

Zinn, J. Mor, V., Castle, N., Intrator, O., & Brannon, D. (1999). Organizational and environmental factors associated with nursing home participation. *Health Services Research, 33(6),* 1753–1767.

Zisook, S., & Shuchter, S. R. (1991). Depression through the first year after the death of a spouse. *American Journal of Psychiatry, 148,* 1346–1352.

Zuvekas, S., & Cohen, J. W. (2002). A guide to comparing health care expenditures in the 1996 MEPS to the 1987 NMES. *Inquiry, 39,* 76–86.

Index